IN DEFENSE OF *UNCLE TOM*

"Uncle Tom" is the most piercing epithet blacks can hurl at one another. It marks targets as race traitors, and that painful stain is often permanent.

Much more than a slur, Uncle Tom is a vital component of a system of social norms in the black community that deters treachery. In this book, Brando Simeo Starkey provocatively argues that blacks must police racial loyalty and that those successfully prosecuted must be punished with the label Uncle Tom.

This book shadows Uncle Tom throughout history to understand how these norms were constructed, disseminated, applied, and enforced. Why were Martin Luther King Jr., Marcus Garvey, Muhammad Ali, Jackie Robinson, Thurgood Marshall, and others accused of racial betrayal? *In Defense of* Uncle Tom answers this and other questions and insists that Uncle Tom is too valuable to discard. Because it deters treachery, this epithet helps build black solidarity, a golden tool in promoting racial progress.

Brando Simeo Starkey is a writer and scholar. He holds degrees from the Ohio State University and Harvard Law School. He was a postgraduate research Fellow at Harvard Law and a Constance Baker Motley Fellow at the Equal Justice Society, and he previously taught law at Villanova Law School and the Thomas Jefferson School of Law.

In Defense of *Uncle Tom*

WHY BLACKS MUST POLICE RACIAL LOYALTY

BRANDO SIMEO STARKEY

CAMBRIDGE
UNIVERSITY PRESS

32 Avenue of the Americas, New York, NY 10013-2473, USA

Cambridge University Press is part of the University of Cambridge.

It furthers the University's mission by disseminating knowledge in the pursuit of education, learning, and research at the highest international levels of excellence.

www.cambridge.org
Information on this title: www.cambridge.org/9781107668348

© Brando Simeo Starkey 2015

First published 2015

Printed in the United States of America

A catalog record for this publication is available from the British Library.

Library of Congress Cataloging in Publication data
Starkey, Brando Simeo, 1982– author.
In defense of Uncle Tom : why blacks must police racial loyalty / Brando Simeo Starkey.
     pages   cm
ISBN 978-1-107-07004-2 Hardback
ISBN 978-1-107-66834-8 Paperback
1. Race discrimination – Law and legislation – United States – History.   2. African Americans – Legal status, laws, etc. – History.   3. Civil rights movements – United States – History.   4. Slavery – United States.   5. Uncle Tom (Fictitious character)   6. Stowe, Harriet Beecher, 1811 – 1896. Uncle Tom's cabin.   I. Title.
KF4757.S725   2016
305.896′073–dc23   2014020982

ISBN 978-1-107-07004-2 Hardback
ISBN 978-1-107-66834-8 Paperback

I dedicate this book to those who danced so I don't have to.

Contents

Acknowledgments

Many have helped me in writing this book. I fear that my memory is far too imperfect to recall them all, but it is good enough to write: Ken Mack, Harwood McClerking, Al Brophy, Ray Block, Lani Guinier, Annette Gordon-Reed, David Wilkins, David Caudill, Kenneth Nunn, Ralph Richard Banks, Michelle Madden Dempsey, Carlton Mark Waterhouse, and my editor John Berger. I thank these folk and hope my recollection won't force me to make awkward and regretful apologies later in life.

Before this book was published, I wrote three law review articles based on this project which appeared in the following journals: *Berkeley Journal of African-American Law & Policy, Georgetown Journal of Law & Modern Critical Race Theory*, and the *Alabama Civil Rights and Civil Liberties Law Review*. To the members of these journals who worked with me, please know that you improved this final product. Also, my research assistant Danielle Gardner did great work for me.

I started writing this book when I was nineteen, after having completed my sophomore year at "The" Ohio State University. When I graduated from Harvard Law School six years later, I had enough for a completed book, but not one that matched my personality and my true feelings about *Uncle Tom*. I think good writing is a product of an author's best self. When I'm at my best, I proffer arguments that make people uncomfortable, maybe a little angry – probably a lot angry, actually. I challenge. I respect audacity and disrespect the conventional wisdom of many. That book would not have made you uncomfortable. That book challenged no readers. An audacious mind had nothing to do with that book.

In 2011, when I was struggling to write as my best self, Penelope Pether provided me great guidance. She was a wonderful law professor at Villanova Law School. She unfortunately will not be able to read this book in its final form. That causes me great grief. But without her warm encouragement, this book would be far worse than it is. A discussion I had with her – a moment I will never forget – made this book bolder and stronger. Some people are going to hate what this book says and perhaps me for writing it. Others will fall on the opposite end of the spectrum. Few will be in the middle, I think. Good. I hope my future ventures stir passions too.

I finally thank my mother, Stephanie Starkey; my father, Sam Starkey; and my brother, Bee Starkey. Everyone has kin. Not everyone has a family. I am lucky to have the latter. And to the most beautiful woman, my wife and my best friend, Wendy, I thank you for being you and the world for letting me find you.

Introduction

IN DECEMBER 1942, a black man named Warren H. Brown denounced black newspapers in a *Saturday Review of Literature* editorial. Brown, director of Negro relations for the Council for Democracy, argued that blacks came in two molds, "Negroes and sensation-mongering Negro leaders." To his discomfort, the latter controlled black newspapers. He believed the "agitators" provided whites an inaccurate portrait of the Negro. These newspapers painted blacks as hungry and thoroughly frustrated with what America served them. When the black man peeked over at the white man's plate, he saw something far more appetizing.

Brown, however, depicted a satisfied lot, believing that "despite his sometimes snail's-pace progress, the Negro knows that in America – for the long pull – he can't lose." Brown was dismayed that black newspapermen excluded this positive picture from their work. In his estimation, these newspapers aggravated racial hostility by portraying blacks as discontent and "Negro first and American second." Brown implored black newspapers to change the images they disseminated and solicited his people to boycott these publications for their "venomous, hate-making policies."[1]

But black newspapers, not Brown, best captured the likeness of black people. Indeed, blacks endorsed their newspapers' sharp criticisms of America. Reacting to Brown's editorial, the *Negro Digest* polled blacks, finding that 86 percent of respondents felt that their newspapers represented their views. The monthly reported, in fact, that many wished the black press was even more aggressive.[2]

---

[1] Warren H. Brown, *A Negro Looks at the Negro Press*, Saturday Review of Literature, Dec. 19, 1942, at 5–6.

[2] Wallace Lee, *Does the Negro Press Speak for Most Negroes in its Opinions?*, Negro Digest, Feb. 1943, at 54.

But beyond simply misjudging blacks' perceptions of race relations, Brown denigrated an important black institution in the Jim Crow era. Writing in the *Michigan Chronicle*, a black newspaper, Louis E. Martin argued that whites had consistently targeted the black press. Acutely aware of the need to monitor blacks to maintain the racial pecking order, whites who perused black newspapers were frequently alarmed by their content and depicted them as extreme. Martin anticipated a black person would parrot whites' criticisms, and Brown became "the long awaited voice of an Uncle Tom courting the affection of his white masters." In a different black newspaper, James A. Hamlett Jr. agreed, stating that Brown was one of the "'Uncle Tom' Negroes" who "tell white people anything … as long as it is something to block the progress of the Negro race."[3]

Both argued that black newspapers encouraged recent racial progress. Martin specifically mentioned President Franklin Roosevelt's executive order outlawing employment discrimination in war industries as well as the Fair Employment Practice Committee, which prohibited companies that practiced employment discrimination from receiving federal contracts. Martin insisted that black newspapers taught blacks to "demand" their rights, and Brown committed racial treachery by rebuking such a vital institution. With one epithet, the two disparaged Brown for taking thirty pieces of silver. Martin and Hamlett participated in a common black cultural practice. They launched *Uncle Tom* at a black person they felt violated unwritten group rules and impeded the race's collective interests.[4]

As the case of Warren Brown shows, *Uncle Tom* is more than just a slur that blacks have hurled at supposed Judases. It is a vital component of a system of social norms in the black community that police racial loyalty. Social norms are the rules that regulate behavior in groups that are enforced through sanction. Blacks have monitored fidelity through the management of "racial loyalty norms" throughout history. This book is a biography of *Uncle Tom*, the most historically significant punishment for defying these norms.[5]

Uncle Tom owes much of its prominence to the cause of black solidarity. By marshalling support for certain goals, solidarity provides blacks a path toward legal gains. By itself, it is inadequate. But in concert with other tools – strategy,

---

3   Louis E. Martin, Negro Digest, Feb. 1943, at 46.
4   Id.; James A. Hamlett Jr., *Week-end Chats*, Plaindealer, Jan. 15, 1943, at 1; Andrew Edmund Kersten, Race, Jobs, and the War: The FEPC in the Midwest, 1941–46 17–18 (2000); Paul Norgen, *Government Contracts and Fair Employment Practices*, 29 Law and Contemporary Problems 225, 225 (1964).
5   Cass Sunstein, *Social Norms and Social Roles*, 96 Columbia Law Review 903, 907 (1996); Christine Horne, *Sociological Perspectives on the Emergence of Norms* found in Michael Hechter and Karl-Dieter Opp, Social Norms 5 (2001).

moral authority, organization, and the like – black solidarity is invaluable. The Montgomery Bus Boycott, the 1960s sit-in movements, and Project Confrontation in Birmingham in 1963 exemplify black solidarity, in tandem with other tools, helping produce civil rights victories. Even when substantive legal gains never eventuate, see, for instance, the antilynching movement, solidarity nonetheless provides a starting point from which to resist subordination. And as law professor Derrick Bell once noted, the mere act of resisting should oftentimes be considered a form of victory. If black solidarity is so valuable in the pursuit of legal triumphs, then social norms that encourage that solidarity are crucial.[6]

My thesis is that blacks should enforce "constructive" social norms to police racial loyalty because doing so helps bolster black solidarity, which is vital in promoting collective legal interests and ability to affect public policy. I follow the life of *Uncle Tom* to demonstrate my thesis. A person is called an *Uncle Tom* for violating a racial loyalty norm that truly exists or a norm that one who endeavors to create new norms, a norm entrepreneur, wants to exist. This signals to the rest of the black community to conform or else face punishment. That is, *Uncle Tom's* power stems from its effects on the broader group, not any effect it may have on the supposed betrayer. Quite simply, *Uncle Tom* deters treachery. Shadowing *Uncle Tom* through black history helps us to understand where and how these norms were constructed, disseminated, applied, and enforced. From there, we can assess their propriety.[7]

These norms arrange into two groups: constructive norms and destructive norms. Constructive norms, on the one hand, help build black solidarity by penalizing individuals for consciously promoting the interests of antiblack

---

6   There is a wealth of literature on the Montgomery Bus Boycott, the sit-in movements, Project Confrontation in Birmingham, and the antilynching movement. See, for example, Jo Ann Gibson Robinson, The Montgomery Bus Boycott and the Women Who Started it (1987); Donnie Williams and Wayne Greenhaw, The Thunder of Angels: The Montgomery Bus Boycott and the People Who Broke the Back of Jim Crow (2006); Randall Kennedy, *Martin Luther King's Constitution: A Legal History of the Montgomery Bus Boycott*, 98 Yale Law Journal 999 (1989); Robert Jerome Glennon, *The Role of Law in the Civil Rights Movement: The Montgomery Bus Boycott, 1955–1957*, 9 Law and History Review 59 (1991); Ruth Searles and J. Allen Williams Jr., *Negro College Students' Participation in Sit-Ins*, 40 Social Forces 215 (1962); Diane McWhorter, Carry Me Home: Birmingham, Alabama: The Climatic Battle of the Civil Rights Revolution (2001); Rosalyn Terborg-Penn, Discontent Black Feminists: Prelude and Postscript to the Passage of the Nineteenth Amendment in The Black Studies Reader 74 (Editors Jacqueline Bobo, Cynthia Hudley, and Claudine Michel 2004); Deleso Alford Washington, *Exploring the Black Wombman's Sphere and the Anti-Lynching Crusade of the Early Twentieth Century*, 3 The Georgetown Journal of Gender and the Law 895 (2002); Derrick A. Bell, *Racial Realism*, 24 Connecticut Law Review 363, 379 (1992).

7   For a deeper discussion of the "norm entrepreneur" see Eric A. Posner, *Symbols, Signals, and Social Norms in Politics and the Law*, 27 Journal of Legal Studies 765, 772–76 (1998).

entities, for exhibiting inexcusable meekness in the face of racism, or for lacking concern for the race. "Destructive" social norms, on the other hand, discipline blacks for behaviors the race should permit, impeding the cause of racial solidarity. These norms overregulate behavior.

I want to clarify what I am not arguing. For one, I am not alleging that social norms that punish "sellouts," on their own, directly caused concrete gains. Because many variables account for racial progress, that position is unreasonable. My claim is, rather, that properly using social norms can help galvanize the black community around important goals. Where evidence supports the contention that social norms did help galvanize the black community, I argue as such. I do not contend, furthermore, that blacks have strategically maintained social norms for racial progress. I endeavor to show, in short, that subordinate groups can advance their collective interests, particularly their legal interests, with intelligent use of social norms.

Apart from my main thesis, I proffer three subsidiary arguments. The first is that blacks have discarded and redrawn conceptions of racial betrayal throughout time. To varying degrees, racial loyalty policing responds to the many methods of racial subordination of a particular era.

The first of three definable periods of *Uncle Tom*'s "post Cabin" career began in 1865 and ended in 1959. During these years, blacks managed various norms to promote racial solidarity. The most prevalent norm was that blacks had to resist segregation. Norms were also constructed to empower blacks to eschew the asserted meek characteristics of Southern Negroes. *Uncle Tom*, furthermore, assailed blacks in various employment contexts. Black clergymen who supposedly advised capitulation too were constantly targeted for *Uncle Tom* punishment. Negroes supporting Herbert Hoover likewise broke norms, resulting in *Uncle Tom* brandings. Blacks in Hollywood, as well, suffered the indignity that inevitably accompanies *Uncle Tom* when playing roles that were considered demeaning to the race. These roles reinforced stereotypes that endorsed racial inferiority and supported legal subjugation.

The second period is from 1960 to 1975. Here, recalcitrance regarding desegregation and a lack of true progress largely propelled the direction in which racial loyalty norms proceeded. During the first period, these norms were, generally speaking, only enforced by one group, those endeavoring to overthrow the racial caste system. But in the second period, we see two groups – integrationists and black nationalists – manage frequently clashing sets of social norms. Integrationists' entire enterprise of norms maintenance was devoted to rallying blacks around the goal of an integrated society that followed the complete dismantling of segregation. Thus, blacks who refused to take part in uprooting the status quo, disapproved of busing, or deprecated the sit-in and protest efforts all broke the social norms promulgated by integrationists.

Whereas integrationists were concerned with introducing blacks into larger society, black nationalists loudly dissented. Nationalists indicted integrationists for betrayal for wanting closer associations with whites who, nationalists averred, refused to remedy their racist past to create an egalitarian future. Militants, preferring more radical strategies, attacked both integrationists and supporters of interracial coalition politics. Malcolm X, who rebuffed racial intermingling, features prominently during this period. Black nationalists, in sum, fashioned racial loyalty norms to push blacks away from white society and toward the creation of a separate black existence.[8]

During these years, moreover, visible hostility between the black community and police officers increased. Blacks, integrationists and militants alike, profoundly distrusted the police. Police departments, in response, hired black officers particularly to police black neighborhoods. Blacks taking such positions, however, were constantly derided as *Uncle Toms*.

The third and final period starts in 1976 and continues to the present day. Overt racism is more relic than reality and Americans overwhelmingly reject discrimination. With federal and state antidiscrimination laws, legal equality is secured. That does not, however, equate to actual equality. Whatever is deemed worth having, blacks have less. This is the central issue of this period, guiding *Uncle Tom's* trajectory. With blacks voting for Democrats nine to one, black Republicans are frequently dismissed as sellouts. As blacks run for all levels of political office, social norms, furthermore, often require complete black support. Being too connected with or favorable toward the prosecutorial side of justice system, which is perceived as rife with racial bias, also makes blacks vulnerable to *Uncle Tom* accusations.

My second subsidiary argument is that as the endeavor of policing loyalty through social norms continued throughout history, destructive norms have increasingly predominated over constructive ones. The best explanation is that social norm managers are now less responsible. Previous enforcers tended to be more conscientious. This has been gradually less true, particularly in the third period. *Uncle Tom* has diverted from its past. It now frequently appears in situations devoid of even a whiff of duplicity.

But what should blacks do with *Uncle Tom*? In the third subsidiary argument, I address what place racial loyalty norms and *Uncle Tom* should have in contemporary society. Killing *Uncle Tom* and ceasing policing loyalty is the

---

[8] Angela Jones, African American Civil Rights: Early Activism and the Niagara Movement 50 (2011).

popular stance. But that's a terrible, potentially disastrous, idea. Rather, blacks must continue to constructively manage social norms, and *Uncle Tom* should be rehabilitated, not deserted. Because constructive social norms and *Uncle Tom* can still help blacks improve their condition, the group must resist any impulse to forsake them. Many malign the very idea of sellout rhetoric. I write, however, in defense of *Uncle Tom*.

I concede, though, that the *Uncle Tom* card is now overplayed. *Uncle Tom* is dealt to nearly every black person who voices conservatism. Publically opposing affirmative action, for instance, is a sure bet to be called an *Uncle Tom*. Yet criticizing the policy is far from treacherous. I hold, nevertheless, that the epithet can still aid in the pursuit of racial progress. In the quest for equality, it is imperative that blacks not sacrifice the race's well-being for personal gain or any other reason. Some are still guilty of this. And there will be more in future generations. Blacks, therefore, must be concerned about potential turncoats. *Uncle Tom* is a baleful epithet with the capacity to bolster racial fidelity. For self-defense, *Uncle Tom* must be retained although not unsheathed habitually. But, racial loyalty norms and *Uncle Tom* must remain in the arsenal because blacks' best opportunity for full emancipatory justice calls for group unity. A race cannot lift itself with turncoats weighing it down.

This book draws from legal history, American history, black studies, sociology, psychology, political science, and other disciplines to make the point that blacks can manage racial loyalty norms to promote their collective legal interests. Among the various fields this work may be linked to, it certainly is what legal historian Alfred Brophy refers to as applied legal history, legal historical scholarship that "speaks to contemporary issues." This book inspects the past to guide present and future generations in their quest for social justice.[9]

But I primarily intend to expand the debate within law and social norms literature. Legal scholars examining the intersection of law and social norms make various arguments. As seen in Robert Ellickson's *Order without Law* (1994) or Lisa Bernstein's work on the diamond industry, one prominent argument holds that disputes can be settled in the absence of law by using social norms. And as seen in the scholarship of Dan Kahan or Cass Sunstein, another argument holds that society can be improved if government, through law, manages social norms in certain contexts.[10]

---

[9]　Alfred L. Brophy, *Introducing Applied Legal History*, 31 *Law and History Review* 233, 233 (2013).

[10]　Robert Ellickson, Order Without Law (1994); Lisa Bernstein, *Opting out of the Legal System: Extralegal Contractual Relations in the Diamond Industry*, 21 *Journal of Legal Studies* 115 (1992); Sunstein, *Social Norms and Social Roles*; Dan M. Kahan, *Social Influence, Social Meaning and Deterrence*, 83 *Virginia Law Review* 349 (1997).

Another story, however, longs to be told, one obscured by the larger law and social norms narrative. My claim is that marginalized peoples can, and often should, contest their legal marginalization by managing norms within their own communities. Finding great potential, perhaps women can unlock a more equal future through the management of social norms. The lesbian, gay, bisexual, and transgendered community too might apply this principle to their plight. Or poor whites in Appalachia, perchance, may see the benefits of my position. This thesis has enormous potential for marginalized groups with varied legal grievances. This book explores how communities can manage social norms to promote their legal interests by examining one community, the black community, and one class of norms, those punishing racial treachery.

Chapter 1 provides the context about black solidarity, how *Uncle Tom* became an epithet and the difference between constructive and destructive social norms. In full, this chapter presents the background and structure on which the rest of the book builds. The following seven chapters examine the three different periods of these social norms: 1865–1959, 1960–1975,

I am not contending that these are the only arguments made within the law and social norm fields. There are countless examples of law and social norms scholarship produced by law professors. This following list is based on an amazing bibliography put together by Christopher Fennell, *Sources on Social Norms and Law*, available at: http://www.anthro. illinois.edu/faculty/cfennell/syllabus/normbib.htm. See, for instance, Eric A. Posner, Law and Social Norms (2002); Eric A. Posner, Social Norms, Nonlegal Sanctions, and the Law (2007); Norms and the Law (Editor John N. Drobak 2006); Lisa Bernstein, *Social Norms and Default Rule Analysis*, 3 *Southern California Interdisciplinary Law Journal* 59 (1993); Richard A. Posner, *Social Norms and the Law: An Economic Approach*, 87 *The American Economic Review* 365 (1997); Dan M. Kahan, *Gentle Nudges vs. Hard Shoves: Solving the Sticky Norms Problem*, 67 *University of Chicago Law Review* 607 (2000); Robert Cooter and Ariel Porat, *Should Courts Deduct Nonlegal Sanctions from Damages?*, 30 *Journal of Legal Studies* 401 (2001); Steven A. Hetcher, *Norm Proselytizers Create A Privacy Entitlement in Cyberspace*, 16 *Berkeley Technology Law Journal* 877 (2001); Dan M. Kahan and Eric A. Posner, *Shaming White-collar Criminals: A Proposal for Reform of the Federal Sentencing Guidelines*, 42 *Journal of Law and Economics* 365 (1999); Dan M. Kahan, *Reciprocity, Collective Action, and Community Policing*, 90 *California Law Review* 1513 (2003); Lawrence Lessig, *The Regulation of Social Meaning*, 62 *University of Chicago Law Review* 943 (1995); Lawrence Lessig, *Social Meaning and Social Norms*, 144 *University of Pennsylvania Law Review* 2181 (1996); Richard H. McAdams, *Signaling Discount Rates: Law, Norms, Economic Methodology*, 100 *Yale Law Journal* 625 (2001); Lawrence E. Mitchell, *Understanding Norms*, 49 *University of Toronto Law Journal* 177 (1999); Lior J. Strahilevitz, *How Changes in Property Regimes Influence Social Norms: Commodifying California's Carpool Lanes*, 75 *Indiana Law Journal* 1231 (2000); Lior J. Strahilevitz, *Charismatic Code, Social Norms, and the Emergence of Cooperation on the File-swapping Networks*, 89 *Virginia Law Review* 505 (2003); Cass Sunstein, *Selective Fatalism*, 27 *Journal of Legal Studies* 799 (1998); Robert C. Ellickson, *Controlling Chronic Misconduct in City Spaces: Of Panhandlers, Skid Rows, and Public-Space Zoning*, 105 *Yale Law Journal* 1165 (1996); Dan M. Kahan, *Between Economics and Sociology: The New Path of Deterrence*, 95 *Michigan Law Review* 2477 (1997).

and 1976–present. Two chapters are dedicated to the first two periods and three chapters are dedicated to the last. Each period has one chapter detailing the social norms that regulated the behavior of non-famous blacks and one doing the same with renowned blacks. The last period also has a chapter about Supreme Court Justice Clarence Thomas. These seven chapters assess the propriety of the various *Uncle Tom* accusations – determining who was and who was not guilty of betrayal – and establish how constructive norms helped blacks' overall legal interests and why destructive norms were imprudent. The final chapter, Chapter 9, explores what blacks should do with racial loyalty norms moving forward. Here I unpack my third subsidiary argument – that blacks should continue enforcing constructive racial loyalty norms to help advance collective legal interests and capacity to influence public policy.

1

Solidarity, Social Norms, and *Uncle Tom*

INTRODUCING *UNCLE TOM*

IN 1934, FISK UNIVERSITY, A BLACK college in Nashville, disciplined one of its students for protesting the school's decision to have student singers perform at a segregated theater. A columnist for the *Baltimore Afro-American*, a black newspaper, commended the student and criticized Fisk for bowing and scraping before Jim Crow. The columnist preferred to burn down all Southern black colleges rather than have the race's brightest young minds learn in "'Uncle Tom' Schools," which train their students to lie down while educators drain their valor to resist racism.[1]

A few months later and nearly 700 miles north, M. Gran Lucas, a black elementary school principal, defended segregation before a National Education Association gathering in Washington, DC. Lucas told the audience, which included President Franklin Roosevelt, that separate schools were best for black children. According to Lucas, black pupils had particular needs that integrated schools could not accommodate. Columnist L. K. McMillan lambasted the speech as one in a series of disgraceful pro–Jim Crow speeches blacks had delivered to national audiences in recent memory. Lucas, like the other speakers, was an "Uncle Tom" more concerned with receiving his "assured pork chops" than black children.[2]

These incredibly rich tales reveal various textures that represent just a piece of the intricate tapestry that is the black American existence. These accounts illustrate the burgeoning race consciousness and black solidarity

---

[1] Flying Cavalier, *Hats Off to Flory*, Afro-American, Mar. 31, 1934, at 15. From now on, when I refer to the *Afro-American* I mean the *Baltimore Afro-American*. A few other cities had their own *Afro-American* newspapers.

[2] L. McMillan, *McMillan Scourges Lucas for Favoring Dual School System*, Afro-American, July 14, 1934, at 14.

before the civil rights movement; they highlight the frequent expectations of racial loyalty; they reveal how the black community managed social norms; and they suggest the sanctioning power of *Uncle Tom*. Each of these separate ingredients, when stewed together, forms the basis of this book.

In this chapter, I provide the background structure upon which the rest of this book will build. First, I narrate how race consciousness and black solidarity arose and argue that blacks should enforce social norms to maintain and build that solidarity. I then champion black solidarity and differentiate between constructive and destructive racial loyalty norms. Next I investigate *Uncle Tom* and detail how a character from a novel became an epithet. Last I defend the continued use of *Uncle Tom*.

CHRONICLING BLACK SOLIDARITY

The story of social norms, racial treachery, and *Uncle Tom* is comprised of various smaller narratives. The foundational narrative, though, concerns what, beyond racism, sparked blacks to enforce racial loyalty. The catalysts are race consciousness – the identification with and loyalty toward one's racial group – and racial solidarity – the end state where the racially conscious unite around shared interests. Strong conceptions of both precede widespread expectations of loyalty.[3]

Our story opens with free blacks in the North in the late 1700s. The first black social movement, which indicates race consciousness and solidarity, was launched by free blacks seeking separate churches in the North. Their campaign for their own houses of worship began when blacks were increasingly present in white Baptist and Methodist pews. A sprinkling of Negroes among a sea of whites triggered no waves. A "mass" of dark faces, however, "caused [Northern whites] to react with the same prejudice as their brothers to the South." Rather than welcome the budding black population, white churchgoers limited their privileges. The movement for black churches, occurring in various Northern cities, encouraged race consciousness and solidarity among freemen.[4]

[3] W. O. Brown, *The Nature of Race Consciousness*, 10 *Social Forces* 90 (1931); W. O. Brown, *Race Consciousness among South African Natives*, 40 *American Journal of Sociology* 560–70 (1935); Alvin J. Schexnider, *The Development of Racial Solidarity in the Armed Forces*, 5 *Journal of Black Studies* 415, 415–16 (1975); William T. Hoston, *Black Solidarity and Racial Context: An Exploration of the Role of Black Solidarity in U.S. Cities*, 39 *Journal of Black Studies* 719 (2009).

[4] Joseph R. Washington Jr., Black Religion: The Negro and Christianity in the United States 187–88 (1966).

A November 1787 incident at St. George's Methodist Episcopal Church in Philadelphia prompted this movement. Several black parishioners were praying in the white section of the church and were dragged away while on their knees. Such episodes precipitated the formation of black churches around the country and the first black national denomination, the African Methodist Episcopal Church. These black churches were hotbeds of political debate and social welfare activities.[5]

The national black convention movement carries our story into the nineteenth century. Before the first national convention in 1830, there had been local variants. At a local convention in Philadelphia, attendees denounced the American Colonization Society's program of transporting free Negroes to Africa. The national convention movement, partly a response to the Cincinnati race riot of 1829, not only gave blacks a place to develop an agenda but also gave "the Black man a sense of identity" and "a feeling of confidence and self-respect." One general movement theme was that free blacks must petition Congress and state legislatures for equal rights. At a particular convention, some argued that blacks must violate the Fugitive Slave Act and assist their fellow brothers and sisters to escape bondage. Convention movement leaders sought citizenship and a place within American society, and the annual gatherings "provided [blacks] with an opportunity to arrive at a common perspective of problems and solutions." The convention movement's worldview disseminated to the masses, leading to blacks debating their problems without the help of sympathetic whites.[6]

The setting of our story is America, to the chagrin of a few. Indeed, some blacks, perhaps most notably Martin Delany, rejected an implicit premise of

[5] Id. at 187–93; Carter G. Woodson, The History of the Negro Church 72–73 (1921); E. Franklin Frazier, The Negro in the United States 79, 520–21 (1957 revised edition); Eddie S. Glaude Jr., Exodus!: Religion, Race and Nation in Early Nineteenth-Century Black America 24–25 (2000); Tomeiko Ashford Carter, *The Sentiment of the Christian Serial Novel: The Curse of Caste; or The Slave Bride and the AME Christian Recorder*, 40 *African American Review* 717 (2006); Richard S. Newman, Freedom's Prophet: Bishop Richard Allen, The AME Church, and the Black Founding Fathers 68–69 (2008); Carol V. R. George, Segregated Sabbaths: Richard Allen and the Emergence of Independent Black Churches 1760–1840 50 (1973); James T. Campbell, Songs of Zion: The African Methodist Episcopal Church in the United States and South Africa (1995).

[6] Frazier, The Negro in the United States 522; John W. Cromwell, *The Early Negro Convention Movement* 3, Occasional Papers No. 9 11 (The American Negro Academy 1904); Early Lee Fox, The American Colonization Society 46–47 (1917); Charles A. Gliozzo, *John Jones and the Black Convention Movement, 1848–1856*, 3 *Journal of Black Studies* 227 (1972); Howard H. Bell, *Expressions of Negro Militancy in the North, 1840–1860*, 45 *Journal of Negro History* 11, 11–12 (1960); Sundiata Keita Cha-Jua, America's First Black Town: Brooklyn, Illinois, 1830–1915 80 (2000); Howard Holman Bell, A Survey of the Negro Convention Movement – 1830–1861 (1969); John Wesley Cromwell, The Negro in American History 45–46 (1914).

the convention movement, that blacks should call America home. Believing that blacks were a nation within a nation, Delany advocated relocation to Africa, South America, or the West Indies. Delany's ideas ruffled white and black abolitionists alike. But like his black intellectual adversaries, he dipped his rhetoric in racial solidarity to rally blacks around his message, claiming that "not until the blacks of all the world unite will the American Negro be free."[7]

Northern pre–Civil War black newspapers further reflect maturing consciousness and solidarity, expanding our story. Black editors, prone to describing blacks regardless of slave status as "brethren," endeavored to uplift the race through the printed word. Black skin defined group membership.

Some editors implored blacks to meet white middle-class values regarding education, temperance, morality, thrift, and genteel social life. They posited that whites would notice and then grant them full equality. Pollyannaish about the eventual success of this strategy, some wrote as early as the 1830s that Negro youths at the time could one day be president. Whites would accept blacks as equals, the theory held, if the subordinate race proved itself. As one black man of the era thought, as long as whites "have nothing to hate in you but good will and piety" then race prejudice would dissipate. Time ultimately disproved the theory. If bigotry was based on a lack of evidence establishing blacks' ability, then their logic was sound. These editors learned a lesson, however, that blacks a century later were forced to relearn: racial discrimination was premised on white supremacy not syllogism. These episodes nonetheless demonstrate that some concluded that because individual aspirations were linked to that of the group, group solutions were required.[8]

The accounts of Northern black abolitionists deepen and add characters to our story, evidencing advancing black solidarity before the Great War. Racial kinship clearly propelled many black abolitionists. Take David Walker, for example. In his *Appeal to the Coloured Citizens of the World* (1829), Walker proclaimed that "we are the most degraded, wretched, and abject set of beings that ever lived since the world began." Blacks were complicit in their own misery, Walker argued, because they "were servile, treacherous, and cowardly." He claimed that these deficiencies hindered blacks' ability to heed his calling for black solidarity regardless of slave status. See abolitionist Henry Highland

[7] Victor Ullman and Martin R. Delany: The Beginnings of Black Nationalism 1, 141–43 (1971); Raymond L. Hall, Black Separatism in the United States 33–34 (1978); Martin R. Delany: A Documentary Reader 320–21 (Editor Robert S. Levine 2003).

[8] Frankie Hutton, The Early Black Press in America, 1827 to 1860 xiii, 32–33, 103–25 (1993); Frederick Cooper, *Elevating the Race: The Social Thought of Black Leaders, 1827–50*, 24 *American Quarterly* 604, 606, 609 (1972).

Garnet for additional proof that solidarity guided abolitionists. In a fiery speech at the 1849 National Negro Convention in Buffalo, Garnet implored his enslaved "brethren" to violently resist their bondage. William Whipper, Underground Railroad operative and editor of the *National Reformer*, a black journal, similarly claimed that blacks must remain in America, partly because their "brethren" were "suffering" in bondage. And the like-minded Harriet Tubman believed that "the good Lord had come down to deliver her people, and she must go and help Him."[9]

Yet the degree of unity still dissatisfied some blacks. Many stories have contrarians, and James McCune Smith is ours. Smith, an abolitionist, wrote Frederick Douglass in 1854, decrying the lack of black solidarity. "[W]e are not united as a people; and the main reason why," he wrote, "is that we are not equally oppressed.... You cannot pick out five hundred free colored men in the free States who equally labor under the same species of oppression." Smith was partially right; blacks endured varying "species of oppression." A slave's life got worse as he moved south. Slaves' experiences, of course, differed from those of free blacks. And bigotry's rain poured heavier in some Northern states than in others. Smith noted, for instance, that blacks could vote in Maine and Massachusetts; the skies were relatively clear. New York had property qualifications. Some states permitted a light-skinned black man to cast a ballot whereas other states did not. But the torrential Illinois disenfranchised blacks. A few states permitted interracial marriage. Others rejected these unions. Some permitted blacks to enter the state without encumbrance. Others required that they post bond. A few blocked their entry altogether. "The result is that each man feels his peculiar wrong," Smith wrote, "but no hundred men feel precisely the same oppression; and while each would do fair work to remove his own, he feels differently in regard to his neighbor's oppression."[10]

Despite Smith's gripes, the chain that joined black Americans was especially durable. The rest of the African diaspora had far weaker links, or sometimes

---

[9] Timothy Shortell, *The Rhetoric of Black Abolitionism: An Exploratory Analysis of Antislavery Newspapers in New York State*, 28 Social Science History 75, 76 (2004); David Walker, Appeal, in Four Articles; Together with a Preamble, to the Coloured Citizens of the World, but in Particular, and Very Expressly, to Those of the United States of America 3, 22–39 (1829); Henry Highland Garnet, A Memorial Discourse 44–51 (1865); Tommie Shelby, *White Supremacy and Black Solidarity: David Walker's Appeal* found in A New Literary History of America (Editors Greil Marcus and Werner Sollors 2009), available at: https://www.academia.edu/882507/White_Supremacy_and_Black_Solidarity_David_Walkers_Appeal; Hutton, The Early Black Press in America 30; R. C. Smedley, History of the Underground Railroad in Chester and the Neighboring Counties of Pennsylvania 251 (1968).

[10] Patrick Rael, Black Identity & Black Protest in the Antebellum North 12 (2002); The Works of James McCune Smith: Black Intellectual and Abolitionist 98–99 (Editors John Stauffer 2006).

no chain at all, just shackles of domination. In many Caribbean and South American countries, the general pattern was a "three-tiered 'caste' system" with enslaved darker blacks at the bottom, "free" mulattoes in the middle, and ruling-class whites at the top. This weed, however, never took root in America, permitting blacks to garden political unity. And in America, blacks cultivated "an understanding of black identity unique up to that point of any place in the world ... [A]ll people of African descent – the slave and the free, the light and the dark, the African and the creole – shared a common oppression that mandated the need for unified political action and hence a unified social identity."[11]

The antebellum South offered limited opportunity for blacks to express race consciousness and solidarity. Our story's pace quickly decelerates, therefore, when chronicling events in slave states. Various slave insurrections perhaps provide the best evidence for black solidarity. Denmark Vesey, a free black man, sought to enlist Rebels for his failed slave rebellion by appealing to the race consciousness among slaves in South Carolina. Vesey could have left for Africa but refused because "he wanted to stay and see what he could do for his fellow creatures in bondage." But the plot was foiled after two slaves informed whites of the rebellion. Executions followed. And Gabriel Prosser, the leader of a Virginia slave rebellion in 1800, thought God called him "to deliver his people from bondage."[12]

After the North and the South split, the bonds between blacks continued to harden, and our story's pace hastens. In 1864, a racial protest organization headed by John Mercer Langston, the National Equal Rights League (NERL), formed in response to segregation and exclusion in the North. In its founding constitution, the organization maintained that through emotional appeals and law when possible, the NERL would work to secure black citizenship. In his address to attendees of the organization's first annual meeting in Cleveland, Ohio, in 1865, William D. Forten explicitly encouraged solidarity. "[T]o accomplish this much-desired end" of legal equality, announced Forten, "we must be a unit." "Together we must rally," he continued, "and forge a chain of consanguinity and interest, reaching around this land of infamy and wrong,

[11] Rael, Black Identity & Black Protest in the Antebellum North 13–14.
[12] Frazier, The Negro in the United States 522; Research in the Social Scientific Study of Religion 106 (Editors Joanne M. Greer and David O. Moberg Vol. 10 1999); The Atlantic Monthly. A Magazine of Literature, Art, and Politics *Denmark Vesey* 731 (Vol. VII 1861); Archibald H. Grimke The American Negro Academy, Occasional papers No 7: *Right on the Scaffold, or the Martyrs of 1822* found in Occasional Papers, Issues 1–22, 23 (American Negro Academy 1970); Benjamin Griffith Brawley, A Social History of the American Negro 86–88 (1921).

and every black man must constitute a link." Forten claimed, furthermore, that the black leaders in attendance must teach the rest of the race that racial progress hinged on "unity of effort." But persuading some blacks to fight for their rights proved difficult for the NERL's Pennsylvania chapter. One "local leader" decried that "'the worst set of men' would 'give there [*sic*] life for a ball game or a parade but when you come to muster them together to get them to advocate their rights or furnish means for others to do it for them, it is like trying to force water to run uphill.'"[13]

One indication of race consciousness and solidarity during the last two decades of the nineteenth century was the formation of the Afro-American League in 1887, which later became the National Afro-American League in 1890. This nonpartisan political protest organization was the brainchild of Thomas Fortune, the editor of the black newspaper the *New York Age*. The organization combated Southern disfranchisement, lynching, funding disparities between black and white schools, Southern criminal justice system abuses, and segregation. Fortune credited the League with sounding "the death knell of the shuffling, cringing creature in black who for two centuries and a half had given the right of way to white men...." Although the organization was ultimately doomed, it's a crucial part of our story; it exemplifies blacks, after Reconstruction, seeking to improve their condition through group enterprise.[14]

But our story's finest evidence of black solidarity in the late 1800s and early 1900s lies with black people themselves. Up until this point, we have focused mainly on the utterances of the prominent. But the day-to-day lives of ordinary blacks provide the best indication of the current of black solidarity flowing through black America, giving blacks the requisite power to contest their marginalization. Black businessmen, for instance, implored blacks that the best of the race patronized black-owned businesses. Kansas City's Business League made it almost criminal for blacks to purchase goods or services from a white business when a black alternative existed. Pure self-interest

---

[13] William F. Cheek and Aimee Lee Cheek, John Mercer Langston and the Fight for Black Freedom 1829–65 430 (1996); First Annual Meeting of the National Equal Rights League, Held in Cleveland, Ohio 33, 39 (1865); Hugh Davis, *The Pennsylvania State Equal Rights League and the Northern Black Struggle for Legal Equality, 1864–1877*, 126 *Pennsylvania Magazine of History and Biography* 611, 612, 617 (2002).

[14] Emma Lou Thornbrough, *The National Afro-American League, 1887–1908*, 27 *Journal of Southern History* 494, 494–96 (1961); Michael L. Goldstein, *Preface to the Rise of Booker T. Washington: A View from New York City of the Demise of Independent Black Politics, 1889–1902*, 62 *Journal of Negro History* 81, 82–83 (1977); Emma Lou Thornbrough, T. Thomas Fortune: Militant Journalist 110 (1972); Harold Cruse, Plural but Equal: A Critical Study of Blacks and Minorities and America's Plural Society 9–10 (1987).

partly compelled these sentiments. A black storeowner benefited when racial
obligation directed black customers into his shop and away from his white
competitors. But, beyond selfish motives, the thinking was that racial liberation had an economic component, and black solidarity – a pulling together
of resources – offered an effective solution. Like one businessman said in
1898, "nothing could be gained by disunited elements, everything by unity
of action." Blacks engaged in various welfare activities, moreover, including "general charity, women's clubs, old folks' homes, orphanages, hospitals,
social and literary clubs, libraries, day nurseries, kindergartens, and settlement
houses." At the dawn of the twentieth century, blacks were a united people. As
historian August Meier wrote, "By [1890] it was clear that the main themes in
Negro thinking of the race problem were that for the most part Negroes must
work out their own salvation in a hostile environment and that, furthermore,
they must be united in their efforts at racial elevation."[15]

The monthly *The Voice of the Negro*, published from 1904 to 1907, is an
integral source for our story, documenting solidarity during the first years of
the twentieth century. Common in *Voice* writings were calls for unity. In his
article "Come Let Us Reason Together," for example, Kelly Miller, a leading
black intellectual, bemoaned the level of disagreement among black leaders.
Miller hoped that in 1906, black leaders would concentrate on where they
agreed rather than on points of discord. "The supreme need of the race,"
Miller explained, "is a consolidation of its forces, so as to present a solid pha-
lanx to the powers arrayed against it." Activist Fannie Barrier Williams, in
discussing the club movement among black women, wrote in the *Voice* that
black women were banding together for "the social uplift of the Negro race"
and instilling a "co-operative helpfulness among colored women."[16]

In 1905, a year after the first issue of the *Voice* was released, W. E. B. Du
Bois and William Monroe Trotter founded the all-black Niagara Movement,
a seminal moment in our story, one worthy of its own chapter. Twenty-nine
of the Talented Tenth – the black intellectual elite – assembled near the border city of Niagara Falls, Canada, to initiate a campaign for abolishing racial
discrimination and segregation in America. The Movement's "Declaration
of Principles" called for "persistent manly agitation" as "the way for liberty,"
not "cowardice and apology." The Niagara Movement fought for full suffrage

[15] August Meier, Negro Thought in America 1800–1915 121–38 (4th edition 1969).
[16] Bethany Johnson, *Freedom and Slavery in the Voice of the Negro: Historical Memory and African-American Identity, 1904–1907*, 84 Georgia Historical Society 29, 40 (2000); Kelley Miller, *Come Let Us Reason Together*, Voice of the Negro, Jan. 1906 at 47; Fannie Barrier Williams, *The Club Movement among Colored Women*, Voice of the Negro, Mar. 1904, at 99.

rights, equality in public accommodations, freedom of association rights, and equal enforcement of the laws "against rich as well as poor, against capitalists as well as laborers, against white as well as black."

Opposing the accommodationist program of Booker T. Washington, during its 1906 convention in Harpers Ferry, West Virginia, the Niagara Movement declared that blacks "shall not be satisfied with less than our full manhood rights." Like the National Afro-American League before it, the Niagara Movement took ownership for installing a fighting spirit in Negroes. At its final annual gathering in August 1909, the organization claimed that "[f]or four years The Niagara Movement has struggled to make ten million Americans of negro descent cease from mere apology and weak surrender to aggression, and take a firm unfaltering stand for justice, manhood, and self-assertion."

The movement did indeed push blacks to insist on equality. The organization's protest ideology eventually dethroned Booker T. Washington's program of accommodation, becoming a blueprint for subsequent civil rights groups. Du Bois subsequently helped found the National Association for the Advancement of Colored People (NAACP), eventually becoming its director of publicity and editor of *The Crisis* in 1910. *The Crisis*, the NAACP's magazine, featured content promoting race consciousness and black solidarity.[17]

World War I was crucial in developing race consciousness and black solidarity in the early twentieth century. In 1919, a year after the war's end, one sociologist wrote that "the old fashioned Negro preferred to go to the white man for everything," but "the new Negro, with growing race-consciousness urges his people to work together and to stand together." Before American involvement in the war, blacks appreciated that they were expected to liberate foreigners while being less than free at home. Blacks supported the war effort, although that support was counterbalanced by demands for legal equality. When the black soldier returned home, however, he remained Jim Crowed and disfranchised, and faced the threat of lynching. Fighting for

---

[17] Sources for the Niagara Movement discussion: W. E. B. Du Bois, *The Talented Tenth* in The Negro Problem: A Series of Articles by Representative American Negroes 33 (Editor Booker T. Washington 1903); Frazier, The Negro in the United States 523–26; *A Century Ago: The Niagara Movement Meets at Faneuil Hall*, 58 Journal of Blacks in Higher Education 93 (Winter 2007/2008); Elliot M. Rudwick, *The Niagara Movement*, 42 The Journal of Negro History 177, 179, 200 (1957); Christopher E. Forth, *Booker T. Washington and the 1905 Niagara Movement Conference*, 72 Journal of Negro History 45, 46 (1987); J. N. Larned, History for Ready Reference: From the Best Historians, Biographers, and Specialists 533 (1910); Jones, African American Civil Rights 49; W. E. B. Du Bois, *The Niagara Movement*, The Voice of the Negro, Sept. 1905 at 619; The Niagara Movement, Declaration of Principles (1905); Joy James, Transcending the Talented Tenth: Black Leaders and American Intellectuals 16 (1997).

democracy abroad followed by postwar disappointment at home bolstered race consciousness. Emmett J. Scott, aide to the war secretary and the highest-ranking black member of President Wilson's administration, contended that World War I sharpened blacks' grievances with the status quo. The black man, according to Scott,

> wants justice in the courts substituted for lynching, the privilege of serving on juries, the right to vote, and the right to hold office like other citizens. He wants, moreover, universal suffrage, better educational facilities, the abolition of the "Jim Crow" car, discontinuance of unjust discriminatory regulations and segregation in the various departments of the Government, the same military training for Negro youths as for white,... the destruction of the peonage system, an economic wage scale to be applied to whites and blacks alike, better housing conditions for Negro employees in industrial centers, better sanitary conditions in the Negro sections of cities, and reforms in the Southern penal institutions.[18]

The story of race consciousness and black solidarity has no natural end; it is ongoing, playing out in the interactions of black folk every day. St. Clair Drake and Horace Cayton demonstrated this in their study of Chicago's South Side Bronzeville neighborhood based on research and interviews conducted in the late 1930s. *Black Metropolis* (1945), their study, will serve as our ending. Interviewees thought that their success in America depended on "presenting some sort of united front against" whites. As one interviewee voiced, "The Negroes might be able to do something if they would stick together." But Bronzeville residents believed that blacks lacked cohesion. Residents offered many explanations. Jealousy was one. A failure of leadership was another. But all agreed; disunity hurt the race. The local community believed that solidarity would enable blacks to form organizations to remedy the race's ills. As one woman said, "the solution of the race problem rests with the race itself. The Negro as a whole must become more race-conscious, and form organizations that will bring the race issue before the public."[19]

Solidarity, according to social science research, is common among subordinate groups. Psychologists have found, for example, that group solidarity arises

<hr>

[18] Loraine Richardson Green, The Rise of Race-Consciousness in the American Negro 5 (dissertation 1919); John Hope Franklin and Alfred A. Moss Jr., From Slavery to Freedom: A History of African Americans 346–54 (7th edition 1994); *Deaths*, The University of Chicago Magazine, Feb. 1996, available at: http://magazine.uchicago.edu/9602/9602BOBDeaths.html; William G. Jordan, Black Newspapers & America's War for Democracy, 1914–1920 36–39; 105; Emmett J. Scott, The American Negro in the World War 411, 458, 459, 465 (1919).

[19] St. Clair Drake and Horace R. Cayton, Black Metropolis: A Study of Negro Life in a Northern City 723–30 (Volume 2 1962).

when low-status groups attribute their subordination to collective injustice, particularly when such groups believe that their disadvantage can be relieved through united effort. Some low-status group members avoid the stigma associated with their group membership, however, by pursuing exit or mobility strategies. An exit strategy enables members to move from lower-status to higher-status groups. Racial passing is an exit strategy. By presenting themselves as white, persons with African ancestry escape the burdens of blackness. An individual mobility strategy encompasses many maneuvers, including making oneself useful to the dominant group at the expense of one's own group in exchange for personal benefits. Treachery allows one to ascend the ladder.[20]

If large percentages of blacks reason that racial progress requires solidarity, impeders of that solidarity would naturally be ostracized. Again, social science literature supports this point. Psychologists report that low-status groups clean "deviants" out of their own nest before contesting their subordination. Deviants are low-status group members shunned for "prevent[ing] improvement in the group's status by blocking the in-group's attempts to bring about social change." Deviants violate group social norms and are consequently sanctioned. By ensuring that their ranks are deviant-free, subordinate groups prepare for intergroup conflict.[21]

In his defense of black solidarity, philosopher Tommie Shelby identifies five elements required for a "robust form of solidarity" that generates collective action: group identification, special concern, shared values or goals, mutual trust, and loyalty. Because group solidarity requires loyalty, blacks must punish those breaching collective obligations. Thus, blacks need rules and ways to enforce them. This is the function of racial loyalty norms. They are enforcement mechanisms. These norms are proscriptive; they instruct people on what not to do.[22] People obey norms for various reasons, including "fear, benevolence, and the desire to fulfill others' legitimate expectations." Some

---

[20] Naomi Ellemers, Henk Wilke, and Ad van Knippenberg, Effects of Legitimacy of Low Group or Individual Status on Individual and Collective Status-Enhancement Strategies, 64 *Journal of Personality and Social Psychology* 766, 777 (1993); Randall Kennedy, *Racial Passing*, 62 *Ohio State Law Journal* 1145 (2001); Henri Tajfel and John Turner, *An Integrative Theory of Intergroup Conflict* found in The Psychology of Intergroup Relations 43 (Editors Stephen Worchel and William G. Austin 1986); Kathy Russell, Midge Wilson, and Ronald Hall, The Color Complex: The Politics of Skin Color among African Americans 73 (1992).

[21] Daan Scheepers, Nyla R. Branscombe, Russell Spears, and Bertjan Doose, *The Emergence and Effects of Deviants in Low and High Status Groups*, 38 *Journal of Experimental Social Psychology* 611, 611–12, 616 (2002).

[22] This should be understood in contradistinction to prescriptive norms, which direct persons to perform certain activities.

obey norms, moreover, to avoid self-imposed discipline like shame and regret. But external discipline is crucial here. That is, the true power of racial loyalty norms is that, if broken, enforcers will deliver embarrassing and often public punishment. Racial loyalty norms can direct blacks away from behaviors that impede group goals. The disloyal will be maligned as race traitors and branded as *Uncle Toms.*[23]

SOLIDARITY – WHAT IS IT GOOD FOR?

Because I advocate that blacks manage racial loyalty norms to forge group unity, obviously I strongly champion black solidarity. The key test is whether it places blacks "in a ... more effectual position[] to address the environment that called [it] forth." It does.[24]

Community dialogues concerning a common problem, racism, precede black solidarity. Whether overt like Jim Crow or the more subtle yet still pernicious racism of today, shared barriers to the complete enjoyment of American democracy's benefits are still discussed among blacks. Through these discussions, blacks endorse collective action and then debate strategies and ideas that will remove that common problem, racism, which binds individual blacks.[25]

Black solidarity can be sculpted with different organizing principles, including a shared history, biological roots, culture, or even a skin color. I believe blacks should organize around a mutual interest in lessening or eliminating the burdens of antiblack racism. Because a society free of bigotry benefits all, this "oppression-centered" solidarity rallies blacks into joint action. I am much less concerned with why one embraces solidarity, though. That one embraces black solidarity because of the allure of cultural sameness, for instance, is unproblematic. Rather than require a specific path, that the journey leads to the proper destination matters most.[26]

When policing loyalty, however, blacks must only focus on oppression-centered solidarity. Monitoring cultural blackness, for example, would stifle black solidarity. How should blackness be defined? What is the authentic black

---

[23] Tommie Shelby, We Who Are Dark 67–71 (2005); Michael Hechter, Principles of Group Solidarity 59 (1987); Cristina Bicchieri, The Grammar of Society, The Nature and Dynamics of Social Norms 42 (2006); Ofer H. Azar, *What Sustains Social Norms and How They Evolve? The Case of Tipping,* 54 *Journal of Economic Behavior & Organization* 49, 50, 59–60 (2004).

[24] Melvin Rogers, *Liberalism, Narrative, and Identity: A Pragmatic Defense of Racial Solidarity,* 6 Theory and Event (2002).

[25] Rogers, *Liberalism, Narrative, and Identity,* at 34.

[26] Shelby, We Who Are Dark 4; Roy L Brooks, Racial Justice in the Age of Obama 82–86 (2009).

culture? What about those not meeting presumed indicia of blackness? These questions will produce answers divorcing instead of wedding blacks. Indeed, blacks reap nothing through prosecutions of insufficient cultural blackness.

But what is antiblack racism? Some, on one hand, may champion a broad interpretation. In May 2004, Bill Cosby rebuked the black underclass for "not holding up their end in this deal." Cosby's thesis was that "the miserable condition of the black poor [was] brought on by their own self-destructive behavior." Cosby's words could be considered antiblack. Others, on the other hand, will defend a narrow meaning, considering only the most repugnant deeds – purposeful sabotaging of black interests – as qualifying. To my mind, to be "anti" means to be hostile to the goodwill of a particular entity. Black solidarity, therefore, requires repudiating actions that are either intended to harm or that can only harm blacks. Cosby's words do not qualify. As tough parenting is no act against a child, even harsh words against one's community must not automatically be considered an instance of antiblack racism.[27]

No one is directed toward specific policy prescriptions under this conception of black solidarity. Blacks need space to debate the merit of varying strategies for racial uplift. Because no person has *the* answer to the many ailments that beleaguer blacks, my goal is to shape an environment where blacks, animated by mutual concern, debate solutions. Unpopular ideas are welcomed. Blacks must insist, however, that whatever "panacea" an individual race member espouses, it be argued intellectually honestly, believing it to benefit the group. Indeed, the championing of any argument must be activated and propelled by pure devotion. Charging one with betrayal when one's policy beliefs are animated by robust fidelity is indefensible, unless those beliefs are so repugnant that no sensible person could ever voice them. But those indifferent to or even antagonistic to the group deserve the treachery label. Bad faith actors should never be permitted to poison the deliberations that blacks must foster.[28]

But, as abolitionist James McCune Smith noted in 1854, blacks do not suffer from the same species of oppression. Since the experiences of the field and house slave, stratification has marked the black existence. Perhaps economics now cause the deepest fissures. Since the civil rights movement, the ranks of the black middle class have swelled. Blacks currently occupy upper-class white-collar positions more than ever. Many are, therefore, less vulnerable to racism. Yet the black underclass has remained large and disillusioned. Solidarity requires "members of a group being able to identify something that they have

---

[27] Michael Eric Dyson, Is Bill Cosby Right?: Or Has the Black Middle Class Lost Its Mind? xi–xvi (2005).

[28] Tommie Shelby makes a similar point in Shelby, We Who Are Dark 247–48.

in common which provides a shared basis for their collective [endeavor]." Economic stratification, however, produces varied interests. The issue then becomes why non-underclass blacks would embrace an oppression-centered solidarity. This problem is exacerbated if E. Franklin Frazier's estimation in the 1950s – that the "black bourgeoisie do not really wish to be identified with Negroes" – remains true. It might. Lawrence Otis Graham, in his 1999 study of the black elite, wrote that "there are those of us who buy into theories of superiority, and who feel embarrassed by our less accomplished black brethren." This is a common frustration for building solidarity; it is more easily maintained through social coercion in homogeneous groups.[29]

Although the black underclass may gain more by signing this communal contract, "secure" blacks gain too. Self-interest compels all to elevate the status of the race; even the highest are a blunder away from a long fall. And the upper and middle classes are sure to reach new heights in a world sans discrimination. The family and friends of secure blacks, moreover, may occupy the lower rungs of society. To support their loved ones, the better off should participate in black solidarity. And last, the black underclass is likely to retain its unenviable status unless all contribute to the group effort. The moral compass points blacks, who all to varying degrees suffer from the effects of race-specific oppression, to assist the most afflicted.[30]

But black solidarity should not be compulsory. If one wants to reject racial obligations, one should be free to make that choice. Some will conclude that black solidarity will stunt their personal liberty and pursuit of happiness. Such folk should be allowed to reject the enterprise. And, more important, blacks must never criticize anyone for eschewing black solidarity. Their ideas are vulnerable to attack like anyone else's. But "opting out" must not expose anyone to rebuke. I assume that all of the persons discussed in the book embraced black solidarity, absent reason to conclude otherwise.

Those rejecting solidarity, however, cannot reap the benefits that the group provides to individual members. That is, blacks should monitor free riders. Here, a free rider is one "who obtains benefits from group membership but does not bear a proportional share of the costs of providing the benefits." Thus, a public intellectual who has repudiated black solidarity but later believes he has been the victim of racism must not ask the broader community to take up

---

[29] E. Ophelia Settle, *Social Attitudes During the Slave Regime: Household Servants Versus Field Hands* in The Making of Black America: Essays in Negro Life & History Vol. 1 148–52 (Editors August Meier and Elliott Rudwick 1969); James D. McGhee, Black Solidarity: The Tie that Binds 5 (National Urban League 1983); E. Franklin Frazier, Black Bourgeoisie 216 (1997); Lawrence Otis Graham, Our Kind of People: Inside America's Black Upper Class 18 (1999).

[30] Graham Crow, Social Solidarities: Theories, Identities and Social Change 116, 121 (2002).

arms in defense. By rejecting black solidarity, he has surrendered any claims to group benefits. But people should have the opportunity to rejoin after having opted out.[31]

Allowing opt-outs addresses potential complications posed by burgeoning ethnic diversity. Blacks from Africa and the Caribbean, or those self-identifying as biracial or multiracial, may bristle at compulsory black solidarity. *Washington Post* columnist Eugene Robinson argued that there are four black communities, one comprising "two nearly Emergent groups – individuals of mixed-race heritage and communities of recent black immigrants – that make us wonder what 'black' is even supposed to mean." As author Malcolm Gladwell once wrote about his mixed heritage, "I have to think about [whether I am black], and turn the issue over in my mind, gaze in the mirror and wonder, as I was so memorably asked, *what* I am." The one-drop rule and the paper bag test are far less relevant in a world where mixed-race Americans push for census categories allowing them to self-classify as multiracial and not just black. Those rejecting a singular black identity, therefore, can opt out.[32]

In three situations, however, blacks should be deemed to have necessarily opted in. The first concerns persons consciously using group resources. Anyone suing under antidiscrimination law, for example, has opted in. Racial justice movements produced legislation like the Civil Rights Act. To bring a Title VII lawsuit but reject solidarity is "free riderism" of epic proportions. Indeed, such a person is willing to fight discrimination against themselves, but no one else, yet avail themselves of laws that black solidarity helped produce.

Second, those using their blackness to legitimate their arguments cannot opt out. Black skin, in race debates, is a commodity. When a black person speaks, listeners assume various things, including that the speaker cares about the group and has its best interests at heart and that the speaker has knowledge through lived experiences. When a black person uses their racial identity to give authenticity to their positions, or fails to challenge others who vicariously do it for them, the use of that commodity affects the rest of the group. To spend that commodity, but repudiate any duty to those who hold it, is another manner of free riderism. That is not to say that all blacks who "talk race"

---

[31] Mancur Olson, The Logic of Collective Action: Public Goods and the Theory of Groups (1971); Robert Albanese and David D. Van Fleet, *Rational Behavior in Groups: The Free-Riding Tendency*, 10 *The Academy of Management Review* 244, 244 (1985).

[32] Eugene Robinson, Disintegration: The Splintering of Black America 5 (2010); Malcolm Gladwell, *Lost in the Middle* found in Half and Half 124 (1998); Kerry Ann Rockquemore and David L. Brunsma, Beyond Black: Biracial Identity in America 39–40 (Editor Claudine Chiawei O'Hearn 2002). To read firsthand accounts of multiracial persons, see Lise Funderburg, Black, White, Other: Biracial Americans Talk about Race and Identity (1994).

must embrace black solidarity. Rather, opt-outs must seek to participate no differently than would a nonblack person.[33]

The third circumstance concerns blacks strategically opting in and opting out to maximize outcomes. Throughout the course of a lifetime, one may seek to benefit by completing tasks for antiblack organizations or gain from using group resources. Perhaps purely theoretical, such cynical ploys must be disallowed nevertheless.

Some black conservatives critique black solidarity. They contend that the goal of the civil rights movement – legal equality – has been secured and socioeconomic disparities are due to blacks' cultural and moral failings, not racism. Proponents of this position argue that black solidarity breeds a culture of victimization, hampering self-improvement. Racial solidarity, they argue, must therefore be eschewed.[34]

The critique crumbles, however, when analyzed. If widespread cultural pathologies permeate within the black community, one can only wonder how black conservatives presume these problems can be corrected. If blacks must reject racial solidarity, black conservatives are then relying on millions of individual epiphanies among the black underclass. The argument is that blacks suffer from group pathologies. But that any solution must exclude group effort is odd. Communal efforts can surely inspire the black underclass to reform behaviors that supposedly stunt advancement. Those endorsing this critique, in fact, should vigorously endorse black solidarity. Indeed, if blacks are guilty of self-sabotage, remedies can be implemented without the help of outsiders.

CONSTRUCTIVE SOCIAL NORMS

Racial loyalty norms arrange into two categories: constructive and destructive.[35] Constructive norms promote racial solidarity; they punish treachery that obstructs the goals of a unified people. Constructive norms are not mutually exclusive. One act, that is, can violate multiple norms.

Destructive social norms, however, discourage solidarity; they overregulate behavior. These norms discipline actors for non-treacherous behaviors. Group rules perceived as illegitimate and overbearing sour efforts to build black solidarity. Thus, destructive norms alienate some blacks from solidarity.

---

[33] This second scenario may actually be another instance of free riderism, but its importance demands that it be treated as a separate category.

[34] Tommie Shelby provides a good synopsis of this argument. Shelby, We Who Are Dark 5. For a discussion of self-sabotage, see John McWhorter, Losing the Race: Self-Sabotage in Black America (2001).

[35] Some social norms, theoretically, could be neutral, but I'm not centrally focused on those.

There are three constructive racial loyalty norms. The first punishes consciously advancing the enemies' interests. The second penalizes inexcusable meekness in the face of racism. And the third censures blacks for lacking concern for the race. Each norm encourages solidarity. If fewer violated these norms in the 1940s, for example, the community would have better positioned itself to challenge Jim Crow. That is, adherence to these norms enhances blacks' capacity to author legal triumphs.

Let's examine these constructive norms separately. There are obvious hypotheticals of a person consciously promoting enemy interests. A black person who clandestinely works for the Ku Klux Klan and infiltrates a racial uplift organization to appease his Klan bosses, for instance, would obviously qualify.

But I use the word "consciously" for a reason. I propose something approaching intent, intent to aid. See, for example, a black prosecutor who seeks the death penalty for a black defendant accused of murdering a Klansman. The prosecutor is not culpable even though the KKK would cheer the decision. A close connection between the motivation to seek the death penalty and the enemy's interest being promoted is required. The prosecutor, more specifically, would need to have intended to please the Klan by his decision. Toiling for white supremacists' approval warrants swift castigation.

Can blacks never work for an antiblack organization? The answer appears obvious: no. It may not, however, be so obvious to some. In 1993, Anthony Griffin, a black attorney for the American Civil Liberties Union in Texas, garnered national attention for representing Michael Lowe, the head of the Texas Knights of the KKK. The Texas Human Rights Commission demanded that Lowe divulge his membership lists. Many will argue that Griffin was merely doing what lawyers must sometimes do, representing the unpopular but defending the sacrosanct. As Griffin himself said, "[W]e can never take the position that the Constitution does not apply to our enemies." In the cause for black solidarity, however, certain vocations cannot carry special privileges or the enterprise will seem inequitable and consequently falter. Group rules must appear fair. Attorneys consider constitutional rights as especially important. The black masses, though, are unlikely to condone an attorney representing avowed racists, particularly when nonblack attorneys are available.[36]

---

[36] Griffin was also the chief counsel to a local NAACP branch. The branch eventually fired him, citing a conflict of interest, of which there certainly was. The NAACP fights white supremacists and their organizations. Its chief counsel cannot, then, represent the Klan.

Richard Delgado, Yes: More Than Speech Was at Stake, 79 *American Bar Association Journal* 32 (1993); Sam Howe Verhovek, A Klansman's Black Lawyer, and a Principle, New York Times, Sept. 10, 1993, at B9; Delida Costin, *Anthony P. Griffin*, 4 *Boston University Public Interest Law Journal* 107, 109 (1994).

The second racial loyalty norm sanctions blacks for inexcusable meekness in the face of racism. Two words are crucial: "inexcusable" and "meekness." Starting first with meekness, here I mean docile and submissive. For example, a black law professor who remains silent when the school's faculty discriminates against black faculty candidates is being meek. Or take a black public intellectual who is too timid to denounce a politician's racist utterance. His inaction signals submissiveness.

Context matters, though. By inexcusable, I limit the scenarios where meekness warrants criticism. Certain competing interests or considerations must moderate our expectations. What if the silent black professor is untenured and fears that agitation might jeopardize his career? Or what if the politician who uttered the racist remark would retaliate in ways that would hurt the public intellectual's earning potential? Although these inactions are submissive, extenuating circumstances render denunciation improper. One must not be forced to jeopardize one's career in order to demonstrate fidelity.

Racial loyalty norms are powerful because they help build black solidarity. Blacks have enormous interest in ensuring that blacks resist, rather than surrender to, racism. A docile underclass will remain an underclass. Many blacks, in fact, believed that resistance was perhaps counterproductive because their suffering would translate to rewards in the afterlife. To fashion a better tomorrow, however, blacks must boldly confront oppression. As legal historian Michael Klarman writes, "One precondition for eventually overthrowing white supremacy was empowering southern blacks to overcome the norms of deference and subordination that many had internalized in self-defense."[37]

The last constructive racial loyalty norm reprimands blacks for not caring about the race. Punishing the uninterested notifies everyone that their investment in the race's well-being is expected. Violators of this norm will typically be uncommitted to eliminating society of antiblack racism.

The threshold question is, what does it mean to not care about the race? To violate this norm, one does not have to hate black people, or be indifferent to their fortune, although that certainly qualifies. One can actually care about the group, in the sense that one roots for its improvement, yet violate this norm. The unfaithful husband still cares for his wife. If she were struck with some deadly disease, he would undoubtedly mourn and fret over her fate. But his infidelity is a blow against their union; it is proof that he is willing to put something above his marriage. To not care about black people is really

---

[37] Michael Klarman, Unfinished Business: Racial Equality in American History 108–09 (2007); Hortense Powdermaker, *The Channeling of Negro Aggression by the Cultural Process* found in The Making of Black America: Essays in Negro Life & History Vol. 2 100–01 (Editors August Meier and Elliott Rudwick 1971).

to abuse the bonds of blackness. This can be achieved through antagonism or apathy toward the black condition but also by committing acts that reveal *gross* impurities in one's devotion to the group. By gross impurities, I mean flagrant offenses against the group that demonstrate the transgressor is an unreliable participant in black solidarity. Thus, if a black person commits such acts against the marriage I hold that the person does not care about the race.

Another question is, what evidence establishes this infraction? Policy positions are usually helpful only in blatant scenarios. Championing, say, Jim Crow segregation is necessarily duplicitous. But since the 1960s, few have endorsed obviously repugnant policies. All persuasive evidence is admissible and might establish the following: close associations with or defending well-known racists, intellectual inconsistency or dishonest arguments that appear more pretextual than sincere, or even a willingness to engage in actions that hurt the broader group. All of these would violate this norm.

Most often the evidence would be circumstantial. Direct evidence generally will be unavailable. The secret diary of a judge that contains admissions of racial desertion will remain hidden. Thus, this endeavor requires proving a state of mind based on indirect data, a difficult task. Even flagrant violators will avoid punishment if norm enforcers must provide direct evidence. In determining racial apathy, the evidentiary burden must therefore be relaxed; the betrayer can hide his transgressions in various ways. A "by a preponderance of evidence" standard is proper; it balances the need to punish betrayal against the fear of wrongful convictions. If, after weighing all available evidence, a race member concludes that it is more likely than not that the accused does not care about the group, then sanction is permissible. Blacks can examine one's utterances and actions to determine whether one cares about the race.

Having outlined the three constructive norms, I must address a couple questions. First, whose values am I applying? Am I holding blacks living a century ago to twenty-first-century conceptions of submissiveness, for instance? This might be unfair because blacks once lived under real threats of physical danger. Some might argue that judging racial treachery by current conceptions is unjust in such circumstances. But evaluating previous generations on their own standards is improper when later generations have exposed the flawed thinking of their forbearers. Take slavery, for instance. That bondage was once accepted must not exonerate former slave owners. In the following chapters, I am investigating whether various actions hindered efforts to build black solidarity. Even if shameful obsequiousness were once more tolerable, that cannot inoculate anyone from criticism. But the facts of a particular era must be part of the equation. Thus, submissiveness might mean something different when lynching was an ever-present danger.

The second question is, how can we relive events so far removed? How can we know all of the facts to determine whether treachery occurred? Often I have enough evidence to conclude if racial loyalty norms were violated. But when information is too insufficient, my language reflects that uncertainty.

By tracing *Uncle Tom*, we can discover how these racial loyalty norms have been managed throughout time. When one is branded an *Uncle Tom* one is being prosecuted for violating a racial loyalty norm. From there, we can assess the propriety of that specific prosecution. That is, we can determine whether the norm was constructive or destructive.

DESTRUCTIVE SOCIAL NORMS

Destructive racial loyalty norms encompass three distinct ideas. The first destructive norm more accurately describes an unsuccessful prosecution of a constructive norm. Indicting someone for furthering the enemy's interest when the asserted enemy is actually a friend is destructive. Charging someone with being inexcusably meek without evidence is likewise destructive, as is lambasting one for racial apathy when one's devotion has been unwavering. All are destructive racial loyalty norms.

The second destructive norm is not technically a norm. Norms have widespread legitimacy in the population where they operate. Indeed, "the very existence of a social norm depends on a sufficient number of people believing that it exists and pertains to a given type of situation, and expecting that enough other people are following it in those kinds of situations."[38] Nearly all blacks agree, for example, that blacks should not work on behalf of the race's enemies. Blacks would likewise concur that inexcusable meekness in the face of racism warrants criticism. Last, few blacks would intervene if harsh criticism befell a black person who announced racial apathy. Blacks understand these to be transgressions.

Some destructive norms, however, are not so widely appreciated. They have failed to reach norm status. For instance, this book includes a 1940s story of a famous black figure being maligned as an *Uncle Tom* for speaking English improperly. Yet being well spoken is not a norm associated with racial loyalty. This is a destructive racial loyalty norm; it is an idea that a norm entrepreneur wanted to reach norm status that also impeded black solidarity.[39]

The third idea refers to a norm that blacks consider a norm, or at least one can convincingly argue that it is a norm. But this norm inhibits the cause of

[38] Bicchieri, The Grammar of Society 2.
[39] Id.

racial solidarity. Take affirmative action, for example. Supporting affirmative action is arguably a norm among blacks. It is, however, destructive; affirmative action should not be a litmus test. Or take interracial relationships. Among some, such pairings are so taboo that the black partner deserves censure. That ought not to be the case. There is no causal link between interracial intimacies and, say, working on behalf of antiblack organizations. All should reject these norms; they are counterproductive, frustrating the organizing of black solidarity.[40]

UNCLE TOM IS BORN

Uncle Tom is the most venomous epithet blacks can hurl at one another. When *Uncle Tom* raises its head and exposes its fangs, its potential targets are consumed with fear. It is a cobra. Few could have fathomed that a character crafted to illustrate slavery's evils would become a phrase marking racial treachery. But it has, and investigating *Uncle Tom* provides remarkable insight into how blacks police racial loyalty through norms.

Uncle Tom, a gendered epithet almost always referring to a black man, has been defined in two ways. The first, the *Servile Uncle Tom*, is obsequious toward whites. The *Servile Uncle Tom's* relationship with whites mimics that of a servant and boss or worse, a slave and master. The *Servile Uncle Tom* is a harsh critique on a black person's character.

Stephen J. Massey perceived an *Uncle Tom* by "his over deferential and respectful behavior toward whites. . . ." Oliver Cox asserted that "Uncle Tom is a passive figure; he is so thoroughly inured to his condition of subordination that he has become tame and obsequious." Peter Nobel explained that "Uncle Tom has long been a figure of contempt and his name associated with a kind of submissive, servile, passive Negro, the 'good nigger' who would not fight against oppression." And Alvin Poussaint characterized *Uncle Tom* behavior as "docile and nonassertive." The *Servile Uncle Tom*, in the real world, relents to oppression. Rather than striving for a more just society, the *Servile Uncle Tom* accepts his unequal lot and subordinates himself to whites.[41]

The second is the *Sell-Out Uncle Tom*, which refers to a duplicitous Negro. A puppet of those wishing blacks harm, the *Sell-Out Uncle Tom* is frequently

---

[40] Rachel F. Moran, Interracial Intimacy: The Regulation of Race and Romance (2001); Randall Kennedy, Interracial Intimacies: Sex, Marriage, Identity, and Adoption (2003).

[41] Stephen J. Massey, *Is Self-Respect a Moral or a Psychological Concept?*, 93 Ethics 246, 252 (1983); Oliver Cox, *The Leadership of Booker T. Washington*, 30 Social Forces 91, 93 (1951); Peter Noble, The Negro in Films 32 (1947); Alvin F. Poussaint, *A Negro Psychiatrist Explains the Negro Psyche* found in Black Protest in the Sixties 132 (Editors August Meier et al. 1991).

taunted. Randolph Hohle reported that liberal blacks during the civil rights era pegged an *Uncle Tom* as "a race traitor who exchanged information on the blacks with whites for his own personal gain." Malcolm X, in his *Message to the Grass Roots* speech, portrayed *Uncle Toms* as white-sponsored "Negroes" who "keep you and me in check, to keep us under control, to keep us passive and peaceful and nonviolent." And Angela Dillard typified *Uncle Toms* as "race traitors, sellouts, and those who pursue their own self-interest over the collective interest of the 'race.'" The *Sell-Out Uncle Tom*, in practice, purposefully fashions himself to be useful in the maintenance of white supremacy. The *Sell-Out Uncle Tom* appreciates the personal benefit in being coopted.[42]

But how did *Uncle Tom* become an epithet? *Uncle Tom* defining racial duplicity, to some, is curious. Uncle Tom was the titular hero of Harriet Beecher Stowe's *Uncle Tom's Cabin* (1852). "Stowe's Uncle Tom," many hold, "was no 'Uncle Tom.'" A slave, Uncle Tom died rather than assist in the recapture of runaways. In 1968, Benjamin H. Alexander, a black educator, defended Uncle Tom, arguing that many "would have you think [that Uncle Tom] was a weakling, a timid old man who said nothing but, 'yassuh, boss, yassuh, boss.' Uncle Tom was no such man." In his invaluable Civil War work, *Battle Cry of Freedom* (1988), James McPherson asserted that "Tom was a Christ figure. Like Jesus he suffered agony inflicted by evil secular power. Like Jesus he died for the sins of humankind in order to save the oppressors as well as his own people." Harvard law professor Randall Kennedy agreed, calling it "ironic" that Uncle Tom connotes racial treachery. A writer to *Ebony* in 1965 went further, arguing that blacks should reclaim Uncle Tom and "put [him] back in his true perspective." Uncle Tom, according to defenders, should be a compliment, not a slight.[43]

Others dismiss Uncle Tom as anything but virtuous. His most prominent critic, novelist James Baldwin, not only detested Uncle Tom, he condemned the entire book. Tom, Baldwin contended, is the novel's only true black male character, but he "has been robbed of his humanity and divested of his sex." Baldwin believed that Tom, as one commenter explained, was "an intellectual and sexual eunuch who gives himself over entirely to martyrdom." The novel, Baldwin penned, "is activated by what might be called a theological terror, the

42 Randolph Hohle, Black Citizenship and Authenticity in the Civil Rights Movement 45 (2013); Malcolm X Speaks: Selected Speeches and Statements 12 (Editor George Breitman 1965); Angela D. Dillard, Guess Who's Coming to Dinner Now?: Multiracial Conservatism in America 29 (2001).

43 Paul F. Boller Jr., Not So!: Popular Myths about America from Columbus to Clinton, 66 (1995); James M. McPherson, Battle Cry of Freedom: The Civil War Era 90–91 (1988); Bill Rowe, *Billy Rowe's Note Book*, Sept. 8, 1973, at 17; Randall Kennedy, Sellout: Politics of Racial Betrayal 5 (2008); Mary J. Brunson, *Misunderstood Uncle Tom*, Ebony, Jan. 1965, at 12.

terror of damnation.... And is no different from that terror which activates a lynch mob.'[44]

Diverging opinions aside, Uncle Tom's pejorative status is unwarranted. Although reasonable minds can disagree about his virtue, Stowe's Uncle Tom should rank low on the list of possible names denoting racial treachery. But *Uncle Tom* is not based on Stowe's Uncle Tom. Rather, *Uncle Tom* is premised on the theatrical performances based on Stowe's work – plays, minstrels, and movies – that perverted the character.[45]

Uncle Tom's Cabin as It Is, the first play based on Stowe's novel, was actually performed while the book was still appearing in serials in the *National Era* and before the book was published in whole. The play's creator, the proslavery Professor Hewett, marketed the show as a response to Stowe's novel. Hewett's version distorted Stowe's work. A white man played Uncle Tom in blackface, which was true for all renditions of the novel until the 1914 movie version. Tom, additionally, was "not portrayed as a martyr ... but with absolute devotion to his master." Hewett's alterations were outlandish. He devised a speech for Tom that betrayed Stowe's Tom: "Sha! I was born a slave, I have lived a slave, and bress de Lord, I hope to die a slave!" The metamorphosis of Uncle Tom began.[46]

Charles Western Taylor's version continued the metamorphosis. In the novel, the worst of the worst slave owners, Simon Legree, murdered Uncle Tom, his slave. The brutal scene was Stowe's vehicle to convince antebellum readers to turn away from slavery. But Taylor's version masked slavery's heinousness. Like many others, it ended with the "Return of Tom" to his Kentucky cabin and his former, benevolent owner. The lore of a harmonious relationship between slaves and their masters pervaded during slavery and afterward. Slave owners selfishly created the tale, "giving it both its kernel of fact (by their numerous kindnesses toward slaves) and its texture of fancy (in their proslavery polemics)." Giving Tom a joyful resolution hides the abomination that is bondage, giving credence to the happy slave myth. Such deviations sullied blacks' opinions of Uncle Tom. Indeed, to make Uncle Tom a happy slave is to render him an enemy of blacks.[47]

[44] Stephen Metcalf, *Uncle Tom's Children: Why has Uncle Tom's Cabin Survived –and Thrived?*, Slate, May 20 2005, available at: http://slate.msn.com/id/2118927/; James Baldwin, *Everybody's Protest Novel* found in Notes of a Native Son 13–23 (1984).

[45] Linda Williams, Playing the Race Card: Melodramas of Black and White from Uncle Tom to O. J. Simpson 78 (2001).

[46] Harry Birdoff, The World's Greatest Hit: Uncle Tom's Cabin 21, 23 (1947).

[47] Sarah Meer, Uncle Tom Mania Slavery, Minstrelsy and Transatlantic Culture in the 1850s 116 (2005); Birdoff, The World's Greatest Hit 25; Williams, Playing the Race Card 78–79; Meer, Uncle Tom Mania 115; William Jackson Kesler II, The Early Productions of the

Writer George Aiken and producer George Howard created the most influential "Tom show," featuring melodrama and blackface humor. Wildly popular, the Aiken-Howard play is considered the most faithful stage adaptation because it best conveyed Stowe's antislavery viewpoint. Although more faithful to Stowe's novel, it remained problematic. One concern was that Tom, again played in blackface, cared more for his white masters than his own family. "Aiken's distortion conveys the attractive (to antebellum whites) notion that the slaves' love for their master exceeded their love for their own families."[48]

Minstrel shows also featured Uncle Tom. For all of the ills the *Uncle Tom's Cabin* plays escorted into American culture, and they were aplenty, the *Uncle Tom* minstrel shows dwarfed them. Whereas the stage plays were mainly performed for melodramatic purposes, the minstrel shows mercilessly mocked blacks. To Frederick Douglass, minstrels were "the filthy scum of white society, who have stolen from us a complexion denied to them by nature, in which to make money, and pander to the corrupt taste of their white fellow citizens." Civil rights activist Dorothy Height likewise criticized minstrel shows for exacerbating racial animosity. But Eric Lott in *Love and Theft* (1995) championed an ambivalent interpretation, holding that minstrels were a form of flattery and derision. Most blacks, nevertheless, find minstrels thoroughly offensive. That too appears true during the time of *Uncle Tom's Cabin* minstrels.[49]

Uncle Tom's Cabin minstrels pervaded before the turn of the twentieth century. In 1879, a newspaper listed the routes of forty-nine traveling performance groups. Twenty years later that number multiplied tenfold. "Tom troupes sprang up like mushrooms overnight. Their managers scoured the country, giving the sturdy play in the backyards of the nation." Stowe's novel provided a never-ending feast to the minstrel industry, becoming its "bread and butter." For when all else failed, audiences would consume a steady diet of *Uncle Tom's Cabin*.[50]

Aiken-Howard Versions of Uncle Tom's Cabin 77–80 (1968); Kenneth M. Stampp, Peculiar Institution: Slavery in the Ante-Bellum South 322 (1975).

[48] Judith Williams, *Uncle Tom's Women*, found in African American Performance and Theater History: A Critical Reader 21 (Editor Harry J. Elam, Jr. et al. 2001); Williams, Playing the Race Card 80; Daniel C. Gerould, American Melodrama 133 (1983); Patricia A. Turner, Ceramic Uncles & Celluloid Mammies: Black Images and Their Influence on Culture 776–77 (1994).

[49] Eric Lott, *Blackface and Blackness: The Minstrel Show in American Culture* found in Inside the Minstrel Mask: Readings in Nineteenth-Century Blackface Minstrelsy 3 (Editors Annemarie Bean et al. 1996); Dorothy Irene Height, Step by Step with Interracial Groups 17 (1946); Eric Lott, Love and Theft: Blackface Minstrelsy and the American Working Class 4–5 (1995).

[50] Birdoff, The World's Greatest Hit 257.

In 1853, the Christy and Wood minstrels began performing *Life Among the Happy*, a lampoon of the novel's subtitle, "Life Among the Lowly." Greatly successful, the duo turned the minstrel into a full-length opera in the spring of 1854. Tom is a happy slave in the opera, which starts with him returning from a revival camp meeting. He castigates "the dandified pretensions of 'free Darkies'" and expresses his love for "Old Kentucky." Christy and Wood never highlighted the horrors of slavery. The entire show, rather, revolved around a "grouping of plantation songs and dances loosely connected by a weak plot...."[51]

Uncle Tom is consistently imaged in the plays, the minstrels, and, as we will see later, the movies, as elderly. Receiving a visual makeover, Uncle Tom was rarely if ever shown as the somewhat strapping gent Stowe describes. Minstrel actor Frank Brower, however, exaggerated it.

> An 1863 text of his skit, picturing Uncle Tom as hard of hearing, simply revolved around repetition, misunderstanding, and Tom's stupidity. In it, Tom was just a decrepit, near-deaf old man who understood little about the world, but who was invigorated by the sound of banjo music to which he compulsively danced. In itself this portrait of a dim-witted, dancing darky was common in minstrel playlets.... Few would have wept for this Uncle Tom – except for laughing too hard.[52]

The Bowery Theatre's 1860 production, like others before it, flirted with the idea of the runaway slave becoming a "disappointed fugitive." The minstrel began with a fugitive slave who returned to the South "satisfied that he has been deceived by an Abolitionist" after having gone up North "to pick up gold in the street." The play also featured "Scorem, a foreigner to the South, and a cruel slaveholder, [who is] reprimanded for his inhumanity, by a real Southerner." The implication – that real Southerners treated their slaves well – further legitimated both the "happy darky" myth and slavery itself. Uncle Tom was sent to the North to rescue Daisy (the novel has no Daisy), who abolitionists kidnapped. There, Tom was appalled because Northern liberalism permitted blacks to become "uppity," causing him to conclude that "the menagerie is broke loose." Tom also saw blacks freezing to death in the North, suggesting that slaves would fare better in slavery's warm comfort. Tom is thrilled upon returning "to de Bressed Old Souf."[53]

Another minstrel show troupe, The New Orleans Serenaders, sang an "Uncle Tom's Cabin Song," which concerned the happy slave's love for his

[51] Gossett, Uncle Tom's Cabin and American Culture 276; Toll, Blacking Up 93.
[52] Toll, Blacking Up 94.
[53] Meer, Uncle Tom Mania 65.

slave quarters where "we played the banjo, sung and tripp'd it lightly": "Oh! How I love my own dear cabin Home." In Dan Rice's *Uncle Tom's Cabin*, Uncle Tom sang about "strange adventures among the Northern States" where he is "cold and stravin' from de elbow to de knee." Tom felt betrayed by abolitionists; they guaranteed him freedom but denied it. "Dey called me brudder Thomas, an' said you're quite secure, / An' locked me up to prove it, till I broke down de door."[54]

Despite segregation, blacks saw these minstrels. New York City's Bowery Theatre advertised seats for blacks in the "Colored Person's Gallery" on playbills. The Nightingale Serenaders' *Uncle Tom's Cabin* minstrel was first performed in Charleston, where the city council prevented blacks from entering the hall. Blacks were nevertheless smuggled in for high prices. The Uncle Tom plays performed in New York's National Theatre too were seen by blacks, usually on a segregated basis. Thus, blacks watched the "theatrical Uncle Tom," and those who had not undoubtedly learned of him second-hand. Because he was such a degrading stereotype, his name came to connote the lowest rung in the black hierarchy. Blacks seeing these minstrels would have had to conclude that being like Uncle Tom was the worst crime committable against the race.[55]

Uncle Tom's Cabin appeared on the big screen in the twentieth century. In 1903, Edwin S. Porter directed a twelve-minute silent motion picture of *Uncle Tom's Cabin*. It was the first movie based on Stowe's novel and had cinema's first black character. Tom was not black, though. Rather he was "a tall, aged, slightly pot-bellied white man in blackface with a fringe of white hair on a balding head." In a silent film, body language is paramount in interpreting the plot and the characters' personalities. In Porter's rendition, Tom was always "bowing and scraping" when in the company of his masters. Even on the big screen, Tom embarrassingly deferred to whites.[56]

In the 1914 version of *Uncle Tom's Cabin*, Sam Lucas, black, played Uncle Tom. This marked the first time a film about blacks featured a black actor, and the use of blackface subsequently waned. James B. Lowe portrayed Uncle Tom in the 1927 movie, becoming the first black actor a studio promoted. Universal Studios initially pegged Charles Gilpin for the role. Unable to rid the script of its inflammatory material, particularly Uncle Tom's docility, Gilpin instead returned to his elevator operator job, reflecting the "defiance

54 Id. at 65, 66–67.
55 Id. at 71; Gossett, Uncle Tom's Cabin and American Culture 271.
56 Williams, Playing the Race Card 87; Turner, Ceramic Uncles & Celluloid Mammies 79; Donald Bogle, Toms, Coons, Mulattoes, Mammies, and Bucks: An Interpretive History of Black in American Films 6 (1994 edition).

on the part of African Americans determined to devise their own revisions of *Uncle Tom's Cabin.*" Before reviewing the film, the *Pittsburgh Courier,* a black newspaper, predicted that Lowe's playing "Uncle Tom" would improve the meaning of the phrase "Uncle Tom Negro." The prediction was wrong. Uncle Tom remained a "genial darky ... with new color but no new sentiments." Bruce Chadwick, in *The Reel Civil War* (2001), agreed, arguing that despite the movie maintaining Stowe's antislavery message, Uncle Tom and the other black characters were played as "fools."[57]

And Uncle Tom was not limited to *Uncle Tom's Cabin* movies. Tom was everywhere. In *For Massa's Sake* (1911), a tom movie, "a former slave is so attached to his erstwhile master that he sells himself back into slavery to help the master through a period of financial difficulties." A review of *So Red the Rose* (1935) contained the headline "Uncle Tom, Will You Never Die." Film historian Donald Bogle flawlessly described the tom character, scribing, "always as toms are chased, harassed, hounded, flogged, enslaved, and insulted, they keep the faith, n'er turn against their white massas, and remain hearty, submissive, stoic, generous, selfless, and oh-so-very kind."[58]

These heinous reproductions controlled how blacks viewed Uncle Tom. Tom was not stereotypically servile in the novel, but became so in the plays, minstrels, and movies. These adaptations buried Stowe's Uncle Tom, who is entombed never to be excavated. For every person who read the novel, fifty watched a secondhand interpretation. And with a lifespan of nearly a century, the stage outshined the novel. It is as if Stowe's Tom never existed. If bombarded with detestable Uncle Toms, blacks would inevitably disdain the name. And such is reality.[59]

But not only did the plays, minstrels, and movies drive blacks' perception of Uncle Tom, they framed that of whites too. Blacks appropriated Uncle Tom as an epithet. Whites, however, used it to describe the helpful or nonthreatening black man as distinguished from the black brute who terrorized whites in the silent film *Birth of a Nation* (1915). This type of usage dates back to the late nineteenth century. An 1885 *Atlanta Constitution* article, for example, recounted the tale of a white man passing a courthouse and seeing "a typical colored man of the old school" whom "de white folks call ... Uncle

[57] Rodney Ayers, *Role of "Uncle Tom" Has been Completed by James B. Lowe*, Pittsburgh Courier, June 18, 1927, at A3; Bruce Chadwick, The Reel Civil War: Mythmaking in American Film 89 (2001); Leab, From Sambo to Superspade 98.

[58] Bogle, Toms, Coons, Mulattoes, Mammies, and Bucks 4–6; Turner, Ceramic Uncles & Celluloid Mammies 84; Edward Mapp, Blacks in American Films: Today and Yesterday 17 (1972).

[59] Gossett, Uncle Tom's Cabin and American Culture 260; Turner, Ceramic Uncles & Celluloid Mammies 83. Turner gives the subheading of 100 years of Uncle Tom, an inexact count.

Tom." In 1898, a *New York Tribune* reporter saw some nice old black men and wrote that "some of the kindly old gray-hair men would have made excellent 'Uncle Toms.'" Or take a fellow named "Uncle Tom" Mosby, an affable Negro adored by whites as detailed in his 1901 obituary. And see a 1907 *Chicago Daily Tribune* article concerning a new vacuum cleaner. It replaced "the old negro and his carpet beater. No longer does the later edition of Uncle Tom knock at your back door and then respectfully ask if your rugs need a beating."[60]

The theatrical Uncle Tom completely altered the titular protagonist, turning him into a bowing and scraping gray-haired old man who loved his benevolent "massa" and his slave quarters. By the late 1800s, the transmutation of Uncle Tom was complete. Uncle Tom had reached pejorative status. The obsequious and happy darky who relished slavery was too much. His name, to blacks, would signify the servile and the duplicitous. But whites saw the theatrical Uncle Tom and appropriated the name to describe blacks who were content with their second-class citizenship. "Good ole Uncle Tom" was the Negro all but a small minority of whites preferred. Despite different vantage points, blacks' and whites' perception of Uncle Tom were similar. In Uncle Tom, whites saw the Negro they always wanted – one never striving to loosen white supremacy's unyielding grip. To blacks, nothing could be worse.

IN DEFENSE OF *UNCLE TOM*

I support extending *Uncle Tom's* life. But I am in the minority. Most want *Uncle Tom* buried. Two viewpoints are dispensed with the goal of either killing *Uncle Tom* or severely handicapping it. Both are too austere, needlessly paralyzing blacks' capacity to meet their political and legal objectives.

Yale law professor Stephen L. Carter, backing the "kill it" position, holds that epithets like *Uncle Tom* stunt intellectual freedom. The fear of the sellout label dissuades blacks from endorsing unpopular positions, Carter contends. He asserts that blacks seek out heretics for excommunication. He wants black dissenters to have the intellectual freedom to espouse whatever beliefs they find valid.[61]

Carter argues that dissenters must fight anyone who dares stifle debate. He insists, "not only must an intellectual refuse to pay the stated price for the right

---

[60] *Uncle Tom's Philosophy*, Atlanta Constitution, Jan. 9, 1885, at 7; *Waiting at Santiago*, New York Tribune, July 24, 1898, at 2; *"Uncle Tom" Mosby Dead*, New York Times, July 18, 1901, at 1; R. C. Wheaton, *Rug Beater Back Number; Gas Engine Ousts Negro*, Chicago Daily Tribune, Nov. 17, 1907, at E6. Interestingly, Mosby used his home to help ex-slaves turn their life around. *Editorial Notes*, New York Observer and Chronicle, July 25, 1901, at 110.

[61] Stephen L. Carter, Reflections of an Affirmative Action Baby 102, 118 (1991).

to think; an intellectual must refuse to acknowledge anyone else's authority to decide that the price must be paid." The "stated price" results from blacks' desire to foster group unity. Carter believes that dissenters are punished for endorsing disfavored positions. He claims the majority dictates what the official positions of the race must be and dissenters are taught to remain silent or be silenced. Carter rebuffs anyone telling him what to think or directing him to muffle his views.[62]

Washington University law professor Kimberly Jade Norwood largely agrees with Carter. She wrestles with cultural practices that produce black groupthink, which mandates that all blacks embrace the policies supported by the majority. She writes, as "a Black law professor, unquestioned allegiance is expected and demanded for all causes deemed to benefit Black America, even at the cost of legitimate debate." To enforce allegiance, the "Soul Patrol" emerges, actively policing the black community, searching for anyone running afoul of "black laws." The Soul Patrol targets black dissenters who, once found, are "de-blacked" and "strip[ped] ... of [their] racial identity."[63]

According to Norwood, nonconformists are punished to pursue racial unity. But unity is unattainable, she concludes. Blacks have varied experiences, leading to diverging viewpoints. Blacks have never spoken with a singular voice, Norwood argues, and never will. Norwood prays that blacks will allow expression without the fear of censure.[64]

Norwood holds, moreover, that this phenomenon is racially discriminatory; racial identity limits the views blacks can espouse. Decrying discrimination only to perpetrate it on fellow blacks who depart from mainstream liberalism is hypocritical, she laments. As Norwood writes, this behavior "has no place within Black America; and it should be vehemently and vigorously opposed within the sacred and hallowed halls of academia."[65]

Carter and Norwood write passionately. But they write in error, many errors in fact. Their biggest one is really obvious: they ironically want to increase debate by banning debate. Norwood specifically advocates tolerance while being intolerant of those who, in her view, stunt debate. Carter takes a similar line, wanting to disabuse the black community of banishing blacks who take unpopular stances. Norwood, and to a lesser extent Carter, wants blacks to be free to voice their views, unless those views police racial loyalty. Why should

---

[62] Id. at 102, 112, 117–18.
[63] Kimberly Jade Norwood, *The Virulence of Blackthink and How Its Threat of Ostracism Shackles Those Deemed Not Black Enough*, 93 Kentucky Law Journal 143, 155, 176, 177 (2005).
[64] Id. at 180, 188–89, 189–92, 198.
[65] Id. at 195–96, 198.

blacks sacrifice debate as to whether certain individuals are *Uncle Toms* in favor of a debate concerning the correctness of the supposed *Uncle Tom's* positions? Why is one debate better than the other? Why does the first debate preclude the latter? And most important, if they want blacks to have intellectual freedom, does not this necessarily mean that there should be space for those who wish to police the community?

This point must be driven home. Some contend that *Uncle Tom* "chills" speech. Supporters of this position reject language that impairs the exchange of ideas, which, they contend, *Uncle Tom* does. But there are a couple counterarguments. First, those holding this position are guilty of their own sins. By making *Uncle Tom* and discussions concerning racial loyalty off limits, they are the biggest "speech chillers" of all. Nothing chills speech more than "you cannot say that." Hypocrisy abounds.

Second, criticizing a person for their speech is not "chilling" speech. It is speech. True, black folk will be less likely to voice an opinion if they predict they will be accused of racial treachery in response. Likewise true, whites will be less likely to voice an opinion if they predict they will be maligned as racist. Yet many who revolt upon the mere specter of *Uncle Tom* would never relinquish the word racist. Why is it permissible to indict a white person for racism, but not a black person for racial betrayal, which, in many ways, is merely racism against one's own group? Hypocrisy keeps abounding.[66]

Those seeking to ban *Uncle Tom* presume that wonderful discussions would blossom but instead wilt under the threat of ostracism. I have two responses. First, *Uncle Tom* is a countermeasure to powerful external interests. It is true. Fearing *Uncle Tom*, people have decided against publically expressing certain positions. Stephen L. Carter argues this in his book *Reflections of an Affirmative Action Baby* (1991). Yet his very presence illustrates that people do take unpopular positions anyway. Although it may seem easier for black "insiders," plenty of black "outsiders" have borne the burden. Many black outsiders, furthermore, would be without their careers had they not boisterously assaulted the black majority. Simply put, defection is rewarded. If *Uncle Toms* did not exist, they would be created. That is not to equate all disagreement with defection. But defection occurs. Thus, *Uncle Tom* should be retained when such behavior is encouraged.[67]

Second, blacks must be allotted both the freedom to etch out acceptable behaviors and the ability to mete out punishment to norm violators. Once

---

[66] Mercedes C. Morno, *Reaction to:* Uncle Tom *and Clarence Thomas: Is the Abuse Defensible? Indefensible,* 2 Georgetown Journal of Law & Modern Critical Race Perspectives 149, 150 (2012).

[67] Carter, Reflections of an Affirmative Action Baby 112.

there is a group, almost by definition, there must be certain acts that carry with them the punishment of expulsion. Practically all countries, for instance, punish treason. This same phenomenon appears in animal species. It is odd that blacks should be forced to battle against basic nature and stifle their survival instincts.[68]

The fatal flaw in Carter and Norwood's position, though, is that they only examine the policy positions of alleged race traitors and find that oftentimes the positions themselves do not warrant group ostracism. Apparently to them, treason only manifests in shameful beliefs. Because those who are routinely assailed as sellouts endorse acceptable ideas, the two professors defend maligned blacks.

Carter and Norwood fail to acknowledge, however, that those antagonistic to the race's well-being can stake out positions that the two find palatable. But I appreciate that even though one can hold tolerable beliefs, the means by which one arrives at such beliefs can be unclean. A black person, for instance, can abhor blacks and consequently support the welfare state, believing it will make blacks reliant on the government much the same way as one who cares so much for his people that one wants to create a social safety net. Carter and Norwood, though, defend both because they only look for racial betrayal in one place. The two fail to comprehend the nuance of treachery.

Any argument that forbids *Uncle Tom* is amiss. The debate should center on where to draw the line, not if there should be one at all. In his book *Sellout* (2008), Harvard law professor Randall Kennedy appreciates this and voices a different viewpoint. Kennedy defends the idea of policing racial loyalty.[69]

But Kennedy finds that sellout rhetoric is wielded recklessly. Kennedy argues that blacks should conserve sellout rhetoric, spending it on blacks clearly guilty of racial treachery. In his book, more specifically, Kennedy condones the unleashing of sellout rhetoric against individuals who willfully or knowingly hurt the black community, a standard that would "give rise to few indictments

---

[68] I agree with Randall Kennedy here when he writes, "If a group exists, there must be some conduct in which a member can engage that is appropriately labeled 'betrayal.'" Kennedy, Sellout 85. The U.S. Constitution defines treason at U.S. Const. Art. III, Sec. 3. For an example of animals punishing treachery, see *Gay Penguins Steal Eggs from Straight Couples*, The Telegraph, Nov. 27, 2008, available at: http://www.telegraph.co.uk/news/newstopics/howaboutthat/3530723/Gay-penguins-steal-eggs-from-straight-couples.html. The article discusses two gay penguins that were ostracized after they were caught stealing eggs from straight penguins. Stealing eggs was a crime against the group for which expulsion was the punishment.

[69] Kennedy, Sellout 85.

for racial betrayal." In practice, however, Kennedy apparently only supports sanctioning champions of "negro slavery" or "Jim Crow segregation."[70]

Although Kennedy's position trumps those supporting *Uncle Tom's* death, he still gets it wrong. The most obvious critique is that his stance mimics that which he discredits. He does not seek to immediately kill *Uncle Tom*, just ditch it in a sweltering desert, allowing it to parish in obscurity. Indeed, if only those supporting separate but equal or slavery have crossed the line, then the line is but a mirage. Limiting *Uncle Tom* to theoretical use strips a device that helps maintain group fidelity from a vulnerable people. *Uncle Tom* having a serious capacity to wound compels many to prefer withholding its application to only the most repugnant. But blacks are then left dangerously exposed to insiders subverting group interests. Blacks should not relinquish *Uncle Tom* to all but the most blatant of scenarios, especially when doing so requires casting aside a powerful phrase.[71]

Some understandably wish the policing of racial loyalty away. It stunts debate. It reinforces myths that all blacks think alike. These positions move many. But they should move no one. *Uncle Tom* and other terms defining racial betrayal are a necessary by-product of having a group. In all settings, groups explicitly or implicitly demarcate the lines of acceptable behaviors. Black Americans, as a subordinate class, particularly need to guard against betrayal. Black dissenters, often co-opted by interests most blacks deem antithetical to their own, wield incredible influence in public debate. Their black skin is used to advance arguments that whites cannot without being labeled racist.

Many will contend that blacks should deal with positions instead of leveling personal attacks. Blacks, however, must reject this false choice. Blacks have enough space to swing *Uncle Tom* that is conjoined with an explanation. More important, policing loyalty deters others from choosing that path. *Uncle Tom*, in other words, discourages racial defection, which is critical for an insular minority. Blacks therefore need the freedom to punish bad faith actors. Completely destroying the *Uncle Tom* pipeline is smarter than dealing with each antagonist who weasels through it.

But *Uncle Tom* must be wielded responsibly. Only upon gathering data demonstrating a violation of a constructive racial loyalty norm is the use of

---

[70] Id. at 85, 137–38, 139, 142, 143; Randall Kennedy and John McWhorter, *Bad Word*, bloggingheads.tv, Feb. 22, 2008, available at: http://bloggingheads.tv/diavlogs/8892.

[71] In his BloggingHeads.tv discussion, Kennedy notes that his definition of treachery "is largely theoretical but it might have some real world purchase.... The boundaries I give are way out.... There are people who would say that, in fact, though not in theory" he bans sellout rhetoric. Kennedy and McWhorter, *Bad Word*, Bloggingheads.tv.

Uncle Tom permissible. Each individual should be allowed to decide whether a particular person has violated a constructive norm. If many conclude that a particular person is an *Uncle Tom*, then that label will stick. And that result would be just, if the conclusions are supported. Those publicly criticizing a person for racial betrayal face heightened pressure to adequately support their accusation. Blacks who misuse sellout rhetoric should be punished for their errors, especially flagrant abusers. There will never be total agreement – various high-profile criminal trials have taught us that people interpret evidence in unexpected ways. But, as subsequent chapters will show, reckless allegations of racial betrayal are particularly salient. Destructive norm managers should be vulnerable to criticism comparable to that received by *Uncle Toms*. They are guilty of the same crime – impeding the cause of racial solidarity, thereby frustrating the race's capacity to direct legal triumphs.

2

Uncle Tom: 1865–1959

THE ORIGINS OF UNCLE TOM

To misuse *Uncle Tom* is to ball up one's fist and drill it right into the epithet's gut. Each punishing body blow saps its power. *Uncle Tom* has taken innumerable haymakers and is now wobbly. As if its eyes are swollen shut, the epithet cannot see the race's true foes and just swings aimlessly. Anyone can be hit with *Uncle Tom* accusations. *Uncle Tom* is a destructive force within black America.

In 2013, for instance, at the National Association of Black Journalists Convention, Hugh Douglas, a former National Football League player, heaved *Uncle Tom* at Michael Smith, his cohost of their ESPN television show, *Numbers Never Lie* (NNL). Douglas was apparently uneasy about the future of NNL after Smith's good friend, Jemele Hill, joined the show. Smith and Hill, both former print journalists, left Douglas apparently insecure as the outnumbered ex-athlete. At a convention-sponsored party at a local club, an inebriated Douglas was headed to the stage, and Smith directed Douglas to not go up to it. Douglas obliged. But after a few minutes, Douglas berated Smith and called him an *Uncle Tom*. As is now common, Douglas reached for the painful slur to settle a personal dispute that had no impact on racial loyalty. That Douglas was intoxicated is fitting because *Uncle Tom* is a punch drunk epithet that blacks should retire, many feel. *Uncle Tom*'s origins, however, were far more auspicious than its president-day status indicates. Black folk must rekindle that lost promise. It is mandatory.[1]

---

[1] Douglas also called Smith a house *nigger*, which is roughly synonymous with *Uncle Tom*. John Koblin, ESPN *Fight: Hugh Douglas Called Colleague Michael Smith "Uncle Tom,"* Deadspin, Aug. 6, 2013, available at: http://deadspin.com/espn-fight-hugh-douglas-called-colleague-michael-smith-1042188473; Robert Littal, *ESPN's Hugh Douglas Allegedly Called Michael Smith an Uncle Tom at NABJ Party*, Black Sports Online, Aug. 6, 2013, available at:

In 1865, as the Civil War was nearing its conclusion, Frederick Douglass addressed the Massachusetts Anti-Slavery Society in Boston. The thesis for his lecture, "What the Black Man Wants," was that black men needed to be enfranchised. Some white abolitionists argued that the time was not right for blacks to vote; slavery needed to be abolished and time needed to pass before the ballot should be extended to the freedmen. Douglass vehemently disagreed, believing that the Negro needed the vote to reach his full potential as an American citizen. If blacks were given the opportunity to compete without whites' negative influence, Douglass insisted, blacks had proven that they would succeed. Douglass stated:

> A great many delusions have been swept away by this war. One was, that the Negro would not work; he has proved his ability to work. Another was, that the Negro would not fight; that he possessed only the most sheepish attributes of humanity; was a perfect lamb, or an "Uncle Tom"; disposed to take off his coat whenever required, fold his hands, and be whipped by anybody who wanted to whip him. But the war has proved that there is a great deal of human nature in the Negro, and that "he will fight," as Mr. Quincy, our President, said, in earlier days than these, "when there is reasonable probability of his whipping anybody."

Douglass's use of *Uncle Tom* to inform the audience that blacks were no different from their white counterparts, and not meek creatures unwilling to defend themselves, marked the birth of *Uncle Tom* as an epithet.[2]

Uncle Tom returned two decades later, still in its infancy. Speaking to the Bethel Literary and Historical Association in New York in March 1883, Walter G. Christopher advocated "prudent and conservative action" in combating the status quo. Agitation was unwise when the race was so severely outnumbered, he believed. Christopher, though, was loathe "to revive the 'Uncle Tom' type of manhood; I despise that as heartily as any one [*sic*]."[3]

In 1887, the *Wichita Globe*, a black Kansas newspaper, was exasperated that some "colored boys or men" were given extralegal horse whippings for disorderly conduct. The *Globe* thought the gentlemen should have been punished according to law and not simply beaten. The Democratic newspaper the *Beacon*, however, delighted in the brutality. Democratic publications, the

http://blacksportsonline.com/home/2013/08/espns-hugh-douglas-allegedly-called-michael-smith-an-uncle-tom-at-nabj-party/comment-page-1/.

[2] David W. Blight, Frederick Douglass' Civil War: Keeping Faith in Jubilee 182 (1991); Frederic Douglass, Selected Address of Frederick Douglass 24–30 (2008).

[3] *The Educational Problem. The False and the True*, New York Globe, Mar. 31, 1883, at 1; Adena Spingarn, *When "Uncle Tom" Became an Insult*, The Root, May 17, 2010, available at: http://www.theroot.com/views/when-uncle-tom-became-insult.

Globe contended, "blame all negroes for what one does and think all negroes are barbarous." The *Globe* employed *Uncle Tom* to convey that blacks were no longer obedient chattel, but citizens with the same legal rights whites enjoyed. "The Beacon," the *Globe* replied, "should remember the days of Uncle Tom . . . are a thing of the past. That will take very well in [places] where they have one law for the white and one for the black."[4]

Uncle Tom was next presented as the butt of an artist's quip. In 1890, the *Freeman*, a black Indianapolis newspaper founded in 1888, published a cartoon with two speaking characters, "Uncle Tom" and his white "boss." The name Uncle Tom was almost certainly selected because the newspaper associated it with docility. In the cartoon, Uncle Tom tells his boss that he captured three "coons" and asks him if he is interested in purchasing them. With only two dead raccoons on the ground, the white boss, dressed with a top hat, a long coat, and a cane – clearly of a higher class – says that he only notices two coons. Uncle Tom responds that there are indeed three, "two coons with the ring tail" and then "the big-eyed [coon]," the black man in tattered clothing standing in the background.[5]

In 1892, the black newspaper the *Plain Dealer* featured an article discussing how the American Negro had been misunderstood. The newspaper claimed that many assumed that blacks were either a "dear faithful Uncle Tom" or a "big, black burly ruffian." Because of this, the word Negro had negative connotations. The newspaper implored blacks to debunk that misperception so that the name Negro becomes "glorious."[6]

Uncle Tom reappeared a year later. Here, a maturing *Uncle Tom* is clothed in more abrasive garb. In 1893, the *Freeman* censured blacks for their lack of political influence. "The trouble with the Negro," the newspaper inveighed, "has been, and is to-day, he's got too much 'Uncle Tom,' good 'humble darkey' stock in his ranks, and not enough of the Nat Turner blood." In the same editorial, the *Freeman* assailed a prominent black businessman who declined to pursue elected office because he feared it might jeopardize the Republicans' chances. He apparently thought his presence might alienate white voters. For "forgetting his manhood . . . to please a handful of white nimcompoops [*sic*]" he was derided as an *Uncle Tom*.[7]

---

4   Wichita Globe, July 30, 1887, at 1. At that time, Democratic was synonymous with the racist South.

5   Emma Lou Thornbrough, Indiana Blacks in the Twentieth Century 13 (2000); *Three of a Kind*, Freeman, Aug. 16, 1890, at 4.

6   *The World Neither Views the Negro Failure Nor Correctly*, Plain Dealer, Jan. 1, 1892, at 1.

7   *"Humble Niggers" in Politics*, Freeman, Nov. 11, 1893, at 4.

In 1895, in Montgomery, Alabama, two white men lingered outside of a black family's home speaking vulgarly. Annoyed, the male head of the household politely asked them to either move or cease using obscenities because his family was inside. Instead of complying, one of the men shot him through his heart. The *Freeman* thought it was particularly wicked that the "assassins" responded with violence to such a "gentlemanly" request, although the newspaper's editors found the request from a submissive black man relatively bold. "It was a stinging rebuke coming from the down-trodden and degraded Negro worthy of Mrs. Stowe's Uncle Tom. Yet how dear! How costly it was!"[8]

Even a cursory examination of these narratives establishes that *Uncle Tom's Cabin* plays and minstrels controlled the meaning of *Uncle Tom*. The commonality in all of these usages is servility, the salient characteristic of the theatrical Uncle Tom. The notion of duplicity, however, had not caught on. *Uncle Tom* was half-baked. At this point, it was more of a flavorful phrase that spiced up a hearty passage than a fully cooked pejorative, even though it was already salted with negativity.

Equally important is that *Uncle Tom* was not yet used as a label. No one, that is, was called an *Uncle Tom*. In 1897, for instance, the *Cleveland Gazette*, another black newspaper, denounced William Hooper Councill, president of the Colored Normal School at Huntsville, a black college. The *Gazette* estimated that Councill placated white racism, seemingly blaming all crime against white women on black males. "Really it is heart-rending," the newspaper sighed, "to note to what depths certain of our so-called leading and educated men will descend to gain popular applause and favor." Although those were harsh words, the newspaper did not brand Councill an *Uncle Tom*. Councill overtly appeased racist Southern Democrats to acquire funds for his school. In 1886, Councill sued a railroad over mistreatment of black passengers and quickly made enemies. Councill did an about face and, in the words of Booker T. Washington, "ha[d] the reputation of simply toadying to the Southern white people." Forty years later, *Uncle Tom* would have been tossed so freely Councill would have thought it was his name. The epithet simply was in its infancy.[9]

Uncle Tom also appeared on the pages of the October 5, 1900 edition of the *Washington Post*, marking one of the first instances that *Uncle Tom* was recorded by a white periodical. The speaker was James Milton Turner, a gifted

[8]   *Stained with Negro Blood*, Freeman, Sept. 14, 1895, at 4.

[9]   *Prof. W. H. Council*, Cleveland Gazette, Sept. 11, 1897, at 2; August Meier, Negro Thought in America 1880–1915: Radical Ideologies in the Age of Booker T. Washington 110, 209–10 (1966); Robert J. Norrell, Up From History: The Life of Booker T. Washington 88–89 (2009).

orator. Like the other early users, he stopped short of calling a specific person
an *Uncle Tom*. Rather, Turner employed the epithet to derogate a segment of
black America. An ex-slave and "forgotten benefactor" for his race, Turner
was minister resident and consul general in Liberia for President Ulysses
S. Grant, making him one of America's first black diplomats. He later represented freedmen in claims against several southwestern Indian tribes. Turner
proudly announced that "boys [by the] hundreds and thousands [are in] the
public school system of our country, and unlike Uncle Tom … they are doing
their own thinking."[10]

Uncle Tom can be seen ten years later in the *Chicago Defender*, one of the
most influential black newspapers. In the 1910 article, the *Defender* discussed
a Fourth of July parade that forced blacks to march tenth in line. The newspaper was outraged that blacks, who the newspaper argued stood up first to
fight in every war, were relegated to the tenth position. Favoring a boycott,
any black participant, the *Defender* printed, was a member of "Uncle Tom's
class … who by their lack of education … cannot rise beyond the scope of an
errand boy."[11]

Prominent blacks, like black newspapers, were crucial in rearing *Uncle
Tom* into the most intimidating epithet that blacks may encounter. In 1919,
for example, Marcus Garvey employed *Uncle Tom* to distinguish the intrepid
from the timid. "From 1914 to 1918," he said, "two million Negroes fought
in Europe for a thing foreign to themselves – Democracy. Now they must
fight for themselves. The time for cowardice is past. The old-time Negro has
gone – buried with 'Uncle Tom.'" Here, Garvey referenced black participation
in World War I and argued that if blacks fought for their country abroad they
could fight for their race at home. Finding sheepishness detrimental to black
advancement, a year later, Rev. George Alexander McGuire, at an address to
Marcus Garvey's United Negro Improvement Association's (UNIA) first convention, declared that "the Uncle Tom nigger has got to go and his place must
be taken by the new leader of the Negro race … not a black man with a white
heart, but a black man with a black heart." McGuire was not the only person that day to employ *Uncle Tom*. Protesters held signs announcing, "Uncle
Tom's dead and buried."[12]

---

10   *Fort Near Every City*, Washington Post, Oct. 5, 1900, at 1; Irving Dillard, *James Milton Turner:
     A Little Known Benefactor of His People*, 19 Journal of Negro History 372, 372, 406 (1934); Gary
     R. Kremer, James Milton Turner and the Promise of America: The Public Life of a Post-Civil
     War Black Leader 195–96 (1991).
11   Christopher Metress, The Lynching of Emmett Till: A Documentary Narrative 25 (2002);
     The Negro in the Tenth Place, Chicago Defender, July 2, 1910, at 3.
12   *Garvey Urges Organization*, Afro-American, Feb. 28, 1919, available at: http://www.iath.vir-
     ginia.edu/utc/africam/afar93at.html; Amy Jacques Garvey, Garvey and Garveyism 46 (1963);

A year later at a UNIA convention in August 1920, Garvey delivered another *Uncle Tom* rift in a speech about the need for blacks to elect a leader of their own who would serve in the "black house." Garvey argued that previous black leaders were "cringing" types and that the race had to reject their leadership. Garvey said, "[w]e are unable to elect a leader to the White House, but we intend to have a black house where one of our race will serve us for a term of four years." This leader, according to Garvey, had to be a true agent for the race or he would be discarded. "The time has come," he announced to a cheering crowd, "when we must cease being Uncle Tom negroes."[13]

By the 1920s, in addition to connoting servility, *Uncle Tom* began to encompass racial treachery. In 1923, a small cadre of black professionals, cynical about the legality of Garvey's UNIA operations, sent a letter to U.S. Attorney General Harry Daugherty voicing their concern. Once Garvey got word, the UNIA responded that "EIGHT 'UNCLE TOM' NEGROES" betrayed Marcus Garvey. A year later, *Uncle Tom* was similarly directed again at someone guilty of "telling on" blacks. George Schuyler, a popular black public intellectual in the early twentieth century, was wrongfully jailed in Vicksburg, Mississippi, because, according to the *Plain Dealer*, an "'Uncle Tom' Negro" gave him up.[14]

Twenty years into the twentieth century, *Uncle Tom* was finally engrained in black vernacular describing both the submissive and the duplicitous. *Uncle Tom* was fully grown. In 1922, a man from Buffalo, for instance, praised a new class of black leaders who "absolutely refuse to play the part of an 'Uncle Tom.'" In 1923, South Carolina Governor Thomas Gordon McLeod wrote that Southern whites greatly respected the "Colored man," which the *Defender* translated as the "'Uncle Tom' type." In 1925, likewise, a man wrote in the *New York Amsterdam News* that the easiest way for blacks to thrive in America was to adopt the "me-too-boss," "Uncle Tom," "you white folks is God's chosen" worldview. Or, take the words of a New Yorker, who was disheartened that dissenters were always susceptible to the *Uncle Tom* label, writing to the *Defender* in 1934. "As the Race is becoming educated and useful not only is the friction between the races increasing," he wrote, "but that within the Race is increasing

"Uncle Tom" in the 20th Century, available at: http://utc.iath.virginia.edu/africam/afin20c.
html; The Marcus Garvey and Universal Negro Improvement Association Papers Volume IV
1 September 1921–2 September 1922 653 (Editor Robert A. Hill 1985).

[13] *Marcus Garvey's Convention Stirs Lively Interest*, Philadelphia Tribune, Aug. 21, 1920, at 1.

[14] The Marcus Garvey and Universal Negro Improvement Association Papers Volume V
September 1922–August 1924 257 (Editor Robert A. Hill 1986); *Geo. Schyler as Holdup
Suspect Says Miss. Mayor*, Plaindealer, Feb. 3, 1923, at 2.

to such an extent that if one dares to disagree with another he is either black-guarded or classed as an Uncle Tom." *Uncle Tom* was everywhere.[15]

These early uses helped raise this prodigious cultural artifact. From a novel's titular hero into the most opprobrious epithet blacks can hurl at one another – this is the life of Uncle Tom. The first Africans were brought to this land in 1619. Although not originally slaves, as decades passed, colonies began enacting laws granting property rights in people. In 1865, after the Civil War, America finally ended the long horror of slavery with the Thirteenth Amendment. Reconstruction followed the war. Although fraught with problems, this era featured unimaginable gains for freedmen. One day property, the next they helped draft former slave states' constitutions. But after Reconstruction, white supremacy, which maintained slavery, reformulated to terrorize blacks and strip them of as many rights as possible. Blacks were lynched, segregated, discriminated against, disfranchised, and forced into peonage. In response, from 1883 to 1959, blacks managed various racial loyalty norms that helped forge solidarity. This chapter follows five contexts: segregation, Southern servility, employment, supporters of President Herbert Hoover, and meek Christian clergymen. With the law and the cultural climate denying them civil and political rights, many blacks thought that the group must coalesce to ameliorate their condition. Not everyone bought into the concept of racial solidarity. Those blacks, refusing to toe the line their more militant brethren drew, were continuously dismissed as *Uncle Toms* for violating racial loyalty norms. During this period these norms were constructive, generally.

UNCLE TOMS LOVE SEGREGATION

Blacks managed racial loyalty norms to promote unity in mounting a sustained challenge to separate but equal. *Uncle Tom*, consequently, rose to cultural prominence in the first half of the twentieth century. In fact, the epithet was hurled in the context of segregation more than any other prior to 1960. The reason is obvious: blacks believed that the biggest impediment to equal citizenship was the Supreme Court's upholding separate but equal in *Plessy v. Ferguson* (1896). As long as segregation was practiced, blacks would never fully participate in American democracy. Jim Crow needed to be toppled by any means necessary. The black community, therefore, heavily monitored behavior affecting segregation. Any black person deemed guilty of violating

---

[15] Eugene W. Scott, *Editor's Mail*, Chicago Defender, Dec. 2, 1922, at 12; *Make Light of Talks of Gov. McLeod*, Chicago Defender, June 9, 1923, at 1; W. P. Bayless, *Current Comment*, New York Amsterdam News, Oct. 7, 1925, at 11; H. A. Clarke, *The Head and the Hand*, Chicago Defender, May 12, 1934, at 14.

racial loyalty norms in the context of racial apartheid was harshly disciplined, frequently with an embarrassing *Uncle Tom* denunciation. The norms here were typically constructive. Indeed, they correctly punished treacherous and submissive actions that truly impeded the race's capacity to subvert the racial caste system. The norms also encouraged the rebellious culture that would empower blacks to emancipate themselves from the straightjacket that was white supremacy.[16]

One of the first times that *Uncle Tom* was employed in the context of segregation in public places was in the *Defender* in 1922. Then, two young black men were thrown out of The Colonial, a theater in downtown Chicago, and arrested. A judge subsequently released them, however, and criticized the employees who ejected them. The two could have launched a retaliatory civil suit but opted not to. The *Defender* heavily criticized that choice. "The white man," the newspaper declared, "has given them the law to fight with and they refuse the weapon. They would rather grovel than climb, yet some people speak of 'Uncle Tom' being dead. He's not. He's only younger." The editors were outraged that with the ability to strike a blow against segregation, the two gentlemen decided to not swing. Such an act was deemed a betrayal. Without knowing why they did not sue, judging the propriety of using *Uncle Tom* in this situation is impossible. But empowering blacks to resist subjugation was important. Managing racial loyalty norms in this fashion was constructive if, that is, the two men elected against a lawsuit because they were too timid to assert their legal rights.[17]

Staying in Chicago, in 1926, the African Methodist Episcopal Zion Church boycotted the International Sunday School convention because of a mandated segregated seating policy. Blacks were going to be relegated either to the gallery or a separate section on the main floor. A representative for the Alabama organization organizing the event said, "we cannot break established rules to satisfy a few Negroes." The AME church members decided to skip the event rather than listen to who they believed to be Christian hypocrites. The *Defender* heralded the decision.

When a black man named J. M. Pepper disagreed, though, he was lambasted. Pepper wrote, "[w]e are too weak, too infirm, for lack of better understanding. Let us then look up to the people who are strong enough to hold us up and have been doing it ever since we were brought to this country." In response, the *Defender* asserted that his thinking "makes Jim Crowism ... possible." The newspaper, that is, envisioned that if blacks refused their domination, and

---

[16] *Plessy v. Ferguson*, 163 U.S. 537 (1896).
[17] *Broken Spines*, Chicago Defender, May 27, 1922, at 2.

fought white supremacy as a group, they could be victorious. Why Pepper was disdained is clear. In arguing that blacks should accept segregation because whites are their superiors, Pepper violated the norm that prohibited inexcusable meekness. And punishment was severe. "There is hope for our Race," the *Defender* concluded, "only when the tribe of Peppers ... has vanished along with Uncle Toms." *Uncle Toms*, in other words, impeded blacks' ability to ameliorate their subjugation.[18]

A few years later, in 1930, the Census Bureau in Washington, DC, segregated its cafeteria. Black workers were forced to eat in a small separate room. When the policy started, one black worker, discontent with being Jim Crowed, attempted to use the whites-only cafeteria, but was rebuffed and told that his "place is on the other side, and you can't do anything about it." All but a few black workers boycotted the segregated cafeteria to the *Baltimore Afro-American*'s delight. That nearly all of the black workers united "prevented many of the 'Uncle Tom' class from patronizing the government's segregated cafeteria." Here the *Afro-American* strategically used a story where blacks opted for racial solidarity to teach the race how it was expected to comport. The *Afro-American* also injected *Uncle Tom* into its argument to let readers know that eschewing this norm came at a price.[19]

In the South, many white eateries denied service to blacks. Others, like lunch counters in Woolworth's department stores, served blacks in segregated seating arraignments only. Woolworth's has garnered historical attention for being the setting for the famed 1960 sit-in demonstrations in Greensboro, North Carolina. Before those demonstrations, though, blacks were often pressured to simply refuse to patronize such establishments. When the *Plain Dealer* was alerted in November 1935 to blacks who ate at a local Woolworth's in Kansas City, Kansas, the paper listed the names of blacks who played "Uncle Tom." Having one's name on an *Uncle Tom* list was assuredly embarrassing. One can imagine sitting at home, reading the newspaper, and seeing one's name listed as an *Uncle Tom* for the entire community to see. If the price for eating at Woolworth's was public humiliation, then few would dine there. *Uncle Tom* was an amazing tool to enlist troops to battle racism. Such maintenance of norms was effective in enlisting troops to battle racism.[20]

By the mid-1930s, *Uncle Tom* was wielded to punish blacks exhibiting cowardice in the face of racism. Edwin B. Jourdain, however, was seen as the

[18] *Ministers Uphold Color Line at Church Congress*, Chicago Defender, Mar. 13, 1926, at 1; J. M. Pepper, *Let's Pity This One*, Chicago Defender, Apr. 10, 1926, at A10; *Another Jackass Brays*, Chicago Defender, Apr. 10, 1926, at A10.

[19] *Clerks Boycott U.S. Jim Crow Cafeteria*, Afro-American, June 13, 1931, at 6E.

[20] *Lines O' Type*, Plaindealer, Nov. 15, 1935, at 5.

antithesis. In 1935, his victory in a councilman's race in Evanston, Illinois, was heralded as a triumph over *Uncle Toms*. Jourdain, a Harvard Business School graduate, created a stir after successfully pushing for the building of a recreation center in the black part of town. Some "Uncle Toms" scolded him for "going too far because the [white] folks don't want us to have a [center]." The rest of the black community reading this story learned that blacks who boldly sought to achieve racial gains against white resistance were revered. The obsequious, however, would be publically censured. In the councilman's race, Jourdain bested two opponents, one white, one black. His black opponent, William H. Twiggs, "entered [the race] by interests described as 'Uncle Tom.'" Twiggs likely agreed to join the contest at the behest of whites seeking Jourdain's defeat. Twiggs's presence could have siphoned black votes from Jourdain, letting the white candidate sashay to victory. Indeed, an effective way to split the black vote was by using an "Uncle Tom" candidate. That did not happen here because the black community united around Jourdain and Twiggs was deemed an *Uncle Tom* for aiding whites who were trying to limit blacks' ability to sit at the table of power.[21]

One way to disseminate racial loyalty norms was to have an important black figure detail exactly how certain treacherous activities impaired the race's ability to solidify around important legal goals. This was true with William H. Hastie. As the civilian aide to the secretary of war, Hastie worked from within the system to desegregate the Army. Speaking to youth organizations in 1940, Hastie alleged that black segregation supporters hurt his effort to change public policy because whites could validate their racism by pointing to like-minded blacks. From around the country, blacks appropriated Hastie's comment to castigate supposed *Uncle Toms*. The *Defender* hailed the remarks as proof "that the 'Uncle Toms' in our midst are compromising our interest and injuring our cause." The *Courier* echoed Hastie's argument, holding that "'Uncle Tom Negroes'… must stop asking for more segregation." Hastie provided black newspapers with the perfect argument to engage the masses on the importance of rejecting the status quo. And *Uncle Tom* was skillfully wielded to encourage all blacks to fight legal subjugation. Either work with the race or face ridicule.[22]

---

[21] *Jourdain Is Re-Elected to Council*, Pittsburgh Courier, Apr. 13, 1935, at 7; Morris Lewis, *Defender Helps Jourdain Win Back Council Seat*, Chicago Defender, Apr. 6, 1935, at 1; John Jordan, *Rambling Rover*, New Journal and Guide, Nov. 3, 1945, at 7; John M. Carroll, Fritz Pollard: Pioneer in Racial Advancement 184 (1998).

[22] Morris J. MacGregor, Integration of the Armed Forces, 1940–1965 19–20 (1981); *The Price of Segregation*, Pittsburgh Courier, Dec. 28, 1940, at 6; *Hastie Says Our "Uncle Toms" Hinder Fight on Segregation in U.S. Army*, Chicago Defender, Nov. 30, 1940, at 1; *The "Uncle*

As with Hastie's thesis about the need for all blacks to oppose segregation, blacks championing solidarity would cite a 1942 victory at the Bureau of Engraving and Printing as evidence that group cohesiveness produced racial gains. That year, the Bureau's cafeteria banned its Jim Crow seating policy. Before the ban, the younger black employees steadfastly stood against segregated seating. Their older coworkers, however, were less antagonistic to the antiquated custom. Thus, when a meeting was convened to discuss the policy, the Bureau's bigwigs picked the older employees as the race's representatives. The tables were turned, though, when the older workers decided to follow the lead of their younger brethren, arguing to end segregated cafeteria seating. Some of the white employees, in response, boycotted the newly integrated cafeteria. The *Defender* lauded the black employees with the headline, "Find No 'Uncle Toms' as Workers Vote Down D.C. Cafeteria Jim Crow." This triumph was a learning tool. By using *Uncle Tom*, the *Defender* instructed blacks on what the penalty would have been if the older blacks violated racial loyalty norms and submitted to Jim Crow. This helped foster unity around the importance of fighting segregation.[23]

We see another constructive use of social norms in 1947, when the all-black play *Carmen Jones* was performed in Kansas City, Missouri. The local NAACP branch boycotted the play because of the Municipal Auditorium's segregated seating policy. In the past, when performances were held there, blacks acquiesced, paying to sit in a segregated venue. This time, however, under the NAACP's leadership, almost all blacks refused to give their dollars to Jim Crow. Thirteen, though, did break the picket lines and each of their names was printed in the *Kansas City Call*. The *Plain Dealer* figured that the picket crossers believed they would go undetected but noted that "we have always had some 'uncle toms' in the race who have felt that they own no responsibility to any one [*sic*] but themselves. Because of their presence, the race's battle is twofold ... we must fight the enemy within in order to build solidarity, unity and strength so that we might hang together to combat the institution of segregation." Using the phrase "the enemy within," the editors for the *Plain Dealer* intimated that the picket crossers did not care about the race and were not committed to purging society of its antiblack elements. In this sense, the boycott violators were indeed guilty of defying constructive social norms. This was a wise sanction because the public rebuke could have

Toms," Chicago Defender, Dec. 14, 1940, at 14; *May Hike Race Quota in Air Corps*, Chicago Defender, July 18, 1942, at 1.

23 *Find No "Uncle Toms" as Workers Vote Down D.C. Cafeteria Jim Crow*, Chicago Defender, Mar. 28, 1942, at 2; Desmond King, Separate and Unequal: Black Americans and the US Federal Government 32 (1997).

helped crystallize the local black community around the need to work cooperatively to improve their condition.[24]

Rosa Parks famously refusing to get out of her seat on December 1, 1955
led to the Montgomery Bus Boycott, a much more historically significant
social protest. Boycott leaders depicted boycott participants as the antithesis of *Uncle Tom*. In so doing, leaders helped bolster solidarity and dissuade
blacks from riding city buses. Ralph D. Abernathy, for instance, claimed that
the "new colored man refuses to be an 'Uncle Tom' for a pat on the back
and special consideration." Perhaps this vigilant management of racial loyalty
norms explained why one speaker, during a meeting for the boycott, said that
"[e]ven the 'Uncle Toms' are tired of being 'Uncle Toms.'" Widespread criticisms of the racially treacherous likely helped drive many blacks into participation. And blacks directing the boycott absolutely had to regulate behavior
in this fashion. Many black ministers in the city were "flagrant opportunists."
Also, some Montgomery blacks' hid income was tied to local white "'angels'
who had supplied them with small favors and token donations." These "neo-
Uncle Tom[s]" were a "special community liability," and the Montgomery Bus
Boycott evidenced how destructive they could be. As Steven M. Millner, an
African American studies professor, put it, "White leaders in Montgomery
used all 'resources' they had at their disposal. For what good are puppets if
they cannot be made to dance when a show starts?"[25]

BLACKS DEEMED TO HAVE VIOLATED racial loyalty norms when residential segregation was at issue were likewise punished. We first turn to Detroit. Many residential properties there included racially restrictive covenants in their deeds.
When a property purchaser signed a racially restrictive covenant he agreed to
never transfer any property interest to a nonwhite. One typical covenant read,
"[a]t no time shall said premises or any part thereof or any building erected
thereon be sold, occupied, let or leased or given to any one of any race other
than the Caucasian, except that this covenant shall not prevent occupancy by
domestic servants of a different race domiciled with an owner or a tenant."

[24] *The NAACP Picket on "Carmen Jones,"* Plain Dealer, Jan. 3, 1947, at 11; John Bush Jones,
Our Musicals, Ourselves: A Social History of the American Musical Theatre 133 (2003);
Sherry Lamb Schirmer, A City Divided: The Racial Landscape of Kansas City, 1900–1960
196 (2002).

[25] Taylor Branch, Parting the Waters: America in the King Years, 1954–63 143–205 (1988);
Dr. Roberta Hughes Wright, The Birth of the Montgomery Bus Boycott 26 (1991);
Montgomery Bus Boycott to Continue Until Victory, Afro-American, Sept. 8, 1956, at 5;
Preston Valien, *The Montgomery Bus Protest as a Social Movement* found in The Walking
City: The Montgomery Bus Boycott, 1955–1956 89 (Editor David J. Garrow 1989); Steven M.
Millner, *The Montgomery Bus Boycott: A Case Study in the Emergence and Career of a Social
Movement* found in The Walking City 476.

The Supreme Court intimated that judicial enforcement of these covenants was constitutional in *Corrigan v. Buckley* (1926). In *Shelley v. Kraemer* (1948), however, the Court finally declared that judges could not enforce them without running afoul of the Equal Protection Clause of the Fourteenth Amendment. In 1923, the Klan insisted that racially restrictive covenants be included in the deeds of properties in any new section in the city zoned as residential. Any desirable part of the city that did not employ racially restrictive covenants achieved the same result through sheer terrorization. If a black person attempted to buy a "white" home, that is, he would be intimidated and forced to areas reserved for blacks.[26]

To further its segregationist aims, the Klan ran a candidate in 1925, Charles Bowles, for a seat on Detroit's nine-man city council (Bowles ultimately served as the city's mayor before being recalled). He was opposed by John W. Smith, the incumbent with an "unusual [record of] square dealing and fairness toward [black] people." For any blacks to support the Klan candidate over a "fair" white one would be highly ironic. But irony abounded. A small group of professional blacks opposed Smith's reelection, although not openly backing Bowles. They did, however, claim that the Klan was "the friend of the Negro and hostile only toward Catholics and Jews." These black supporters were scolded as *Uncle Toms* for consciously furthering the Klan's interests. The *Defender* said they must be either one of two types – handkerchief heads or copper heads. The former is "the hat in the hand" type, whereas the latter "fights the fight of the enemy against his own blood." Fighting the Klan, the Supreme Court, and local policy makers was enough. Blacks could not afford to fight their own too.[27]

As was true in the previous story, elections were often viewed as opportunities to prove allegiance. In 1935 in Grand Rapids, Michigan, such an opportunity arose when a known segregationist, Harry C. White, campaigned for a ward commissioner office. Blacks were the swing vote. White, knowing this, assiduously courted them. His Jim Crow instincts, however, frequently seeped through. Indeed, he once told a black audience that "Negroes should not attempt to live in white neighborhoods if white people objected." The *Defender* wanted black voters to show that segregationists could not count on

---

[26] Joe T. Darden, Richard Child Hill, June Thomas, and Richard Thomas, Detroit: Race and Uneven Development 110–12 (1987); Clement E. Vose, Caucasians Only: The Supreme Court, the NAACP, and the Restrictive Covenant Cases vii (1968); *Corrigan v. Buckley*, 271 U.S. 323 (1926); *Shelley v. Kraemer*, 334 U.S. 1 (1948); *Detroit Faces Klan Issues in Election*, Chicago Defender, Oct. 24, 1925, at 1.

[27] Wilbur C. Rich, Coleman Young and Detroit Politics: From Social Activist to Power Broker 235 (1999).

their support. Before the election, the newspaper threw down the gauntlet, declaring that "the returns from the colored precincts ... will determine whether Grand Rapids' Race citizens are Uncle Toms, with chocolate éclair backbones, or whether they are willing to fight for their rights with that most powerful of weapons, the ballot."[28]

Knowing how frequently blacks in Grand Rapids were notified that they were expected to not vote for a segregationist is now impossible. But if it were abundantly clear that voting for White would be equated to treachery, blacks would more likely unite against a political candidate so antagonistic to their interests. Alerting blacks that they would be ostracized for pulling the lever for a white supremacist was a constructive way of forging racial loyalty; anyone who used suffrage rights thusly was liable for violating the norm that prohibited blacks from consciously promoting the enemies' interests. In any event, White lost, receiving about 200 of the 1,500 black votes. Blacks who voted for White were called "Uncle Toms" who "baited their votes for beer."

RACIAL LOYALTY NORMS, IN THE context of segregation, were most commonly enforced when education was at issue. Wise blacks understood that the racial caste system required easily manipulated pawns and the learned are difficult to capture. Indeed, as early as 1910 blacks used *Uncle Tom* to censure those hindering efforts to stop public school segregation. That year, the *Defender* railed against "negroes of Georgia" working with the "southern society of Chicago" to create a segregated school in the city. One black woman, Mary T. Johnson, specifically drew ire. After raising $50,000, black and white Georgians visited the "homes of the ignorant" with a petition claiming "what a fine thing it is to have their daughters and sons teaching in their own schools, and how well their children would get along without fights and without having white folks calling them names." The *Defender* implored the city's "better families" to kill the fledgling movement, calling on "the better thinking class of the race" to reject Mrs. Johnson and her comrades' pleas and send them back to Dixie. The *Defender* wanted to repel the wave of Jim Crow from cresting in Chicago. In order to delegitimate the endeavor and its proponents, *Uncle Tom* was employed. "When we are in touch with Mrs. Johnson we will show her the back door to Chicago and have her beat it back to her dear old southern home, where all the Uncle Toms ... should be." More important, the newspaper pointed to a theme in the use of *Uncle Tom* that continues to this day – the idea that white supremacists will transform a black person into an instrument

---

[28] *Grand Rapids Citizens Unite to Defeat Candidate Who Fostered Discrimination*, Chicago Defender, Mar. 23, 1935, at 4; *Jim-Crow Exponent Loses in Michigan*, Pittsburgh Courier, Apr. 13, 1935, at A3.

to sabotage black progress. "Still here, where he sees the race making such strides[,] he takes in our own and hurls them against us to frustrate our plans and put us to the bad."[29]

In 1916, J. E. Boyd, founder and superintendent of the Texas Normal Industrial Institute for black youth, issued a statement endorsing segregated schooling. The *Defender* denounced him, writing, "Like Uncle Tom of 'Cabin' Fame This Man is Ready to Submit to Anything a White Man Tells Him – Men of This Stripe Not Even Fitted To Train Skunks Much Less Children." One can never be certain of Boyd's motivations in publically espousing segregation. Perhaps he honestly supported it. Maybe he was a puppet of segregationist whites. Uncertainty dominates. What's true, though, is that segregation ensured jobs for black educators like him. Indeed, many blacks personally benefited from the racial caste system, creating conflicting interests. Often wielded like a sledgehammer, *Uncle Tom* obliterated these conflicts. Many, in any event, willingly assisted in perpetuating segregation, rationalizing that separate but equal kept blacks employed. Popular black columnist for the *Pittsburgh Courier* George Schuyler once remarked on this phenomenon. Schuyler contended that "Uncle Tom Negroes" advanced this argument and did not justify segregation. Boyd and black educators like him, Schulyer would have argued, needed to be rebuked for furthering the goals of white supremacists. To those who concur with this argument, this was a constructive use of social norms.[30]

But racial solidarity does not mean total unison of thought. Blacks are permitted to disagree about solutions to their various problems. Among the transgressions that racial solidarity forbids, though, is the individual who sabotages group interests for personal gain. Thus, if Boyd were positioned to help desegregate schools but demurred because he enjoyed a comfortable situation, then criticizing him for treachery was warranted. But here, Boyd could have plausibly concluded that, in 1916, school integration was a fool's paradise. Boyd could have seen desegregation as ideal, but the time was unripe, and thus he tried to play a bad hand as best he could. And if he thought this way he infringed no constructive racial loyalty norms. Another explanation could be that Boyd generally preferred segregated education, reasoning that all-black schools were better for black youth. This too was an acceptable argument. Yet, if Boyd came out in favor of school segregation to ingratiate himself to local whites, hoping to procure some personal benefit, then the punishment was fair.

---

[29] *Jim Crow School in Chicago*, Chicago Defender, Nov. 12, 1910, at 1.

[30] *J. E. Boyd Says Keep the Race Down*, Chicago Defender, Feb. 5, 1916, at 1; George Schulyer, *Views and Reviews*, Pittsburgh Courier, Oct. 10, 1931, at 10; George Schuyler, *Views and Reviews*, Pittsburgh Courier, Mar. 24, 1934, at 10.

Blacks in Atlanta likewise grappled with supposed *Uncle Toms* in their effort to improve education for their children. In 1916, the city's board of education decided to save enough money to open a new white high school by eliminating seventh grade for blacks. The previous year, the board cancelled eighth grade education for blacks and funneled the saved funds toward white education. With no high schools for their children, Atlanta blacks were incensed, particularly because they, like whites, paid property taxes to fund public education. For the first time in the city's history, blacks were going to protest and contacted the NAACP. Walter White of the NAACP, in his autobiography, recounted that, even before the local black community petitioned the organization, racial loyalty norms were violated when "some informer – a local Uncle Tom – had rushed to the board of education" to let the whites know of their plans.[31]

In 1927, the Klan convinced a New Jersey city to relocate its black students to a segregated school housed in a church. The *Courier* lauded the parents of thirty black children for refusing to enroll their kids into the segregated school. The parents of five children who allowed their kids to attend, however, were dismissed as *Uncle Toms*. The *Courier* argued that acceptance of segregation only emboldened white supremacists. "If it were not for these spineless Negroes," the newspaper stated, "who are ever ready to surrender to segregation for the sake of a job for their daughters or to escape taking a manly position, we would not have so many of these battles to fight." The *Courier* depicted the five parental groups as either buckling to pressure or accepting the thirty pieces of silver in exchange for helping ease Jim Crow into the North. The *Courier* understood that segregationists had resources to pull blacks in their direction. Blacks lacked financial means, though they did have *Uncle Tom* and social norms that could help discourage racial defection.[32]

Although the criticism was understandable, the parents did not violate any of the three constructive racial loyalty norms. Some might argue that the parents' decision was submissive and displayed a lack of concern for the race, or that maybe it even helped the race's enemies. But the alternative appears to be that their children would not receive any education. Every parent has a right to ensure that their children receive some form of pedagogy. This does not seem to be an instance of racial treachery.

Although a problem in the North, the impact of segregated education reverberated disproportionately on Southern terrain. In the 1930s, the NAACP

[31]   Walter Francis White, A Man Called White: The Autobiography of Walter White 29–30 (1948).
[32]   *Jim Crow in Jersey*, Pittsburgh Courier, Mar. 19, 1927, at A8.

deemed North Carolina fertile ground from which to uproot *Plessy*. A central
goal for the NAACP's North Carolina activities was to equalize pay between
black and white teachers. "Separate but equal" was a misnomer; separate and
unequal was more fitting. Black teachers in segregated schools knew this well.
Indeed, in North Carolina, for instance, a white teacher with eight years of
experience had a salary ceiling of $720 a year but an identical black teacher
could only hope to make as much as $560.[33]

Local whites, fearing the NAACP's possibility for success, revived the specter of the carpetbaggers – Northerners disrupting the "happy" arrangement
between Southern blacks and whites. Through newspapers articles and letters
to the editor, whites attempted to intimidate and divide the black population,
charging the NAACP with meddling in the state's affairs. The "Uncle Tom"
elements of society generated some dissent, black newspapers detected, but
most backed the NAACP's goals. As the *Courier* noted, "[o]bservers in the state
are convinced that with a few 'Uncle Tom' exceptions, all North Carolinians
desire the program of the N. A. A. C. P. carried out. Many timid souls[,] who
do not come out in the open for fear of the 'good white folks,' are secretly cheering on the N. A. A. C. P." The *Afro-American* noted that some "Uncle Toms,"
to prevent the NAACP's success, wrote letters to the local papers, saying that
"the good white folks" will continue to be friends of blacks and that outside
instigation was harmful. Here, it appears that the asserted black "Uncle Toms"
violated all three constructive norms.[34]

Another goal for the NAACP in North Carolina was to integrate the state's
colleges and graduate schools. In May 1932, the association announced that
it would combat the problem through litigation. The NAACP had reasoned
that the wisest strategy to dismember Jim Crow in schools was to start with
postgraduate college education and then work its way down. In 1933, Thomas
Raymond Hocutt attempted to enroll in University of North Carolina's (UNC)
all-white pharmacy school. Hocutt's effort to attend UNC commenced an
eighteen-year plan to integrate the state's graduate and professional schools.
UNC denied Hocutt admission and the NAACP, along with local attorneys,
filed suit on Hocutt's behalf. Their objective was to invalidate the state law that

---

[33] *North Carolina Factions Unite Behind Program*, Pittsburgh Courier, Dec. 2, 1933, at A3;
Demand Equal Pay for Carolina Teachers, Chicago Defender, Sept. 23, 1933, at 2; *Fight to
Enter N. C. U.*, Chicago Defender, Feb. 25, 1933, at 4; *Mandamus in North Carolina "U" Case
Denied: To Appeal Decision*, Pittsburgh Courier, Apr. 8, 1933, at 2; *"Boogey Man" Cry from
North Carolina Brings a Big Laugh*, Pittsburgh Courier, Nov. 18, 1933, at 2; *NAACP to Fight
Unequal N.C. Salaries*, Afro-American, Sept. 23, 1933, at 17.

[34] *North Carolina Factions Unite Behind Program*, at A3; *NAACP to Fight Unequal N.C.
Salaries*, at 17.

prevented blacks from attending publically funded all-white universities even when the state lacked similar separate but equal educational opportunities.

The state's segregationist leaders were predictably obstructive. But the state's black educators, who were scrambling to keep their schools running in the midst of the Great Depression, also opposed the plan. Ferdinand Douglass Bluford, the president of the all-black North Carolina Agricultural and Technical College, wrote Walter White to ascertain if the NAACP was in fact attempting to integrate education. White, the NAACP's head at the time, said that was indeed the mission. White argued that blacks had to think about the race's group rather than personal interests. "The dual school system," White predicted, "will eventually be abolished."

If integration was going to occur, black educator James Edward Shepard decided, it would do so in spite of his disruption. Hocutt graduated from North Carolina College for Negroes in Durham. Shepard was that college's president and he refused to forward Hocutt's transcript to UNC. Hocutt's case was then tossed on the technicality that he failed to fully comply with application procedures. NAACP attorneys Thurgood Marshall and William Hastie believed their case against UNC was "sound" and Marshall denounced Shepard as a "first-class Uncle Tom." Others in the NAACP claimed that Shepard and other influential blacks in the state were "Uncle Tom-ing." Undeterred, Shepard used the threat of integration to get more money from the state legislature and used those funds to create graduate programs at his college. Although bolstering the educational opportunities for North Carolinian blacks was commendable, Shepard's selfish sabotaging of a lawsuit against segregation was reprehensible. Branding Shepard an *Uncle Tom* announced to the rest of the community that replicating his actions came with a heavy price, censure for violating group norms.[35]

The NAACP's goal to equalize pay for black educators was realized with *Alston v. School Board of City of Norfolk et al.* (1940) when the Fourth Circuit Court of Appeals held that pay disparities between black and white teachers in Norfolk, Virginia, violated the Equal Protection Clause. The NAACP, thereafter, used *Alston* to equalize public education throughout the South. Purported "Uncle Toms" in Georgia, however, attempted to coax black

---

[35] Sources for this and the preceding paragraph are as follows: Glenda Elizabeth Gilmore, Defying Dixie: The Radical Roots of Civil Rights, 1919–1950 256 (2008); Augustus M. Burns III, *Graduate Education for Blacks in North Carolina, 1930–1951*, 46 Journal of Southern History 195, 195–96 (1980); Juan Williams, Thurgood Marshall: American Revolutionary 75 (1998); Patricia Sullivan, Lift Every Voice: The NAACP and the Making of the Civil Rights Movement 168–69 (2009); Kimberley S. Johnson, Reforming Jim Crow: Southern Politics and the State in the Age before Brown 156 (2010).

educators to accept unequal pay. Indeed, black Georgian educators tried to "slip[] through" an "Uncle Tom resolution" at a state meeting for educators that stated that blacks would not seek salary equalization. The black educators were upbraided for accepting inequality and opting to not pursue the race's goals for unadulterated equality.[36]

In Louisville, black teachers similarly refused to insist on equal pay. Daisy Lampkin, an NAACP field secretary, delivered speeches in the city concerning the 15 percent pay differential between black and white teachers. In one speech, she argued, "it is unfair for you who teach in Louisville to receive a difference in salaries. When you have had the same instruction, teach the same subjects and hold the same certificates." Lampkin's point – that blacks were not treated equally – failed to incite black teachers to organize around injustice. In fact, her actions angered some. W. H. Perry, president of the local black teachers' union, told the city's superintendent that although some teachers were moved by Lampkin's pleas, most were not. The black teachers likely did not want to upset whites, realizing nothing perturbed them more than "uppity Negroes" crying about their unequal lot. In a November 1937 letter to NAACP litigator Charles Hamilton Houston, Lampkin reported that the lack of progress was owed to "spineless" "Uncle Tom Leadership in Public Schools." *Uncle Toms*, that is, were to blame for blacks' inability to unite to address inequality.[37]

Gaines v. Canada (1938) was an important victory on the road toward eventual success in *Brown v. Board of Education* (1954), an early positive sign of the propriety of the NAACP's litigation strategy. Lloyd Gaines was refused admission to University of Missouri's law school because of race. The Supreme Court ruled in his favor, deciding that Missouri had to either create a black law school or admit him to the all-white University of Missouri. But the stubbornness of Jim Crow resurfaced when Missouri set up a black law school in St. Louis, oddly enough, with the help of educated blacks. The *Courier* was outraged and derided the "Uncle Toms" who helped segregationists build an inferior separate law school. The *Courier* wrote that "[e]ducational Uncle Toms" followed their directives and "[s]uddenly a Law School, trumpeted as equal to the long-established University of Missouri Law School, was set up in

---

[36] *Alston v. School Board of City of Norfolk et al.*, 112 F.2d 992 (4th Cir. 1940); Scott Baker, *Testing Equality: The National Teacher Examination and the NAACP's Legal Campaign to Equalize Teachers' Salaries*, 35 History of Education Quarterly 49 (1995); *Uncle Toms Fail Georgia Teachers*, Afro-American, Apr. 19, 1941, at 8.

[37] Luther Adams, Way up North in Louisville: African American Migration in the Urban South, 1930–1970 (2010); Women and the Civil Rights Movement 1954–1965 33–34 (Editors Davis W. Houck and David E. Dixon 2009).

an abandoned hair-straightening emporium in St. Louis ... and Negroes were found to solemnly hail it as 'de same ting.'"[38]

Lloyd Gaines himself saw his legal battle to integrate colleges and professional schools in Missouri as a struggle against *Uncle Toms*. In February 1939, Gaines, while speaking in a Kansas City church, declared "[w]e should no longer accept Uncle Tom habits of asking for this and that. We are supposed to do something about what we don't like." Some blacks, however, disagreed with Gaines's efforts of changing the law through litigation. A black lawyer from Tennessee wrote to the *Plain Dealer*, arguing that blacks should instead take their grievances to the state legislature. He, of course, was dismissed as an *Uncle Tom* for criticizing the ambition of overturning *Plessy*.[39]

As Missouri did after *Gaines*, before *Sweatt v. Painter* (1950) ultimately reached the Supreme Court, in 1947 Texas hastily cobbled together a makeshift black law school as a last-ditch effort to avoid integrating University of Texas School of Law. Texas State University for Negroes School of Law (TSUN), which the *Afro-American* derisively called the "Texas JC (Jim Crow) Law school," consisted of three rooms in a basement across the street from the state capitol. Three blacks quickly enrolled in the school: Henry E. Doyle, Virgil C. Lott, and Fornie Ussery Brown. Heman Sweatt, the plaintiff in the NAACP's lawsuit, refused to enroll because, in his words, "I don't believe in segregation." Doyle, though, defended his enrollment at TSUN and stated that he was uninterested in battling segregation. He aspired, rather, to get a legal education, which he concluded was comparable to that offered at University of Texas School of Law. Doyle was satisfied and wished that people would leave him alone. Some thought that whites gave him a custodian-secretary job to help him attend school. Although a poll found that a majority of black Texans favored segregated law schooling, those blacks who helped bankroll *Sweatt* considered Doyle an *Uncle Tom*. Thurgood Marshall called the school "Uncle Tom's Cabin" (now the school bears his name, the Thurgood Marshall School of Law at Texas Southern University). Marshall compared Sweatt and Doyle, saying, "[o]n the one side we have a Negro American and on the other side we had the remnants of a Negro slave." A correspondent for

---

[38] A. Leon Higginbotham Jr., Shades of Freedom, Racial Politics and Presumptions of the American Legal Process 165 (1996); Rawn James Jr., Root and Branch: Charles Hamilton Houston, Thurgood Marshall, and the Struggle to End Segregation 120–21 (2010); Arnold G. Parks, Lincoln University: 1920–1970 89 (2007); We Shall Overcome: A History of Civil Rights and the Law 203–04 (2008); *Toy Universities*, Pittsburgh Courier, Jan. 6, 1940, at 8; *Missouri ex rel. Gaines v. Canada*, 305 U.S. 337 (1938).

[39] *Lloyd Gaines Speaks to Students Here*, Plaindealer, Mar. 3, 1939, at 1; *Educated Cowards*, Cleveland Call and Post, Mar. 9, 1939, at 6; P. L. Harden, *Tenn. Lawyer Fires Another Blast on Equal Protection*, Plaindealer, Mar. 15, 1940, at 6.

the *Afro-American* wrote that Doyle "is looked upon as a Benedict Arnold who has sold his race down the river for a mere \$25-a-week job on the State's payroll, and a 'basement legal education.'"[40]

Doyle's critics had a convincing argument that he violated constructive racial loyalty norms. In the late 1940s, blacks were fully vested in a legal challenge against Jim Crow. Led by the NAACP, blacks were asserting their full citizenship rights, arguing that separate but equal violated the Equal Protection Clause. In order to successfully claim that Sweatt was granted equal protection, Texas had to prove that TSUN was equivalent to University of Texas School of Law. Doyle's presence at TSUN helped the state's segregationist attorney general argue that the new law school was equal. The state attorney general even used Doyle as an exemplar product of segregated education. In announcing that he was not interested in dismantling segregation, Doyle told the rest of the black community that he was uncommitted to the racial struggle. Black Texans, in other words, justifiably concluded that Doyle proved that he was unconcerned about the race when he disclaimed any interest in the race's antisegregation battle. The case of Doyle, however, establishes that *Uncle Toms* can be retrieved. After he graduated, he litigated against segregation, including a lawsuit to desegregate the public cafeteria in Houston's main courthouse.[41]

Similarly, in Oklahoma during the period when *Sipuel v. Oklahoma* (1948) was making its way toward the Supreme Court, some blacks refused to embrace the legal challenge to segregation. In *Sipuel*, Ada Sipuel sued Oklahoma for admission into Oklahoma University College of Law. Roscoe Dunjee, editor of the state's only black newspaper, testified during the initial trial for *Sipuel* that he opposed antimiscegenation laws. Those laws, which made interracial marriages illegal, were declared constitutional in *Pace v. Alabama* (1883) and

---

[40] Marguerite L. Butler, *The History of Texas Southern University, Thurgood Marshall School of Law: "The House that Sweatt Built: Douglass Hall*, 23 Thurgood Marshall Law Review 45 (1997); *Woman Withdraws, 2 Men at Texas JC Law School*, Afro-American, Feb. 14, 1948 at 18; Thomas D. Russell, *"Keep Negroes Out of Most Classes Where There Are a Larger Number of Girls": The Unseen Power of the Ku Klux Klan and Standardized Testing at the University of Texas, 1899–1999* found in Robert W. Gordon and Morton J. Horwitz, Law, Society, and History: Themes in the Legal Sociology and Legal History of Lawrence M. Friedman 316 (2011); Dwonna Goldstone, Integrating the 40 Acres: The 50-Year Struggle for Racial Equality at the University of Texas 23 (2006); Gary M. Lavergne, Before Brown: Heman Marion Sweatt, Thurgood Marshall, and the Long Road to Justice 139, 219 (2010).

[41] Michael L. Gillette, *Blacks Challenge the White University*, 86 Southwestern Historical Quarterly 321, 330 (1982); Thomas R. Cole, No Color Is My Kind: The Life of Eldrewey Stearns and the Integration of Houston 40–41 (1997). The black law school, ironically, might have forced the state to integrate because maintaining a separate law school quickly became prohibitively expensive.

were legal until the Supreme Court ruled them unconstitutional in *Loving v. Virginia* (1967). Until *Loving*, though, the South and border states clung to such laws, reflecting their biggest fears: sex between black men and white women. After Dunjee's testimony, a white newspaper blared a paranoid headline reading, "Negro Editor Wants to Marry White Women." Blacks in the area were disgruntled with Dunjee after his testimony. Dunjee disclosed that "Uncle Tom Negroes in Oklahoma City said that I had ruined everything." Local blacks likely feared that his statement would rile the white folk. Dunjee probably thought, however, that these blacks were more interested in mollifying whites than in supporting a movement for change. The Supreme Court's siding with Sipuel in her quest to integrate University of Oklahoma's law school told Dunjee that the white liberal was a better defender of blacks' rights than blacks were. "That is," he wrote, "a dangerous situation!"[42]

As *Gaines* and *Sweatt* instruct, Southern states were very eager to create ersatz schools for blacks to attend rather than integrate graduate and professional schools. These Supreme Court decisions, in any event, were seen as triumphs over *Uncle Toms*. Dr. David D. Jones, president of Bennett College, thought that white educators were putting up a fight, but recent Supreme Court decisions were giving *Uncle Toms* "cause for pause." Reputed *Uncle Toms* might have paused, but they quickly regrouped, once again making themselves useful in the maintenance of dual-race school systems. Asserted *Uncle Toms*, for instance, helped get blacks fired. Segregationists were very eager to locate blacks connected with the NAACP and inflict punishment on them, economic and even sometimes physical. Alabama tried to enforce a statute that required the NAACP to disclose its membership lists but it was held unconstitutional in *NAACP v. Alabama*. In Savannah in the early 1950s, five black schoolteachers were fired after their NAACP membership was disclosed. A local black man who opposed integrated schools alerted the white superintendent of the NAACP connections of the fired teachers. The local NAACP head, W. W. Law, said that "Uncle Tomism" and racism was to blame for their dismissal.[43]

Other blacks took a more direct approach to resuscitate segregation and defy racial loyalty norms. In 1951, New Mexico's state legislature debated the future of the state's optional public school segregation policy that

---

[42] *Pace v. Alabama*, 106 U.S. 583 (1883); *Loving v. Virginia*, 388 U.S. 1 (1967); *Uncle Toms Hit by Roscoe Dunjee*, Cleveland Call and Post, Mar. 13, 1948, at 1B.

[43] *End of Second-Class Citizenship Now in Sight, Educators, Lawyers Agree*, Afro-American, June 24, 1950, at 19; Gilbert Jonas, Freedom's Sword: The NAACP and the Struggle against Racism in America, 1909–1969 161–62 (2005); *Four Ga. Teachers Fired for NAACP Activity*, Afro-American, Sept. 8, 1951, at 5.

affected approximately ten cities. Repealing the law would have allowed
affected black children to attend white, and almost assuredly, better-funded
public schools. The senate's judiciary committee heard the testimony of
six blacks. Four opposed repealing the law. During his testimony, one
schoolteacher asked the legislature to not "disturb us." He continued, "We
have peace and enjoyment in our schools. You put our children together
and there will be a race war. You'll be putting the white man against the
black man." The *Atlanta Daily World* assailed him and the other three as
"Uncle Toms."[44]

Mississippi's Clyde Kennard, similarly, was considered willing to eat a meal
even if he starved the rest of the race. His asserted singular focus on self-
interest angered many blacks, who dismissed him as an *Uncle Tom*. Kennard,
a Korean War veteran, returned to his hometown of Hattiesburg before completing his degree at the University of Chicago. He wanted to continue his
education at Mississippi Southern College (now the University of Southern
Mississippi), an all-white school near where he lived. Because he had to care
for his mother after the death of his stepfather, he had to attend a nearby
university and no black school was. Some argued that Kennard, in response,
devised a plan to become the "perfect Negro" to ingratiate himself to local
white leaders and convince the state to make an exception and permit his
enrollment at the white college. Kennard wrote a letter to a white newspaper
affirming his support of "States Rights," the Southern mantra connoting the
desire to keep the federal government from "meddling" in their affairs. He
also affirmed his stance against forced integration and rebuffed the NAACP's
offer to fight his case in court. Kennard even spoke to the governor, who told
him that he should wait until after the elections to pursue a spot at the college. He did. Using "the 'Uncle Tom' approach did get Kennard considerable
mileage – though it didn't get him in school," the *Defender* quipped. It got
him framed and imprisoned instead. The White Citizens Council set him up
on a bogus reckless driving charge and planted whisky in his car. Mississippi
was under prohibition at the time. His application was then rejected because
of irregularities.[45]

Although some announced *Uncle Tom's* death on May 17, 1954, *Uncle
Tom* excoriations survived *Brown v. Board of Education*. The jubilation that

44 *Negroes Split on School Bias Bill in New Mexico*, Atlanta Daily World, Mar. 15, 1951, at 8.
45 *He Wanted to Go to College in Mississippi and Wound up in Prison*, Chicago Defender,
    Nov. 24, 1962, at 9; John Dittmer, Local People: The Struggle for Civil Rights in Mississippi
    80–83 (1995); George A. Sewell and Margaret L. Dwight, Mississippi Black History Makers
    131–32 (1984); Gordon A. Martin Jr., Count Them One by One: Black Mississippians Fighting
    for the Right to Vote 16 (2010).

followed the decision was tempered by the reality that the NAACP faced the enormous challenge of integrating school districts against virulent white resistance. In addition to those local whites, the NAACP fretted about the potential ploys of Southern *Uncle Toms*. Dr. Channing H. Tobias said that the organization was going to be aggressive in dealing with "congenital 'Uncle Toms'" who benefited from Jim Crow. In this mold were the presidents of black colleges Texas State University and Prairie View College. Both presidents speaking to the Texas Commission of Higher Education declared that blacks preferred segregated schools. Walter White assailed them as blacks who were more concerned about keeping their jobs than trying to help black students.[46]

After Reconstruction, white supremacy pivoted from slavery toward racial apartheid to subjugate the black population. Blacks were second-class citizens. But many were not content with their inferior positioning. The only way the race would ever reach full citizenship would be by demanding and fighting for it, as a group. Separate but equal was not a problem with individual solutions. Blacks had to dedicate themselves to the cause of changing a truth of American democracy: Black skin functioned as a disability. Required here, then, was a device to compel blacks to join the struggle. This was the purpose of racial loyalty norms. By regulating behavior, blacks taught the race how to wage effective campaigns for their rights and to do so as a unified people. The enterprise did not operate perfectly; some blacks, as mentioned, were charged with disloyalty when it was not warranted. On the whole, though, the practice of using racial loyalty norms to punish race traitors in the context of segregation was enormously constructive and, quite simply, the right move for blacks during the Jim Crow era.

UNCLE TOMS LIVE IN THE SOUTH

Amid the South's legal and social climate, *Uncle Tom* sensibilities were frequently imputed to Southern blacks. As one wrote poetically, "you can take Uncle Tom out of the Southland, but you can't take the South out of Uncle Tom." Those using *Uncle Tom* in this context demeaned supposed Southern meekness, realizing that timidity crippled the effort to construct the solidarity necessary to challenge oppression. *Uncle Tom*, in other words, was used to rebuke blacks for exhibiting inexcusable submissiveness in the face of racism.

---

[46] *Congratulations, Councilman*, New Journal and Guide, June 22, 1957, at C15; *Walter White Blasts Byrnes, "Uncle Toms*," Cleveland Call and Post, July 10, 1954, at 3A; *NAACP to War on "Uncle Toms*," Philadelphia Tribune, July 3, 1954, at 1.

The mores of Southern blacks, many believed, ruined blacks' prospects to collectively craft a better future.

Many Southern blacks, however, contended that their Northern brothers were too demanding because the South had a way of exterminating the boisterous Negro from its soil. Some, that is, felt that supposed Southern Negro servility was a justifiable survival tactic. As one black Southern leader remarked, "They should come down here and feel the fears, uncertainties, and utter dependence of one of us in their bones," adding that if Northern blacks moved South, they "would be [as] cautious and pussyfooting as we are." V. F. Calverton, a white left-wing intellectual, agreed, observing that blacks had to be *Uncle Toms* to survive in the South. To demand equality under the law, Calverton wrote, was to render oneself the "bad nigger." And history informs that bad *niggers* lived short in Dixie.[47]

Some whites not only preferred *Uncle Toms* but contended that they actually best served blacks' interests. In this vein, U.S. Army Colonel John H. Sherman argued in an article entitled "If I Were a Negro" that *Uncle Toms* were more likely to procure rewards for the race than their aggressive counterparts. Sherman wrote that "the day is past where a minority group can improve its lot by agitation and violence. A minority of ten per cent cannot compel a majority by any means other than by friendly persuasion." Assertive blacks believed that Southern blacks agreed. Militants, for their part, thought the group must insist on legal equality and that *Uncle Toms* placated the South for centuries with no gains. Only by demanding their rights, they concluded, would blacks ever receive them.[48]

In short, in this context, blacks managed racial loyalty norms to empower blacks into accepting that meekness had no place in a self-respecting people trying mightily to secure goals as a group. To the extent that racial loyalty norm managers were indicting all Southern blacks with treachery, that was unfair and destructive. Any use of racial loyalty norms that failed to appreciate the real physical and economic threat under which Southern blacks lived was likewise misguided. Norm enforcement in this context, however, was generally constructive because these norms put blacks on notice that submissiveness was disfavored.

A very early example of supposed Southern meekness occurred in Atlanta in July 1920. Then the *Chicago Defender* assailed a black man, the assault

---

[47] Ralph Matthews, *Watching the Big Parade*, Afro-American, Aug. 24, 1935, at 6; Myrdal, An American Dilemma 770; V. F. Calverton, *The Negro* found in America Now: An Inquiry into Civilization in the United States 485 (1938).

[48] *Officer Urges Race to Be Subservient*, Afro-American, Aug. 24, 1946, at 7; *Claims Negro Leaders Should be "Uncle Toms,"* Philadelphia Tribune, Aug. 24, 1946, at 13; *Uncle Tom Solves Nothing*, Afro-American, Aug. 31, 1946, at 4.

stemming from a lynching episode, in an article entitled "Give Purse to Race Betrayer 'Uncle Tom,' Who Led Innocent Man to Mob, Rewarded by Lynchers." That innocent man, Philip Gathers, was lynched for supposedly murdering a white woman, although he denied any involvement. Gathers claimed that he drove a white man to the location where a white woman was already slain and that the white man forced him get out of the buggy at gunpoint. He was then, according to Gathers, told to "run down the road." Gathers said that he was ignorant of the events until a friend later told him that the sheriff was looking for him because he was wanted for murder.[49]

That's where the supposed "Uncle Tom" came in. Buck Stevens, according to the *Defender*, "acted as a stool pigeon and betrayed Philip Gathers, a member of his Race" when he led a white mob to Gathers. Once found, Gathers was then burned at the stake in the public square. His body was drenched in gasoline and a high school-aged girl set him aflame. For his reward, local whites honored Stephens with a cashier's check for $10.11. The white mob collected the money after Gathers's body was torched and dismembered, cut into separate pieces, and distributed "among the throng ... [of] men, women and children." Along with the check, Stephens received a letter that quintessentially captured white supremacy. The letter stated that:

> The citizens of Pineora and Marlow give to you, Buck Stephens, this check for so faithfully turning up Phillip Gathers, the much wanted black brute who murdered Miss Jaudon in our county. We do this to show our appreciation of the Negroes who are loyal to our best interests and common good. The southern white people are the best friends of the Colored Race and their co-operation in helping to bring criminals to Justice will greatly help to make an end of the unmentionable crimes committed upon our white women. We know you agree with the cool, calm manner in which was lynched the brute Gathers.[50]

Supporting a charge that Stevens was guilty of racial treachery seems incredibly difficult. Indeed, although he may have been submissive, many would conclude that Stevens had an excuse. No defense surpasses "help us or we'll kill you." But Gathers came to Stevens's home asking for food and then Stevens alerted authorities. Apparently Stevens, under no threat or coercion, voluntarily led a vengeful mob to Gathers. Under these circumstances, that the *Defender* would loathe Stevens, particularly because he was paid for essentially Negro-catching services, is understandable.[51]

---

[49] *Give Purse to Race Betrayer "Uncle Tom," Who Led Innocent Man to Mob, Rewarded by Lynchers*, Chicago Defender, July 3, 1920, at 1.

[50] Id.; Donald L. Grant, The Way It Was in the South: The Black Experience in Georgia 318 (2001).

[51] *Burned at Stake Then Shot by Mob*, Kingsport Times, June 22, 1920, at 1.

In attempts to "cure" the Southern Negro, the *Defender* advocated that Southern blacks migrate northward where "a man is paid a man's wage for a day's work and given a chance to spend his earning as he pleases, just like any other man." Those remaining in the South were considered unthinking for jeopardizing their lives and livelihood, according to the *Defender*. Another black publication urged blacks to "get out of that hell hole." When the editors of the *Defender* in 1923 read in a New Orleans newspaper that white businessmen rewarded blacks who remained as sharecroppers with a barbeque, they excoriated those blacks for "trading freedom and a man's wage for a mess of hog meat!" Those prizing pork over dignity were called *Uncle Toms*.

The *Defender* neither believed that the North monopolized the best race members, nor fathomed that all blacks below the Mason-Dixon Line were obsequious. They did, however, maintain that Dixie was a poor breeding ground for independent thinkers. State-sponsored segregation, overt racism, and lynching, the *Defender* probably thought, weakened the Negro's mettle. Southern blacks, the newspaper found, were "cramped – they lack freedom, and their children are brought up under an environment that leads to a perpetuation of the 'Uncle Tom' spirit." The *Defender*, therefore, hoped that blacks migrated northward.[52]

Whereas most ran away from *Uncle Tom* accusations, P. B. Young, the *Norfolk Journal and Guide's* editor, considered *Uncle Tom* a compliment. Young, of course, was Southern. In 1923, Young endured *Uncle Tom* accusations for supporting a United Daughters of the Confederacy plan to erect a monument to mammies near Lincoln's memorial. The mammy monument, which nearly came to fruition, sprang out of the nostalgic feeling for the Old South on the part of those who wanted to return to "an imagined history of beneficent antebellum slavery and southern gentility, a time when ... whites were good stewards of their land and their laborers, and black people loved them." Although agreeing that black mothers deserved commemoration, the *Washington Tribune* found the monument disrespectful and that Young's blessing highlighted his "'Uncle Tom' spirit." Young responded as though he was ignorant of what an "Uncle Tom spirit" was; he lauded "Uncle Tom" as "generous and genteel" and hoped that more would emulate him. But the suggestion that Young was weak willed was deeply unfair. By the 1930s, Young

[52] The sources for this and the preceding paragraph are as follows: *Burned Hog Meat Given Uncle Toms*, Chicago Defender, Sept. 1, 1923, at 13; *Negroes, Leave the South!*, The Messenger, Mar. 1920, at 2; *Let's Make It 3,000,000*, Chicago Defender, June 13, 1925, at A10; Charles A. Simmons, The African American Press: With Special References to Four Newspapers, 1827–1965 31–32 (1998).

and his newspaper had proven to be among the strongest agents for civil rights and racial justice in the South.[53]

Another supposed embarrassment occurred in 1928 when 200 members of the Ex-Slaves' Association held their annual convention in Birmingham, Alabama. During their convention, the ex-slaves sang spirituals and, according to the *Defender*, reminisced about the "happy days" of captivity. The *Defender* thought the display carried the detestable odor of minstrelsy and was confounded that freedmen would commemorate an institution where blacks were torn from their loved ones and deemed property. The newspaper argued that these ex-slaves were *Uncle Toms* and labeled their gathering an "Uncle Tom Convention." The leader of the group, Simon Phillips, was specifically derided as "the enterprising Uncle Tom who organized the association and who has been president for 17 years." The *Defender* correctly pegged Phillips as a former bondsman who fondly remembered the days of slavery and adored his former master, considering him the best slave owner in the world. Indeed in *Old Massa's People* (1931), a book featuring slave narratives, Phillips depicts "plantation life" as "fine living." The *Defender* pointed to a silver lining: The ex-slaves were necessarily old and therefore the Grim Reaper was near. Nonetheless, the *Defender* was sad that the Thirteenth Amendment applied to them. With blacks like Phillips, the newspaper complained, segregation would remain, illustrating how legal concerns frequently propelled *Uncle Tom* charges.[54]

One of the ways Jim Crow justice was maintained was through the use of the all-white jury. In *Williams v. Mississippi* (1898), the Court gave Southern states free reign to exclude blacks from juries until *Norris v. Alabama* (1935), where the Court held that prolonged black absence from juries established an Equal Protection Clause violation. *Norris* overturned the decision of one of the Scottsboro boys, nine black youths accused of raping two white women. After the decision, states could not purposefully exclude blacks from juries as easily as before. According to the *Cleveland Gazette*, when Norris was retried, Alabama put an "Uncle Tom Negro" on the jury to comply with the Court's holding. Presumably, the "Uncle Tom Negro" acquiesced to racism.[55]

[53] *See Lincoln's Spirit*, New York Amsterdam News, Mar. 14, 1923, at 12; *Editorial Article*, New Journal and Guide, Mar. 10, 1923, at 4; Henry Lewis Suggs, P. B. Young, Newspaperman: Race, Politics, and Journalism in the New South, 1910–1962 94 (1988); Micki McElya, Clinging to Mammy: The Faithful Slave in Twentieth Century America 116–17 (2007).

[54] *Uncle Tom Convention*, Chicago Defender, Aug. 11, 1928, at A2; Orland Kay Armstrong, Old Massa's People: The Old Slaves Tell Their Story 33–34 (1931).

[55] *Williams v. Mississippi*, 170 U.S. 213 (1898); *Norris v. Alabama*, 294 U.S. 587 (1935); Clarence Norris, The Last of the Scottsboro Boys: An Autobiography (1979); The Man from Scottsboro:

Other Southern state criminal justice systems began interviewing a few blacks for possible jury service in the wake of *Norris*. But blacks were sometimes unwilling to serve. In 1935, the *Afro-American* published an article entitled "Uncle Tom Jurors Duck Service," excoriating potential black jurors in Memphis. Five prospective black jurors were examined in circuit court but all of them purposely avoided service. They were likely afraid; black jurors were often targets of physical retribution. In 1910, for instance, a black man was abducted at night and beaten two days after a black man sat on an Alabama jury. But to many blacks, refusing to serve on juries was lamentable. The NAACP thought that jury commissioners were intentionally picking *Uncle Toms* with meek reputations.[56]

Possibly, white jury commissioners purposefully chose only those blacks for jury service who were known to be submissive. That notwithstanding, a per se criticism of blacks for dodging jury service in the Jim Crow South was destructive norm management. Sanctioning docility is constructive only when the behavior is inexcusable. Yet the threat of physical violence was all too real for black jurors. Constructive social norms must not require blacks to stare down the threat of physical punishment. Blacks are less likely to willingly embrace black solidarity if such fearlessness is required.

Other *Uncle Tom* accusations were unfair. In 1937 in Apalachicola, Florida, a black man was accused of attempted assault on two white women. The women were picking blackberries near the local airport when a black man reportedly assaulted them. A manhunt ensued and the suspect was arrested. A mob was all set to lynch him, but ultimately did not. After the man's life was spared, the black leaders in the city wrote a resolution praising Governor Fred Cone, the mayor, and other officials. For this, those leaders were likened to *Uncle Tom*.[57]

But was charging these leaders with betrayal fair? The most potent attack is that they legitimated whites' ability to lynch blacks. If whites are hailed for not lynching, the implicit suggestion is that the right to lynch exists. Some might contend, furthermore, that praising a white mob for treating blacks in a way

---

Clarence Norris and the Infamous 1931 Alabama Rape Trial, in His Own Words (1997); *Norris*, 294 U.S. 587; *Uncle Tom Negro; Scottsboro*, Cleveland Gazette, Nov. 16, 1935, at 2.

In *Swain v. Alabama*, 380 U.S. 202 (1965), however, the Court deferred to Southern prosecutors in using peremptory challenges to strike blacks from juries. *Swain* was overturned in *Batson v. Kentucky*, 476 U.S. 79 (1986).

56 *Uncle Tom Jurors Duck Service*, Afro-American, Sept. 28, 1935, at 3; Gilbert Thomas Stephenson, Race Distinctions in America Law 254 (1910); Michael J. Klarman, From Jim Crow to Civil Rights: The Supreme Court and the Struggle for Racial Equality 268 (2004).

57 Richardson, *"Leaders" Criticized for Lauding Florida's Anti-Negro Governor*, Pittsburgh Courier, June 19, 1937, at 3.

the law mandates was obsequious. The other side, however, had a retort. The decision to commend the aforementioned whites could be considered a realistic response under the circumstances. Whereas those criticizing the resolution did so from afar, blacks actually living there could have been expressing sincere gratitude that a man was not killed. Lynchers were rarely prosecuted. And if the accused in this case was lynched, likely no one would have been punished. One can reasonably contend that the resolution was adequately calibrated to lessen the likelihood that the next accused black man would fall victim to the unbridled rage of a white mob ignited by unsubstantiated charges. Thus, returning to the original question, the evidence is insufficient to support the charge that the city's leaders violated constructive norms. Their meekness was not inexcusable.

Whereas some thanked whites for not victimizing blacks, this next man, for personal gain, actually called upon the local white supremacist power structure to abuse blacks. He, as expected, endured condemnation for duplicity. In July 1939 in Live Oak, Florida, the Klan went on a rampage, assaulting black residents frequenting a particular jook joint. The black victims deserved it for their "rowdiness near white churches" according to a local white newspaper. The person who unleashed the Klan was villainized. The brutality frightened blacks into purchasing guns. An unnamed black man, who ran a competing jook joint, was the villain. He convinced his white boss to call upon the KKK to brutalize blacks who patronized their jook joint competition, believing that all of the business would flow to his establishment afterward. That unnamed man was assailed as an *Uncle Tom*. With blacks like this, solidarity would be hard to forge, ensuring segregation would last for the foreseeable future.[58]

Hurling *Uncle Tom* at blacks who appeased segregationists is expected, but some uses of *Uncle Tom* in this context might appear odd to contemporary readers. In 1937, for example, the *Defender* excoriated black students at the University of Chicago who created a "Negro club." The newspaper blamed Southern blacks who moved north but retained Southern sensibilities. The black students reported that they "feel funny among so many white folks." The *Defender* was intolerant of their worldview, wanting the clubs discontinued. "Those students," the *Defender* wrote, "who prefer to inaugurate a program of segregation at the university should pack bag and baggage and go back South where that type of education is the custom, and where they can absorb without interference such back-door philosophy that has produced thousands of Uncle Toms among us."[59]

---

[58] *Klansmen Stage Raid; Beat Negroes Found on Streets*, Atlanta Daily World, July 26, 1939, at 1.

[59] *U of C Students Told to Ban South's Ideals*, Chicago Defender, Oct. 23, 1937, at 15.

Today, though, *not* participating in black clubs might invite accusations of racial betrayal largely because the law and social conditions have changed. Legal and societal factors, in other words, color behavior in the black community. The *Defender* likely anticipated that segregationists would aver that such clubs evidenced that even blacks preferred racial separation. Now, without fearing the restoration of segregation by law, the current concern is blacks eschewing the race's cultural activities, suggesting racial desertion. This example illustrates how the law and the racial climate combine to form a wheel that steers what comportments will be associated with racial treachery, and, by extension, how blacks will configure *Uncle Tom* as a mechanism to punish crimes against the race.

Those criticizing Southern blacks surely would cite a black man's attempt to run for political office in North Carolina as evidencing Southern meekness. This case also demonstrates constructive management of racial loyalty norms. In 1938, M. K. Tyson announced his candidacy for the state legislature. A group of blacks, however, wanted to work with whites to dissuade him. The *Afro-American* argued that whenever blacks tried to uplift the race in the South, "whites ... get a bunch of snoopers together" to stunt progress. Tyson was, in the paper's estimation, immensely qualified and therefore should be free to pursue elected office. The *Afro-American* possibly believed that a black legislator might be able to make changes from within the system. Those blacks thwarting Tyson's pursuits were worse than white segregationists, the paper argued. "There will come a time when our communities will chase our Uncle Toms to cover. They do not belong in forward-looking society."[60]

The Negro Chamber of Commerce of North Carolina's executive secretary, Ned Davis, brought treachery to new heights (or lows) in a 1941 speech at a white South Carolinian businessmen's club. Davis told the audience that whites will always be the "masters" if blacks remain in their proximity. To Davis, "Negro" and "nigger" were synonymous, and both "want to stay in our places." Davis further claimed that he encountered blacks who should have been kept in bondage. With the white audience, the speech was a hit. Local blacks, however, were incensed and started a movement to oust him from his job to ensure that he would no longer have a position "which gives him enough prestige to makes his utterances described variously as 'Uncle Tom' and 'handkerchief head.'"[61]

Or take H. W. Newell, commenting on the President's Committee on Civil Rights report in 1947. Newell claimed that intelligent Southern Negroes

---

60 *Uncle Toms with Us Yet*, Afro-American, May 14, 1938, at 4.
61 A. M. Rivera Jr., *Speech Shocks City*, New Journal and Guide, Nov. 15, 1941, at 1.

wanted to keep segregation for the time being, saying that "all they want is to be left alone." Newell believed that desegregation might work in the future, but that segregation had not run its course. He also asserted that blacks were treated better in the South than in the North. The *Afro-American* reported the speech with the headline "Uncle Tom Lives."[62]

But did Newell engage in racial treachery by arguing that, in 1947, segregation was preferable to integration? Many scholars argue that pursuing integration was a tactical mistake for civil rights lawyers. This argument holds that blacks would have been better served by pursuing a separate black existence rather than live in an integrated society that treated blacks unfairly. But Newell's argument was far different. Newell claimed that Southern blacks were treated better than were Northern blacks. With Southern blacks being lynched, disenfranchised, and subject to racist social etiquettes, no sincere black person would utter those words. Newell was cozying up to Southern whites. He lauded them for being better than their Northern peers and defended the continuance of segregation. Doing both of these things would undoubtedly ingratiate a black person to Southern whites. Assuming there were no extenuating circumstances, Newell's servility earned him the *Uncle Tom* label.

The stereotype of black Southerners wilting under Southern bigotry is perhaps best seen in the case of Charlie Fitzgerald and his wife, Sarah. In Myrtle Beach, South Carolina, Mr. Fitzgerald was a successful businessman and a "well-known Negro leader." In 1948, he and Sarah, the city's only registered black voters, asked the mayor to remove their names from the voter roll. Mr. Fitzgerald commented that he did not think it was "the right time" for blacks to vote and whites and blacks would continue to get along if "outside agitators" did not interfere. Charlie made sure to alert his white friends to their decision to unregister. The *Plain Dealer* recounted the story under the headline "'Good Ole Uncle Tom' Says Time Not Ripe for Negro Voting." The Fitzgeralds' voluntary relinquishing of their suffrage rights surely charmed the local whites with whom they were likely trying to build and maintain valuable relationships. That blacks had to give up rights to secure economic vitality perfectly illustrates the stifling racism of the Jim Crow South and how it cramped the black condition.[63]

As was true in the context of segregation, racial loyalty norms directed at Southern meekness were largely constructive. Southern culture pressured blacks into comporting subserviently. For instance, S. I. Hayakawa, who later

---

[62] *Tenn. "Leader" Says He Likes Segregation*, Afro-American, Nov. 15, 1947, at 18.
[63] *"Good Ole Uncle Tom" Says Time Not Ripe for Negro Voting*, Plain Dealer, Aug. 20, 1948, at 6.

became a U.S. senator, was shocked and ultimately disturbed by Southern blacks' behavior when visiting the Deep South in the 1940s. He writes, "having gone down to the Deep South, I am now privileged to know better what is meant by the contemptuous Northern Negro expressions, 'Handkerchief Haids' [*sic*] and 'Uncle Toms.'" During his trip, one elderly black man was strikingly deferential. The man was on crutches and walking down the street, but stopped, took off his hat, and waited for Hayakawa to pass. Hayakawa, Asian American, penned, "It's not that [he] took me for white. I suppose, so much as the fact that they knew I wasn't Negro and therefore decided to take no chances." If this reflected Southern Negro behavior, an intervention was an absolute necessity. Linking this behavior to racial treachery and notifying blacks that they would be harshly rebuked for submissiveness was an excellent first step. This was not necessarily a conscious endeavor. The argument is not that underneath every use of *Uncle Tom* was a conscious effort to make blacks more militant. But it was effective in empowering blacks into resisting oppression.[64]

UNCLE TOMMING FOR A JOB

The principal issue in this context is how blacks comported in employment settings amid a society that limited their autonomy in the labor market. Southern states skirted the central aims of the Thirteenth Amendment by curtailing black workers' autonomy. In cities, although the state could not discriminate without running afoul of the Equal Protection Clause, private employers were practically unfettered in discriminating against black laborers. This was true because both the state and the federal governments ignored employment discrimination until the 1940s. The inadequate antidiscrimination laws that some states passed were under-enforced, though most states passed no such laws, especially Southern ones. Some Southern locales, in fact, enacted statutes discriminating against black workers. The federal government's first antidiscrimination efforts were President Roosevelt's executive orders of the early 1940s. These orders, however, failed in combating widespread discrimination. The Great Depression and its disproportionate effects on black workers ensured that there would be few jobs for the scores of unemployed blacks. Some blacks urged solidarity to uplift black spirits while petitioning the federal government to alleviate chronic black unemployment. Other blacks, to endure a racially hostile land, were deemed guilty of betraying the race, and *Uncle Tom* accusations often arose.

[64] S. I. Hayakawa, *Second Thoughts*, Chicago Defender, Jan. 6, 1945, at 11.

That blacks were vulnerable to employment discrimination affected black behavior in various ways. One effect was subservience. Marcus Garvey once remarked that blacks themselves erected most of the obstacles on the road to racial advancement. Booker T. Washington also perceived this, pegging the "crabs in a basket" mentality as one hindrance. This described the phenomenon that, when a black person approaches success, other blacks reflexively attempt to prevent it, pulling the crab back down to the bottom of the basket. Along these lines, one black commenter contested that "[t]he greatest handicap our group has are [sic] these relics of bygone days, these 'Uncle Toms' who think by belittling their own that they can curry favor with the cracker element of the South." Fully appreciating that white supremacy favored obsequious and treacherous blacks, many took the cue and behaved accordingly. When that happened, the menacing *Uncle Tom* unveiled its long talons, producing deep gashes.[65]

Blacks were often their own worst enemy. After one Chicago business began hiring blacks, the *Defender* investigated why other businesses that mainly served blacks typically hired only whites. The *Defender* determined that some black customers actually dissuaded the hiring of blacks. Blacks consistently jeered the black worker who the previously mentioned business hired. "They seem to resent his services," the *Defender* reported, "despite the fact that he has proved himself efficient." Those exhibiting this "tomfoolery" were called Judases. The newspaper further contended that it was "the duty of all of us not only to ridicule but also to ferret out and utterly destroy this remnant of the days of Uncle Tom. It is against our race that these servile plotters work their dirty conspiracies." Here, writers at *Defender* alerted their readers to the existence of a problem – blacks who bemoaned the presence of black workers – and implored the race to stamp out that mindset. In doing this, the newspaper helped build solidarity around the notion that blacks sabotaging employment opportunities for other blacks was perverse. This racial cohesion was crucial for blacks not only dealing with labor dilemmas, but other crises as well.[66]

Many were justifiably concerned that *Uncle Toms* hampered progress in the workforce. Those concurring held that some acted slavishly to meet white employers' preferences. No self-respecting black person would want to adhere to this dehumanizing, but nonetheless favored, archetype. But a job was a job and blacks had few options. Many, therefore, had to choose between dignity

---

[65] *Too Much Talk*, Chicago Defender, Feb 7, 1925, at 12; Conversations with Ralph Ellison 127 (Editors Maryemma Graham and Amritjit Singh 1995); Cary D. Wintz, African American Political Thought 1890–1930 177 (1996).

[66] *Object to Own Race*, Chicago Defender, Apr. 2, 1921, at 15.

and work. Blacks wanting both gainful employment and their pride intact, in turn, admonished those who raced to the bottom. Blacks, in short, were implored to not comport like *Uncle Toms* and reminded that their behavior was subject to racial loyalty norms.

Uncle Tom, in this context, generally referred to those making it harder for other blacks in the workforce. Sometimes the "Uncle Tom" was an unprofessional worker. Other times the "Uncle Tom" was an employee who whites fancied because he was compliant with his subordination. Both *Uncle Tom* varieties were disdained for impeding the progress of the proud black worker who was professional and decorous. As the *Plain Dealer* wrote, "the Negro race does not appreciate the 'uncle Tom' type of Negro who will harbor segregation and jimcrowism to hold a job.... 15 million Negroes in America are more important than any ten or 15 Negroes on a jim crow job." The racial loyalty norms that were typically violated here were the norms against inexcusable meekness and furthering the enemies' interests. As true with segregation and Southern meekness, norm management here was usually constructive.[67]

In 1911, a letter to the editor printed in the *Defender* directed train porters to act professionally. The writer exclaimed that "monkey porters and Uncle Tom[s]" frustrated other blacks' ability to find employment. In 1912, the *Defender* told black porters to "discharge your duty like a man ... and cut out that Uncle Tom act." Porters were arranged into two categories, the "subservient [and] cringing" *Uncle Tom* type and those who were "dignified [and] business-like." Relatedly, in 1913, the *Defender* similarly derogated asserted *Uncle Toms*. "It has been reported," wrote the *Defender*, "that a train porter has been dismissed from the service of a railroad company in Chicago for playing 'Uncle Tom.' You are not with the companies to amuse passengers; you are there to serve them; such porters should be in vaudeville, not on the passenger trains." Those criticizing "Uncle Tom" porters realized that white employers would project the faults of one black worker onto the entire race. Ensuring that each black worker was exemplary helped hire the next black person.[68]

Uncle Tom was also appropriated to scold those who mistreated fellow blacks while on the job. In 1917, for example, the *Defender* accused some porters with "Old Uncle Tom in their systems" of offending black women. In 1930, the *Defender* was fed up with Southern *Uncle Tom* brakemen, workers who

---

[67] *Arrest Windy City Gang Milgrams Store Practices Democracy in Employment*, Plain Dealer, Sept. 13, 1946, at 1.

[68] John R. Winston, *In the Railroad Center*, Chicago Defender, Feb 4, 1911, at 2; Chicago Defender, July 20, 1912, at 2; *The Railroad Porter*, Chicago Defender, Dec. 8, 1923, at A12; Chicago Defender, Apr. 12, 1913 at 7.

inspected trains and helped the conductor. Many Southern black brakemen reportedly assumed that only whites could afford luxury accommodations. Thus, whenever they saw black passengers, they told them, "Your coach is in front, next to the baggage car." Being racially profiled as undoubtedly poor was humiliating and worsened because the profiler was black. These reputed *Uncle Toms* were chastised for disgracing their brethren.[69]

This vexing behavior revealed itself in other employment settings. A 1930 *Courier* article provides a fascinating instance. The *Courier* discussed black employees who spotted blacks attempting to pass for white in segregated places. This leads to an intriguing question: Who committed racial betrayal? One might depict the "passer" as the real *Uncle Tom*. Eschewing racial membership, after all, could be interpreted as an affront. Or perhaps passing could be viewed as blacks attempting to "pull one over" on whites by enjoying something their skin color would ordinarily preclude. Returning to the original question, who was the wrongdoer? The *Courier* chose the black employees. "[A]lthough we are depressed," the newspaper's editors wrote, "we are not at all surprised by the news from Washington, D.C., that a number of these submarine Negroes who ... are so low they could walk under a rug with a beaver hat on, are finding employment 'spotting' Negroes who 'pass for white for Nordic owners of theaters, stores and hotels.'"[70]

While the norm against inexcusable meekness does not compel blacks to sacrifice their livelihood for the race's interests, these "submarine" Negroes were closely tied to the maintenance of white supremacy. Indeed, their duties helped enforce segregation. For their decision to assist whites in promulgating separate but equal, they violated the norm against furthering the enemies' interests. Being too sheepish toward a white boss might draw criticism but, depending on the circumstances, it might be unwarranted if the behavior was necessary to ensure the paycheck that keeps food on the table. But consciously taking a job so intertwined with the maintenance of segregation was validly ripe for derision.

---

[69] *Complain of Treatment by Railway Employes (sic)*, Chicago Defender, Mar. 17, 1917, at 9.
[70] *Submarine Negroes*, Pittsburgh Courier, June 14, 1930, at 10. Arthur F. Raper, The Tragedy of Lynching 356 (2012).

The *Courier* wrote that a just punishment for their "Uncle Tom tactics" was to force them to live their life in Honey Grove or Sherman, Texas. On May 16, 1930, Sam Johnson's corpse was found in Honey Grove after he was lynched by a mob of 2,000 whites. During the same month, the Sherman Riot of 1930 occurred when a black man named George Hughes was burned in the vault of the local courthouse. His body was then retrieved, drug, hung, and set afire again after he was accused of raping a white woman. It was overkill, but the ire the submarine Negro drew underscores how serious some blacks were about the need for all blacks to organize around the goal of resisting oppression.

Although, as in the previous tale, blacks accepted degrading work, sometimes blacks were permitted to occupy positions of authority. Some blacks, however, refused to accept them as superiors. That this occurred was no lie trumped up by white employers to justify employment discrimination. It was real. And this self-sabotage had to be sanctioned, for it hindered the upward mobility of the race. A 1932 survey established this. Indeed, hundreds of surveyed blacks affirmed their refusal to take orders from a member of their own race. In one government department, for instance, a qualified black female supervisor presided over a largely black workforce. The black employees disobeyed her instructions, creating an untenable work environment. When a white woman replaced her, operations resumed normalcy. Or take what transpired when a wholesale business put a black foreman in charge of other blacks. The black workers formerly worked under a white man. They followed him "without question." But when the black foreman took over, the black workers became uncooperative.[71]

Famed scholar Carter G. Woodson reported that twenty years of research established blacks' preference for white bosses. "This is true," Woodson scribed in 1932, "largely to the fact that slaveholders taught their Negroes that they were as good or better than any other Negroes and, therefore, should not be subjected to any member of the race." If anyone ordered them around it should be whites; they are blacks' superiors. This subservient mentality violates constructive racial loyalty norms. Woodson also believed whites preferred the black worker who only obeyed them, writing that whites "have little trouble with the Uncle Tom Negro worker who still has the attitude of the slave in salaaming and kowtowing to the white man." Woodson concluded that such thinking hurt the race economically. "Inasmuch as the Uncle Tom class is more acceptable to the employers themselves this makes the probability of advancing Negroes" to leadership employment positions unlikely.[72]

That *Uncle Toms* hindered "the good black folk" from procuring employment was widely believed in the North and South. Fred Poindexter from Chicago sent a letter to the *Defender*, averring that whites preferred Southern blacks because they accepted lower wages and were "more humble and submissive to the boss than the average northern Negro." Southern blacks, Poindexter further argued, tolerated slurs and demeaning remarks more than their Northern counterparts. Poindexter concluded, "I ... am greatly concerned because proud, intelligent, dignified Negroes ... with principles are

---

[71] Carter Woodson, *Tells Why the Negro Cannot Move Forward*, Pittsburgh Courier, Jan. 39, 1932, at 5.

[72] Id.; *Are They Men or Mice?*, Kansas American, Jan. 10, 1941, at 2.

not liked by the white bosses and in so many cases are not given jobs at all when an Uncle Tom can be hired instead." A "Nashville citizen," writing in the *Courier*, too perceived that whites favored *Uncle Toms*. The citizen witnessed this phenomenon at employment agencies, writing "[e]ven when a job is available, they stand and look at us like we are monkeys in a cage. The office might be filled to capacity and this is still the condition all day long. Then in walks some 'Uncle Tom' sort of fellow and they pass the job out to him." Trust was the apparent issue. Whites trusted blacks who acquiesced to white hegemony.[73]

The *Defender*, though, was disgusted with "Uncle Tom workers" and featured a cartoon in 1927 entitled "People We Can Get Along Without." This cartoon depicted a black worker, with his hat in his hand, talking to a white man who is sitting behind his desk. The caption reads, "The 'Uncle Tom' postal employee who spends all of his spare time trying to 'stand in good' with the superintendent by carrying tales to him." The *Chicago Defender*, sixteen years later, again highlighted the same behavior. "'Uncle Toms,'" the newspaper noted, "insure job security by running to their bosses with answers they want, and with tales about other [employees]."[74]

But such *Uncle Tom* denunciations, those aimed at curtailing asserted subservience on the job, were not necessarily examples of constructive norm management. Denouncing blacks who sought to further themselves by lying about other blacks to their white employers exemplifies constructive racial loyalty norm management. And the same holds true for blacks who gratuitously painted their black colleagues in a negative light, realizing that white bosses fancied the self-styled black informant. Tying a heavy price to exploiting antiblack sentiment for personal gain helps build the group solidarity crucial to accomplishing legal goals. But blacks attempting to be favored employees by being overly deferential were guilty of breaking no constructive racial loyalty norms. The stereotypical "yessuh boss" retort might have signaled servility, but such gestures were often required amid a racist society. Indeed, blacks often had to meet the social mores of the era – meekness in particular – to hold on to a job, especially in the South. Criticism of these individuals would be deeply unwarranted. The use of *Uncle Tom* during this period, though, was generally constructive in employment situations.

[73] Fred Poindexter, *The People Speak*, Chicago Daily Defender, Jan. 9, 1957, at 9; *What the People Think*, Pittsburgh Courier, June 3, 1950, at 32.
[74] *People We Can Get Along Without*, Chicago Defender, June 4, 1927, at 4; Charley Cherokee, *National Grapevine*, Chicago Defender, Feb. 6, 1943, at 15.

If blacks lacked solidarity, it would be apparent in the context of unions. During the Great Depression, when blacks suffered under staggering unemployment levels, the Steel Union wanted to align with black leaders to get blacks to join. White and black union leaders agreed that an interracial alliance was mutually beneficial. Black leaders worried, however, that weak racial unity could hinder the effort. In 1937, Robert L. Vann, the editor of the *Courier*, said that "[i]n your way, this time as always, you'll find stool pigeons and Uncle Toms of your own race, employed by the companies. You've got to fight them, blast them out." Vann highlighted the central reason why *Uncle Tom* was useful. Emboldened blacks could ameliorate their subjugation. The fear of being branded as an *Uncle Tom* nudged blacks toward self-empowerment.[75]

The case of the Brotherhood of the Sleeping Car Porters (BSCP) also illustrates how racial loyalty norms build solidarity. The BSCP was the black Pullman car porters' union formed in the early 1920s. Most onlookers found car porters servile. They were the grinning blacks who served food and fluffed pillows. Porters were an unlikely symbol of black strength and industriousness. But black porters quickly redrew their image after successfully forming a union to battle the powerful Pullman Company. Because the Pullman Company was the country's largest employer of blacks, some blacks thought the race was indebted to it. The Pullman Company, though, was rabidly anti-union. Blacks who organized the BSCP were seen as waging an unwinnable war. When triumphant, the BSCP became an archetype of the "New Negro." In creating the union, members skillfully mastered racial loyalty norms and *Uncle Tom* to deride black opponents and forge cohesion. Black porters who supported the BSCP were the "new Pullman porter" who rejected the "uncle Tom idea[,] . . . the psychology of let well enough alone."[76]

The Pullman Company used blacks to disrupt the BSCP when it was in its infancy. These blacks were important for the Pullman Company's goal of thwarting the unionization of black workers. One writer described them as the "'big house' Negro," recalling the age of slavery. Others argued that they suffered from the "Uncle Tom, me-too-boss, hat-in-hand psychology which arises from the belief that a Negro has no rights a white man is bound to respect . . . that Negroes can't be trusted to deal fairly with each other, that they will lie and steal and talk loud from the big gate, but have no courage to act." A. Philip Randolph, once head of the BSCP, claimed that there were

---

75 *Phil Murray Urges Negro Workers to Join Great Steel Union*, Pittsburgh Courier, Feb. 13, 1937, at 1.
76 William H. Harris, The Harder We Run: Black Workers since the Civil War 77–78 (1982); A. Philip Randolph, *The New Pullman Porter*, The Messenger, Apr. 1926, at 109.

"too many Uncle Toms in the service. With their slave psychology they bow and kowtow and lick the boots of the Company officials, who either pity or despise them." Randolph said these men "are always afraid that somebody will rock the boat, that *the good white folks will get mad.*" On another occasion, Randolph claimed that the Pullman Company was "accustomed to the happy-go-lucky, easy going Uncle Tom type of Negro porter who would grin, say 'yessa boss' and shuffle along."[77]

Randolph and Chandler Owen cofounded the *Messenger*, a race-conscious socialist magazine. The monthly aggressively advocated for the unionization of black porters and liberally applied *Uncle Tom* to demonstrate how black workers were supposed to act. One *Messenger* issue, for instance, featured a conversation between a "New Porter" "who has realized the necessity of having strong unions in order to better the Negro worker's lot" and the "Uncle Tom Porter" who exemplified the "let's not cause any trouble" attitude. An exchange between the two men is as follows:

NEW PORTER: White folks are no different from any other kind of folks, pop. It all depends on how much *power* you got, and you can't get power unless you are *organized*. You know the old joke about the farmer not bothering *one hornet* because of the fear of the *rest* of the *hornets standing behind him*. Well, that's all we porters got to do – *stick together*; be *all for each and each for all*.

UNCLE TOM PORTER: But, son, you know des *"niggers"* ain't like *hornets*, day ain't gwine to *stick*.

N.P.: That's nothing but the slave psychology in you, Pop. You don't think a black man can do anything a white man can do. That's all bunk, pop. Get that stuff out of your noodle. This is the 20th Century. Understand that "a man's a man." A Negro can do anything he is big enough to do. When you're right, pop, and got "guts," you can stand up and look any man in the face and spit right square in his eyes if he tries to give you any *hot stuff* about your rights.[78]

The *Messenger* also ran political cartoons to promote unionization, and editors again used *Uncle Tom* to further their efforts. Eleven cartoons featured

77 *Local Theatrical Managers Eager to Help Pullman Porters' Brotherhood*, New York Amsterdam News, July 11, 1928, at 10; A. Philip Randolph, *Pullman Porters Need Own Union*, The Messenger, Aug. 1925, available at: http://www.iath.virginia.edu/utc/africam/afes92at. html; A. Philip Randolph, *The Porters Union, Unrest and Pullman*, Black Worker, Feb. 15, 1930, at 1.

78 Theodore Kornweibel Jr. No Crystal Stair: Black Life and the Messenger, 1917–1928 xvi (1975); Alan Dundes, Mother Wit from the Laughing Barrel: Readings in the Interpretation of Afro-American Folklore 199–205 (1973).

a character named Uncle Tom who was straight out of minstrelsy. Uncle Tom was drawn as a big-lipped darky who was servile toward the white-run Pullman Company – a relationship that mimics a slave and his master. The comic beat readers over the head with one simple message: Don't be an *Uncle Tom*!

Not all black periodicals at the time, however, endorsed the *Messenger's* views. At least one, the *Argus*, argued against the unionization of black workers. The St. Louis newspaper dissuaded black workers from comparing their wages to their white counterparts, telling readers that whites always out-earned blacks. Randolph's response was succinct and caustic: Mr. Mitchell, *Argus's* editor, was the "*Idiot-orial* Uncle Tom of St. Louis." Randolph's critique was well founded. Imploring blacks not to pursue equal pay was a submissive betrayal indeed.[79]

In 1933, the Pullman Company, with the BSCP solidifying its power, made a last desperate effort to replace the BSCP with a company-controlled union. The company union, ostensibly, would be an agent for the black porters. But insidiousness lurked beneath the surface. It was a ruse. That union would have actually done the bidding of the Pullman Company, denying black porters a true representative. It was a clever trick. The BSCP feared that blacks would fall for it and succumb to the Pullman Company's scheme that "good ole Uncle Tom" aided. "All efforts to intimidate, browbeat and bully porters and maids in any way, direct or indirect, to [accept the Company union], by high or petty officials, stool-pigeons or Uncle Tom Company men of the Pullman Company, should be immediately reported." George Schuyler wrote that forming the Brotherhood was "an uphill fight all the way, beset as the organization was on all sides by mercenary Uncle Tom Negroes." The company union never went into effect. *Uncle Toms* were defeated.[80]

The ability to pursue gainful employment was necessary for all races in America. But because of the intense racism directed at them, blacks were unable to procure work with the same freedom as did whites. Being less free, for blacks, was an unfortunate yet accustomed place. This inability to fully flex one's muscles produced various ailments. The most sanction-worthy ailments were that some refused to work for other blacks and some dissuaded the hiring of members of their own race. This worldview, premised on the idea that whites were superior, violated the constructive racial loyalty norm against inexcusable meekness.

---

[79] William H. Harris, Keeping the Faith: A. Philip Randolph, Milton P. Webster, and the Brotherhood of Sleeping Car Porters, 1925–37 42–44 (1991); A. Philip Randolph, *Reply to the Argus*, The Messenger, Dec. 1925, at 384.

[80] *Porters, Maids Fight Alleged "Fake" Elections*, Pittsburgh Courier, Oct. 28, 1933, at 4; George J. Schuyler, *View Reviews*, Pittsburgh Courier, June 8, 1935, at 12.

Another ailment was that some black workers comported in ways that they believed whites preferred. Some blacks, more specifically, were subservient to appease white employers. Criticizing blacks for such behavior is complicated. Everyone needs a job. And if currying favor with the white boss helped keep the paycheck that fed one's family, then nothing inexcusable is afoot. The problem arises, however, when the servility is part of a personal mobility strategy designed to profit from antiblack sentiments. The office informer is an example. He recounts, to his boss, his colleagues' unflattering stories to be "the company's most favored Negro." Punishing this behavior was constructive; such censure notified blacks that those pursuing this tactic would be rebuked and dissuaded others from walking down this disfavored path. The loyalty enforcement efforts in this context were generally constructive. On the whole, norm managers helped build solidarity that served as a launching pad to remedy American society of its antiblack elements.

UNCLE TOM VOTED FOR HERBERT HOOVER

"No one," W. E. B. Du Bois once remarked, "in our day has helped disfranchisement and race hatred more than Herbert Hoover." Despite getting a majority of the black vote during both of the presidential elections in which he ran (1928 and 1932), President Hoover was abhorred by many leading black intellectuals of the day. Perhaps their expectations were too high. After all, as secretary of commerce and director of the relief efforts during the Mississippi Flood of 1927, Hoover was, many blacks charged, "insensitive to the plight of black sharecroppers and their abuse by local whites during the crisis."

By 1928, blacks had been loyal Republicans for decades. That bond was cemented during the Civil War era. A Republican president emancipated the slaves; Republicans administered Reconstruction; and Republicans drafted the postwar amendments. Democrats, though, were viewed as the Southern proslavery party. And, after the Civil War, Southern Democrats left no trick behind in attempts to fetter black freedom. But as Republican electoral success depended less on Northern blacks, the Republican Party distanced itself from blacks and began wooing Southern white voters. President Hoover's dour countenance became this new hostile face of the Republican Party.[81]

---

[81] The sources for this and the previous paragraph are as follows: Rita Werner Gordon, *The Change in the Political Alignment of Chicago's Negroes during the New Deal*, 56 Journal of American History 584, 590 (1969); Philip A. Klinkner and Rogers M. Smith, The Unsteady March: The Rise and Decline of Racial Equality in America 124 (2002); John M. Barry, Rising Tide: The Great Mississippi Flood of 1927 and How It Changed America 320 (1997).

Republicans long dreamed of unlocking the Democratic South. The Republican Party did just that in 1872, wining 53 percent of the vote. But after Reconstruction, the GOP had difficulty attracting Dixie voters. By the 1920s, after little success in winning Southern states in presidential elections, the GOP distanced itself from blacks and courted Southern whites. Embracing white supremacy was a precondition to appealing to Southern white voters. And Southerners required that Washington, DC, permit them to "handle their Negroes" as they saw fit. President Hoover followed the boilerplate template to appeal to Southern voters, and blacks were largely ignored. Some disagree with this interpretation, holding that President Hoover steered the ship with black interests in mind also. Elite black opinion at the time, however, was that Hoover was navigating a Southern strategy and tossed blacks overboard.

During the 1928 election, Hoover worked with Republican state "lily-white" delegations to assemble a formidable and durable Southern presence. As William Howard Taft noted, Hoover sought "to break up the solid South and to drive the negroes out of Republican politics by backing 'Lily-White' Republican organizations in the South." "Lily-Whites" were Southern white Republicans who favored an all-white party and excluded blacks from their ranks. "Lily-whitism" dates back to the 1870s, but failed to pick up steam until Theodore Roosevelt supported it in 1912 over the "black-and-tan" interracial coalitions. By the 1920s, lily-white factions existed in every Southern state.[82]

Hoover's Democratic opponent in the 1928 presidential election, New York Governor Al Smith, was Catholic. Many Americans at the time, especially Southerners, harbored stifling anti-Catholic prejudices. Hoover's plan to crack the Democratic South worked. Hoover became the first Republican presidential candidate since Reconstruction to poach solid Democratic Southern states (Hoover won Florida, Tennessee, North Carolina, Texas, and Virginia). Many Republicans believed that Hoover's success meant that the party could abandon black voters. Hoover then stepped up the party's lily-whitism, and, in his first year in office, made no significant black appointments.[83]

Historically, Hoover is most associated with impotence during the Great Depression. Most economists find that the Great Depression started in the

---

[82] The sources for this and the previous paragraph are as follows: James J. Kenneally, *Black Republicans during the New Deal: The Role of Joseph W. Martin, Jr.*, 55 *The Review of Politics* 117, 117 (1993); Donald J. Lisio, Hoover, Blacks and Lily-Whites: A Study of Southern Strategies (1985); Vincent P. de Santis, *Republican Efforts to "Crack" the Democratic South*, 14 *Review of Politics* 244, 244–45 (1952).

[83] Klinkner and Smith, The Unsteady March 123–24; Richard B. Sherman, *Republicans and Negroes: The Lessons of Normalcy*, 27 *Phylon* 63, 67–68 (1966).

United States with the stock market crash in 1929, which led to massive
unemployment and economic despair. In 1927, however, the black unemployment rate rose and by 1929, 300,000 black industrial workers were unemployed.
The Depression hit everyone hard. But the pneumonia that whites endured
was yellow fever to blacks. They had lower wages. They worked jobs dispropor-
tionally affected by the Depression. And they faced racial discrimination on
a scale that ethnic Europeans did not. Indeed, during the Depression, blacks
were fired to give whites jobs. The Depression, therefore, was harder for blacks
to withstand. As Du Bois noted, "we Negroes were the first and severest suf-
ferers from depression and the last to be relieved." Hoover was seen as ineffectual in getting the country moving again as it mired in economic futility. But
because blacks were doing especially poorly his failures were seen through an
even more jaundiced lens.[84]

Possibly, Hoover's biggest affront to blacks was his nominating a reputed racist to the Supreme Court. After Associate Justice Edward Terry Sanford died,
Hoover tapped Judge Johnston Jay Parker from North Carolina as his replacement. The NAACP was alarmed that a Southerner was pegged. Association
officials were initially heartened that Parker found in favor of a black man who
tried to buy a home in a white neighborhood. But the NAACP's Walter White
discovered that as the Republican nominee in North Carolina's 1920 gubernatorial race, Parker endorsed a plan to amend the state's constitution to include
a grandfather clause. Parker also reportedly said that "[t]he participation of the
Negro in politics is a source of evil and danger to both races and is not desired
by the wise men in either race or by the Republican Party of North Carolina."
After learning of that remark, White sent a telegram to Parker seeking clarifi-
cation. After three days of silence, the NAACP board of directors approved the
decision to oppose Parker's nomination.[85]

Despite Parker's past, when his nomination was announced, his confirmation was assumed. Supreme Court justices are rarely rejected. And reputed
antiblack bigotry certainly did not bar confirmation in the 1930s. White told
the White House of Parker's previous statements and implored the administration to withdraw Parker's nomination. Hoover ignored White. White

[84] Charles H. Martin, *Negro Leaders, the Republican Party, and the Election of 1932*, 32 *Phylon*,
     85, 85, 86 (1971); Michael C. Dawson, Behind the Mule: Race and Class in African-American
     Politics 102 (1994).
[85] Richard Kluger, *The Story of John Johnston Parker: The First Demonstration of Negro Political
     Power since Reconstruction*, 46 *Journal of Blacks in Higher Education* 124, 124–25 (2004–05);
     Richard L. Watson, Jr., *The Defeat of Judge Parker: A Study in Pressure Groups and Politics*,
     50 *Mississippi Valley Historical Review* 213, 218 (1963); Kenneth Goings, The NAACP Comes
     of Age: The Defeat of Judge John J. Parker 23–24 (1990).

thought someone like Parker could never settle disputes with a "dispassionate, unprejudiced, and judicial frame of mind which would enable him to render a decision according to the Constitution." That Hoover would appoint someone deemed anathema to blacks increased the tension. Parker's nomination would eventually be derailed by a confluence of forces aside from the NAACP's ambition to kill his appointment, including organized labor and Democrats wanting to stave off any attempt by Hoover to woo Southern white voters. Although the NAACP's effect on Parker's failed nomination was likely small, the organization's efforts empowered blacks to collectively fight against national events moving away from their interests.[86]

When Hoover ran for reelection, he continued marginalizing blacks in the party. By 1932, the percentage of blacks at the Republican National Convention was the smallest of the century. All of the state committees in the South were lily-white; the black-and-tan factions had been outgunned. The party's platform, moreover, was watered down when it came to black issues. The NAACP fought for the party's convention platform to include "forthright denunciation" against discrimination, lynching, and the lily-white movement. The platform, instead, expressed traditional language of "friendship for Negroes." Walter White, who described Hoover as "the man in the lily-white House," called the platform "flapdoodle" and went on to say that "no one familiar with the Republican Party's recent record with regard to the Negro can take this plank seriously." For this reason, and others, the *Pittsburgh Courier* claimed that "the president treated fish on a fishing trip better than he had representatives from any black group."[87]

No twentieth-century Republican president lived up to Lincoln's name. Theodore Roosevelt gave blacks hope; he appointed blacks to federal offices and consulted Booker T. Washington on racial matters. But his dishonorable discharge of black infantrymen in Brownsville, Texas, soured black opinions. William Howard Taft continued that troubling legacy. He, for example, refused to appoint federal officers who might meet disapproval in their communities, which meant few black appointments. Taft also ignored segregation, disfranchisement, lynching, and other Southern abuses. Picking up where Taft left off, Presidents Harding and Coolidge only appointed a few blacks to federal posts and continued the policy of segregation in the civil service. Harding, Coolidge, and Republican Congresses, moreover, ignored

---

[86] Kluger, *The Story of John Johnston Parker*, at 125; Watson, *The Defeat of Judge Parker*, at 214, 219; Nancy J. Weiss, Farewell to the Party of Lincoln: Black Politics in the Age of FDR 16 (1983).

[87] Martin, *Negro Leaders*, at 86–87; Kenneally, *Black Republicans during the New Deal*, at 118.

disfranchisement. The anger with Hoover was simply a building antagonism directed at the Republican Party that erupted during his only term.[88]

In 1921, for instance, seven years before Hoover's election, the *Negro Star* caught wind of Republicans excising blacks from Southern state parties. The newspaper, though, figured that the state parties would allow a few *Uncle Tom* blacks to remain. In 1922, the NAACP's publication the *Crises* credited black organizations for convincing blacks to desert the GOP because Republicans neglected Negroes. These organizations, the *Crises* stated, showed "party leaders that the 'Uncle Tom' type of black man is an extinct specimen of humanity." A year later, blacks openly questioned their ardent support of the Republican Party and packaged *Uncle Tom* with the message that if the party continued to ignore their concerns, blacks must abandon it. As one commented, "The Republican Party needs to [realize] that the Negro of today is not UNCLE TOM of forty years back. The Negro voter is and will demand thru his leaders some of the tangible fruits of political victory and a smaller Degree of political promises made in the heat of excited campaigns."[89]

These usages of *Uncle Tom* alerted the community that their behavior was being monitored, that the race was unwilling to tolerate political treacherousness. Blacks were expected to strongly support the race's legal and political rights. Anything short would be punished. In doing so, racial loyalty norms managers were building a more unified black populace by reducing the number of blacks willing to accept their unequal lot.

During the campaign season of 1928, as Hoover telegraphed that should he win, he would be an enemy of the Negro, the black intellectual class used every tool including *Uncle Tom* to unwed blacks from the Republican Party. Black elites surely understood that Hoover was cozying up to lily-white Republican organizations in the South. Shortly before Hoover's election, columnist Kelly Miller assailed blacks who would return to the GOP's trough and vote again for another Republican. In a poetic screed, Miller wrote:

> Those past middle age, the over-optimistic, who somehow believe that the spirit of Abraham Lincoln will be reincarnated in the Grand Old Party, the timid and hesitant who rather endure the ills they have than risk those they know not of; those of the slavish Uncle Tom type of temperament, the cunning and crafty, who hope to gather in the crumbs of the favor which

---

[88] Weiss, Farewell to the Party of Lincoln 4–6; Kathleen Dalton, Theodore Roosevelt: A Strenuous Life 321 (2001); Edmund Morris, The Rise of Theodore Roosevelt xvii (2010).

[89] *Republicans Planning to Bar Negros in the South*, Negro Star, June, 3, 1921, at 6; *The Looking Glass*, The Crises, Jan. 1922, at 129; *People; Parties; Campaign; Republican*; Party, Negro Star, Aug. 10, 1923, at 4.

fall from the white master's table, will adhere to the Republican standard, though the dry land turn to sea.[90]

Over Miller's objections, blacks supported Hoover's candidacy, those who could vote at least. Kelly's anti-Republican sentiments, however, were foreshadowing. Hoover frequently transgressed, weakening blacks' long-term Republican Party identification. Supporting an unresponsive president and political party was linked to racial treachery. Blacks needed politicians to promote racial equality. Blacks who seemingly countenanced the Hoover administration's deplorable treatment were dismissed for racial betrayal.

In 1930, for example, the Hoover administration sent a contingent of "Gold Star Mothers" to France to visit the graves of their sons and husbands buried there during World War I. The black women were to be sent, not with white mothers, but on a separate Jim Crow ship. One black mother was disgusted, saying, "As a Gold Star Mother who happens to be colored I wish to protest against the gratuitous insult in the attitude of the War Department in segregating colored Gold Star Mothers.... We who gave and are colored are insulted by the implication that we are not fit persons to travel with other bereaved ones.... We are set aside, Jim Crowed, separated and insulted." In July 1930, about fifty-six black mothers boarded their separate ship to France to visit their fallen loved ones. But fifty-three stayed behind, protesting the segregated arrangement. The NAACP complained to President Hoover that the War Department was "jim-crowing" the ladies. Secretary of War Hurley responded that "no other big line would book them" and that if they could find a white group that would welcome them then the War Department would permit the arrangement.[91]

The NAACP petitioned the Hoover administration to integrate the ships. Once that failed, the association organized a boycott. The mothers who defied the boycott were chided, as were black religious leaders who supported the administration's segregation policy. The executive secretary of the New York Urban League sent a letter to the NAACP voicing gratitude for the organization's antisegregation efforts and for disparaging servile blacks. "The most intelligent Negroes in America," the letter read, "now look to the N.A.A.C.P. for guidance and policy in matters of discrimination and segregation. Yet there

[90] Weiss, Farewell to the Party of Lincoln 16; Kelly Miller, *As the Negro Goes to the Polls,* New York Amsterdam News, Oct. 31, 1928, at 16; Edward O. Frantz, The Door of Hope: Republican Presidents and the First Southern Strategy, 1877–1933 239 (2011).

[91] *We Are Insulted,* Time, June, 9, 1930, available at: http://www.time.com/time/magazine/article/0,9171,739449,00.html?promoid=googlep; *Black Pilgrims,* Time, July 21, 1930; John W. Graham, The Gold Star Mother Pilgrimages of the 1930s: Overseas Grave Visitations by Mothers and Widows of Fallen U.S. World War I Soldiers (2005).

seem to be enough 'Uncle Toms' to convince even the administration of our national government that they are spokesmen appointed by God."[92]

In 1932, President Hoover was up for reelection. Some black newspapers tried to ensure that blacks deserted him. Many needed no convincing. One black person, looking back, said, "Hoover killed my taste for Republicans." Others, however, needed to be coaxed away from the Republican Party. In a two-party system, if Republicans lost, Democrats won. Some blacks were so accustomed to hating Democrats that they believed whenever that party was in power "the South is in the saddle and ... the Negro is trodden under foot." Undeterred, some continued to believe that blacks should not vote Republican. In July 1932, for instance, the Republican Party was to hold its national convention in Chicago. In February, the *Courier* predicted that many Uncle Toms would sit in the "back entrance of the G.O.P. band wagon," supporting the "Hoover Jim Crow administration." The *Courier*, that is, argued that to support Hoover was an act of treason. The newspaper doubted that self-respecting blacks would vote for Hoover. The nomination of Judge Parker to the Supreme Court, the lack of acknowledgment of the horrors of lynching, and all the other indignities the Hoover administration perpetrated led the *Courier* to ask rhetorically, "How in the name of God [could] any member of our group in the face of these inhuman insults [possibly] have the nerve to ... sound the praise of this Administration?"[93]

In June, however, the *Courier* backpedaled, forecasting that blacks would bypass the Republican convention. The "race men" at the *Courier*, in just a few months, changed their mind and concluded that the miserable previous four years would revamp the political behavior of black Americans. "The flies will not swarm this year," according to the paper. Blacks have "no interest in Mr. Hoover," the paper continued, "and unless some interest is created between now and November, the Negro will be found far off the reservation.... We predict now that those who do attend will represent ... the Uncle Tom, the slave, and the blind."[94]

Blacks harshly criticized the Hoover administration when it appointed Norman Armour, a white diplomat from New Jersey, to serve as envoy to Haiti in August 1932. The White House choosing a white man was met with disgust and

---

[92] *"Uncle Toms" Who Approve Jim Crowing of Gold Star Mothers Scored by Urban League*, Pittsburgh Courier, July 19, 1930, at A8.

[93] Lawrence Gordon, *A Brief Look at Blacks in Depression Mississippi, 1929–1934: Eyewitness Accounts*, 64 Journal of Negro History 377, 381 (1979); Kelly Miller, *Kelly Miller Asks What Would the Negro Lose by Triumph of Democrats*, Pittsburgh Courier, May 7, 1932, at A1; *Flays Hoover's "Jim Crow" Administration*, Pittsburgh Courier, Feb. 6, 1932, at A2.

[94] *The Flies Won't Swarm*, Pittsburgh Courier, June 11, 1932, at 10.

further suggested that blacks were "out in the cold." The *Defender* compared Hoover to President Theodore Roosevelt, who had appointed Henry W. Furniss, black, to this post previously. Roosevelt was heralded as someone who did not use race as a "bar to the recognition of character and fitness." But Hoover "can only visualize Uncle Tom, [who] has long since [died]." Teddy Roosevelt, as mentioned earlier, also supported the lily-white groups over their black-and-tan counterparts. Thus, to use him as a champion of egalitarianism seems odd. But that Roosevelt was lauded as embodying racial fairness demonstrates both how little blacks expected of their politicians and how disappointing Hoover was.[95]

Less than a month before the 1932 election, black Hoover backers held a public meeting at Pittsburgh's Pythian Temple to rally support for their candidate. Their plan was scuttled when Dr. C. A. Ward took to the rostrum. Ward lambasted the Republican Party, denouncing them as racists "pull[ing] the cover from the hidden evils from which the Negro now suffers at the hands of the Republican party." John M. Marguess, who headed the event, even admitted that Hoover had been a disappointment. And with that, the Roosevelt supporters in the audience took over, and not even "the feeble effort of the Uncle Toms," wrote the *Courier*, could turn the event back to its original purpose.[96]

On November 8, 1932, the presidential election was held with Hoover suffering a lopsided defeat to Franklin Roosevelt. Most blacks, however, voted for Hoover. In fact, despite all of the intellectual class's grievances with Hoover, he received a higher percentage of the black vote in 1932 than he did in 1928.[97] Many blacks, nevertheless, believed that Hoover's defeat and the new Roosevelt administration marked a possible turning point for the race. The words of W. H. Ferris here are worth recalling. "Those black leaders in the Republican Party who thought President Hoover had only to pose with them six weeks before the election to hold the Negro vote ... will be supplanted by new colored leaders [who have] vision and courage.... [This will result in] the passing of the Uncle Tom, handkerchief head, hat in hand and 'me too boss' Negro leadership. Out of the ashes of the old leadership a new Negro leadership ... will rise Phoenix like." Ferris's vision of a new dawn in black leadership eventuated, to some degree, though certainly not during the 1930s. His hopeful words, in any event, reflect how miserable some blacks felt about Hoover's America.[98]

95   *Mr. Armour to Haiti*, Chicago Defender, Aug. 20, 1932, at 14; *Armour Appointed Minister to Haiti*, New York Times, Aug. 14, 1932, at 14.
96   *Hoover Meeting Turns Roosevelt*, Pittsburgh Courier, Oct. 22, 1932, at 3.
97   Kevin J. McMahon, Reconsidering Roosevelt on Race: How the Presidency Paved the Road to Brown 27 (2010).
98   W. H. Ferris, *Bishop Jones Sees a Dawn of New Day for Leadership of Negroes Under Roosevelt*, Pittsburgh Courier, Dec. 17, 1932, at 3.

Blacks managing racial loyalty norms in this context concluded that the group should abandon political parties that did nothing for them and especially those that actively pursued racial subordination. The race, many felt, needed politicians who championed a bold vision for civil rights and equality. That vision was unlikely to materialize in the early twentieth century. But blacks, so the argument went, should never support politicians who refused to advocate for their rights.

Sanctioning blacks as *Uncle Toms* for supporting Hoover was complicated, though, because the alternative, the Democratic Party, was hardly a strong supporter of black rights at that time. There is, in fact, something to the argument that Republicans were a lesser of two evils, and criticizing black Republicans for backing a party that was the alternative to the Democratic Party with its Southern segregationist wing might have been unwise. But during a time when blacks had learn to insist on their rights, censuring blacks for strongly backing a politician and a political party that contributed to blacks' second-class citizenship was constructive. If norm managers were trying to build solidarity among blacks, permitting race members to approve of politicians who supported disfranchisement and racial apartheid would have ruined their endeavors. For blacks to support Jim Crow politicians while fighting Jim Crow would have been wildly inconsistent.

But norm management could have been destructive during this period, the 1920s and 1930s. Criticizing blacks for supporting racially egalitarian politicians obviously would have been. But the same held true for those who backed politicians who, although ardent champions of civil rights, refused to pander to white supremacy for votes. These are the sorts of officeholders that blacks should have attempted to sway. In effect, a line existed. Supporting segregationist politicians crossed it.

UNCLE TOM IN THE PULPIT

A robust church could have aided tremendously in building the racial solidarity important in improving the Negro condition. As Kelley Miller wrote in his book *Out of the House of Bondage* (1914), "The uplift of the negro ministry means the uplift of the negro life; the downpull of this ministry means the pulling down of the people. The most effective way to improve the general moral, industrial and social tone of the race is to elevate its pulpit."[99]

In 1919, the *Messenger* declared the Negro church a failure. Whereas in 1906, W. E. B. Du Bois argued that the black church's failure was linked to

---

[99] Kelly Miller, Out of the House of Bondage 214 (1914).

the immorality of black ministers, according to the *Messenger* the problem was that the church's chief concern was profits. A lesser but real concern was that many black churches were part of denominations controlled by white capitalists who were uninterested in racial justice. The church, the *Messenger* concluded, avoided political discussions "unless some good, old Abraham Lincoln Republican desire the vote of the Negro, and is willing to pay for educational propaganda." The *Messenger's* solution was for the church to discuss issues of politics, labor, and government so that blacks could improve their lot. "The New Negro demands a new church," one that helps "a people who are lynched disfranchised and jim-crowed."[100]

Some scholars have argued that religion has long fueled black resistance. Historians Eugene Genovese and Albert Raboteau found that religion was vital in slaves' survival and rebellion. And black churches proved instrumental in mobilizing black political participation, with the black church often serving as the home base for strategists during the civil rights movement in the 1950s and 1960s.[101]

Not all, however, share this benign interpretation of the black church. Originally having the religion of their former African tribes, blacks adopted the religion of their white captors in the New World. Ronny E. Turner argues that during slavery, some whites controlled black ministers, who convinced their brethren into comporting in a manner that pleased slave owners. Slave owners greatly feared both Nat Turner-style rebellions and organized escapes. Some slave owners used Christianity to help dominate their bondsmen. And the minister was often a tool to manipulate blacks to prevent insurrections or escapes. Indeed, "Through the minister the slave owner controlled black religious activities and for the most part precluded organized resistance or rebellion by slaves." Martin Delany, in that vein, also criticized the black church for teaching "subservience in the face of oppression."[102]

Some argue that this legacy continued after slavery. That, instead of empowering the black masses to resist white supremacy, religious leaders taught their parishioners to bear rampant racism and focus on the afterlife. This latter

---

[100] *The Failure of the Negro Church*, The Messenger, Oct. 1919, at 6; W. E. B. Du Bois, *The Minister*, Hampton Bulletin, Sept. 1906, at 91–92.

[101] Fredrick C. Harris, Something Within: Religion in African-American Political Activism 6 (1999); Albert Raboteau, Slave Religion: The "Invisible Institution" in the Antebellum South (1978); Eugene D. Genovese, Roll, Jordan, Roll (1974); Charles V. Hamilton, The Black Preacher in America (1972); Aldon D. Morris, The Origins of the Civil Rights Movement: Black Communities Organizing for Change (1984); Gary T. Marx, *Religion: Opiate or Inspiration of Civil Rights Militancy among Negroes?*, 32 American Sociological Review 64, 64–65 (1967).

[102] Ronny E. Turner, *The Black Minister: Uncle Tom or Abolitionist?*, 34 Phylon 86, 86 (1973); Glaude Jr., Exodus! 19.

form of accommodationist religious teaching might have greatly benefited bondsmen. It very well may have made slavery endurable. But after emancipation, blacks needed empowerment.[103]

Black clergymen who dissuaded their parishioners from active resistance ingratiated themselves to powerful whites. Looking back, Bobby Miller in 1979 forcefully argued that religion was once an opiate in black America. "The Black Church," he penned, "was developed in slavery, nourished on a diet of white supremacy, and weaned on 'Uncle Tom' politics.... Black churches ... solely ... keep Blacks from becoming radicalized about the here and now." Another writer concurred, stating, "It was only when the Negro preacher advised patience and forbearance among his congregation that he came to earn 'considerable good will among the whites.'" Alternatively, when a black preacher tried to enlist race members in a war against degradation, the well of white support quickly dried up.[104]

The central critique of the *Uncle Tom* preacher during this first period was that he sold out the race for white dollars, usually to fund the church. He was not a leader the race chose, but a figure whites propped up to pursue their interests – the maintenance of black subordination, Jim Crow, white supremacy, and everything that naturally grows from those evil seeds. Rev. Taschereau Arnold said it well when he wrote in the *Atlanta Daily World* in 1947 that "[t]he mission of these Uncle Toms is to tell Negroes 'things will get better some sweet day.' Some of them will sell you 'down the river' for the sake of their stomachs." The use of racial loyalty norms was undeniably constructive against such preachers.[105]

Many blacks averred that the preacher had a special role in the black community; that from behind the pulpit he was uniquely situated to disseminate valuable lessons. Rather than concentrate on the afterlife or, as one in 1929 put it, "the people 'on the other side of the river,'" the black preacher could have instructed on "the great need" of black people – complete freedom. This archetype was diametrically opposed to the *Uncle Tom* preacher, who was an "opportunist" and "afraid to speak his convictions." One writing in 1927 noted that "even today the white South liberally supports our churches and our 'Uncle Tom' ... type of preachers [who] are ... their pets."[106]

[103] Keith Andrew Winsell, Black Identity: The Southern Negro, 1830–1895 203–04 (PhD dissertation 1971).

[104] Bobby Milles, *The Failure of Christianity to Liberate the Black Community*, Sun Reporter, Nov. 29, 1979, at 4; Joseph H. Fichter, *American Religion and the Negro*, 94 Daedalus 1085, 1089 (1965).

[105] Rev. Taschereau Arnold, *On the Reel*, Atlanta Daily World, Dec. 20, 1947, at 3.

[106] *The Economic Freedom Needed by Race, Claim*, Pittsburgh Courier, July 6, 1929, at 8; Stearns S. Peake Jr., *Observations*, Chicago Defender, June 18, 1927, at A2.

Others reported that black clergymen were frequently disloyal. In 1929, for example, Dr. George C. Parker, editor for the *Christian Index*, argued that blacks needed a message of economic freedom and black men of the cloth were failing to provide it because they were more concerned with their own personal success. "The worst thing in the world is a cowardly, time-serving, grinning, bowing Negro preacher," Parker said, "who will sell his race and his manhood for measly dollars. The time has passed for the 'Uncle Tom' type of preacher, for the man who is an opportunist, for the man who is afraid to speak his convictions."[107]

Sometimes preachers were assailed for servility and cowardice in the face of brutal racism. We see an example of this in the summer of 1920 in Paris, Texas. Herman Arthur, a black World War I combat veteran, persuaded his brother Irvin and the rest of their family to stop sharecropping. The brothers lived with their father, Scott, mother, Violet, and two sisters. They decided to move. They were disenchanted with the constant debt under sharecropping. Their white landowners, Will Hodges and his father, J. H., thought that the Arthur family was lazy and "slack about work." Will and J. H. were concerned that the Arthur family was preparing to leave while owing a huge amount of advance money. On July 1, Will and J. H. visited the Arthurs' shack. After learning that the male family members were absent, they kicked over the cook stove and food and said they would return the following day to speak with the brothers. When they arrived the next day, Herman and Irvin were both present and the family was packing a truck to leave. Will and J. H. exposed their guns and a shootout occurred. Who shot first? Accounts vary. But after the last shot rang, Will and J. H. were dead.[108]

Knowing black men had no right to self-defense, Herman and Irvin fled to Oklahoma. Paris was consumed with finding the two brothers, and armed groups spread throughout northeast Texas and southeast Oklahoma searching for them. The other family members were taken into custody to prevent their communication with the brothers. In a later interview, a member of the Arthur family disclosed that "the whole county was stirred up and started talking that if they couldn't find the boys then they would just kill the rest of the family."[109]

---

[107] *Pittsburgh C.M.E. Conference Meets*, Afro-American, June 29, 1929, at 5.

[108] The Paris News, July 6, 2007, available at: http://theparisnews.com/story.lasso?ewcd= dfb62e60790f9430; Walter L. Buenger, The Path to a Modern South: Northeast Texas between Reconstruction and the Great Depression 167 (2001); Ralph Ginzburg, 100 Years of Lynching 139–40 (1988); Thad Sitton and James H. Conrad, Freedom Colonies: Independent Black Texans in the Time of Jim Crow 165–66 (2005); Chad Louis Williams, Torchbearers of Democracy: The First World War and the Figure of the African-American Soldier 298 (PhD dissertation 2004).

[109] Buenger, The Path to a Modern South 167–68.

On July 6, a posse finally captured the two brothers in Oklahoma aided by Pitt McGrew, black. Contrary to advice, the brothers were brought back to the local county jail. Angry whites assembled outside the prison and District Judge Denton failed to convince them to disperse. With sledgehammers, the mob ambushed the jail and removed Herman and Irving and dragged them to the site of their previously prepared executions. A crowd of about 3,000 witnessed the two brothers tied to a stake and burned to death. The macabre continued. The mob then chained their charred remains to a pickup and caravan and paraded their burnt corpses through the black sections of town, screaming "Here are the barbecued Niggers! All you Niggers come out and see them and take a warning." No one was ever charged with a crime.[110]

In the wake of the incident, the *Defender* printed an article lambasting Rev. C. N. Hampton, a "prominent minister" in Paris. Right after the incident, from his pulpit, Rev. Hampton asserted that whites had not done anything against blacks. Hampton also implored his parishioners to remain in the South, and he refused to contribute to funds the local black community collected to send the Arthur family to Chicago. He even, allegedly, went so far as to try to prevent the sale of black newspapers that reported the lynching. In fact, Hampton opposed blacks reading black newspapers because it makes readers angry with whites. The *Defender* believed that he acted with an eye toward wooing whites who could help him fund the building of a new church. Thus, it appears that Hampton was both inexcusably submissive and guilty of furthering the enemy's interests, by purposefully attempting to keep blacks docile in exchange for personal benefits from whites. Hampton, in fact, demonstrated his unconcern for the race. True, he may have cheered for the race's uplift. But his devotion to the group – that is, his black solidarity – was fatally compromised if he tried to make local blacks a milquetoast people in order to fund a new church for himself. For running afoul of possibly all three constructive racial loyalty norms, the *Defender* fairly derided Hampton as an *Uncle Tom*.[111]

As the case of Rev. Hampton established, when a black preacher publically placated white bigotry, he violated constructive racial loyalty norms and *Uncle Tom* accusations inevitably and rightly followed. See the case of Oscar De Priest. Chicago's De Priest was the first black congressman elected in the twentieth century. The Republican representative and his wife became embroiled in controversy when First Lady Lou Henry Hoover invited De Priest's wife to the

---

[110] Dahleen Glanton, *Running North: A Family History*, Chicago Tribune, Feb. 12, 1998, at 4; Williams, Torchbearers of Democracy 299.

[111] *Brand Minister a Traitor in Texas*, Chicago Defender, Sept. 11, 1920, at 1.

White House in 1930. A Virginian preacher criticized him for permitting his wife take up the offer. In response De Priest said, "[a]s far as I'm concerned ... Uncle Tom Negroes should all be dead."[112]

This shunned group included many others, like "Uncle Tom" preachers in Tampa who came to the *Afro-American's* attention in 1932. The leadership of the local African Methodist Episcopal church refused to condemn segregated railroad transportation in the South. The newspaper claimed that reduced fares and "other concessions" were the price for treachery. Part of the deal, apparently, was that the bishops had to implore blacks to continue using the railroads in order to get their payoff. This proved to the *Afro-American* that *Uncle Tom* preachers are "too easily bought." These preachers, if the reports were true, were rightly denounced for racial treachery. By using their authoritative position to promote segregated companies that were providing them financial rewards, those Tampa preachers demonstrated their willingness to betray the group for dollars.[113]

When Rev. J. M. Williamson of Mississippi in 1936 told a white editor of the *Jackson Daily News* that blacks' education should stop at the eighth grade, he became "the safest Negro leader in Mississippi." Williamson contended that a high school education, for blacks, was excessive. "We are trying to teach them too high," he insisted, "carrying them further than they are able to go." Teaching black boys and girls a trade, rather, was a better use of resources. Although his words ingratiated him to white Mississippians, blacks rightly denounced him as an *Uncle Tom* for his treachery and meekness.[114]

Black preachers were repeatedly rebuked, sometimes by other preachers. Rev. Harten of Brooklyn bemoaned that some comrades courageously criticized vague notions of injustice from their pulpits but when a specific issue arose, their mettle suddenly softened. As he said in February 1941, "there are some colored ministers in the Metropolitan area who are famous for making speeches before Negro audiences [but] when there's a protest against the whites, these same pulpit parasites, Uncle Tom Handkerchief Heads, are used as a go between." Here Rev. Harten criticized some black preachers for lacking the backbone to say to the white man's face what he said behind his back.[115]

---

[112] E. W. Baker, *DePriest's Address at the Douglass Day Dinner*, Afro-American, Mar. 1, 1930, at A2; William Edward Leuchtenburg, Herbert Hoover 89 (2009); Davis S. Day, *Herbert Hoover and Racial Politics: The De Priest Incident*, 65 Journal of Negro History 6 (1980).

[113] *Bishops Dodge Jim Crow Issue*, Afro-American, Apr. 2, 1932, at 20; *Jeers and Boos Halt Committee Probing Riots*, Afro-American, Apr. 27, 1935, at 12.

[114] *Minister Says Colored Schools Should Quit at the Eighth Grade*, Plaindealer, June 12, 1936, at 2.

[115] *Rev. Harten Back from South Arouses Huge Crowd with Sermon*, New York Amsterdam Star-News, Mar. 1, 1941, at 8.

A year later, Rev. A. W. Wormack similarly faulted his brethren, arguing that many ministers sought to please whites who offered them financial rewards. Wormack thought black preachers should have singularly focused on the race instead of currying favor with whites who were uninterested in the welfare of black people. "We have too many men in the pulpit among us who are still Uncle Toms, who sell the race for a donation, and for their family and relatives to get on certain pay rolls," Wormack said, "while the masses of people are in slavery and starving." Harten's and Wormack's critiques were the sort of public pronouncements that pushed black preachers to be true and devoted leaders of a united people.[116]

An archetype of the *Uncle Tom* preacher very well could have been Rev. I. G. P. Johnson. Johnson, according to a very sympathetic 1942 article, listed twelve principles that blacks should embrace for happiness and prosperity. Among the most notable are: "the Southern white man is the Negro's friend"; "265 years ago [the white man] brought the Negro from a savage and heathen state to his present standing in the world"; the fact that blacks are doing better than any other "dark race" is "owe[d] to the American white man." Many blacks who knew him likely added a thirteenth principle: Rev. Johnson is an *Uncle Tom*.[117]

Uncle Tom accusations continued to fly during the 1940s. During World War II, Alabama Governor Frank M. Dixon announced that he would refuse any war contract containing a nondiscrimination clause, griping that "federal agencies are attempting to force social equality upon the South." After his statement, the local chamber of commerce attempted to get twelve black leaders to endorse Dixon's position by signing a telegram. The telegram read in part:

> Our past and present relations with our white people are satisfactory and we do not want any strife to mar our pleasant relationships.... This is a time for war against foreign enemies, not for war against Southern civilization, and your clear understanding of this fact and your determination to prevent that which it is sought to accomplish, is in harmony with the best traditions of Southern statesmanship.[118]

Few blacks would have described Alabama race relations in the 1940s as "pleasant." To convince twelve black leaders to endorse Dixon's Jim Crow

[116] *Minister Scores Clergy in Race Relations Sermon Sun*, Atlanta Daily World, Feb. 15, 1942, at 6.
[117] *Rev. Johnson's "Uncle Tom" Program Is Endorsed by Mississippi Editor*, Chicago Defender, Apr. 11, 1942, at 5.
[118] *Dixon's Negro Support Evaporates*, Chicago Defender, Aug. 8, 1942, at 1.

policies, moreover, would have been exceedingly difficult. But that's where Rev. E. M. Wilson came in. Wilson called eleven other black leaders, and when those leaders picked up the phone, Wilson handed the phone over to a local white leader who asked each to endorse the statement in order to "avert a race riot [which was said to be] imminent." When the black leaders hesitated, they were threatened. Each black leader finally endorsed a telegram that was a watered-down version of what was eventually sent to the governor. The leaders charged Wilson with chicanery, with one relaying that "If I hadn't [signed the telegram,] Reverend Wilson would have gone back and said something that would have hurt me in my business." Citizens in Gadsden were outraged and planned to act against Wilson. One hoped that they could run him out of town. Wilson had deep connections with the local white community and even was attempting to set up an army commission as chaplain for himself. He was also rumored to have a secret state job. The "local progressive elements" declared that "the colored people of this city do not consider Reverend Wilson a leader but an 'Uncle Tom' of the most dangerous type. He is definitely not a representative of the Negro group in Gadsen [*sic*]."[119]

Another Alabama minister brought criticism on himself stemming from the contents of a letter. In 1943, Rev. J. A. Brodie was accused of writing an "'Uncle Tom' letter." In the letter, Brodie argued that all blacks born in Dixie desire to live among Southern whites because blacks' only friend "is the Southern white man." He disclosed, furthermore, that he preached the need for blacks to improve their skills as servants, cooks, laundresses, and waitresses. Brodie even thanked whites for slavery, saying that "whatever may be said of the hardships of slavery, it must be acknowledged that slavery was a blessing to the Negroes. It must be admitted that the slave owners turned out four million men, women and children better trained in trades, industries, morals, manners and religion than any other four million people since." Many blacks wondered if Brodie had a hidden motive, and the *Defender* thought it had uncovered it. Supposedly Brodie, needing $1,000 for his church, concluded that a tribute to the virtues of Southern whites and thanking them for the privilege of slavery would do the trick. If the *Defender* correctly uncovered his ulterior motives, Brodie was right. He raised the cash. "Judas got his 30-pieces of silver," the *Defender* wrote. "Rev. Brodie got his $1,000."[120]

In 1946, after blacks in Atlanta participated in the Democratic primaries, Rev. J. T. Dorsey of Mt. Zion Baptist Church mollified local whites. Just two

---

[119] Id.

[120] *Slavery Was a Blessing*, Chicago Defender, Dec. 18, 1943, at 14; Pastor, *What the People Say*, Chicago Defender, Dec. 18, 1943, at 14; *"Uncle Tom" Letter from Minister Draws Press Fire*, Atlanta Daily World, Dec. 26, 1943, at 4.

years prior, *Time* magazine reported that no blacks voted in the state's white primary. Dorsey knew that Southern whites believed that suffrage should have been whites only. As a black religious leader, the white power structure very well might have paid him a visit for an explanation as to why the "uppity Negroes" were not staying in their place. Dorsey, perhaps in response, or maybe as a preemptive measure, drafted a conciliatory letter that he distributed to church members and printed in the local paper. He wrote:

> God made us black, but he didn't make us bitter. He filled our hearts with humility, but not hate. The Negro is not greedy, he is grateful. The White man brought the Negro to the South, and the good white people of the South have made him what he is today. For all of the good things done for us, we are grateful.... Now the white man says the Negro can vote.... We will do the best we know how. Good white people, won't you help us? Please don't hate us.

For his inexcusable meekness, Dorsey was derided as a turncoat. The headline of a *Cleveland Call and Post* article about the preacher read, "'Uncle Tom' Leader Kneels While Negroes Vote."[121]

In 1947, Rev. A. L. Roach of Cleveland was labeled a "belly-crawling, handkerchief-headed Uncle Tom." John O. Holly, the labeler, headed a local black self-help organization. Holly blamed Roach for the Cleveland Trust Company not hiring blacks for white-collar positions. Holly's organization picketed outside of the bank's offices to protest asserted employment discrimination. George Gund, the bank's president, then had a "pleasant" meeting with Holly and two other black leaders. They and Gund compromised and Gund agreed to implement hiring changes within two weeks. Before the two-week period was over, however, Gund called Holly and told him that whatever deal they had was off because, in his words, "[s]ome of your leaders say we are being fair with your people." One of those "leaders" was Rev. Roach, who, according to Holly, interjected because he wanted a bank loan. Holly said that Roach was "the kind of Negro we've got to get rid of" and framed his treachery as scourge on blacks' present and future. Holly criticized Roach for choosing personal advancement over that of the race, which appears true based on the evidence. Roach, in an effort to get a bank loan, subverted the goal of inclusive hiring practices for a major employer. He was uncommitted to the cause of racial justice. He did not care about the race.[122]

---

[121] *Tension Rising in Georgia as Talmadge, with Klan Backing, Plans "Rebel" Cabinet*, Cleveland Call and Post, July 27, 1946, at 5B; *White Primary*, Time, July 17, 1944, available at: http://www.time.com/time/magazine/article/0,9171,885498,00.html.

[122] Russell Jackson, *Charges Intervention of Minister Encouraged Cleveland Trust Bank in Rejection...*, Cleveland Call and Post, Nov. 29, 1947, at 1A.

The *New York Amsterdam News* similarly criticized Rev. Henry Hugh Proctor for servility and treachery when he delivered a reputedly racist screed. Proctor scoffed at the idea of black entertainment venues being brought to Brooklyn. "Soon," he declared in a white Southern newspaper, "if the community does not take steps against them, there will be more of these cabarets, and then colored night clubs, blind tigers, speakeasies and all the rest of the evil night life." But his issue was not with how these locales affected blacks. No, Proctor fretted over his belief that if blacks participated in these activities they would become incubators of vice and immorality and they would then spread pestilence to whites. "The colored folk," he warned, "go into white homes as domestic servants. And they carry their disease and crime with them." The *Amsterdam News* presumed that Rev. Proctor made the statements to get white donations. The newspaper countered that "the real trouble with Brooklyn is not the influx of Harlem people. It is not the influx of West Indians. It is the influx of Uncle Toms." A reader wrote in to agree with the newspaper's assessment of Rev. Proctor, declaring that those opposing his removal from New York were "dumb fool[s]" just like him. Two weeks later, 5,000 people assembled at a local temple simply to denounce him.[123]

Before becoming the first black man to run for president in 1960, Rev. Clennon King was a history professor at Alcorn College in Mississippi. In 1957, King wrote a series of columns in segregationist Jackson newspapers that called for more "Uncle Toms" within black leadership and that criticized the NAACP. Student president Ernest McEwen, in response, said that "Alcorn College died at 12:55 p.m. today!" Students loudly protested King and boycotted classes. In the wake of their students' noise, the school's all-white board of directors fired the school's black president for not controlling the protests and for his asserted tacit sympathy with the students. The students labeled Rev. King an *Uncle Tom*. Black newspapers recounted tales of Alcorn's "'Uncle Tom' Prof." And the *Philadelphia Tribune*, a black newspaper, wrote "[t]he day is past when Negroes are going to permit 'Uncle Toms' to wax fat by preaching that the time is not ripe for integration."[124]

With clergymen occupying a high platform from which to help uplift blacks from their subordination, they were often held to a heightened standard.

---

[123] *Uncle Toms*, New York Amsterdam News, Mar. 12, 1930, at 20; *The Man in the Street*, New York Amsterdam News, Mar. 19, 1930, at 20; Charles T. Magill, *5,000 Hear Rev. Proctor Denounced*, New York Amsterdam News, Mar. 29, 1930, at 13.

[124] *'Uncle Tom' Prof Out at Strife-Torn Alcorn*, New Journal and Guide, Mar. 16, 1957, at 20A; *Down With "Uncle Toms,"* Cleveland Call and Post, Mar. 16, 1957, at 1A; *"Uncle Tom" Prof's Alcorn Row Recalls Union Flop*, New Journal and Guide, Mar. 16, 1957, at 20A; *Students Resent "Uncle Tom,"* Philadelphia Tribune, Mar. 19, 1957, at 8; Adam Fairclough, A Class of Their Own: Black Teachers in the Segregated South 378 (2007).

When they fell below the mark, they were frequently bombarded with *Uncle Tom* denunciations. As in the previous contexts, racial loyalty norms here were managed quite constructively. The black clergymen, that is, typically were guilty of betrayal when they were so accused. With the race needing leaders to help author a strategy for full emancipation, blacks had to rebuke supposed servants of God whenever they served themselves instead.

ANALYSIS

No one can inflict more pain than family. This made *Uncle Tom* especially caustic. It also made it valuable in sanctioning those defying racial loyalty norms. Blacks during this period had scant legal protection, and social marginalization from whites was brutal. Subordinated groups typically have to participate in their own emancipation. Blacks suffering under American apartheid especially had to orchestrate their own liberation; outsiders were not going to do it for them. That blacks needed to push for equality pressured all to assist the effort. With their liberty at stake, many aggressively policed the community's behaviors. Blacks had to demand full citizenship and make no concessions. If blacks got even a whiff that a fellow race member was willing to accept less, oral punishment was swift. W. O. Brown said it well in 1931:

> Since the race conscious are sensitive they naturally resent anything that impugns the status of their race. Hence they protest vehemently against the notion of their inferiority as a race. Any definition of status for the race that implies subordination angers and hurts them. And any type of behavior on the part of members of their race that implies the subservient attitude to other race they condemn.[125]

Perpetuators of the status quo realized the danger in blacks collectively fighting to break their shackles. Opponents of black freedom, therefore, co-opted select blacks to undermine blacks' interests from within. Other blacks simply eschewed racial solidarity and comported in ways the race concluded hindered its well-being. In this context racial loyalty norms were necessary. With few resources, social norms were among the best options blacks had in creating unity. *Uncle Tom* as a sanctioning tool became something blacks had to ponder before they committed treason. As the pejorative was hurled with increasing frequency, it became the most feared in-group

---

[125] W. O. Brown, *The Nature of Race Consciousness*, 10 *Social Forces* 90, 92 (1931).

slur. Norms and *Uncle Tom*, in a racially hostile world, became helpful in forging solidarity.

Tracing *Uncle Tom* from 1883 to 1959 establishes that norms could help blacks improve their legal interests and ability to affect public policy. Any strategy to reform American society hinged on blacks working cooperatively. Because blacks feared the *Uncle Tom* label, the epithet helped dictate behavior.

This argument is most evident in the context of segregation. The tale of racial loyalty norms when segregation was at issue reveals how fervently blacks sought to dismember Jim Crow. State legislatures and cities and even the federal government subordinated blacks. White attitudes likewise ensured that blacks never fully participated in American democracy. Blacks, in response, attempted to reform society and purge the most insidious element – segregation. Racial loyalty norms were important because group cohesiveness was a precursor to dismantling separate but equal. Those blacks failing to sufficiently resist subordination were deemed traitors to the cause. With such high hopes stemming from desegregation, blacks who shared white Southerners' antipathy toward reordering society were almost automatically deemed race traitors. Segregation was the most important reason why *Uncle Tom* was such a ubiquitous epithet, but it certainly was not the only.

Particularly telling was the 1922 story of two young men who were ejected from a downtown Chicago theater. The *Defender* was aghast to learn that the two chose not to pursue legal remedies against the theater and maligned them as *Uncle Toms*. The event suggests that blacks were beginning to realize that they needed to become active participants in their progress movements. Those who did not incurred a penalty. That blacks needed to strongly insist on equal rights explains William H. Hastie's remark that blacks needed to cease "asking for more segregation" if the race wanted to dismantle *Plessy*. And the widespread reaction to Hastie's words – blacks from around the country cited his comments as proof that *Uncle Toms* were jeopardizing the race's interests – showed that blacks truly believed that they could reform America through united effort. Blacks likely thought that solidarity was insufficient by itself but was, nonetheless, a solid base on which to build future success. Thus, the blacks who voted for Charles Bowles, the Klan candidate who ran for a city council seat in Detroit, for example, were branded as race traitors precisely. Many concluded that such blacks committed the sort of treachery that would prevent racial uplift. Similarly, James Edward Shepard, the president of a black college in North Carolina, who refused to release Thomas Raymond Hocutt's transcripts so that he could wage a legal battle to integrate the pharmacy college at University of North Carolina, was heavily criticized.

He consciously helped segregationists and showed an unwillingness to participate in the long journey toward desegregation.

In some scenarios, however, judging whether racial treachery occurred is difficult. Although criticizing blacks during the Jim Crow era for favoring segregation may seem proper, one had valid reasons for preferring racial separation. In that vein, Texas educator J. E. Boyd's 1916 public endorsement of segregated education is worth recalling. Perhaps Boyd was truly acting at the behest of segregationist whites. But, in the second decade of the twentieth century, one could defensibly argue black children in Texas were much better off in separate, rather than integrated, schools.

Some, but not many, usages of *Uncle Tom* in this context were obviously destructive. The New Jersey parents who enrolled their children in a segregated school, perhaps, faced the most unjust criticism. The year was 1927, and the Klan had persuaded a New Jersey town into segregating its schools. The *Courier* indicted the black parents who enrolled their children in the new black school for racial treachery. But no evidence supports the charge. The parents should not have been blamed for trying to ensure that their children received an education. This unfair use aside, the norm managers were quite constructive in their enforcement of racial loyalty norms.

Also important in the development of racial loyalty norms during this period was the characterization of Southern blacks as meek. Indeed, Southern blacks found themselves under attack by race members who castigated them for their reputedly servile behavior. Northerners reprimanded Southerners for their reticence in actively combating Southern bigotry. Doing so not only invigorated Dixie's Negroes to battle their oppression, but it also reminded Northern blacks of the type of mindset that would be vilified. To make the argument that being aggressive could help improve the plight, contending that Southern blacks contributed to their own subordination by being submissive was incredibly helpful. Blacks managing racial loyalty norms in this context, as was true in the case of segregation, helped promote a mindset that would be beneficial in procuring legal goals.

Recall the Fitzgerald couple from Myrtle Beach, South Carolina. They were the only black registered voters in the area and asked that their names be stricken off of the voter rolls because the time was not right for black suffrage. Southern blacks simply could not comport this way if they wanted to participate more fully in American life. Racial loyalty norms were maintained to propel blacks to liberate themselves. Perhaps the most culpable reputed *Uncle Tom* in this context was Rev. C. N. Hampton who, after the Arthur brothers were lynched in Paris, Texas, acquiesced to local whites and refused to do anything to help the fleeing Arthur family, all while saying that blacks in the area were not treated poorly. Also instructive was the case of M. K. Tyson who wanted to run for office in North Carolina in 1938. Some blacks, though, wanted to work with whites to dissuade him from running. The *Afro-American* derided those unnamed blacks as *Uncle Toms*. These narratives, as do others, show how blacks maintained norms that helped discipline the race and promote racial loyalty.

Supposed *Uncle Tom* actions in employment contexts created serious problems, many believed. As blacks languished at the bottom of the economic ladder, subservience and disloyalty frustrated the race's ability to climb up. If blacks hampered the race's economic interests, then the group would remain disproportionately and perpetually destitute. Blacks who told white employers not to hire black employees and black employees who refused to work under a fellow Negro, therefore, were vehemently scolded as *Uncle Toms* for defying racial loyalty norms. Leaders of the BSCP, likewise, realized how helpful social norms could be in both regulating black behavior and compelling blacks to take stances that were believed to further the race's overall interests. As in other contexts, racial loyalty norms helped blacks forge solidarity that could help in combating legal oppression.

In this period, furthermore, stubborn supporters of Herbert Hoover were likewise found guilty of racial treachery. Blacks – those with suffrage rights at least – were long supporters of the Party of Lincoln. But the GOP, concluding that attracting Southern whites was a better electoral strategy, pushed blacks out of the party. Neither party, Republicans nor Democrats, offered blacks much, but norms were managed in a manner that punished blacks who ignored the rampant racism of the GOP and supported Herbert Hoover.

Black religious leaders were heavily monitored by loyalty police as well. Rev. E. M. Wilson might have been the most egregious offender. Wilson was the Alabama clergyman who deceived fellow reverends into signing a letter supporting Alabama Governor Dixon's position against antidiscrimination language being included in war contracts. Also blameworthy were the Tampa preachers who refused to condemn segregated railroads because they were receiving benefits from railroad companies. Black clergymen occupied a prime position from which to offer leadership. A devout people, blacks deferred to their religious leaders whose messages carried added influence. That power accompanied the expectation that they were racial agents. Religious figures could help blacks contest the imposition of second-class citizenship by empowering the masses and selling the race on the propriety of black solidarity. Indeed, because many blacks supported racial unity, black religious figures were very exposed to reproach because they were perfect potential organizers of black resistance movements. Thus, even a hint of betrayal was enough to invite

Uncle Tom accusations that punished transgressions and raised the price of betrayal.

Tracing *Uncle Tom* establishes that the epithet and racial loyalty norms greatly affected local conversations between blacks during this period. *Uncle Tom* influenced debates in black communities about what needed to be done to remedy racial marginalization. *Uncle Tom* was not tossed around merely to injure a target, but rather it was used to signal to the larger group that certain actions and beliefs would be punished by a people who desperately wanted to change their circumstances. That black people regulated behavior might explain the gradual shift among them to demand equality in the first half of the twentieth century. Many blacks participating in the Montgomery Bus Boycott, for instance, perhaps did so in part because they realized they would be branded as race traitors had they not.

Along those lines, when the NAACP decided to pursue desegregation through litigation, attorney William Hastie reported that black communities were going to pursue desegregation with or without the NAACP's help. Black communities in the South, that is, were fed up with segregated schooling to such a point that they would have gone ahead even with no NAACP help. This probably had much to do with black newspapers for nearly half a century telling their readers that only *Uncle Toms* will not battle segregation. Injustice has an ugly face. But too does the man who sits idly by, awaiting its end. Social norms and *Uncle Tom* rallied blacks to stand up, retrieve their arms, and put up a fight.[126]

---

[126] Richard Kluger, Simple Justice: The History of *Brown v. Board of Education* and Black America's Struggle for Equality 293–94 (2004).

3

The Unwitting Pioneers

UNCLE TOM AND THE NEGRO LEADER

RACIAL TREACHERY MUST BE UNCOVERED and punished. This gospel flowed through the veins of the black community. Blacks, therefore, intently monitored the race's most visible – the famous. Many take their cues from, or at least are influenced by, the most acclaimed and prominent members of their group. If black elites, so to speak, violated racial loyalty norms with impunity, the masses were increasingly likely to stray too. Their heightened prominence, moreover, amplified the damage of betrayal. If a renowned black figure publically endorsed Jim Crow, for instance, those frightful words could crush blacks' morale. And foes of racial progress would appropriate the comments to defend the empire that white supremacy built. The racial treachery of famous blacks, in short, could imperil the race's interests in exaggerated ways. Thus, policing racial loyalty carried obvious benefits. By proscribing certain behaviors and actions, blacks helped prod the group's most visible persons into being productive racial agents and stop the spread of the disease that all *Uncle Toms* carry. Perhaps this explains why famous blacks during this period were victimized more by destructive norms than the black masses. Indeed, this chapter contains more unwarranted *Uncle Tom* denunciations than the previous. The over-vigilance is understandable, but must be rejected. Studying the mistakes of yesteryear can guide subsequent generations.

The famous blacks who most needed monitoring were black leaders. Here, a black leader refers to someone whose voice has special influence in dialogues, whether national or local, concerning racial uplift. A leader who violated constructive norms imperiled the race's legal interests and ability to influence the debates that drove public policy. Blacks, consequently, had to ensure their absolute dedication to the cause of racial progress.

Booker T. Washington was perhaps the first leader to encounter *Uncle Tom's* scowl. His prosecutor was Thomas Miller, president of a black college, State College in Orangeburg, South Carolina. Miller did not directly call Washington an *Uncle Tom*; the earliest uses were not of that sort. But Uncle Tom the character was unmistakably dispatched to disgrace Washington's good name. Miller asserted that whites' "ideal Negro is a meek and humble man like the good old Uncle Tom." "We," he continued, "look upon Uncle Tom as a mythical character and despair of seeing his counterpart in real life … But, miracles of the century, in Booker T. Washington we have an Uncle Tom in real life." Miller's indictment of Washington was damning.

> In every attempt that has been made to degrade and humiliate the Negro, to rob him of his civil and political rights, to curtail his educational privileges and opportunities, to reduce him practically to helpless and hopeless peonage and serfdom in the Southland, in short in every attempt made to dethrone the Negro from his humanity and wrest from him the scepter of manhood, Booker T. Washington sees nothing but "blessings in disguise." Why, I really believe that if the entire Negro race in America were to be submerged in slavery again, Booker T. Washington's head would be lifted above the troubled waters and turbulent seas; his grave majestic, Jove-like countenance would be seen, and from his wise lips would issue forth some philosophic declaration, or glittering generalization, or grandiloquent platitude, or eloquent commonplace, proclaiming that enforced servitude was part of the grand plan that the Divine Providence had in store for the Negro. Great heavens, was ever such faith and patience seen since the days of Job; such love since the days of Christ, and such humility since the days of Uncle Tom?[1]

Suffering under debilitating racism, blacks had to fashion a strategy for complete emancipation. As the preeminent Negro leader of his day, Washington was influential. In his famed 1895 "Atlanta Compromise" speech, Washington averred that blacks erred in fixating on politics when the race should have set its sights lower. "Ignorant and inexperienced," he claimed, "it is not strange that in the first years of our new life we began at the top instead of at the bottom; that a seat in Congress or the state legislature was more sought than real estate or industrial skill; that the political convention or stump speaking had more attractions than starting a dairy farm or truck garden." Only after proving themselves would blacks acquire equal rights, Washington felt. And he accepted that as proper.

Washington's message to the all-white crowd was unmistakable. He implored blacks to abandon their political rights and accept segregation while

---

[1] William Henry Ferris, The African Abroad 90–91 (1913).

committing themselves to developing labor and trade skills. "The wisest of my race understand," Washington insisted, "that the agitation of questions of social equality is the extremest folly, and that progress in the enjoyment of all the privileges that will come to us must be the result of severe and constant struggle rather than of artificial forcing." Washington appreciated that white Southerners, above all else, wanted blacks to capitulate to white supremacy. Preserving the racial hierarchy and segregation was paramount, and Washington preached acquiescence, saying that "[i]n all things that are purely social we can be as separate as the fingers, yet one as the hand in all things essential to mutual progress."[2]

Washington was conciliatory. The final years of the nineteenth century were brutal for freedmen. Lynching, segregation, disenfranchisement, and Jim Crow justice all reduced the value of the Emancipation Proclamation and the Thirteenth Amendment. Yet Washington's "Atlanta Compromise" overlooked this misery and drew an incomplete picture of American race relations. He discussed black servants taking care of elderly whites, but ignored blacks being slain while attempting to vote. He recounted black domestics rearing white children but disregarded black peonage. Washington described Negroes as "the most patient, faithful, law-abiding, and unresentful people that the world has seen" for a reason. He wanted to convey that blacks posed no threat. Slavery, violence, discrimination – that was the past. All was forgiven. The slate was clean. And a deal was offered: Allow blacks to pursue economic advancement and the race will repay whites by not voting, surrendering to segregation, and forgetting about civil rights.[3]

Southern whites immediately heralded Washington's speech. In his autobiography, *Up From Slavery* (1901), Washington recounts that Governor Rufus Bullock and other whites rushed to praise him on stage afterward. Southern newspapers cherished his words and lauded his wisdom. That Washington's address allowed for an interpretation that satisfied the two separate camps among Southern whites propelled the adoration. White supremacists understood Washington as relinquishing any claims blacks might make for civil, social, and political rights, and everyone else heard a path toward racial reconciliation.[4]

---

[2] Id. at 223, 240; Rayford Whittingham Logan, The Betrayal of the Negro, from Rutherford B. Hayes to Woodrow Wilson 278–79 (1997); C. Vann Woodward, Origins of the New South, 1877–1913 357–58 (1971); Manning Marable, Living Black History: How Reimagining the African-American Past Can Remake America's Racial Future 83 (2006).

[3] Washington, Up From Slavery 221.

[4] Id. at 225; Raymond W. Logan, The Negro in the American Life and Thought: The Nadir 1877–1901 280 (1954). W. E. Burghardt Du Bois, The Souls of Black Folk: Essays and Sketches 42–43 (1903).

W. E. B. Du Bois's critique of the "Atlanta Compromise" speech best explains why Washington was prosecuted for betrayal. Du Bois acknowledged that Washington was the most influential Negro of his era. He even credited Washington for standing up for his race in the face of ills such as lynching. Yet Du Bois concluded that Washington's program of racial accommodation was disastrous.[5]

Washington, according to Du Bois, wanted blacks to abandon the pursuit of political power, civil rights, and higher education and instead "cast down [their] buckets" and learn a trade. Du Bois contended that Washington's argument – that blacks should pursue economic success and not full citizenship rights – was a "submission" that required blacks to accept their own inferiority. And, as Du Bois wrote, "In the history of nearly all other races and peoples the doctrine preached ... has been that manly self-respect is worth more than lands and houses, and that a people who voluntarily surrender such respect, or cease striving for it, are not worth civilizing." Washington's views, Du Bois contended, led to increased efforts to disfranchise and segregate blacks. To be clear, Du Bois did not blame discriminatory laws on Washington. Rather, he chided Washington's worldview for helping ease in a period during which blacks had their Fifteenth, Fourteenth, and Thirteenth Amendment rights violated.[6]

Du Bois, furthermore, condemned Washington's conciliatory tone. Du Bois thought that blacks were obligated to speak truthfully about race relations. Only after honest appraisal of the country's failures and successes could America come to treat everyone equally. Du Bois's biggest grievance, though, was that Washington prioritized economic matters over political rights, when he believed that the latter were a precondition for the former. As the scholar asked rhetorically, "Is it possible, and probable, that ... [blacks] can make effective progress in economic lines if they are deprived of political rights, made a servile caste, and allowed only the most meager chance for developing their exceptional men?" The problem with Washington's program for black advancement was that it conceded segregation, disfranchisement, and racial discrimination for space to pursue economic matters, when, in fact, total equality was a necessary condition to actually thrive economically.[7]

This situation, however, underscores the complexity and contradictory nature of human beings. The image of Washington as the pure accommodationist misses the larger man. Although the "Atlanta Compromise" may

[5] Id. at 41.
[6] Id. at 50–51.
[7] Id. at 51–52.

have appealed to whites because it seemingly advocated the abandonment of suffrage rights, Washington fought against a proposed Georgia law, the Hardwick bill, which would have disfranchised blacks. The race-neutral bill would have entrusted white registrars with the duty to prevent blacks from registering to vote. During an 1899 interview, Washington decried such legislative acts. He maintained that "[n]o state can make a law that can be so interpreted to mean one thing when applied to a black man and another thing when applied to a white man." Such laws, he argued, were unconstitutional. He softened his comments by holding that the bill would hurt whites more than blacks because such laws also disfranchised poor white men. But behind the scenes, Washington petitioned local blacks in Atlanta to resist the measure, and with the aid of Du Bois, oddly enough, Washington helped organize the black community against the bill. The measure was ultimately rejected.[8]

Similarly, in 1908, Washington began clandestinely funding a legal challenge to Alabama's 1903 peonage statute. The fruit of his money was the landmark *Bailey v. Alabama* (1911) Supreme Court decision that invalidated that law. Although Washington's hands were all over the decision, the broader public never detected his fingerprints. One newspaper editor mistakenly wrote that "[a]s far as can be learned, no negro ... took a hand in" *Bailey.* These stances add color to the complexion of the man. As Washington biographer Louis R. Harlan observed, "Washington's secret stiletto thrusts at the huge body of institutionalized white supremacy did not substantially change its shape or force, but they were clues, to the few who knew about them, of Washington's thought and feeling, and of a stouter heart than his bland public manner suggested."[9]

The key questions here are obvious. Was Thomas Miller right in likening Booker T. Washington to an *Uncle Tom*? Did Washington actually violate constructive racial loyalty norms? Those answering yes might argue that Washington furthered the interests of the race's enemies by publicly calling for blacks to withdraw from the pursuit of political, civil, and social equality. That the racist South adored his "Compromise" perhaps validates the argument.

Washington's strategy for racial progress, though, was nuanced. His ultimate goal was legal equality. But he contended that the best strategy for realizing that goal was to focus first on economic uplift and not outwardly protest

[8]   *Washington Urges Equal Treatment*, The Atlanta Constitution, Nov. 10, 1899, at 7.
[9]   Id.; *Bailey v. Alabama*, 219 U.S. 219 (1911); Robert J. Norrell, Up From History: The Life of Booker T. Washington 188–89, 405–06 (2009); Pete Daniel, *Up From Slavery and Down to Peonage: The Alonzo Bailey Case*, 57 Journal of American History 654, 654 668 (1970); Louis R. Harlan, Booker T. Washington: The Wizard of Tuskegee, 1901–1915, Volume 2 250–51 (1983).

legal oppression. Any strategy for racial equality had to appreciate the required decades of toil. The journey was never going to be short. And Washington was not asking blacks to give up rights they already possessed. Blacks were denied civil and political rights. Washington believed the best approach to acquire those rights was that upon blacks proving themselves economically, whites would voluntarily grant them full citizenship. Washington's aim was complete equality. Thus, fathoming that he furthered the race's enemies' interests by trying to implement a strategy that he hoped would have resulted in what blacks' antagonists feared most – the elevation of the Negro – is hard. Washington, moreover, helped attack laws that subordinated blacks, further establishing that he was no friend of white supremacists. By attempting to implement a strategy for full emancipation, Washington had proven himself an agent for black Americans.

Others might argue that because Washington was inexcusably meek, Thomas Miller's harsh criticism was valid. That argument, however, is also unconvincing. Washington's "Atlanta Compromise" was accommodating because it advocated that blacks abdicate the mission for legal and social equality. But that fact is insufficient to render him inexcusably meek. More is required. Second-class citizenship was the manifestation of race hatred directed at blacks. The belief that if blacks proved themselves economically that race hatred would dissipate was reasonable in the 1890s, a time when blacks were the victims of violence and degradation. Although in the 1960s no black leader should have advanced this viewpoint, the argument was precisely what blacks should have been debating in the late 1800s as they tried to work their way toward full American citizenship. Constructive racial loyalty norm management rebuffs the notion that blacks must be united in thought. If Washington was wrong, then his idea should have been rejected.

But not every argument is within bounds. If, for instance, Washington contended that blacks should reject the pursuit of equality because they were naturally less capable, then Washington would be deserving of rebuke. But nothing of the sort happened here. Washington's racial program did not render him inexcusably meek.

The last possible argument against Washington is that he did not care about the race. Or more precisely, perhaps Washington's black solidarity was markedly impure. That this is false is too clear for argument. Washington's life was dedicated to the uplift of black people. That he arguably chose a bad strategy does not mean that his devotion to black folk was unchaste, particularly because good options for racial progress in the late 1800s were nonexistent. Booker T. Washington, in short, was no *Uncle Tom*.

As Du Bois critiqued Washington, Marcus Garvey did the same to him.
And Du Bois's nemesis freely discharged *Uncle Tom* salvoes. Du Bois was
arguably the most constant civil rights voice in American history. Marcus
Garvey, the fiery Jamaican who sought racial separatism, was his adversary.
One should have expected tension between the two. They were, after all, two
men headquartered in New York City selling blacks two different solutions
to the race problem. Du Bois, on the one hand, helped found the Niagara
Movement and later the NAACP, which guaranteed that the key to blacks'
success was reforming American practices and institutions. Garvey, on the
other hand, contended that true emancipation could only occur in Africa.
Both wanted a better reality for blacks. Du Bois believed in demanding equal
protection under the law. Garvey swore that whites snickered at those stout
requests. Blacks, Garvey pronounced, could only progress with self-reliance.
He founded the UNIA for blacks to "establish a country and Government
absolutely their own." Garvey pled for blacks to flee America and create
an enviable African civilization. Du Bois, however, regarded defection as
defeatism.[10]

Garvey remarked that the "the effigy of Du Bois and his type should be
placed alongside that of Uncle Tom, because as a fact he is of the same mentality." Du Bois was an *Uncle Tom*, according to Garvey, largely for two reasons. First, Garvey held himself out to be a true race warrior and insisted that
Du Bois was a toady for white folks. Along those lines, Garvey claimed that
Du Bois was "purely and simply a White man's nigger" and "the white man
Negro, who had never done anything yet to benefit Negroes." Similarly, in his
newspaper the *Black Man*, Garvey wrote that Du Bois "belongs to that school
of thought that would hitch the Negro onto the white man's coat tail with the
hope that one day the Negro will put on the white man's cast-off coat." Here,
Garvey criticized Du Bois for rejecting racial separation and instead preferring integration and seeking to reform American society.[11]

[10] Raymond Wolters, Du Bois and His Rivals 146, 161 (2002); Edmund David Cronon, Black
      Moses: The Story of Marcus Garvey and the Universal Negro Improvement Association
      16–18 (1960). Garvey was not the only person to brand Du Bois as an *Uncle Tom*. Ben Davis
      Jr., a militant black lawyer who defended Angelo Herndon, denounced Du Bois for racial
      treachery. Davis labeled him, along with Kelly Miller and George Schuyler, as *Uncle Toms*
      who were great at "fooling the Negro masses … and keeping them from fighting against their
      real oppressors." *Ben Davis, Jr., Calls Schuyler, DuBois Prostitutes and Miller "Uncle Tom" in
      Assuming Editorship of Liberator*, New Journal and Guide, July 7, 1934, at A4.
[11] Elliott M. Rudwick, W. E. B. Du Bois: Propagandist of the Negro Protest 216–21 (1968);
      The Marcus Garvey and Universal Negro Improvement Association Papers Volume VII
      November 1927–August 1940 630 (Editor Robert A. Hill 1990); Raymond Wolters, Du Bois
      and His Rivals 155 (2002); Arnold Rampersad, The Art and Imagination of W. E. B. Du Bois
      16 (1976); Marcus Garvey, *The American Negro*, The Black Man, June 1935, at 5; Elliot M

The second factor was that Garvey thought Du Bois was self-hating. Du Bois's membership with the NAACP, an interracial organization controlled by white liberals and mixed-race blacks, agitated Garvey. He called the NAACP as antiblack as "Southern crackers" because "their program is race assimilation which will in another hundred years wipe out this Negro race and make a new race which will not be Negro in any degree." Further supporting Garvey's contention that Du Bois was an *Uncle Tom* was a UNIA document that claimed:

> Du Bois represents a group that hates the Negro blood in its veins, and has been working subtly to build up a caste aristocracy that would socially divide the race into two groups: One the superior because of color caste, and the other the inferior, hence the pretentious work of the National Association for the Advancement of "Colored" People.... The whole staff was either white or very near white, and thus Garvey got his first shock of the advancement hypocrisy. There was no representation of the race there that anyone could recognize. The advancement meant that you had to be as near white as possible, otherwise there was no place for you as stenographer, clerk or attendant in the office of the National Association for the Advancement of "Colored" People. After a short talk with Du Bois, Garvey became so disgusted with that man and his principles that the thought he never contemplated entered his mind – that of remaining in America to teach Du Bois and his group what real race pride meant.[12]

On another occasion, Garvey asserted that Du Bois tried to mask his black ancestry. "Sometimes we hear he is a Frenchman and another time he is Dutch and when it is convenient he is a Negro.... Anyone you hear always talking about the kind of blood he has in him other than the blood you see, he is dissatisfied with something, and ... if there is a man who is most dissatisfied with himself, it is Dr. Du Bois." Garvey's brand of nationalism and solidarity implored blacks to organize around a shared ancestry. Racial mixing inherently frustrated his goals. On this narrow point, Du Bois biographer David Levering Lewis vindicated Garvey's underlying message. Lewis reported that Du Bois, to Harvard trustees, misrepresented his mother as being mulatto, for example. "This subtext of proud hybridization is so prevalent in Du Bois's sense of himself," Lewis wrote, "that the failure to notice it in the literature about him is as remarkable as the complex itself."[13]

Rudwick, *DuBois Versus Garvey: Race Propagandists at War*, 28 *Journal of Negro Education* 421, 424 (1959).

[12] Wolters, Du Bois and His Rivals 159; David Levering Lewis, W. E. B. Du Bois: A Biography of a Race, 1869–1919 148 (1993); More Philosophy and Opinions of Marcus Garvey 57 (Editor Amy Jacques-Garvey 1st Edition 1977).

[13] Rudwick, W. E. B. Du Bois 216.

But the idea that Du Bois was a sellout is indefensible. The best line of attack Garvey offered was that Du Bois, for some reason, embellished his white ancestry, leading to the possible conclusion that Du Bois preferred whiteness. Du Bois had a color complex. He was one of many Negroes who fell prey to "white is right" messages widely transmitted throughout American culture. That does not mean, however, that Du Bois ran afoul of racial loyalty norms. Indeed, the evidence with which Garvey sought to indict Du Bois fell far short of that necessary to sustain a charge that Du Bois violated any of the three constructive racial loyalty norms.

And like Washington and Du Bois before him, Marcus Garvey was dismissed as an *Uncle Tom*. Robert Minor, the labeler, was a white communist. Normally a white person's use of *Uncle Tom* would be irrelevant to a discussion concerning blacks' intra-racial policing. But because Minor's critique was endorsed by a meaningful segment of the black population and because Minor participated in conversations about black folk, his usage is important; it likely means that some blacks too branded Garvey as an *Uncle Tom*. But more significant is that some blacks strongly denounced Garvey for treachery for similar reasons as did Minor, although they did not call him an *Uncle Tom* directly. Using Minor's denunciation as an entry point for a larger discussion on Garvey is helpful in understanding intra-racial dialogues concerning betrayal in the 1920s.

Minor criticized Garvey for advocating immigration to Africa, describing the idea as historically championed by bigoted whites. The most notable example was the American Colonization Society, which wanted to transport free blacks in America to Africa. Minor tied this history to Garvey, arguing that he repackaged the same racist product.[14]

But more important, Minor censured Garvey for placating Southern bigots. With the UNIA dithering after failed ventures, Garvey went to the South where one had to navigate social mores. Garvey ingratiated himself to white supremacists as a cost of doing business there. In 1921, for example, Republican President Harding delivered a speech in Birmingham, announcing that the Republican Party had officially abandoned all pretense of supporting social equality. Harding declared, "Men of both races may well stand uncompromisingly against every suggestion of social equality.... Racial amalgamation there cannot be." Garvey, in response, told Harding that "[t]he Negroes of the world... greet you as a wise and great statesman ... All true Negroes are against social equality." In Raleigh, Garvey thanked Southern whites for "lynch[ing] race pride into the Negroes." In New Orleans, he declared that America "is a white man's country. He found it, he conquered it and we can't

---

[14] Robert Minor, *The Handkerchief on Garvey's Head*, The Liberator, Oct. 1924, at 20–23.

blame him because he wants to keep it. I'm not vexed with the white man of the South for Jim Crowing me because I'm black. I never built any street cars or railroads. The white man built them for your own convenience. And if I don't want to ride where he's willing to let me then I'd better walk." Garvey even distributed a questionnaire to senators to gauge their interest in assisting blacks repatriating Africa.

White supremacists and Garvey had an obvious interest convergence. Both wanted blacks gone. Thus, they had so much common ground that Garvey once met a high-ranking Ku Klux Klan official. After the meeting, Garvey went north and parroted some of the Klan's riffs about America being a "white man's country" and that the world sneered at blacks because they lacked accomplishments. Garvey also argued that blacks must not fight the KKK; their "[n]umerical disadvantage ... is too great." Garvey's method to stop the world's derision was to make Africa enviable. Garvey, in short, used racist taunts to convince blacks that Africa, not America, was the setting for their better future.[15]

Du Bois contended that Garvey's pronouncements rendered him "either a lunatic or a traitor." He was, Du Bois felt, "without doubt, the most dangerous enemy of the Negro race in America and in the world." Du Bois further remarked that "[n]ot even Tom Dixon or Ben Tillman or the hatefulest enemies of the Negro ever stooped to a more vicious campaign than Marcus Garvey, sane or insane, is carrying on." Instead of fighting white supremacy, Du Bois averred, Garvey "is groveling before it and applauding it," describing him as "a little, fat black man, ugly, but with intelligent eyes and big head." He was "a demagogue, a blatant boaster, who with monkey-shines was deluding the people and taking their hard earned dollars." Rather than interpreting Garvey as using racism as an impetus to convince blacks to leave America, according to Robert Minor, Garvey was simply an "Uncle Tom." Minor wrote:

> In short, Garvey did everything that was humanly possible and left no boots unlicked in the effort to make himself a "white man's nigger" in the eyes of the white ruling class, and at the same time a "Negro Moses" in the eyes of the suffering black masses.

And so Garvey's shield reads one side: "Deport the damned niggers to Africa," and on the other side: "Let us go to our glorious Homeland in Africa."[16]

---

[15] Judith Stein, The World of Marcus Garvey: Race and Class in Modern Society 153–54 (1986); Theodore G. Vincent, Black Power and the Garvey Movement 191 (1975); Cronon, Black Moses 194–95; Wilson Jeremiah Moses, Creative Conflict in African American Thought: Frederick Douglass, Alexander Crummell, Booker T. Washington, W. E. B. Du Bois, and Marcus Garvey 275 (2004).

[16] Rampersad, The Art and Imagination of W. E. B. Du Bois 148–49; Minor, *The Handkerchief on Garvey's Head*, at 20–23; Colin Grant, Negro With a Hat: The Rise and Fall of Marcus

Unlike with Washington and Du Bois, the argument that Garvey was an *Uncle Tom* was true. Garvey cared about the race. He was not racially apathetic or antagonistic to black folk. And his devotion to black solidarity was pure. Thus, no one can fairly rebuke him for not being sufficiently concerned about the lives of Negroes.

True, insisting that blacks immigrate to Africa was doing work that pleased white supremacists who objected to blacks' continued presence in America. Blacks should not, however, eschew strategies for racial progress simply because their foes may rejoice upon its successful implementation. Concluding that 1920s America was simply too hostile and the best option would be to plant one's roots in one's ancestral homeland was reasonable. If Garvey was wrong in championing his "back to Africa" movement, then his error should have been criticized. His possible miscalculation here did not render him an *Uncle Tom.*

Garvey's placation to Southern bigotry, however, deserved vociferous condemnation. He met with the Klan, a terrorist organization whose members' hands were stained crimson with the blood of blacks. He excused segregation on trains, arguing, falsely, that blacks had no involvement with the building of railroads. He even thanked whites for lynching race pride into blacks. In short, he validated the worst that white supremacy offered. It very well might have all been a cynical ploy to rev up his efforts to implement his evacuation plan. As one delegate of a UNIA convention said, "The Klan is a help to this movement by increasing the membership, by making the black man think of Africa." But that reasoning fails to exonerate him for his crimes against the race.

Many felt, moreover, that Garvey's possible strategy was deeply unwise. As William Pickens once told Garvey, "You say in effect to the Ku Klux: All right! Give us Africa and we in turn concede you America as a 'white man's country'! In that you make a poor deal; for twelve million people you give up everything and in exchange get nothing." That Garvey concluded he had to parrot racist comments to further his plans should have caused him to rethink his overall strategy. Washington's momentary submission to white supremacy as part of a long-term strategy was permissible. Amid the early twentieth century marked by virulent racism, accommodation to Jim Crow was perhaps a necessity. But Washington did not endorse the racist premises that undergirded the marginalization of blacks. Thanking whites for lynching race pride into blacks, however, is a step much too far. For walking down the path of the inexcusably

Garvey 380 (2008); Stein, The World of Marcus Garvey 153–56; David Levering Lewis, W. E. B. Du Bois: The Fight for Equality and the American Century 1919–1963 148–49 (2001); Wolters, Du Bois and His Rivals 168.

meek, the man who has posthumously become a symbol for black solidarity was fairly criticized for racial betrayal. Marcus Garvey was an *Uncle Tom*.[17]

Other, less prominent, black leaders were derided as *Uncle Toms* as well. Dr. Robert Russa Moton, or "Tuskegee's Uncle Tom," was often considered treacherous. Moton succeeded Booker T. Washington as the head of the Tuskegee Institute in 1916. Though Washington's shine dwarfed that of Moton, the successor's shadow was large nonetheless. Moton had more pull with American leaders than perhaps any other black leader of his day. As one historian commented, "Moton was the white man's biggest Negro." He used a program of racial accommodation to purchase his clout with powerful whites. Accommodation was Moton's way. Although dedicated to racial equality, Moton "pursued his cause in private, seeking to influence whites with calm reason, knowing that angry rhetoric would merely alienate them." He was an accommodationist partly because Tuskegee was financed by Northern philanthropic organizations who agreed with the dominant Southern viewpoint that segregation and disfranchisement best quieted racial disharmony. During his inaugural address as Tuskegee's president, Moton reiterated that he supported Washington's belief that hard work, thrift, and education, not protest politics, was the key to racial progress. His conciliatory manner was further displayed after his wife was ousted from a seat on a Jim Crow railroad luxury sleeping car. Moton remained silent afterward, delighting Southern whites. Moton even took a trip to France in 1919 at the request of the War Department to investigate complaints of the black soldiers and grievances against them. While there, Moton supposedly told the soldiers that, upon their return to America, they should not challenge discrimination and disfranchisement.[18]

As time went on, Moton's public pronouncements against racism grew more biting. During his acceptance speech for the NAACP Spingarn Medal in 1932, for instance, Moton delivered a caustic takedown of racial discrimination and American hypocrisy. But for some, the idea that he was an *Uncle Tom* had calcified. Moton, for reasons similar to Booker T. Washington, however, was not an *Uncle Tom*. He was merely a conservative voice. At the time, his brand of conservatism was a defensible argument to proffer to the broader black community. Moton surely could have taken a more aggressive tone earlier in his career. Indeed, perhaps he should have been criticized for not being

---

[17] Sources for this paragraph and the preceding one are as follows: Vincent, Black Power and the Garvey Movement 209; Stein, The World of Marcus Garvey 164.

[18] *For Dr. Moton's Critics*, Atlanta Daily World, June 2, 1932, at 6A; Adam Fairclough, *Tuskegee's Robert R. Moton and the Travails of the Early Black College President*, 31 Journal of Blacks in Higher Education 94, 94–99 (2001).

more militant and finding his voice too late. His not doing so, though, was not treacherous.

Columnist George Schuyler of the *Pittsburgh Courier* criticized the NAACP's decision to reward Moton, "the spiritual descendent of Uncle Tom," with the prestigious Spingarn Medal. In 1934, Schuyler called Moton "a 20th century edition of Uncle Tom," who fled Alabama when the Klan paraded through Tuskegee's grounds, leaving the students, administrators, and faculty to fend for themselves. The *Messenger* too condemned Moton for political accommodation. To the publication, Moton was "ignorant of the fact that progress has taken Place among any people in proportion as they become discontented with their position and adopted methods to change that position." Moton's personality, some argued, depended on his location. Black newspapers portrayed him as an "Uncle Tom" in the South, but as a true race man in the North. Looking back in 1940, the year of Moton's death, Du Bois said that he once deemed Moton an "Uncle Tom" and a "white folks' nigger." Du Bois claimed that Moton possessed a puerile belief in the fairness of whites, but Du Bois thought that his criticism and that of others helped Moton to eventually find both his voice and "a stronger and more tenable platform."[19]

Another black leader of the early twentieth century, Kelly Miller, was denounced as an *Uncle Tom*. Miller, a man of many hats, was the dean of the College of Arts and Sciences at Howard University, a traveling lecturer, an essayist, and a syndicated columnist. Born in 1863 in South Carolina, Miller was a moderate sympathetic to Booker T. Washington's program, although he dissented in some aspects. In the 1920s, Miller's leadership position in the black community was waning as he found his voice being muffled amid louder, more militant tones. For instance, he stood against labor unions. Black socialists, in response, ridiculed him as a member of the "Old Crowd." Miller, generally, insisted that blacks plot a humble course of action in the face of racist headwinds. Miller thought of himself as practical. He opposed, for example, the Robert F. Wagner-Edward P. Costigan antilynching bill in the early 1930s, believing that white racist attitudes were too engrained for the bill to be effective.

[19] *For Dr. Moton's Critics*, at 6A; George S. Schuyler, *Views and Reviews*, Pittsburgh Courier, May 12, 1934, at 10; George S. Schuyler, *Views and Reviews*, Pittsburgh Courier, Nov. 17, 1934, at 10; Robert Russa Moton of Hampton and Tuskegee 140 (Editors William Hardin Hughes and Frederick D. Patterson 1956); Lerone Bennett Jr., *Chronicles of Black Courage*, Ebony, July 2002, at 158; W. E. B. Du Bois, *Moton of Hampton and Tuskegee*, 1 Phylon 344, 350–51 (1940); Robert Russa Moton, Finding a Way Out: An Autobiography 209 (1921); *Robert Russa Moton*, The Messenger, Aug. 1917, at 31–32.

In 1933, he and Carter G. Woodson, a renowned black scholar of the early twentieth century, had a protracted disagreement during which Woodson dismissed Miller as an *Uncle Tom* and a pox on the race. Woodson accused Kelly of seeking to marginalize the former's efforts to procure equality for blacks. Woodson claimed that Kelly tried to link his work to "the back-to Africa movement or with the so-called radical element of the Race." Only the slave mind, held Woodson, could reframe the vigorous pursuit for justice as radical. Woodson dubbed Kelly an "Uncle Tom Negro." To Woodson, the servile Kelly was satisfied with whatever crumbs whites sought fit to put in his bowl. Worse yet, Woodson averred that Kelly tried to personally profit from segregation. "I insist," Woodson wrote, "that we must fight on for equality and justice even if some of us must thereby suffer and die. [Kelly] would feast upon the profits of segregation as a patient gulps down the opiates which facilitate his dying."

Woodson further plunged the shiv. While in Texas, Woodson noticed that Jim Crow laws were not always enforced. On some modes of transportation, he was allowed to sit wherever he pleased. This signaled, to Woodson, that perhaps the South was attempting to become more enlightened. Woodson took this as an opportunity to again charge Miller with betrayal. "If Kelly Miller, the Uncle Tom of the Potomac, does not watch out the South will get rid of most of its Jim Crowing by the time he and his coworkers thoroughly establish it in the East and North." Based on the available information, accurately determining the fairness of targeting Kelly is challenging. Seemingly, a disagreement between two people escalated and sellout rhetoric was unfortunately used.[20]

Another well-known black thinker of the era was George Schuyler, who, as mentioned, once branded Moton as an *Uncle Tom*. Schuyler was a columnist for the *Messenger* and *Pittsburgh Courier* in the first half of the twentieth century, and was often dubbed the "H. L. Mencken of Negro journalism." During his stint with the *Messenger*, Schuyler grew increasingly conservative. Claude McKay, the Jamaican-American poet and writer, once called him "the supreme advocate of Uncle Tom Do nothingness." Schuyler harshly criticized communism. He was particularly disparaging of black communists' tactics

---

[20] The sources for the Kelly Miller discussion are as follows: Carter G. Woodson, *Uncle Tom and His Coworkers*, Chicago Defender, Feb. 35, 1933, at 11; Carter G. Woodson, *Smiling through Texas*, Chicago Defender, Mar. 4, 1933, at 11; W. D. Wright, *The Thought and Leadership of Kelly Miller*, 39 Phylon 180 (1978); August Meier, *The Racial and Educational Philosophy of Kelly Miller, 1895–1915*, 29 Journal of Negro Education 121, 121–27 (1960); Bernard Eisenberg, *Kelley Miller: The Negro Leader as a Marginal Man*, 45 Journal of Negro History 182, 184–85 (1960).

of going to the South to protest when their only success was "getting [blacks] beaten up, jailed, deported, or killed."

Angelo Herndon, an infamous black communist, abhorred Schuyler. Herndon was arrested in Atlanta in 1932 for attempting to incite an insurrection. Schuyler at first appeared to be concerned for Herndon and blacks like him. But a year and a half later, Schuyler wrote, "Herndon is out on bail and will probably skip it, like all the rest." The Communist Party was livid, believing the columnist took a swipe at its *cause célèbre.* Black communists portrayed Schuyler as a weak-willed Negro who was reticent to fight racism. Herndon, in the Communist Party newspaper the *Daily Worker,* wrote that Schuyler "never missed your opportunity to betray the struggles of the Negro people." "Who is the Uncle Tom?," he continued. "It is you, George Schuyler, belittling the program of struggle, advising subordination and submission in the face of attacks by the white rulers, knifing in the back the fight to free the Scottsboro Boys and myself."[21]

To many, Mississippi newspaperman Percy Greene was an archetype *Uncle Tom.* Greene was not a national black leader but was influential in Mississippi, being the editor of a popular black newspaper, the *Jackson Advocate.* Greene, in fact, called himself an *Uncle Tom* because he thought they were better for the race. "The greatest need for the Negro in Jackson, Miss., and the rest of the South is more and more Uncle Toms," Greene once wrote. Finding a Negro who embodies "selling out" more than Greene is tough. Perhaps Greene's most sanction-worthy offense was accepting money from the Mississippi State Sovereignty Commission, a pro-segregation white supremacist organization. Sovereignty commissions and White Citizens' Councils were business-class equivalents to the coach-seat Ku Klux Klan. And Green was their right-hand black man. From 1956 to 1967 Greene was known to have taken $6,397 as a "troubleshooter" for the commission, though he likely received more because many of his payments were in cash and off the books. He wrote letters, telegrams, and articles espousing its pro-segregation positions for his newspaper *Jackson Advocate.* Nothing appears to have been too far for Greene. As a writer for the *Advocate,* he used his columns to sabotage the desegregation

21 The sources for George Schuyler are as follows: Claude McKay, *Schuyler Lashes Here and There Like Mad Dog – Bites Everybody,* Pittsburgh Courier, Dec. 4, 1937, at 14; Oscar Renal Williams, George S. Schuyler: Portrait of a Black Conservative 92–95 (2007); Ann Rayson, *George Schuyler: Paradox Among "Assimilationist" Writers,* 12 *Black American Literature Forum* 102, 102 (1978); Sam G. Riley, Biographical Dictionary of American Newspaper Columnists 292–93 (1995); George Schuyler, *Views Reviews,* Pittsburgh Courier, Aug. 25, 1934, at 10; Kendall Thomas, *Rouge Et Noir Reread: A Popular Constitutional History of the Angelo Herndon Case,* 65 *Southern California Law Review* 2599, 2599–600 (1992).

goals of Martin Luther King, Harlem Congressman Adam Clayton Powell Jr., and influential Mississippi blacks. Greene, in short, took money from racists and did their bidding.[22]

Columnist Robert M. Ratcliffe thought he had Greene figured out.

Percy is a businessman. He publishes a weekly paper, the Jackson Advocate. He needs the white man's business. If he doesn't get any advertisements in his paper, he'll go broke. He won't be able to eat. White businessmen stopped advertising in his paper when he was fighting for the NAACP. They even cut off his paid political speeches.

Percy likes power and he likes money. So he drops the NAACP and comes out for segregation. Percy is a nice, tough guy. What he's saying about more Negro "Uncle Toms" is a lot of hogwash. We don't believe he believes all this malarkey. We really believe he'd like to be back on the battleground, fighting for the rights of Negroes. He's that type of man.

Ratcliffe, in other words, asserted that Greene curried favor with segregationists as a tactical play for money. When Greene supported James Meredith in his quest to gain entrance to the University of Mississippi, however, his white financiers deserted him.[23]

Greene's once solid relationship with the black community was tarnished after he began criticizing the NAACP's integrationist efforts. After *Brown*, Greene started denouncing the association and asserted that it had communist ties. The Mississippi State Sovereignty Commission learned about Greene's views and quickly teamed up with the newspaperman to further a pro-segregation agenda. The commission began to write editorials in the *Jackson Advocate* under Greene's byline and elicited funds on Greene's behalf for him to go around the country and spread pro-segregation messages. With his informants, Greene was able to infiltrate civil rights meetings and report findings. Greene even advised the commission on how to deal with Martin Luther King's Southern Christian Leadership Conference (SCLC). He counseled local white newspapers to give the SCLC "the silent treatment" when the group met in the state.[24]

Greene had a kindred spirit and black ally in the 1950s in Mississippi in Rev. H. H. Humes. Humes, like Greene, was a local leader and the editor of a black newspaper, the *Delta Leader*. After *Brown* and *Brown II*, the NAACP had to

---

[22] Juan Williams, *Percy Greene and the Mississippi Sovereignty Commission*, 28 *Journalism History* 66, 70 (2002).

[23] *Editor Says South Needs "Uncle Toms,"* Atlanta Daily World, Jan. 31, 1957, at 2; Robert M. Ratcliffe, *Behind the Headlines*, Pittsburgh Courier, Feb. 9, 1957, at 15; Robert E. Baker, *Decision Time Nearing for Rigid Mississippi*, Washington Post, Sept. 11, 1962, at A4.

[24] Williams, *Percy Greene and the Mississippi Sovereignty Commission*, at 67–68.

bring subsequent lawsuits to desegregate school districts that continued to maintain dual-race school systems. Humes hoped that the NAACP would lose its fight, arguing that segregation offered the same opportunities to black children as it offered to whites ones. "If you have a white school," Humes declared, "well-staffed with white teachers, it is no different democratically than a Negro school, well-staffed with Negro teachers if both offer the students the same thing." Humes said that the majority of blacks agreed with him and wanted separate schools. And dissenters, Humes believed, would find themselves dissatisfied after its implementation. The president of the Mississippi NAACP, responding to Humes, said, "[w]e will not accept the Negro Uncle Tom … We will work toward the goal of full freedom, full integration … and see to it that the vicious system of segregation is challenged until it is removed." After another black editor attacked White Citizens' Councils, Humes replied that the editor was a "pseudo-liberal."[25]

Humes copied Greene's signature formula for treachery and worked on behalf of the Mississippi State Sovereignty Commission. Humes attended a civil rights gathering in Greenville, Mississippi, and reported his finding to the commission. Humes even paid a stenographer to create a transcript of the proceedings at the Regional Council of Negro Leadership in April 1957. A prominent commission insider referred to Humes and others as the "good" Negroes and said that "we owe a debt [of] gratitude to our negro friends who have been cooperating so fully." The insider gave Humes and others credit for the "meeting of agitators" being "such a grand flop."[26]

After a while, people learned of the activities of Humes and Greene and they quickly fomented terrible reputations as boisterous segregation supporters. And that reputation sealed their fates. Blacks in droves cancelled their subscriptions and called Humes a "white man's nigger" and an "Uncle Tom." Dr. T. R. M. Howard called Humes "the biggest Uncle Tom in the state" and called both Humes and Greene "Uncle Toms of the first magnitude." Jackie Robinson wrote that Greene "betrayed his race" and was "making a fool out of himself." The *Defender* strongly rebuked Humes, hoping it "will serve as a warning to Uncle Toms in every profession. For mass opinion today is clearly for racial progress on every front – and indeed racial integration." The *Defender*, in other words, correctly understood that racial loyalty norms were powerful teaching tools; they instructed blacks on how to act and notified blacks of the price of racial betrayal. One incurred a cost in being an *Uncle Tom* – public condemnation. Unlike Greene, Humes rejected the *Uncle Tom*

---

[25] *"Uncle Toms" Scored in Mississippi School Fight*, Plaindealer, Nov. 20, 1953, at 7.
[26] Kennedy, Sellout 50–51.

label and countered that his critics stifled diversity of thought in the black community. But no human has the audacity and skill to sell that canard. His excuse was specious. Greene and Humes violated all three constructive racial loyalty norms and were the sorts of people who should have been harshly rebuked. They were fairly branded as *Uncle Toms*. It truly was the right move, the only move.[27]

Racially treacherous leaders possessed the potential to injure an untold number of people; their betrayal could thwart the aims of the entire race by seriously disabling blacks in fighting racial discrimination and various forms of legal oppression. Disloyal commentary that infiltrates into national debates, moreover, could shape a national mood that found blacks' unequal lot permissible. Blacks, therefore, had to heavily monitor their leaders. Policing them, furthermore, was an effective exercise to empower the masses in two important ways.

First, the debate propelled blacks to see their condition as amendable, thereby driving them from complacency into action. After all, if a black person concluded that a leader was damaging the race's interests by being treacherous, the person necessarily believed that a different course of action might produce better results. And second, assessing the character of a leader invites introspection. By asking if, for instance, Booker T. Washington was an *Uncle Tom*, one might ask the question of oneself, leading to a population more likely to resist the shackles of white supremacy.

Leaders were more likely to be falsely accused than the masses. That does not mean, however, that policing loyalty was inherently wrong. Rather, the unfortunate application of destructive racial loyalty norms should be studied to ensure that such wrongs are not committed in the future. The key lesson to be learned here is that racial loyalty does not mean unison of thought; blacks must be given the intellectual space to devise solutions. As true for everyone, the black leader who is truly disloyal is uncommitted to ridding society of its antiblack elements. A leader who shares that commitment should be permitted to outline their strategy for racial progress. From there, blacks can debate the propriety of the strategy.

THE *UNCLE TOMS* IN THE SYSTEM

"It is indeed to be regretted that the most successful Negroes in getting the ears of the high officials are those of the 'Uncle Tom' type." The idea that

---

[27] *Dixie School Battle Explodes!*, Pittsburgh Courier, July 30, 1955, at 13; *Humes Denies "Tom" Label, Raps NAACP*, Chicago Defender, Aug. 6, 1955, at 5; *Our Opinions*, Chicago Defender, Oct. 1, 1955, at 9; Williams, *Percy Greene and the Mississippi Sovereignty Commission*, at 68.

Uncle Toms rather than true "race men" were invited to the bargaining table to advocate for the group pervaded during this period. Blacks could drive to full equality on two main avenues. First, blacks could agitate and reform the system from the outside. Or, second, blacks could stop racist outcomes the system produced by fixing it from within. Those chosen few in a position to pursue the latter path shouldered a heavy burden. Typically the only black person in the proverbial room, they carried the race's aspirations. When blacks believed that their ambassadors' shoulders were too weak for that heavy responsibility, they enforced racial loyalty norms and played one of the few cards they had, *Uncle Tom*.[28]

Often, the easiest path to enter the system for blacks was to take "Jim Crow jobs," political appointments that were given to blacks to handle "black matters" in government. In 1921, Charles R. Forbes was made the director of the U.S. Veterans' Bureau and appointed Dr. John R. A. Crossland as the "special expert" in the department to attend to the interests of black veterans. During the Harding administration, Perry Howard, a well-connected black Republican, occupied a similar position as special assistant to the attorney general. The *Appeal*, a black newspaper based in St. Paul, Minnesota, labeled them both *Uncle Tom* politicians. The *Appeal* figured that if blacks persisted in accepting Jim Crow jobs, then segregation would continue. Blacks wanted their leaders to combat Jim Crow. But these positions were premised on segregation being a mainstay in American life. Thus, anyone who took a Jim Crow job actually had a vested financial interest in its perpetuation. Under this rationale, why Crossland and Howard were branded as *Uncle Toms* is understandable.[29]

But requiring that blacks not take such positions was destructive. So-called Jim Crow jobs were often blacks' only way in the door to make change from the inside. Blacks should have been eager at the prospect of a black insider. Crossland, for instance, could have petitioned his boss on desegregating veterans' hospitals. Insiders should not have been criticized just because they were insiders. Rather they should have been held to the same standards as everyone else.

Howard, however, infringed constructive norms as well. In 1925, while special assistant to the attorney general and a Republican national committee-man, Howard faced virulent denunciation for serving as general counsel to the Pullman Company in its battles with the BSCP, the black porters' union. Howard, himself a former Pullman porter, claimed that the communist-led

[28] *Fort Scott, Kansas*, Plaindealer, Oct. 6, 1922 at 2.
[29] Special Expert, The Appeal, Oct. 22, 1921, at 2.

"radical organization" embarrassed America. The author of a letter to the editor published in the *Afro-American* labeled Howard an "Uncle Tom," a "mercenary," and a "b[la]therskite and skunk" who was not "fit to be a Negro" who hopefully would "'pass over' to the whites." The author equated working for the Pullman Company to peonage and sympathized with black porters' desire for a fairer deal.[30]

More prominent individuals were Howard detractors too. In 1926, the *Messenger* reported that a white Republican urged the publication to stop attacking Howard. Editors A. Philip Randolph and Chandler Owen, though, rebuffed the request. The newspaper argued that simply having a black person on the National Republican Committee was unsatisfactory. Instead, the *Messenger* would "rather have a white man there than to have a worthless, unscrupulous, Uncle Tom Negro there." The *Messenger* undoubtedly agreed with a communist publication that disparaged Perry as an "Uncle Tom politician, who boasts of his lackey service for" the Republican Party who also constantly betrayed the race for jobs from Wall Street employers.[31]

By serving as counsel to the Pullman Company to hamper the efforts of black porters to better their lot, Howard furthered the enemies' interests and established that he was unconcerned about the status of black Americans. Howard, in short, was guilty of racial betrayal. The Pullman Company mistreated its black employees. The company only hired blacks to serve as porters and maids, the lowest-paying positions. These workers had to perform some duties for which they were not paid, and, moreover, had to use large shares of their wages to pay for lodging, uniforms, and food. Though the Pullman Company was not akin to, say, the Klan, it clearly discriminated against black workers. The company, furthermore, fought the black porters' union so intently because it wanted to keep discriminating against them. Thus, Howard's representation was effectively an effort to protect the company's discriminatory ways. Needless to say, blacks cannot assist employers in their maltreatment of black laborers.

Now some might contend that Howard was merely advocating on behalf of his clients. But black attorneys cannot be authorized to use their skills to help a business subjugate black workers. If lawyers are allowed to ensconce employment discrimination while also being inoculated from charges of treachery, then the very idea of racial solidarity is mocked and other blacks

---

[30] *Perry Howard Calls Pullman Porters Red*, Afro-American, Oct. 17, 1925, at 1; George Saranac, *Letter to the Editor*, Afro-American, Oct. 24, 1925, at 9; A. *Philip Randolph Answers New Questions for Perry Howard*, The Messenger, Dec. 1923, at 381.

[31] *The National Republican Committee and Perry W. Howard*, The Messenger, Feb. 1926, at 52; Communism and Socialism Pamphlets 26–27 (1948).

would justifiably feel that the group norms are perverse and consequently illegitimate.[32]

A black man as high in Republican ranks as Howard was unusual, as was assistant solicitor with the U.S. Post Office. But William C. Hueston, a former magistrate judge in Gary, Indiana, beat the odds. He did not, however, avoid *Uncle Tom*. Hueston was supposedly a sellout for speaking on behalf of Republican Senator James E. Watson at a political event in 1932. Watson had previously been a member of the Ku Klux Klan and voted for Judge John J. Parker for the Supreme Court, who the NAACP aggressively opposed. Watson, though, supported Hueston's bid to become an assistant solicitor. At a campaign event, a black onlooker was appalled that Hueston championed an avowed anti-Negro politician, proving that "[t]here are plenty bandannas in the country still." "The only difference in the bandanna now," he continued, "is that the Uncle Toms have pulled off their overalls and put on a stove-pipe hat and a swallow-tail coat, but they are bandannas none the less."[33]

By lauding Senator Watson, Judge Hueston lit a smoke signal that notified blacks that he rejected black solidarity, making him a natural target for *Uncle Tom* derision. In 1926, Sen. Watson was embarrassed before the country when William M. Rogers, a Klansman, testified before the Senate that Watson was a card-carrying member of the Klan. Although Hueston had accomplished many great feats on behalf of black Americans, a black citizen of the era could reasonably equate public support for Watson with racial treachery. One has no reason to conclude that Hueston had nothing but the utmost adoration for his people. Yet one who has endorsed a Jim Crow politician has given his critics enough ammunition to support the charge that his devotion to the race contains gross impurities. His black solidarity was tainted. Thus, the onlooker who witnessed Hueston laud a senator with Klan ties and a dastardly voting record had the requisite evidence to conclude that Hueston's black solidarity was compromised and therefore violated the norm that punishes blacks for lacking concern for the race.[34]

Much closer to the levers of power was Chicago congressman Oscar DePriest. Under that extra pressure, *Uncle Tom* indictments were sure to form. DePriest aggressively wielded *Uncle Tom* himself, once remarking that the black community had too many "Uncle Toms" and they needed "to be dead in heaven or some other place." But he encountered someone who outflanked

---

[32] *Perry Howard*, Afro-American, Oct. 17, 1925, at 9.

[33] L. Coles, *This Reader Thinks Judge Hueston Wears a Bandanna Handkerchief on His Head*, Afro-American, Feb. 6, 1932, at 16; *William C. Hueston Appointed to Post in Solicitor's Office*, Afro-American, June 7, 1930, at 1.

[34] *Declare Watson Carried Klan Card; Had Evans Backing*, New York Times, Oct. 2, 1926, at 1.

him, Herbert Newton. A prominent communist in Chicago's South Side neighborhood, Newton opposed DePriest during the 1932 election. Newton had reasons for censuring DePriest. He claimed that DePriest: spoke on the floor of Congress against unemployment insurance; supported a bill that would have established a segregated school in North Dakota; never voiced support for the Scottsboro Boys; and, as a landlord, evicted black tenants because they were behind in their rent. Although DePriest was typically thought of as an aggressive black politician, the tale establishes that black insiders would always have critics. DePriest, in any event, likely ignored Newton's taunts. Newton, after all, received less than 2 percent of the vote.[35]

During the 1934 midterm elections, however, DePriest faced his first black major party opponent, Democrat Arthur Mitchell. Professing fidelity to the New Deal as the solution to the Great Depression, Mitchell defeated DePriest. The loss startled the NAACP. As the only black congressman, DePriest was close with the organization. Claude Barnett, the head of the Associated Negro Press and a Chicago resident, told the NAACP that despite Mitchell seeming "friendly" and "intelligent" he was an *Uncle Tom* upon closer inspection. Barnett also alerted the NAACP to the remark of a white editor of the *Jackson Daily News*, Frederick Sullens. Sullens said that he was thrilled that DePriest would no longer roam the halls of Congress and that Mitchell was a "white man's nigger." The notion that Mitchell was an *Uncle Tom* spread thereafter. The case against Mitchell was that he continuously proved a tool for whites and was uninterested in working on behalf of blacks. The portrait of Mitchell as an *Uncle Tom* was completed in 1935 after he said he could "see Italy's viewpoint, too" regarding the country's invasion of Ethiopia. The *Courier* excoriated Mitchell for excusing an unprovoked invasion of a black country and demanded that he become more informed and either reflect black thought or keep quiet. His statement, the paper characterized, was "like an Uncle Tom trying to carry water on both shoulders." A norm that forces blacks to parrot the community's popular opinion, however, is destructive.[36]

Six years later, Mitchell again felt the misery that *Uncle Tom* accusations breed. This time, though, he deserved it. Congressman Mitchell wrote a letter to President Franklin Roosevelt endorsing Senator James F. Byrnes of South Carolina for a Supreme Court vacancy. The NAACP was taken aback because

[35] *Calls DePriest "Uncle Tom,"* Afro-American, July 16, 1932, at 3; E; Hazel Rowley, Richard Wright: The Life and Times 94 (2001); Baker, *DePriest Cancels Address to North Carolina Tailors,* Afro-American, May 3, 1930, at A1; *DePriest Urges Voters to Enter Dem. Primary,* Afro-American, May 30, 1931, at 17.
[36] *Congressman Mitchell Sees the Italian Viewpoint in the War,* Pittsburgh Courier, Oct. 12, 1935, at 1.

Byrnes was anathema to the civil rights community for his pro-segregationist positions. Byrnes was not a rabble-rousing segregationist like many of his contemporaries. He did, nonetheless, defend Jim Crow. For Mitchell to have supported his nomination was viewed as a slap in the face to blacks. According the NAACP, Mitchell's letter "takes us back to Uncle Tom days."[37]

Mitchell was not a particularly powerful congressman and President Roosevelt was likely to disregard his wishes. He could have, therefore, chosen any legal thinker he wanted. For a black politician to publically champion a pro-segregationist politician for the Supreme Court was wrongheaded. When black Chicagoans who voted to send Mitchell to Congress learned that he wanted Byrnes to be one of the nine justices to decide the constitutionality of the various laws that subjugated them to second-class citizenship, they could justifiably conclude that their congressman violated the norm that punishes blacks for lacking concern about the race. His treachery matched that of Judge Hueston.

Other blacks were indicted for abdicating their responsibilities toward the group. Take Clarence R. Pope, an official for Harlem's Works Project Administration (WPA) in the late 1930s. During the Great Depression, everyone struggled to find employment, especially blacks. FDR's New Deal ushered in a host of government projects designed to revive the floundering economy. The WPA was one. But when Harlem's WPA bureau was found to have been giving jobs earmarked for blacks to whites instead and at inflated salaries, local citizens and groups were outraged. Many caught flak and the black project supervisor, Clarence Pope, had his racial loyalty questioned. Pope, some believed, betrayed "the best interests of approximately 1,200 Negros workers on the project." Because of his "'Uncle Tom' attitude' ... [which was] detrimental to the welfare of the Negro workers," some argued that he should be replaced. When blacks had alarmingly high unemployment rates, while also facing increasing job discrimination, Pope was an obvious and appropriate target for *Uncle Tom* criticisms. Indeed, because he gave away jobs marked for blacks to whites instead, he violated the norm that required blacks to care about the race. Few blacks would have imagined that a black man shepherded a program that stripped them of employment opportunities, possibly for some sort of personal reward.[38]

---

[37] Dennis S. Nordin, The New Deal's Black Congressman: A Life of Arthur Wergs Mitchell 71 (1997); Robert J. Schneller, Breaking the Color Barrier: The U.S. Naval Academy's First Black Midshipmen and the Struggle for Racial Equality 73–75 (2005); Weiss, Farewell to the Party of Lincoln 88; *Rap Mitchell's Endorsing of Judge Byrnes*, Chicago Defender, June 28, 1941, at 4; *James F. Byrnes and the Politics of Segregation*, 56 *The Historian* 645, 645–54 (1994).

[38] Edgar T. Rouzeau, *Enlist Congressman's Aide in Fight against Discrimination*, Pittsburgh Courier, July 17, 1937, at 4.

In 1945, assistant to Secretary of War Stimson Truman H. Gibson made a huge verbal gaffe after seemingly criticizing blacks in the 92nd Division during World War II. Gibson said that "most of the 92nd Division officers killed in combat have been Negro officers, which reflected more credit on their courage than their judgment. The best answer is to appoint officers, not because they are colored or white, but because they are good, and the division is trying to do that." Columnist George Schuyler, who himself had suffered *Uncle Tom* accusations, assailed Gibson. Schuyler depicted Gibson as espousing the racist arguments that had been used to keep blacks from serving alongside whites. To blame the higher casualty rates of black junior officers on their lack of judgment was "an unforgiveable slur," according to Schuyler. Gibson, moreover, blamed "the alleged failure" of the 92nd Division on the "handicaps of excessive illiteracy and inadequate training," and because "many of them lack a clear conviction of what they are fighting for." Schuyler said that Gibson was "an appeaser and one of the Nouveau Uncle Toms since taking office" who should resign.

Others joined in to brand Gibson as an *Uncle Tom*. One woman insisted that Gibson should have been deemed an *Uncle Tom* for even accepting the position as aide to the war secretary after William Hastie resigned from the same post after being unable to change the War Department's segregation policies. Gibson's comments were reputedly so reprehensible that he was "branded beyond deliverance." Soldiers, of course, were likewise disgusted. One veteran said that "Gibson is one man I hate and he is an Uncle Tom," and another said that, absent his resignation, Gibson's title should be changed to "Uncle Tom Appeaser."[39]

Three years later, Gibson had another public brush with *Uncle Tom*. In 1948, a couple of years before the Korean War, the Senate Armed Services Committee held hearings on selective service legislation. A. Philip Randolph testified during the hearings and told the senators that even during war blacks might choose civil disobedience over service if segregation continued. Randolph, in fact, said that he might personally advocate that blacks not participate. His words startled the committee members. Oregon Senator Wayne Morse said that Randolph's pronouncements were treasonous. Randolph retorted that he "would anticipate Nationwide terrorism against Negroes who

[39] George S. Schuyler, *View and Review*, Pittsburgh Courier, Mar. 31, 1945, at 7; Julius J. Adams, *Truman Gibson: "Uncle Tom" or Useful Public Servant*, New York Amsterdam News, Apr. 14, 1945, at 2A; Mary Ruth King, *Blasts "Uncle Toms" Who Sell Out Race*, Chicago Defender, Apr. 14, 1945, at 12; *A Former Soldier, 92nd Not a Failure But Gibson Is*, Chicago Defender, Apr. 28, 1945, at 12. Coxswain James B. Arnold, *What the People Say*, Chicago Defender, Apr. 14, 1945, at 12.

refused to participate in the armed forces, but I believe that that is the price we have to pay for the democracy that we want.'[40]

Gibson testified afterward and strongly disagreed with Randolph. He told the senators that he expected blacks to be patriotic and participate in any war effort. In response, Harlem Congressman Adam Clayton Powell called Gibson a "rubber stamp Uncle Tom." In his memoir, Gibson maintained that Randolph's views were imprudent. Gibson argued that Randolph discounted the social zeitgeist of the era because blacks sitting out in a war effort would result in them being labeled traitors. Randolph "ignored the political atmosphere of those years," Truman insisted. "African Americans rejecting the call of their country would be denounced as traitors. That was the last thing we needed if we hoped to build on whatever gains we had made in World War II."[41]

Branding Gibson an *Uncle Tom* for arguing that blacks should participate in a possible war effort was destructive. Gibson's belief that sitting out a war would damage blacks' overall interests was a reasonable position and in no way suggested that his dedication to the race was compromised. Whether blacks should fight abroad while being discriminated against at home was an issue that blacks should have debated. As long as debate participants were truly dedicated to lessening racial marginalization, then criticizing those who favored involvement was deeply unfair.

William Levi Dawson replaced Arthur Mitchell as the congressional representative of Illinois' first district (Chicago). During Dawson's tenure, Harlem's Adam Clayton Powell, in many ways, was the unofficial congressman of black America. Whereas Powell was an agitator, Dawson was anything but. Dawson's temperament and his relative silence on white supremacy constantly produced *Uncle Tom* accusations. As one wrote in 1945, "in spite of Congressman Powell's weakness for making ... irresponsible statements from time to time, he is no 'Uncle Tom.' On the other hand, Mr. Dawson's intense desire to play ward politics in order to get along with his white colleagues, often causes him to veer very close to being an 'Uncle Tom.'"[42]

Powell and Dawson had bad blood, with the former frequently maligning the latter as an *Uncle Tom*. One of their clashes occurred after the 1952 National Democratic Convention's party platform omitted strong support for civil rights. Senator Herbert Humphrey, a staunch supporter of civil rights, told

---

[40] George Lipsitz, Rainbow at Midnight: Labor and Culture in the 1940s 340 (1994).
[41] Truman K. Gibson, Knocking Down Barriers: My Fight for Black America: A Memoir 230–31 (2005).
[42] Earl Brown, *Timely Topics*, New York Amsterdam News, Dec. 29, 1945, at 8.

Powell that the platform was weakened because "Congressman Dawson made a speech which killed every effort of any of us to do anything to improve [it]." Powell was incensed. The sabotage of the platform, Powell stated, resulted from Dawson's "Uncle Tomming" from "behind closed doors." Powell criticized "Chicago's Uncle Tom" further: "If the National Democratic Committee dares to bring William Dawson into this town at any time during the election they might as well forget trying to carry Harlem or New York State. One thing we Harlem Negroes decided a long time ago: We don't want any Uncle Toms north of 110th Street." Powell said he refrained from deriding Dawson for eight years, but his destruction of the civil rights platform was inexcusable.[43]

If Dawson hindered the efforts to strengthen the pro–civil rights rhetoric in the party's platform, then that would have been racial treachery. Powell's portrayal, however, excluded important nuance. In 1952, any Democratic Party platform had to get by the Southern pro-segregationists, the so-called Dixiecrats. Dawson's speech may have irked Northern liberals. But it helped secure Dixiecrat support. And although the plank might not have been as strong as what Powell and Humphries wanted, it was, at the time, the most pro–civil rights plank in the party's history. It thus appears that questioning Dawson's racial loyalty was quite misguided, and that he was unsuccessfully prosecuted for violating constructive norms. He may have contributed to the weakening of the platform, but he very well might have concluded that weakening the platform was necessary. Powell was well within his rights to criticize Dawson if he believed the Chicago congressman erred. To charge Dawson with betrayal, however, was destructive and unfair.[44]

Also illuminating of how the black insider always operated under the threat of *Uncle Tom* is the story of E. Frederic Morrow and the so-called kissing case. Morrow was an administrative aide and advisor to President Dwight Eisenhower. Reporters, however, joked when he was named administrative officer for special projects that his most important task would be assigning parking places for White House staff members. An obituary described Morrow as an outspoken proponent of equal rights and integration, a man who pushed for minority and female inclusion into the Republican Party.

But in 1958, amid the kissing case in Monroe, North Carolina, Morrow was branded as an *Uncle Tom*. The incident involved two young black boys – David "Fuzzy" Simpson, seven, and Hanover Thompson, nine – who were invited

---

[43] Evelyn Cunningham, *Adam Powell Blasts Rep. Dawson Again*, Pittsburgh Courier, Aug. 9, 1952, at 20; *Powell Hits Dem Plank, Dawson*, Chicago Defender, Aug. 9, 1952, at 1; *Sabotage of Rights Plank Blamed on "Uncle Toms,"* St. Joseph Gazette, Aug. 4, 1952, at 1; Christopher Manning, William L. Dawson and the Limits of Black Electoral Leadership 124–25 (2009).

[44] *Dawson Guides Rights Plank Through*, Afro-American, Aug. 2, 1952, at 2.

to join a group of five white children, two of whom were girls. A kissing game ensued between Thompson and white eight-year-old Sissy Sutton. After learning of the event, the police arrested Simpson and Thompson, who were later convicted of rape. Simpson received twelve years; Hanover received fourteen. During the height of the controversy, Morrow wrote a letter to the black newspaper the *Los Angeles Tribune* stating that President Eisenhower would be unable to intervene on behalf of the two boys. Morrow also defended himself from scrutiny by noting that his duties in the White House were unconnected to race relations matters and the president's record on race. He attempted to dispel the notion that he was "being used as a cat's paw to secure full justice before the law." The *Tribune* realized that Morrow lacked clout to get presidential intervention. But the newspaper believed Morrow was chosen to deliver the public response because the administration hoped a black messenger would mollify the community. In light of that, the paper wondered why he stayed in the administration rather than quit. The paper concluded he "was nothing but an *Uncle Tom*" for remaining.[45]

The *Los Angeles Tribune* erred in denouncing Morrow for remaining with the Eisenhower administration. He violated no constructive racial loyalty norm. If Morrow discouraged the president from intervening to prove that he could be as tough on blacks as any white man could in hopes that he would personally benefit, then sanction would have been proper. But that did not happen here. If Morrow did resign in protest, the symbolism and narrative would have been powerful. But to not do so is not tantamount to racial treachery. He still could have used his insider status to petition on behalf of black folk. Morrow was victimized by destructive racial loyalty norm management.

The racial loyalty norm management for black insiders was more constructive than it was for black leaders. That black insiders were more prone to racial treachery has an easy explanation. By becoming a participant in longstanding institutions, the black insider reached a level that the overwhelming majority of the race never could. Their attachments to the black community likely weakened as they functioned in a world with few black faces. Perhaps some lost sight of white supremacy's salience because their status inoculated them from many manners of discrimination. Others might have realized the

45   E. Frederic Morrow, *First Black Aide At White House, Dies*, Jet, Aug. 8, 1994, at 16–17; Kennedy, Interracial Intimacies; 196–97; Timothy B. Tyson, *Robert F. Williams, "Black Power," and the Roots of the African American Freedom Struggle*, 85 Journal of American History 540, 551–52 (1998); *President's Aide Morrow Nothing But an Uncle Tom*, Los Angeles Tribune, Jan. 16, 1959, at 8; *Mail Box Pure Quirk of Chance Tribune*, Los Angeles Tribune, Jan. 16, 1959, at 8; *Mail box Republican Aide to Republican County Committeeman-Over*, Los Angeles Tribune, Jan. 23, 1959, at 9.

personal benefits to be reaped from being useful in maintaining the status quo. Both explanations evidence an abandonment of racial solidarity organized around the concept that all blacks must be committed to ridding society of its antiblack elements. These were the sorts of figures who would not advocate on behalf of blacks in various contexts. Thus, to protect their legal interests, blacks were wise to monitor insiders to ensure fidelity to the mission of resisting racial subordination. As each of these insiders operated, they appreciated the expectation that they would remain racially loyal. This could only help foster black solidarity among a class of individuals whose vocations put them in close proximity with influential decision makers. Moderating the behavior of black insiders, in short, could only help blacks in their quest to uproot a cruel legal regime.

UNCLE TOM PUTS ON A SHOW

Uncle Tom frequently tormented black entertainers. To reshape American society, blacks grappled with pernicious stereotypes that permeated at home and abroad. The underlying argument is that it is morally more defensible to suppress a race that is inferior than do the same to one that is undeniably equal. Much like supposed innate inferiority was used to justify slavery, it too could excuse racial apartheid.

American culture regularly promulgated stereotypes about blacks. Here, three are especially salient. The first held that blacks were content with domination. This meant that legal equality was misguided because blacks actually preferred subordination.

The second depicted blacks as needing legal restraint; for if free, their savage bestial instincts would be uncaged, producing white victims. This rendered segregation laws compulsory. This stereotype was infamously featured in D. W. Griffith's racist silent film *The Birth of a Nation* (1915). President Woodrow Wilson, after a White House screening of the film, reputedly remarked, "It's like wiring history with lightning. And my only regret is that it is all terribly true." Wilson biographer Jon Milton Cooper disputes the veracity of the statement, but nonetheless argues that Griffith intimated that the president endorsed his film. If Americans thought the chief executive believed propaganda depicting blacks as brutes, racial progress had little chance until that stereotype was exposed as a lie.[46]

---

[46] Gadwick, The Reel Civil War 113; John Milton Cooper, Woodrow Wilson: A Biographer 272 (2009).

The third stereotype mocked blacks as two-dimensional cartoons and not well-rounded people with the same aspirations and most important, the same intellectual capabilities as whites. If popular culture corroborated any of these three stereotypes, Jim Crow needed not worry about a deathbed.

The issue here is that many felt that black entertainers promoted these stereo-types that reinforced laws that subjugated the race. That is to say, when black entertainers played dehumanizing roles, they legitimated the racial hierarchy. To recreate America so that it truly lived up to the ideals of the Declaration of Independence – that all men were created equal – black entertainers had to eschew stereotypes that even hinted at blacks' inferiority. Indeed, much like Frederick Douglass's 1854 speech that debunked the myth of innate Negro inferiority that justified slavery, blacks needed to stop playing demeaning roles that validated second-class citizenship.[47]

In the entertainment industry context, racial loyalty norms were frequently managed to maintain an image that blacks found dignified. When discussing a black play in Chicago, for instance, a writer fondly noted that "[t]here are no mammies or Uncle Toms in the play." When the *Philadelphia Tribune* praised entertainers Leon Gardner and Harold Simpson, the newspaper specifically mentioned that they did not "Uncle Tom" but rather offered a "smart" and "entertaining" show. An ex-slave named Colonel Howard Divinity, in con-trast, was deemed an embarrassment because he allowed whites call him "Champeen Chicken Thief of the Confederate Army." Comic relief for poor whites, he wore a tag around his neck that read, "If lost, return to any point in Mississippi and he'll get home from there." The *Defender* branded him a first-class "Uncle Tom," and implored readers to not fret because while blacks like him still roamed, the "grim reaper will soon end their worries as well as stop them from worrying us."[48]

As was true of the "Champeen Chicken Thief of the Confederate Army," names blacks chose for themselves typically fueled *Uncle Tom* sanctions. Dave Peyton, writing in the *Defender*, for instance, reviewed Lawrence Harrison and his orchestra who performed in Chicago in the summer of 1928. Although Peyton opined that the band had "improved wonderfully," their name – the Alabamians – disturbed him. He declared, "We do not have to take these Uncle Tom names if we have the [goods]." Peyton wanted blacks to avoid

---

[47] Frederick Douglass, *The Claims of the Negro Ethnologically Considered* found in Frederick Douglass: Selected Speeches and Writings 282–98 (Editor Philip S. Foner 1999).

[48] A. L. Jackson, *The Onlooker*, Chicago Defender, Apr. 28, 1923, at 12; *New Novelty Act on Eastern Tour*, Philadelphia Tribune, June 21, 1934, at 11; *A Few of 'Em Still Left*, Chicago Defender, Nov. 3, 1923, at 1.

debasing themselves with names that not only disparaged the individual performers, but the entire race.[49]

In 1929, Armond W. Scott, who later became a judge in Washington, DC, scolded supposed "Uncle Tom" comedians who lampooned the race to appease whites. Scott argued that these comics were self-interested – willing to disparage blacks if that furthered their careers. Scott, that is, rebuked blacks for not caring about the race. Similarly, a Harlem actor named William Smith assailed many black play producers because they "exploit [their] race for the benefit of [themselves] and the white backers." Smith insisted that blacks ignore these *Uncle Toms* because they hurt the race.[50]

White appetites were a large part of the problem. Many only consumed black arts and entertainment that met prejudiced expectations of blackness. Some blacks, therefore, felt they had to suppress part of themselves – their full humanity – in order to receive white support. In that vein, Kelly Miller assailed whites for only acknowledging blackness if it was presented submissively or crudely. Presentations of proud and dignified Negroes, however, were repudiated. The case of a nude Paul Robeson statue was evidence, Miller contended. In the summer of 1930, the Philadelphia Art Alliance, fearing racial controversy, refused to allow a display in the Rittenhouse Square of a nude statue of Robeson, a black actor and activist. Although white nudity was never barred, black nudity apparently was. Miller wrote that "there is no place for the cultured and refined Negro in high social life, he cannot be rectified in art. No refined, cultured lady or gentleman under cover of Negro face or features hang on the walls of the parlors of the elite, nor in the salons and art galleries." Miller claimed this was true because whites only envisioned blacks as deferential servants, comic buffoons, or *Uncle Toms*.[51]

This held true for music as well. In 1934, one white reporter considered Noble Sissle's band too "sophisticated" and wondered why more "colored bands don't follow Cab Calloway and his Di-de-ho style." The reporter, apparently, rejected classy black performance. Such terrain was reserved for whites. The *Pittsburgh Courier*'s James E. Bowen framed this as another example of "narrow-minded whites" who could only appreciate the "'Uncle Tom' attitude."

[49] Dave Peyton, *The Musical Bunch*, Chicago Defender, June 2, 1928, at 6.
[50] No *Jokes in the Douglass Speeches*, Afro-American, Mar. 2, 1929, at 6; *Don'ld Heywood Flayed by Actor for New Play*, Afro-Americans, Sept. 10, 1932, at 10.
[51] Kelly Miller, *Negro Nudity in Art*, New York Amsterdam News, June 11, 1930, at 24; Scott Allen Nollen, Paul Robeson: Film Pioneer 29 (2010); Philip S. Foner, Paul Robeson Speaks 30 (1978).

Bowen, and those who agreed with his critique, likely wanted to fashion a better image of the group that affected blacks' legal status.[52]

Whereas some blacks sought to heighten the opinion of the American Negro through performance, others bowed down, picking up the humiliating portrayals that most blacks wanted to remain discarded. Many deemed the willingness to play stereotypes for money indefensible. More confounding, however, were those who did it for free. Arthur Davis, writing in the *New Journal and Guide* in 1935, criticized blacks who turned their race into comic fodder on the *Major Bowes Hour*, a popular radio program. Davis understood why some blacks submitted to racism and took jobs in show business that offended their dignity. But, he wrote, "I for the life of me ... cannot understand why perfectly normal, intelligent Negroes, who ordinarily speak fairly decent English, will go to New York for Major Bowes' Hour and make fools of themselves talking brokenly about ham, pork chops, etc., and get nothing for it." Davis wondered if the radio show sought out blacks or if *Uncle Toms* volunteered their services. One reader, in a letter to the editor, agreed with Davis, writing that nothing was funny about portraying the race as being satisfied with having a "bite to eat and a roof over our heads." The reader was correct. Such performances misrepresented blacks as being content with their unequal lot as did the *Uncle Tom's Cabin* minstrel shows. Only this time the blacks made the quips themselves. Such denigration reinforced the social caste system and the laws that undergirded it.[53]

With careers at stake, many blacks appreciated those who refused to play up stereotypes to make it in the entertainment industry. This was particularly true for Hollywood films. In countless pre-1960 newspaper articles, blacks lamented that Hollywood portrayed them, not as three-dimensional persons, but as *Uncle Toms*. In a 1937 article, J. A. Rogers noted that he had only watched one American film with a non-"Uncle Tom" black character – *Arrowsmith* (1931), based on Sinclair Lewis's Pulitzer Prize-winning 1925 novel. "Care, however, was taken to show that he was a foreign Negro." Apparently American audiences would reject an American black in a non-*Uncle Tom* role.[54]

A huge concern of Rogers was the international implications of these pictures. American cinema was not confined to the country's borders. The world watched it. These films heavily shaped foreign perceptions of black Americans

---

[52] James E. Bowen, *Noble Sissle and Ethel Waters Steal Spotlight as '34 Radio Sensations But Whites Knock 'Em*, Pittsburgh Courier, Feb. 3, 1934, at A1.

[53] Arthur P. Davis, *Cross Currents*, New Journal and Guide, Dec. 28, 1935, at 8; Alice Buster, Letter to the editor, *Clowning Not Appreciated*, Afro-American, Apr. 8, 1939, at 14.

[54] J. A. Rogers, *Rogers Attacks Anti-Negro Propaganda of Movie Industry*, Pittsburgh Courier, May 1, 1937, at 14, Joseph McBride, Searching for John Ford: A Life 186 (2001).

and not for the better. Porter Roberts, writing in the *Courier*, agreed. He criticized the naiveté of "all [the] Negroes who claim that 'Uncle Tom' type of motion pictures don't influence the different nationalities to treat them like dogs when they visit other countries!"[55]

Some argued that Hollywood's negative portrayal of blacks was intentional. Earl J. Moris wrote of actress Theresa Harris in *Toy Wife* (1938), whose best scenes were omitted and, therefore, she was depicted less humanly. Morris concluded that the reason for deleting those scenes was because "she would have endeared herself to the world and the race would have been proud of this fine artists [*sic*]."

J. A. Rogers called for a boycott. Earl Moris too saw black solidarity, organization, and money as an answer to the "Uncle Tom role" problem. He, however, opted for positive reinforcement, wanting blacks to support movie companies that favorably depicted blacks. When *The Duke Is Tops* (1938) was released, blacks were pleasantly surprised by what was called "beyond doubt the most lavish and outstanding all-Race picture released to date." According to one movie reviewer, "The elimination of parts so commonly injected into many major pictures that represent the Race in Uncle Tom fashion is most gratifying." Moris's strategy would have required blacks to support this movie to convince Hollywood that it could make money by making films with respectable black characters. This strategy carried obvious legal benefits. Heightening the image of the Negro could only help the race's efforts in securing the total bundle of rights American citizenship had to offer.[56]

In 1940, a deal was supposedly struck after the black press' steady criticism, establishing how black solidarity organized around antipathy toward *Uncle Toms*, in this case theatrical *Uncle Toms*, could produce gains. Hollywood guaranteed films "showing the 'real side' of the Negro." Arthur Dreifus, a film director, said, "I share the opinion … that the Negro, through his papers has prove[d] that he will not tolerate being exploited and ridiculed on the screen and feel that in order to produce successful all-colored pictures, a company must film stories showing the true side of the race." Dreifus's comment demonstrates that black newspapers' efforts of enforcing racial loyalty proved beneficial. By painting actors' decisions to portray stereotypes as a form of treachery, black newspapers helped drive a message.[57]

---

[55] Rogers, *Rogers Attacks Anti-Negro Propaganda of Movie Industry*.
[56] Id.; Porter Roberts, *Praise and Criticism*, Pittsburgh Courier, Dec. 24, 1938, at 21; Earl J. Moris, *Should Negroes Ban White Motion Pictures*, Pittsburgh Courier, Sept. 24, 1938, at 21; The Scribe, *Scribe Puts Okay on "Duke Is Tops,"* Chicago Defender, Nov. 5, 1938, at 19.
[57] L. D. Wright, *The Weekly Watchtower*, Atlanta Daily World, Feb. 5, 1940, at 6.

Black newspapers' messages resonated if letters to the editor reflected the black populace's mood. A man named Arthur Williams, for instance, writing to the *New York Amsterdam News*, stated that blacks should not appear in movies at all if they were relegated to demeaning terrain because the "Uncle Tom days are gone." Williams' letter correctly identifies the *Uncle Tom* problem as a two-way street. Black actors were forced into "Uncle Tom, uneducated, or jitterburg roles if [they wanted] to work." If blacks continued to play *Uncle Toms*, though, studios had no motive to improve. As a spokesman for Columbia Pictures remarked, "as long as there are colored persons ... willing to play Uncle Tom roles or through buffoonery to barter the dignity of their race, it seems likely that Uncle Toms and buffoonery will continue." Some blacks, consequently, implored black entertainers to pursue less glamorous vocations absent a Hollywood epiphany. Some, like Canada Lee, had the *Uncle Tom* elements of a script excised as he did in *Lifeboat* (1944). And Lena Horne altogether refused to play an *Uncle Tom* role in the Broadway production *St. Louis Woman* (1946). Lee and Horne, though, were exceptions. They were able to maintain their careers. But others were not so lucky. Theresa Harris, a reputedly great dancer, actress, and singer, refused to take "Uncle Tom roles" and became unemployable. Taking a stand on principle is difficult if it makes one's dream profession unavailable.[58]

But black folk, however, no longer sat silently. Movie boycotts and protests were common in the early 1940s. In 1942, for instance, blacks picketed *Tales of Manhattan*. Many believed that the film featuring Paul Robeson, Ethel Waters, and Eddie "Rochester" Anderson contained *Uncle Tom* characters. Black movie stars, subsequently, strategized at Anderson's home to dissuade any further picketing of *Tales of Manhattan* and other pictures. With their plan devised, the actors responded that their roles were not "disgraceful." Appreciating the institutions that nourished these protests, the stars claimed, rather unconvincingly, that the black press was not truly interested in procuring better parts for black actors. If black newspapers endeavored to improve

---

[58] Nell Dodson, *Behind the 8-Ball*, New York Amsterdam News, Dec. 16, 1939, at 13; Verna Arvey, *Wiling to Barter Race Dignity, Perpetuate Uncle Tom*, Afro-American, Feb. 19, 1944, at 8; Margaret Goss, *Voice of the People*, New Journal and Guide, June 10, 1944, at C8; Harry Levette, *Canada Lee Has "Uncle Tom" Phrases Cut from Script in Fox's "Lifeboat,"* Afro-American, Sept. 11, 1943, at 10; *Deny Lena Horne's Movie Career Halted*, Cleveland Call and Post, Oct. 13, 1945, at 1A; Herman Hill, *"'Rochester,' Theresa Harris Teamed Anew in 'What's Buzzin,' Cousin' Film,"* Pittsburgh Courier, July 31, 1943, at 20; Daniel J. Leab, From Sambo to Superspade: The Black Experience in Motion Pictures 130 (1976); Arthur Williams, *Racial Exploitation*, New York Amsterdam News, Sept. 17, 1938, at 10; *Would End Movie Evil*, Pittsburgh Courier, Nov. 5, 1938, at 14.

the black image in cinema, insisted the black actors, they would have used their revenue to create a black-owned studio for black actors.[59]

Mightily as they tried, black entertainers unsuccessfully kept the masses out of their affairs. The NAACP launched a campaign to advance a better image of the race in popular culture. In 1943, the *Afro-American* hosted a round-table discussion with prominent black actors concerning black treatment in Hollywood and the NAACP's enterprise of bettering black portrayals in films. The black actors generally felt that the NAACP could not reform Hollywood and predicted that movie studios, rather than provide blacks better roles, would provide them no roles at all. The actors were particularly incensed that the NAACP failed to consult them first. And again, black actors rejected assertions that their roles belittled the race. Clarence Muse, one roundtable participant, was unsure why he had a reputation for playing *Uncle Tom* roles. "Just what do we mean by 'Uncle Tom' roles," he inquired, concluding that "[t]hose whom the race would destroy they first call 'Uncle Tom.'"[60]

As blacks in America squabbled over the matter, blacks in the military stationed abroad entered the debate. Their words further corroborated the argument that agitation was required. During World War II, black soldiers were stationed all over the world, including countries that showed these films. Without any contact with American blacks, these pictures negatively shaped how these soldiers were perceived. As Langston Hughes, who called for blacks to stop playing "Uncle Toms for celluloid white folks," once wrote, these films were "why so many otherwise uniformed people all over the earth think so disparagingly of the American Negro." Many soldiers agreed, reporting that the locals thought poorly of them based on American cinema. Because the movie industry generally embraced the War Department's desire to showcase "national unity," many films included "throw-in" black characters. Movies being more inclusive worsened locals' opinions of blacks. More roles did not mean better roles. And the roles were definitely not better. According to a 1945 study of 100 films with black characters, in seventy-five instances blacks were played disparagingly. Only in twelve cases were blacks portrayed favorably. As Edward Mapp wrote, "Although more Negro performers acted in films, the specter of the old stereotype prevailed."[61]

59 *Film Stars Answer Charges by Public Protesting "Uncle Tom" Roles*, Chicago Defender, Aug. 29, 1942, at 7; Polly E. McLean, *Mass Communication, Popular Culture, and Racism* found in Racism and Anti-Racism in World Perspective 97 (Editor Benjamin P. Bowser 1995).
60 Ralph Matthews, *The Truth about Hollywood and the Race Issue from the Actors' Viewpoint*, Afro-American, Jan. 9, 1943, at 11.
61 Langston Hughes, *Negro Digest*, Apr., 1943, at 19–20; Leab, From Sambo to Superspade, at 119; Mapp, Blacks in American Films 34.

During the Second World War, many black enlisted men implored black actors to rebuff "anti-Negro roles." Pvt. Charles W. Brown Jr., for instance, wrote to the *Associated Negro Press* with the call that his plea be published in black newspapers around the country. Brown's words, which are worth quoting at length, establish that he felt black actors were violating racial loyalty norms.

> [W]e embarked on a certain island at a designated time; when I say we, I am referring to a company of Negro marines. Of course we didn't expect a great deal of hospitality from the inhabitants of the island but everyone of us looked forward to a little consideration and understanding. Instead, the majority of the people were very hostile towards us; and they didn't falter in accepting ignorant and untrue fables of our people and their character. Consequently we were determined to fight all of our handicaps in any way and reasonable methods possible. Yes, we fought this menace by every means, with our hands and minds.
>
> . . .
>
> For instance, there is the picture called "The Flame of Barbary Coast," with a part in it for a Negro maid which should have never been accepted by a Negro for reasons of character expressed. There are many other examples such as Hattie McDaniel's role in the picture "Hi Beautiful." We were so ashamed of the part that we decided to select an individual to write a letter expressing the feelings of other GI's and ourselves toward those Uncle Tom parts (typical thought and attitude taken by most Negroes who are faced with such untrue and unjust portrayals of the character of the Negro as a whole). I so happened to be the one selected.
>
> Our main purpose of [wanting] this article printed in every colored paper is to give the people who accept these parts the advantage of reading and apprehending our embarrassment. In doing so, it may alter their decision in playing such roles in the future.[62]

Another man stationed in the Philippines penned a similar letter that the *Daily World* printed in 1945. "That Uncle Tom stuff is all over the islands here," the soldier reported. "It's true, actors must live, but if these Uncle Tom plays don't stop, the Negro race will never be respected and only hated throughout the world. We are trying hard to build our race up, but Negro actresses like Hattie McDaniel are making it almost impossible." Similarly, stationed in New Guinea, Julius W. Hill penned a missive to the *Defender* that hits a harmonious note. After seeing the movie *Three's a Family* (1943) featuring Hattie

---

[62] *Marines Say Films Poisoning Native Islanders Toward Race*, Atlanta Daily World, June 6, 1945, at 1.

McDaniel, many black infantrymen walked out of the theater. Hill wrote the letter to reveal to black actors that their work impacted the world. "Negro actors and actresses," he argued, "whose 'Uncle Tom' performances continue to give all racial groups an erroneous impression of the Negro race, should be just as seriously condemned as white actors and actresses whose performances are of a similar nature." The "Uncle Tom role" erected a towering perception that even the most captivating barrage of words could not topple. Although this dilemma was not unique to those stationed in the Pacific Islands, indeed, it was felt elsewhere, the eloquence of the soldiers stationed in those Asian nations is moving. If black actors had considered their pleas, they might have reconsidered their part in tarnishing the black image overseas.[63]

NAACP executive secretary Walter White, in 1945, spoke on how the Hollywood cinema damaged the black soldier's psyche. "It wouldn't be a bad idea," he pronounced, "for some of our colored movie 'stars' to see and hear the reaction, particularly of Negro soldiers, to their portrayal of the imbecilic 'Uncle Tom' roles." White warned black actors to react to the angst among black soldiers if they "hope[d] to remain in the films."[64]

Amid the large outcry, the NAACP created a Hollywood bureau that reviewed films and judged their content. The goal was "to counter the 'Uncle Tom' trend." The organization hoped to replicate the Catholic Church's Legion of Decency model, a Hollywood lobby that promoted Catholic interests in Tinsel Town. Unfortunately for the NAACP, many black actors battled the bureau even before it was constituted. Some actors, like Clarence Muse, wanted sway within the group. The problem, however, was that the same performers who sought influence embarrassed black soldiers and the race at large with their "disgusting Uncle Tom roles." The brainchild of this venture, Walter White, though, brushed off black actors' concerns and was singularly focused on his goal of creating a Hollywood more responsive to the sensibilities and concerns of blacks.

Many blacks thought that these actors feared that their careers would be damaged, that they would no longer be able to play maids or slow-witted janitors. "Perhaps Hattie McDaniel and Louis Beavers would no longer cavort in servants' uniforms and Clarence Muse himself might not be called upon to put on a grass skirt and prance about as a jungle savage, ostensibly portraying an African." Being self-interested and pursuing the vocation of one's choosing

---

[63] *Letters to Editor*, Atlanta Daily World, Aug. 24, 1945, at 6; Julius W. Hill, *GIs Overseas Resent Movie "Three's a Family*," Chicago Defender, July 28, 1945, at 12; Charles H. Loeb, *Our GI's in S. Pacific Fiercely Resent "Uncle Tom" Roles*, New York Amsterdam News, Sept. 1, 1945, at 1A.

[64] Walter White, *People, Politics and Places*, Chicago Defender, Mar. 24, 1945, at 13.

is not inherently wrong. People become angry, however, when the livelihood of the few negatively affects the entire race. A writer in 1946 captured the issue brilliantly, writing, "What is more important – jobs for a handful of Negroes playing so-called 'Uncle Tom' roles or the welfare of Negroes as a whole?" The NAACP made its decision: group above individual.

The actors, however, revealed a different concern: their careers. The Los Angeles branch of the NAACP hosted a dinner for black actors and actresses to give them an opportunity to air their grievances. Many of them were concerned that the NAACP's venture would reduce the amount of work they would get. One actress, for example, flatly stated that she wished to make a comeback and if that comeback involved a maid's outfit she would don it eagerly. But perhaps black actors wrongly discounted the possible benefits the bureau could have had on their careers. The outside pressure might have reformed Hollywood, resulting in roles that black actors would have found more desirable. The black masses, nevertheless, firmly backed White and the NAACP. One implored White to "[s]mash Hollywood's practice of using Negroes" for debasing roles. Another commented that "[t]hese 'actors' … and 'actresses' … are more like white man [*sic*] operating machines who don't give a thought to the fact that they harm Negroes more than they help them."[65]

The NAACP's efforts extended to the television show *Amos 'n' Andy. Amos 'n' Andy* started as a radio show program created by Charles Correll and Freeman Gosden, two white men. With whites doing the voice acting, the radio program featured black characters speaking in broken English. To the chagrin of many blacks, the show played up racial stereotypes. Immensely popular, the program eventually made its way to the silver screen using black actors, debuting June 28, 1951. The character Amos most embodied the *Uncle Tom* stereotype, being portrayed as a dim-witted ineffectual black man. The NAACP along with Students for Democratic Action (SDA) attempted to get the show cancelled, believing that it furthered the stereotype that blacks were "either stupid, lazy, dishonest or 'amusing.'" The SDA argued that the show hurt democratic societies because all ethnic groups must be valued in a democracy. Opponents of *Amos 'n' Andy* wanted to get the show cancelled because black folk were simply tired of being "constantly depicted as 'mammys' or 'Uncle Toms.'"[66]

---

[65] Sources for this and the preceding paragraph are as follows: *White Pledges NAACP to Finish Fight on Movie "Uncle Tom" Roles*, Chicago Defender, Mar. 2, 1946, at 3; *Hollywood and Walter White*, Chicago Defender, Feb., 23, 1946, at 14; Walter White, *People, Politics and Places*, Chicago Defender, Mar. 9, 1946, at 15.

[66] Bart Andrews and Ahrgus Julliard, Holy Mackerel!: The Amos 'n' Andy Story 15–18, 58 (1986); Angela M. S. Nelson, *Black Situation Comedies and the Politics of Television Art* found in

The issue is obvious: Was criticizing black actors for playing *Uncle Tom* roles proper? If a black actor accepted a role that negatively portrayed the entire race, has that actor violated any constructive racial loyalty norms? The question is difficult, but, particularly in pre-1960s America, the answer was yes.

Blacks rightly deduced that demeaning stereotypes disseminated through popular culture were inextricably linked to racial oppression. Black solidarity, although not requiring unison of thought, forbids blacks from disparaging the race before the entire world. Amid rampant racial subordination, blacks had a right to insist that no one humiliate the group through popular culture. Much of the criticism in this context was really a plea to black actors to refuse *Uncle Tom* roles. That is, the theatrical characters themselves were considered *Uncle Toms*, but not the individual actors. Ridiculing movie characters provided a vivid picture to every one of the actions and behaviors worthy of censure. The outrageous docility and the apparent contentment with second-class citizenship were impermissible mindsets for blacks. Assailing such characters as *Uncle Toms* let all blacks see the types of people who would be ostracized, empowering blacks to adopt attitudes that would be more advantageous in terms of eliminating society of its antiblack elements.

SOME ENTERTAINERS, HOWEVER, WERE DIRECTLY labeled as *Uncle Toms*. Bill Robinson was one such performer. Robinson was a popular tap dancer and actor in the 1930s and 1940s. From the grandson of a slave to tap dancing with Shirley Temple, "Bojangles" had an unlikely life. Uncle Billy, another of his nicknames, was most known for his roles opposite Temple. True to the times, Robinson played bootlicking butlers and slaves who tap danced when called upon. For instance, in *The Little Colonel* (1935), Temple's father becomes incarcerated and Uncle Billy uses his "educated feets" to raise money for them. He played *Uncle Tom* roles, many blacks felt, and was personally derided often. Some called him an *Uncle Tom* for personifying stereotypes even when he was not being forced to by Hollywood executives. During a Cleveland performance in 1941, for instance, black youths heckled him, telling him to shut up and dance. Robinson began the show telling off-color jokes about a black soldier. "We don't want to hear that old 'Uncle Tom' stuff," one yelled, "we came here to see you dance." The belief that Robinson was a sellout was so common that in 1944, a black high school principal refused to let Robinson address his student body because he deemed him an "Uncle Tom."[67]

Cultural Diversity and the U.S. Media 83 (Editors Yahya R. Kamalipour and Theresa Carilli 1998); *Protests Increase over Amos 'N' Andy, Atlanta Daily World*, July 24, 1951, at 3.

[67] *The Pulse of the Public*, New York Amsterdam News, Dec. 3, 1949, at 1; *"Bojanagles" in a Fit of Temper as Hecklers Heckle "Uncle Tom" Jokes*, Chicago Defender, Nov. 1, 1941, at 6; Joseph D. Bibb, *Sylvester's Mule*, Pittsburgh Courier, Apr. 29, 1944, at 7.

Actor Stepin Fetchit, born Lincoln Theodore Monroe Andrew Perry, named after four presidents, also failed to appreciate that playing *Uncle Toms* exacted a price. By the mid-1930s, he was among Hollywood's most bankable black actors. But he played coons, "no account niggers, those unreliable, crazy, lazy, subhuman creatures good for nothing more than eating watermelons, stealing chickens, shooting crap, or butchering the English language." And he played the role well. In film, he was subservient and mindless, allowing his characters to be palatable to a Jim Crow society. In fact, his characters were so simplistic, they did not respond to the pervasive racism that abounded; they were unaware of its existence.[68]

Dissonance marked how Stepin Fetchit was regarded. Many whites ate his shtick by the trough load. More blacks abhorred it. And civil rights organizations, particularly the NAACP, effectively ended his career. Dancer Leonard Reeds reported that the NAACP considered Fetchit an "Uncle Tom" and blacks in show business understood that the organization targeted him. Even his own son called him an "Uncle Tom." Fetchit asserted that his roles did not hurt the race. In fact, during an interview where he denied that he was an "Uncle Tom." Fetchit claimed that he had done more than anyone for the race, "including Booker T. Washington." The man who coined the catchphrase, "Yas'm, I's a-comin'.... Feets do yo' stuff," however, ended his life dismissed as an *Uncle Tom*.[69]

Clarence Muse was in the mold of Robinson and Stepin Fetchit. The actor was ridiculed during the early twentieth century for playing degrading stereotypes. Muse appeared in more films than any other black actor in history. But his knack for procuring work in Hollywood resulted in him being considered "Hollywood's perennial Uncle Tom." Film historian Donald Bogle was more sympathetic. "The fact that he played tom characters cannot be denied," Bogle conceded. "The fact that he played those figures with great intelligence and thoughtfulness," he continued, "has often been overlooked." Though Muse may have been a fine actor, he was stigmatized for playing spineless servants in movies and was further criticized for defending Hollywood's treatment of blacks. Indeed, he claimed that he "belong[ed] to the only profession where there is no discrimination." Later in life, Muse was asked why he accepted

---

[68] Donald Bogle, Toms, Coons, Mulattoes, Mammies, & Bucks: An Interpretive History of Blacks in American Films 8, 38–44 (2001 Edition).

[69] Id.; Champ Clark, Shuffling to Ignominy: The Tragedy of Stepin Fetchit 70, 89, 120, 126 (2005); Michael Carter, *Stepin Ftchit: Lincoln Peary Says He's No Uncle Tom; Feels He Has Helped Race Relations*, Afro-American, May 26, 1945, at 5; Mel Watkins, Stepin Fetchit: The Life and Times of Lincoln Perry 108 (2006); Alex Berlyne, *Lancashi Hotpot Hotpot*, The Jerusalem Post, Apr. 11, 1997.

Uncle Tom roles. "A lot of you people have called me an Uncle Tom, but I have something to tell you," he responded. "You were as dumb as I was. You were the audience and you laughed at what I did."[70]

Supposed *Uncle Tom* entertainers were not just actors. Musicians too were ridiculed. In 1942 in Rome, Georgia, singer Roland Hayes defended his wife from being insulted by a white shoe store clerk. Hayes, then, was severely beaten. After the altercation, Hayes said he was not upset and affirmed his "love" for Georgia. W. E. B. Du Bois, by contrast, said that the attack on Hayes proved that it was "the small southern town where racism is most deeply embedded." Upon hearing of the event, Governor Eugene Talmadge said that whites treated blacks well in Georgia and affirmed that Jim Crow was a permanent fixture. "If the Negro does not like this, my advice to him is to stay out of Georgia," Talmadge declared. The *Cleveland Call and Post* wrote that Mr. Hayes and "all the Uncle Toms like him" likely enjoyed the governor's declaration. "Hayes may love Georgia," the paper continued, "but the crackers in that state don't love him except when he stays in what they outline as his place.... The Negro race would love Roland Hayes more if he would only conduct himself as a real man and love Georgia less." Some, understandably, wanted him to be outraged. Hayes's genteel response, however, was not inexcusably meek. He had every right to feel his and his family's lives' were in jeopardy. Constructive racial loyalty norms maintenance does not require blacks to stand up to physical threats to prove themselves faithful members of the group.[71]

Singer Nat King Cole appears to have had a similar outlook to that of Hayes. Indeed, Cole was branded as an *Uncle Tom* for exhibiting composure rather than indignation after a failed abduction on stage. Cole was a popular and musically gifted mid-century singer. But blacks sometimes questioned his judgment. Some might have believed that he vindicated their unease in the late 1950s when he performed in front of a segregated audience in Alabama. To many, singing in front of a segregated audience was to condone it. And many viewed Cole as having stamped the seal of approval on Jim Crow's forehead. Contrast Cole with Ray Charles when the latter refused to sing in front of a segregated crowd in Georgia, which led the state to ban him from performing there. Charles's decision was viewed as a defense of black dignity whereas Cole's decision was a hindrance to racial progress. If wanting to avoid ridicule,

---

[70] C. Gerald Fraser, *Clarence Muse, 89; Acted in 219 Films*, New York Times, Oct. 17, 1979, at D23; Clarence Edouard Muse, Contemporary Black Biography, Volume 21, Apr. 1999; Frank Manchel, Every Step a Struggle: Interviews with Seven Who Shaped the African-American Image in Movies 205–06, 209 (2007).

[71] Mary Young, W. E. B. Du Bois: An Encyclopedia 100 (2001).

Cole should have mimicked Charles. Instead, he was called an "Uncle Tom" and a "traitor." Thurgood Marshall said, "[a]ll Cole needs to complete his role as an Uncle Tom is a banjo." Cole's worldview was simple. He was an "entertainer," not a "political figure." "In my way," he once said, "I may be helping to bring harmony between people through my music." I find Cole's decision to perform in front of a segregated arena in the 1950s permissible, largely because of when he did it. Had this happened in the 1960s, with blacks showing that more aggressive measures were successful, I would find playing in front of a segregated audience condemnable.[72]

Another musician of the era accustomed to *Uncle Tom* taunts was jazz musician Louis Armstrong. With his trumpet and distinctive unmelodic voice, "Satchmo" firmly placed jazz within America's collective musical soul. His musical acumen, however, failed to mask his perceived character flaws. His on-stage persona – the excessively grinning, bug-eyed melodramatic quality – aroused a bad yet familiar taste in black mouths. It tasted like minstrelsy. He was seen as *Uncle Toming* his way to the bank – ingratiating himself to whites and parlaying that into prosperity. Black music professor Michael White reported that Armstrong's "stage mannerisms, his garbled speech and his handkerchief and all of that seemed to be throwbacks to the Uncle Tom image." As one argued, "Armstrong may be a great musician, but there is no doubt that he is a Great Uncle Tom."[73]

Miles Davis implicitly belittled Armstrong in a 1962 *Playboy* interview. Although he did not name him, Davis clearly targeted Armstrong and his signature smile. "I ain't no model, and I don't sing or dance, and I damn sure ain't no Uncle Tom just to be up there grinning," Davis remarked. Unlike Davis, musician Dizzy Gillespie attacked Armstrong by name, stating that he was "a white man's nigger, an Uncle Tom debasing the aspirations of the jazz elite." Another time, in 1957, Gillespie derided Satchmo for his "Uncle Tom-like subservience," further claiming that "[n]owadays no cat should be a Tom." Singer Billie Holiday said, "'Sure Pops Toms, but he Toms with class." Some unnamed bebop musicians disagreed with the contention that he was a classy Tom, arguing that he was simply "an old Uncle Tom, laughing and telling naughty jokes and carrying on as if he were in a minstrel show. He was … an embarrassment." Even Thurgood Marshall referred to Armstrong as "the No. 1 Uncle Tom." And

[72] Jonathan Yardley, *The King of Sing*, Washington Post, Jan. 16, 1985, at D2; Don Wheeldin, *Sun Reporter*, Mar. 7, 1970, at 8; Hedy Weiss, *The Nat King Cole Story (Unforgettable)*, Chicago-Sun Times, Nov. 3, 2000, at 46. Daniel Mark Epstein, Nat King Cole 258–59 (1999); Richard Iton, In Search of the Black Fantastic: Politics & Popular Culture in the Post-Civil Rights Era 68–69 (2008).

[73] Dennis Persica, *HAPPY 100TH, SATCHMO!*, Times-Picayune, Aug. 4, 2001, at 1.

like Nat Cole before him, Armstrong performed before segregated audiences, which too led to *Uncle Tom* denunciations. Writer Gerald Early, however, tried to vindicate him, averring that Armstrong was nothing more than a casualty of the zeitgeist. "Armstrong was perceived mistakenly as an Uncle Tom. He was liked too much by white audiences, and that made him suspect to us. To a more militant, post-World-War-II African-American community, he seemed a link to minstrelsy that we were ashamed of."[74]

Rather than ascertaining if each of these individuals was an *Uncle Tom*, a more fundamental question concerns whether black entertainers violated constructive racial loyalty norms if they portrayed belittling stereotypes. Did accepting a movie role, for instance, that played up racial stereotypes violate constructive racial loyalty norms? I say yes. To accept those roles is to at least have gross impurities in one's devotion to black folk. A caveat to constructive norms is that they do not mandate that blacks sacrifice their livelihood for the interests of the race. But taking a part in a movie that demeaned the race was not your average vocation. A postal employee who remained silent on racial discrimination in the workplace did not have the same level of cultural resonance as did a black actor who embarrassed the race in a film viewed by millions across the world. The black community was well within its rights to insist that black actors not further humiliating stereotypes in popular culture. If black actors chose to do so anyway, with the harms such movies inflicted on blacks' legal interests, they established their lack of concern for the race. Also true, black actors were inexcusably meek in accepting humiliating roles. To accept a role that mocks one's racial identity is to condone racial belittlement.

THE *UNCLE TOM* OF SPORTS

Sports stars are not leaders, at least not in the traditional sense. Few turn to them to provide answers to the pressing problems of the day. They do not typically partake in national dialogues concerning the problems vexing the race. But athletes do, however, attract attention. Their racial treachery, therefore,

---

[74] *Miles Davis: A Candid Conversation With the Jazz World's Premier Iconoclast*, interviewed by Alex Haley, Playboy, Sept. 1962; *Letters from Our Readers; "Dig"race Race Case Satchmo*, The Plain Dealer, Mar. 29, 1957, at 7; Leonard Lyons, *Lyons Den*, Daily Defender, May 15, 1957, at 5; *"Satchmo" Tells Off Ike, U.S.*, Pittsburgh Courier, Sept. 28, 1957, at 33; Richard Cook, *Top of the Pops*, New Statesman, Aug. 21, 2000; Laurence Bergeen, Louis Armstrong: An Extravagant Life 439 (1997); Joan Indiana Rigdon, Two Score and Ten Years Ago: Brown v. Board of Education, *DC Bar*, available at: http://www.dcbar.org/for_lawyers/washington_lawyer/may_2004/brown.cfm; Michael Anthony, *"JAZZ" Centurion*, Star Tribune, Jan. 7, 2001, at 1F.

has disastrous potential. And thus blacks had an enormous interest in ensuring their fidelity. The racial loyalty norm management in this context, though, proved quite destructive. Studying the destructive norm management in this context provides helpful guidance. More pointedly, what follows is a demonstration of how to not manage racial loyalty norms.

In October 1934, University of Michigan played Georgia Tech in football in Ann Arbor. Willis Ward, black, was both a track and football star at Michigan. Georgia Tech, though, refused to play against black players. Earlier that year, when the two schools negotiated, Georgia Tech's officials maintained that a potential football matchup was contingent on Ward not participating. As Georgia Tech's coach declared, "Public sentiment in the southeastern states simply demands that no team in this section play against a Negro athlete." Michigan accommodated Georgia Tech and barred Ward from competing. Because Ward remained on the team he was criticized as an *Uncle Tom*. The *Atlanta Daily World* reported that Ward was frequently deemed "spineless." "Many," according to the newspaper, "feel that any player who knuckles down under a raw deal such as this, when he has won the right to play by beating out all of the white players on his team is a coward and an 'Uncle Tom.' He should've turned in his uniform in protest against the decision."[75]

Six years later, history repeated itself. In 1940, New York University's halfback Leonard Cornelius Bates was prevented from playing in an away game against the University of Missouri. This was familiar to NYU. In 1929, halfback Dave Myers was barred from a football game against the University of Georgia. The *Afro-American* noticed that Myers was suspiciously out of the lineup in an away game against West Virginia Wesleyan earlier in the season and predicted the same would occur in other games NYU had scheduled against Jim Crow schools. The newspaper was right. While many criticized NYU for acquiescing to Georgia's Jim Crow policy, the *Defender* assailed Myers. Noting that around Harlem, he was "yellow … [with] no backbone," the *Defender* compared him to other athletes who took a stand and prayed that he followed suit. The newspaper "call[ed] upon Myers to quit making a laughing stock out of his Race. If Meehan (NYU's football coach) refuses to allow him in the Georgia game the entire Race looks for Myers to hand in his uniform and be a man."[76]

---

[75] Charles H. Martin, Benching Jim Crow: The Rise and Fall of the Color Line in Southern College Sports, 1890–1980 30–31 (2010); Chico Renfroe, *This and That in Sports*, Atlanta Daily World, Apr. 24, 1980, at 9.

[76] Raymond Schmidt, Shaping College Football: The Transformation of an American Sport, 1919–1930 151–53 (2007); Donald Spivey, *"End Jim Crow in Sports" The Leonard Bates Controversy and Protest at New York University, 1940–1941* found in Sport and the Color

Although the *Defender* stopped short of calling Myers an *Uncle Tom*, others did not extend that same courtesy to Leonard Cornelius Bates a decade later. Many begged Bates to quit the team in protest. As the cases of Ward and Myers demonstrate, Southern mores frequently forced black collegiate athletes out of sporting events. And universities usually assumed that black student athletes would comply. Many blacks lived vicariously through its stars and wanted Bates to declare his unwillingness to be cast aside whenever society deemed his – and by extension their – presence unwelcome. But when NYU publicized a private letter authored by Bates, he obviously was not going to be the archetype for black militancy. Bates wrote that before committing to NYU, he knew that he would be unable to participate in games in Missouri pursuant to an existing arrangement between the universities. Making a cultural stand was not Bates's concern. Rather his "concern has been to gain a college education. Football is a secondary matter," he wrote. The *Defender* wrote that his letter was reminiscent of the "me too boss" type of black man with "his hat in his hand." Others went for the jugular and called him an "Uncle Tom."[77]

Because Ward, Meyers, and Bates were supposedly guilty of the same crime, the propriety of the charge can be appraised jointly. Remaining at a university that expected blacks to disappear whenever their skin color was unwarranted very well might be a submissive action. But their competing interests – a degree from a great university – should have inoculated them from charges of racial treachery. Blacks should not have expected the three to sacrifice their education to make what would have been a bold stance. They did not, in other words, violate any constructive racial loyalty norms. As was true for Willis Ward, charging Bates with racial treachery was destructive. Student athletes choose their colleges when they are teenagers. Asking a person that young to give up a scholarship to make a cultural stand is unreasonable to expect and wrongheaded to ask.

Even sports superstars were indicted for running afoul of racial loyalty norms. A few months after the Bates incident, perhaps the first black sports star for which both blacks and whites cheered, boxing great Joe Louis, was tagged as an *Uncle Tom*. In 1941, Arthur Reed, the head of a fledgling black business, criticized the "Brown Bomber." Reed, an inventor, made a brake that he wanted to produce, but he failed to convince blacks to buy stock for his company. Louis, as well as other black stars, participated in a 1941 Urban League-sponsored radio program that petitioned companies receiving defense contracts to hire blacks. After the program aired, Reed's business issued a leaflet entitled "Claim Your Heritage" that specifically derided Louis for daring to ask companies to employ blacks while he wasted his money on an extravagant lifestyle. Reed, the leaflet's apparent author, was right about Louis's spending habits; the fighter lived lavishly. But Reed depicted Louis's consumption as treasonous. Reed contended that Louis, and other celebrities, were obligated to invest in the black community. The leaflet asserted that "our most worthy champion [has] no background but that of the average poor Negro, yet thousands of the same class of which they were birthed stand by and see them squander thousands of dollars on such things as golf links, amusement farm, riding academy, club houses and petty insurance companies." Because the spendthrift Louis did not assist the black community, he was an *Uncle Tom*, according to Reed.[78]

Monitoring blacks' spending habits, however, is a bridge much too far. Such norm maintenance impeded the cause of black solidarity. Making spending habits a component of racial loyalty would surely cause many blacks to reject any rallying cries for group unity.

Arthur Reed was a struggling businessman who was likely lashing out at those more successful. And because evidence is lacking of anyone else during this era having their loyalty questioned on this ground, this critique was probably widely rejected, never fully taking hold to reach "norm status." In fact, the *Philadelphia Tribune's* sarcastic tone in the article about Reed's grievances indicates that his assessment was categorically rejected.

When Louis was called an *Uncle Tom* a few years later, the *Defender* went beyond the *Tribune's* passive aggressive sarcasm and actively rebuked his indicter. Joe Williams, a black sportswriter, called boxers Joe Louis and Joe Walcott "the two venerable Uncle Toms of the ring" in 1948. The *Defender* was apoplectic. What Williams's specific gripes were is unclear, but the *Defender* strongly defended the two boxers. "Without being over sensitive concerning sports writers' attempts to be clever, it must be pointed out that Williams, writing on this topic are neither clever, witty nor comical. They are just plain nasty." After Joe Louis beat Max Schmeling in 1938, the black community had found its new cultural hero. If one was going to accuse him for treachery,

---

[78] Richard Bak, Joe Louis: The Great Black Hope 259–62 (1996); *Louis Called an "Uncle Tom,"* Philadelphia Tribune, Apr. 17, 1941, at 13.

then the evidence had to be convincing or the misguided prosecutor would be reprimanded for his false accusation.[79]

The *Defender* likely protected Louis because he did nothing deserving censure. But speaking in public in a stereotypically ignorant manner was a more common ground for criticism. Blacks in the first half of the twentieth century (and even arguably today) were viewed by many nonblacks as always representing the race. One black person's embarrassing trait was projected onto the entire group. Realizing this, blacks often required the best of their public figures. Falling short of this standard sometimes led to *Uncle Tom* allegations.

For instance, illiterate boxer Beau Jack discovered this when he was assailed for his unpolished speaking style. Observers joked that Jack would frequently respond to interview questions with something to the effect of: "I glad I win ... ev'rthing's all right up heah." Sportswriter Don DeLeighbur wrote that Jack carried an unwelcomed "Uncle Tommish" manner into boxing.[80]

But not just Jack's unpolished speech drew censure. Two years later in 1946, Jack was photographed shining the shoes of a white golfer, Byron Nelson, during the Masters Tournament at the Augusta National Golf Club. The club did not admit blacks, likely rendering the incident all the more scandalous. Columnist Fay Young wrote about the episode. Alongside his column was the photograph of Jack "grinning like a hyena" while "playing shoeshine boy." It was "a role of pleasing the Crackers down in Georgia" and below the photograph read the caption "Uncle Tom Beau." Smelling a possible publicity stunt, Young told Jack that it was "time he [learned] his A, B, Cs," perhaps implying that he was ignorant on how to be a black man in the public eye. Jack used to work at Augusta National shining shoes and waiting tables before he became a boxer. The white golfers to whom he endeared himself financed his start as a boxer. He was likely being nice to the men who had played an instrumental role in his life. Jack, nonetheless, erred in helping promulgate a "happy darky" image that reinforced the supposed propriety of blacks' second-class citizenship. That blacks would lament his public persona is understandable. Jack's detractors, nevertheless, failed to make the case that he violated constructive racial loyalty norms. He was unrefined. But refinement has little to do with racial loyalty. Jack's prosecutors lacked evidence establishing that he was treacherous.[81]

The case of Beau Jack at August National instructs that blacks expected dignified behavior from their sports stars. Harlem Globetrotter Reece "Goose"

---

[79] *Louis, Walcott Called "Uncle Toms,"* Chicago Defender, July 10, 1948, at 11.

[80] Don DeLeighbur, *See Beau Jack Handlers Trying to "Freeze" Title,* Afro-American, Feb. 19, 1944, at 19; John Strege, When War Played Through: Golf during World War II (2006).

[81] Fay Young, *Through the Years,* Chicago Defender, Apr. 27, 1946, at 10.

Tatum failed to heed that lesson, a misstep resulting in similarly unfair *Uncle Tom* denunciations. Tatum was a two-sport athlete, playing baseball in the Negro Leagues for the Birmingham Black Barons and the Cincinnati Clowns. But Tatum was most known as the Globetrotter with the unusual frame and mannerisms. One said of him, "He talked slow, walked funny and looked like a circus freak.... His body seemed all out of proportion, with arms so long." Tatum garnered notoriety for his clownish antics. In 1929, the Globetrotters began integrating stunts and comedic routines in their games for which they became famous. In 1942, the team hired Tatum, who took that showmanship to new heights. Not all loved his antics, including sportswriter Alvin Moses, who railed, "GOOSE TATUM, if you should go to Philly or Rochester ... for God's sake CUT OUT THE UNCLE TOMING WILL YOU FELLA?"[82]

A year after Jackie Robinson shattered baseball's color barrier in 1947, Hall of Fame catcher Roy Campanella became his teammate for the Brooklyn Dodgers. Robinson was highly critical of Campanella's acceptance of segregation. Campanella did not believe he could change racism. It was to be endured, not bucked. On one occasion, Robinson tried to pick a fight with an umpire he dubbed a "Negro-hater." Campanella ran up to him saying, "Don't start trouble Jackie.... Let's not take any chances. It's nice up here [in the Major Leagues]." Campanella relished the opportunity to play on the highest stage and refused to jeopardize that. Robinson was different. He felt obliged to fight injustice. His polar opposite, Robinson deemed Campanella subservient and an *Uncle Tom*.[83]

Robinson and Campanella, according to rumors, frequently argued in the clubhouse. On television, Robinson denied this, instead depicting their relationship as nonexistent. "I didn't like Campy's attitude towards racial matters," Robinson disclosed. "So therefore we had nothing to do with each other." Further explaining his feelings, Robinson said:

> Remember last year when they were bombing in the South? Roy made a statement that it was the people seeking integration who were responsible. It hurt all of us very much because you just don't come out with such statements where people are violating laws. The only thing that we're doing is

[82] Robbie Butler, The Harlem Globetrotters: Clown Princes of Basketball 16–19 (2002); Larry Powell, Black Barons of Birmingham: The South's Greatest Negro League Team 50–51 (2009); Alvin Moses, *In the World of Sports: Beating the Gun*, The Plain Dealer, July 25, 1947, at 4; Strege, When War Played Through; David Owen, The Making of the Masters: Clifford Roberts, Augusta National and Golf's Most Prestigious Tournament 233–35 (2003).

[83] Arnold Rampersad, Jackie Robinson: A Biography 165–66 (1997); *How Fate Claimed a Great Career*, Sunday Mail, Apr. 22, 1990.

asking that we be allowed to live where we choose. And for one of us to say it's the people seeking integration who are responsible for the bombings, that does a good thing for the Ku Klux Klan.[84]

Sportswriter Dick Young, white, provided insight into how Campanella's racial outlook endeared him to whites. "Few thought of Campanella as a Negro," Young revealed. "There was no race consciousness about the man. He had grown up playing baseball with whites and against whites. Mixing was never a problem for Campy. He was accepted most everywhere." Sportswriters enjoyed Campanella because with him they could just talk about baseball without having to wade in uncomfortable racial matters. But with Robinson, they were constantly aware that he was black. Dick Young told Robinson this and Robinson replied that he would rather be respected than be a "handker-chief head."[85]

As Dick Young explained whites' preference for Campy, A. S. "Doc" Young gave the black perspective. Doc described Campanella as:

a Dale Carnegie disciple who believes in "getting along" at all costs, in being exceedingly grateful for any favor, or any deed interpreted as a favor.

Jackie, on the other hand, is an aggressive individualist who is willing to pay the price, and once having paid it in full does not believe that effusive "thank yous" are a necessary tip.[86]

The best case against Campanella was that he was inexcusably meek. His detractors might claim that his acceptance of racism while playing baseball was racially treasonous. Although blacks might have hoped that Campanella was a race warrior, choosing to not fight racism may have been meek, but it was not inexcusable. Campanella, as his statement to Robinson suggests, likely feared that he would potentially be out of Major League baseball if he came off as the rabble rouser. If that was indeed his fear, then not being a race warrior was not treacherous.

Robinson charged Campanella with placating bigoted racial attitudes, and others leveled the same criticism upon him. Indeed, in 1953, Jackie Robinson organized an all-star baseball team that included a number of whites that was to play a game in Birmingham, Alabama. The state, however, prohibited interracial sporting competitions by law. When told to keep the white players from participating, Robinson complied and later did the same in Memphis. The sentiment in certain segments of the black community was that Robinson was a "disgrace to the race" and an *Uncle Tom*.

[84] J. A. Rogers, *History Shows...*, Pittsburgh Courier, Mar. 15, 1958, at A9.

[85] Id., Jackie Robinson, I Never Had It Made: An Autobiography 109–11 (1972).

[86] A. S. Doc Young, *What's Behind the Campanella-Robinson Feud?*, Los Angeles Sentinel, Jan. 31, 1957, at C3.

Columnist Eddie Burbridge wrote that upon learning that Southern cities forbade interracial sporting events, Robinson should have cancelled the exhibitions. His critics feared that his acquiescence to segregation empowered the South to maintain the status quo. Robinson, many felt, could deliver a blow to Jim Crow but chose to take the money and bow to Southern edict instead. Robinson's supposed *Uncle Tom* behavior symbolized a hindrance in the race's ability to reform its legal subordination. But calling Robinson an *Uncle Tom* here was destructive norm management. Whether Robinson should have cancelled the competition is an important discussion to have. But his choosing to hold the event rather than call it off in no way established racial betrayal.[87]

Norms were not managed constructively against black sports figures. The reason is quite clear. Their relationships to the types of conversations and issues that elicit well-supported accusations of racial betrayal were tangential at best. Sports figures' primary duty is athletic accomplishments. They do not operate in the arena where racial politics is central. That is not to say that black athletes could never be *Uncle Toms*. If for instance, a black athlete in the 1930s publically endorsed an antiblack politician, then his behavior would evidence a betrayal of racial solidarity. The basic lesson to learn here is that unless an athlete weighs in on salient issues of the day, they have unlikely betrayed the race.

ANALYSIS

The racial loyalty norm management for famous blacks was not as constructive as it was for the rank and file. One explanation might be that famous blacks were held to a higher standard and their behavior was more closely monitored. Any misdeeds, after all, had the potential to affect more than the black masses. Their actions were available for all to see. Also true is that no matter what famous blacks did, at least one person would always find some fault and then hurl *Uncle Tom*. But policing loyalty still had much potential to empower blacks into building black solidarity. When the behavior of famous blacks was at issue, the general point remained: constructive racial loyalty norms helped forge the solidarity that would be useful in obtaining racial progress. *Uncle Tom* was used in the framework of a larger argument about how blacks should comport to better their plight.

---

[87] *Jackie States the Case*, Chicago Defender, July 30, 1949, at 6; Eddie Burbridge, *Layin' It on the Line*, Los Angeles Sentinel, Dec. 3, 1953, at A10; Roi Ottley, *Ottley Says Jackie Robinson Incident Stirs South Side*, Chicago Daily Tribune, Nov. 22, 1953, at SWA4.

Undoubtedly the three most important figures to be sanctioned with *Uncle Tom* accusations were Booker T. Washington, W. E. B. Du Bois, and Marcus Garvey. Of the three, that Washington was called an *Uncle Tom* is the least surprising. The most influential black man of his era has been repeatedly branded a sellout posthumously. *Uncle Tom* has followed him to his grave. His indicter, Thomas Miller, criticized Washington for being subservient to whites and acquiescing to racial subordination. Miller's harsh criticism was based on Washington's accommodationist statements like that seen in his "Atlanta Compromise" speech. Although Miller's critique is perfectly in line with the sorts of cultural regulations that blacks erected elsewhere, Washington lived in a complicated era and lived a complicated life. For instance, although he seemingly wanted blacks to eschew the ballot box, he surreptitiously backed efforts against black disfranchisement in Georgia. The case of Washington displays that efforts to police the behavior can be extraordinarily tricky if you fail to take stock of the full man.

W. E. B. Du Bois was called an *Uncle Tom* by Garvey. But Garvey's sanctioning of Du Bois was likewise destructive. A cynical, perhaps wise, mind might conclude that Garvey branded Du Bois an *Uncle Tom* largely because the two were adversaries. But taking his words at face value, Garvey considered Du Bois an *Uncle Tom* because the latter believed in interracial coalitions and integration while working for the NAACP. But the NAACP's program – contesting segregation, lynching, and other social ills – was the sort of ideas the black community should have debated.

Oddly enough, the epithet directed at Marcus Garvey was the most appropriate. Garvey, though a black nationalist, went to the South and bowed down to white supremacy. Robert Minor, a white communist, noticed it, as did others including Du Bois, and deemed Garvey a sellout. Garvey's kowtowing to Southern bigots was the exact behavioral pitfall that blacks knocked about Southern Negroes. Thus, the man who is a popular posthumous symbol for blackness was, among the three, most properly labeled an *Uncle Tom*.

The most censure-worthy asserted *Uncle Toms* of this first period were Percy Greene and Rev. H. H. Humes. The two black newspapermen from Mississippi took money from avowed racist organizations to counteract the work of racial uplift organizations. That such persons existed highlighted the importance of blacks wielding such language to not only punish the traitorous, but also rally blacks around the need to oppose their racial subordination and the entities striving so hard to inure it.

The black leader typically conducted his work outside of the powerful institutions that implemented America's racial policy. There were, though, some blacks within such structures. In pre-1960s America, the black insider, however, was a rare bird. A strain of thought in the black community criticized blacks who chose positions in government that limited their duties to "black affairs." But that was unfair. Blacks had few opportunities to work within the system. The community should have relished the chance to have someone from within with the potential to articulate its grievances.

Perhaps the black insider who most clearly defied racial loyalty norms was Perry Howard, a special assistant to the attorney general. Howard, a former Pullman porter, served as counsel to the Pullman Company in the company's effort to beat back the efforts of black porters to unionize. Howard took a pretty mendacious route of branding the black porters as communists in his efforts to defend a company that was discriminating against black workers. Also deserving criticism was Clarence R. Pope, an official for Harlem's WPA. Pope was in charge of providing jobs to black workers but gave the jobs to whites instead. These two gentlemen violated constructive racial loyalty norms.

Some black insiders, however, were victims of destructive norm management. The case of Chicago congressman William Dawson is particularly interesting. A fellow black congressman, Adam Powell, called him an *Uncle Tom* for delivering a speech that Powell argued weakened the civil rights language in the Democratic Party's platform during its 1952 convention. But Dawson's words allowed the Southern Democrats to sign off on the plank that, importantly, contained the toughest stance against racial discrimination in the party's history. Branding him an *Uncle Tom* in that circumstance was unjust. The problem here, as was often true, was that a difference in opinion was unfortunately equated to racial treachery.

Perhaps the most constructive norm management of famous blacks was that within the entertainment industry. The connection between black images promulgated in entertainment contexts and racial subordination was unmistakable. White supremacy sought to sustain itself by depicting blacks as savages, servants, and buffoons. If blacks were less endowed than whites, then their second-class citizenship was not unjust; it simply reflected God's plan. Pressure, therefore, was exerted on blacks who made their living in show business to portray the race in the best possible light to undermine this rationale for discrimination. The most indelible pressure was that applied by black men stationed abroad during World War II who were forced to deal with the calamitous effects of these movies – the poor treatment that resulted from the tarnished image of the American Negro. As in other contexts, a tension between self-interest and group interest existed. Black entertainers often focused on their own careers and averted their eyes from the mounting evidence that their decisions hurt the entire race. *Uncle Tom* was constructively used to punish blacks who chose their profession over the long-term interests of the race.

Blacks had a right to defend their public image from those profiting off such stereotypes, particularly because negative portrayals in popular culture furthered their subordination.

The most destructive racial loyalty norm management was directed at sports figures. Boxing great Joe Louis, for instance, was called an *Uncle Tom* for spending his money lavishly and not investing in the black community to help the struggling masses mired in a racially hostile land. Louis should have been allowed to use his money how he saw fit without having his racial loyalty questioned, but at least Reed made a critique that had some relationship to racial oppression. The same can be said of boxer Beau Jack, who was called an *Uncle Tom* in the 1940s for being inarticulate and for shining the shoes of golfer Byron Nelson. Although the use of *Uncle Tom* was harsh, one must remember that during that era, blacks combatted stereotypes that they were intellectually inferior beings who were best suited to occupy the lower levels of society. When put into the proper context, why Jack was ridiculed is understandable although destructive.

4

Uncle Tom: 1960–1975

UNCLE TOM VERSUS THE INTEGRATIONISTS

WITH SEGREGATION'S GRIP LOOSENING, some black integrationists during the early 1960s unclenched their fists and began flirting with the idea that *Uncle Toms* no longer needed to be fought. *Uncle Toms*, once threatening civil war, were suddenly no longer an intra-racial foe, it seemed. Indeed, less than a decade after *Brown*, black integrationists – the folk who previously bemoaned the presence of *Uncle Toms* – began to publically muse that their adversaries were no longer present to hinder their good work.

In this vein, Dr. Robert C. Weaver, chairman of the NAACP's board of directors, proclaimed in 1960 that Southern sit-in efforts indicated that "'Uncle Tom' is being destroyed as the stereotype of the American Negro." And after the 1960 Civil Rights Bill's passage, Weaver claimed that the NAACP was "softening up Uncle Tom for the knock-out blow." Leslie W. Dunbar, head of a Southern civil rights organization, insisted that "Jim Crow cannot live without Uncle Tom, and Uncle Tom is dying fast." Dr. C. Eric Lincoln, a professor and expert on the black church, also asserted that *Uncle Tom* was practically dead. "The image of Uncle Tom, the Negro who passes out the white man's favors and helps keep his people down, is an image that is gone now," declared the academic. "Uncle Tom," Lincoln further pronounced, "is [no] longer an effective agent of class control, nor can he any longer deliver even the fractional benefits which made him a power in the Negro community."[1]

Similarly, in 1960, black Memphis newspaper the *Tri-State Defender* claimed that "[a] new day is dawning in the consciousness of the opressed

---

[1]   Curt Swenson, *NAACP Asks White Support in Strategy*, Chicago Daily Defender, June 23, 1960, at A4; New York Amsterdam News, June 25, 1960, at 1; Wallace Terry, *Wilkins Sees Possibility of Shift to GOP by Negroes*, Washington Post, Mar. 30, 1963, at A4; *Line Principles of Democracy with Actions, Lincoln Urges*, Atlanta Daily World, Apr. 5, 1962, at 2.

[*sic*]. The hat-in-hand Negro is no more; there are no more accommodating, grinning Uncle Toms. The Negro no longer begs for his rights; he demands them with all the solemnity at his command." John Jordan, likewise, writing in the *New Journal and Guide* in 1961, saw Southern blacks no longer willing to patronage discriminatory stores as signaling that the South was a "land where Uncle Tom used to live."[2]

In these folk's estimation, by the early 1960s, the vultures were closely stalking *Uncle Tom*, awaiting their moment. *Uncle Tom* was not yet comatose; a smidgen of vitality plodded through its limbs. But many keen witnesses foretold *Uncle Tom*'s impending death. Racial loyalty norms had been effectively enforced, apparently, and *Uncle Tom* was nearly breathless. This development suggests that some believed that black solidarity was sturdy because racial treachery was practically obsolete. This delighted observers because a united black people was well positioned to contest the legal imposition of second-class citizenship.

Uncle Tom's death, however, never came. It was as alive as ever. And integrationists needed to remain on guard; *Uncle Tom* never dropped its arms. Particularly in the early 1960s, blacks who mightily strove to dismantle segregation lashed out at those seeking to aid recalcitrant whites maintain the status quo. Such blacks were often attacked for violating racial loyalty norms. The accusations were generally constructive. The targets here primarily impeded black solidarity. Holding up such persons to public censure facilitated racial unity and helped the quest to uproot the legal installation of racial segregation.

NAACP attorney Constance Baker Motley continued to believe that *Uncle Tom* still roamed. While persuading Southern black educators to support the NAACP's school desegregation efforts, Motley beseeched black teachers to "bury every Uncle Tom." She hoped that "every segregationist has been dethroned in the courts. Every Uncle Tom has lost his job on Mr. Charlie's payroll, and we have wrought a miracle and have put down every foe of integration, both white and black." To Motley, battling *Uncle Toms* and regulating behavior was as necessary as ever. Her words were a sage call for solidarity. Motley realized that group unity helped her civil rights lawyering.[3]

Six black women in Birmingham further verified, to some, that *Uncle Tom* had yet to perish. In December 1955, blacks started a yearlong bus boycott in

---

2 *The Sorry Sight in the Senate*, Tri-State Defender, Mar. 12, 1960, at 6; John Jordan, *This Is Portsmouth*, New Journal and Guide, Apr. 15, 1961, at C22.
3 *AFL-CIO Union Makes Overtures to Teachers Ass'n*, New Journal and Guide, Aug. 8, 1964, at A16.

the city. Like most Southern cities, Birmingham segregated its buses by law. After those laws were found unconstitutional, city officials passed an ordinance that permitted the Birmingham Transit Company to set its own seating policy. The Transit Company's policy required blacks to board the bus from the rear and whites from the front. Seeking to maintain segregation, the city passed the duty to implement Jim Crow from government hands to private hands, hoping its ploy would survive constitutional attack.

Lambasting "an unholy conspiracy" between local politicians and the Transit Company, local black clergymen pressed blacks to disobey the policy. One of those clergymen was Rev. Calvin Woods. In turn, police chief Bull Conner charged Woods with violating the state's antiboycott law. Woods was eventually convicted and sentenced to jail for six months and fined $500, but he was later exonerated after his successful appeal. During his original trial, though, six black women testified against him. Those six women were congregants of his church and in January 1960, the 250-member church voted to expel them. "I love them," Woods said, "and I would like for them to love me, but they proved they didn't love anybody." The *Philadelphia Tribune*, a black newspaper, reported the events in a headline that read, "Ala. Church Expels Female 'Uncle Toms.'" A week later, the *Tribune* remained delighted that the females were ousted because "'Uncle Toms' are being exposed for what they are."[4]

If *Uncle Toms* still lived, they certainly would have been spotted in Mississippi – the home of Percy Greene and Rev. Humes – where racism was perhaps most stymieing and where white supremacists paid blacks for their disloyalty. And spotted in Mississippi they were. In 1961, James Meredith sought to attend the all-white University of Mississippi. Although many blacks considered Meredith's bold ambition a step toward equality, not all did, including Rev. J. W. Jones, a black Baptist minister. Jones, in fact, discouraged Meredith from enrolling at Ole Miss. He argued that it "will cause a setback in harmony between white and colored races. He will be doing us harm. We will not be ready for a long time to try to compete on a fully equality basis." The minister was dismissed as an *Uncle Tom* for his indefensible meekness.[5]

4   *Browder v. Gayle*, 142 F. Supp. 707 (M.D. Ala. 1956); *Browder v. Gayle*, 352 U.S. 903 (1956); *Woods v. State*, 116 So. 2d 400 (Ala. Ct. App. 1959); Andrew M. Manis, A Fire You Can't Put Out: The Civil Rights Life of Birmingham's Reverend Fred Shuttlesworth xx–xxi (1999); Wilson Fallin Jr., The African American Church in Birmingham, Alabama, 1815–1963: A Shelter in the Storm 157 (1997); Jet, Jan. 14, 1960, at 24; *Ala. Church Expels Female "Uncle Toms,"* Philadelphia Tribune, Jan. 2, 1960 at 2; *Female "Uncle Toms,"* Philadelphia Tribune, Jan. 9, 1960, at 4.
5   *"Uncle Toms" Still Open Big Mouths*, Pittsburgh Courier, Oct. 6, 1962, at 4; Charles W. Eagles, The Price of Defiance: James Meredith and the Integration of Ole Miss (2009).

Many undoubtedly would have found objectionable Rev. Jones's decision to deter Meredith from endeavoring to integrate Ole Miss. But those actively conspiring with staunch segregationists were more disconcerting. Blacks contesting segregation in Mississippi were surprised that some blacks dared to work on behalf of White Citizens' Councils, segregationist organizations filled with professional whites, a "country club klan" of sorts. Those reputed traitors were constructively maligned as being worse than "Uncle Tom[s]" for serving as "paid Negro informers who report to the citizens council or sovereignty commission any signs of 'racial agitation.'" Charles Evers, a Mississippi civil rights leader, too noticed *Uncle Toms* in his midst while attempting to organize blacks to participate in their own government. He described an *Uncle Tom* as "a guy who'll run back and tell the white people on other Negroes. He's the man who's grinning when he's not tickled – just grinning and scratching when he doesn't itch."[6]

Although not in Mississippi, Wetumpka had a similarly embarrassing racial past. In 1966, the nation's eyes were on the small Alabama town outside of Montgomery when city officials refused to bury Jimmy Williams, a black soldier who had been killed in Vietnam, in the city's cemetery. Williams was the city's first Vietnam casualty, but city officials offered no condolences to his family. The cemetery's black section had no space available and the city refused to bury him in the whites-only section. Williams was ultimately buried in Andersonville National Cemetery in Georgia.

A year later, Wetumka was again under the spotlight for a suspicious set of deaths of blacks in the local county jail. In December 1960, Matthew Wilkerson died in jail the day after he had been critically injured in a car accident. In November 1966, William Edward Young too died in jail after the ill Young was not taken to the hospital. A few months after Young's death, James Earl Motley was clubbed to death in the same jail. Jimmy Williams's father wanted the black population to take collective action against the city's rampant racism. He had little hope, however, that local blacks would heed his advice. "Negroes here," he said, "are too afraid to launch a civil rights movement, and there are too many Uncle Toms who tell the white man everything." Such uses of *Uncle Tom* alerted blacks that the most valuable members were eager participants in the struggle against discrimination, encouraging engagement in joint enterprise.[7]

---

[6] Charles Cobb, *Beginnings*, Mississippi Free Press, Sept. 29, 1962, at 2; Charles Evers, Evers 167–69 (1971) Neil R. McMillen, The Citizens' Council: Organized Resistance to the Second Reconstruction 1954–64 xii (1994 edition).

[7] *Alabama Jail Deaths Touch off Investigations*, Los Angeles Sentinel, Dec. 29, 1966, at A7; James E. Westheider, Fighting on Two Fronts: African Americans and the Vietnam War 73

But *Uncle Toms* were not just a Southern bugaboo; they caused Northern blacks great consternation too. A particular reputed *Uncle Tom* was so vexing that the head of the Hempstead, Long Island NAACP branch, Rev. Robert C. Chapman, resigned in 1960. The purported *Uncle Tom*, Rev. Clinton Boone, divided the black community, or at least he tried. Three years before Boone's arrival, the city hired its first black teachers after the NAACP mobilized the black community. The organization hoped to continue making racial gains through black solidarity. But Boone attempted to vanquish such aspirations, telling his congregation to reject the NAACP. As he derogated the organization, Boone positioned himself to be the mayor's friend. Boone was thought to be purposefully stunting black progress to cozy up to the mayor and reap personal benefits. Boone was ridiculed as one of the city's "Jet Age Uncle Toms."[8]

If Boone sacrificed group progress for personal reward, he was correctly assailed for violating the norm that requires blacks care about the race. Boone seemingly had no qualms about sabotaging blacks' interests to further his own ambitions, compelling locals to make an example of him lest others pursue similar treasonous paths. Boone was probably too far gone; the *Uncle Tom's* soul dies hard. But the local community could convince others not to replicate his treachery by rendering him a pariah. And, by branding him an *Uncle Tom*, they marginalized him. He was no longer a voice that local blacks would pay attention to.

Northern clergyman Archbishop Clarence C. Addison of the African Universal Church was similarly an enemy to integrationists. In 1963, Addison told a black organization that "God is the author of segregation; the devil is the author of integration." Instead of pursuing integration, Addison advocated that the black man heed the directive of Booker T. Washington and "pull himself up by his own bootstraps." He also assailed the NAACP's characterization of Southern blacks as oppressed because of his "figures" that supposedly established that black Southerners fared better economically than blacks elsewhere. One must distinguish typical black nationalists, who condemned bigotry and argued that blacks should go it alone from Addison, who excused bigotry. Indeed, Addison supported Southern states' overly complicated rules implemented to disenfranchise blacks. "You've got to qualify for anything," he claimed. He even spoke at an event sponsored by a local

(1997); Jeff Frederick, Stand Up for Alabama: Governor George Wallace 151–52 (2007); Jack Nelson, *Alabama Records Show Deaths in Elmore Jail*, St. Petersburg Times, Dec. 29, 1966, at 10A.

[8] *Uncle Tom Charges Leveled at Clergy*, New York Amsterdam News, May 21, 1960, at 22.

white supremacist politician in Lakewood, Ohio, headlined by KKK Imperial Wizard James R. Venable. At the "hate get-together" Addison claimed that blacks had "just as good a chance as any white man" in America. Civil rights groups called him "the world's biggest 'Uncle Tom.'"[9]

Addison, who detractors believed was a black white supremacist, earned such sanctions and, unsurprisingly, "found some approval from conservative white political groups." He promoted the interests of intractable whites by defending disenfranchisement and denying the ill effects of bigotry. He was inexcusably meek for defending racism. And he displayed that not only did he harbor gross impurities in his devotion to black folk, but he was apathetic or even antagonistic to the group. Addison violated all three constructive norms.[10]

John H. Perry, a black school board president in Englewood, New Jersey, was the target of ire in 1963. Black parents criticized Perry for the slow stroll to integration in the school district over which he presided. The breaking point, apparently, was an elementary school that remained 98 percent black nine years after *Brown*. Three black residents led the charge against Perry, calling for his resignation and that of two white members of the five-member board. The residents were "tired of this man being used as a figurehead of integration when in reality he is no more than a tool of those who are denying the Negroes their rights." "It is with great disgust," they continued, "we have noted that time after time Mr. Perry has joined forces with the two segregationists … to vote against integration." Their aim was simple; they wanted to oust the supposed *Uncle Tom*. The residents implied that Perry purposefully delayed integration and was unconcerned about the damage his treachery wreaked on black schoolchildren. Perry, that is, was accused of being unconcerned with his fellow race members. Whether he had truly erred is difficult to determine. But their frustration is understandable.[11]

Although some disputed that *Uncle Tom* was dying off, others declared that it was actually changing its stripes, but remained nonetheless a dangerous animal. No longer was an *Uncle Tom* a timid member of the black underclass. An *Uncle Tom*, rather, was a learned Negro whose tutelage became a wrecking

[9] Allen Howard, *Arrested White Picketing Segregationist Speech*, Cleveland Call and Post, July 6, 1963, at 3A; *"Uncle Tom" Heckler Gets Trial Postponed*, Cleveland Call and Post, Aug. 24, 1963, at 5A; Congressional Record – House of Representatives, *KKK in the North*, June 23, 1966, at 14021.

[10] Encyclopedia of African American Religions 28 (Editors Larry G. Murphy, J. Gordon Melton, and Gary L. Ward 2013).

[11] *N.J. Integrationists Rip Boycott; Rap "Uncle Tom" Negro School Board Head*, Chicago Daily Defender, Feb. 25, 1963, at 6.

ball used to tear down his race. One person at a rally asserted that *Uncle Tom* was not dead but "has just gone to college and put on an Ivy League suit. The hat in his hand [may] be cleaner but it means the same thing." A letter to the editor in the *Defender* in 1960 similarly noted that fifty years prior, *Uncle Toms* were "so-called unlearned Negroes ... but today about 95 percent of the 'Toms' are found among the so-called learned Negroes. Most of them would sell their mothers or sisters for a pat on the back from some white person – right or wrong." Reverend A. Leon Lowry, a Tampa pastor, agreed, saying that "the Southern white man's 'good Negro' is gone ... but now there are Dr. Toms, Rev. Toms and Mr. Toms." A South Carolinian preacher remarked that *Uncle Toms* are "too often ... teachers and preachers doctors and lawyers.... They are well known and people listen to them. And too often they don't speak for us." The *Pittsburgh Courier*, similarly, ran an article in 1962 stating, "In case you don't know, an Uncle Thomas is an Uncle Tom with a college degree and Brooks Brother suit." This line of thinking reveals that some blacks once believed that the unassertive black masses were once the race's biggest liabilities. But the situation had changed. Blacks had to fear their educated brethren most.[12]

Beyond the usage of *Uncle Tom* to attack blacks opposing integration, the epithet was pitted against blacks in the context of busing. Because of residential segregation, unless children were sent to schools far from their homes, public schools would remain segregated even absent the discriminatory intent of government decision makers. Many school districts implemented busing programs to comply with a federal court desegregation order. Some mainstream civil rights organizations, particularly the NAACP, favored busing to achieve integration. Blacks who disagreed with busing sometimes endured *Uncle Tom* ridicule. The true race warriors, so the argument went, supported busing because integration assured black children an education as good as that of their white counterparts. Those who rejected that argument, however, purportedly acquiesced to whites who endeavored to bar black children from attending school with their sons and daughters.[13]

An example of this supposed acquiescence occurred in early 1970s Atlanta. After a federal court determined that Atlanta public schools had

---

[12] Gerald D. Bullock and Samuel R. Stratton, *1,000 Labor Leaders Move Toward Equality*, Daily Defender, June 6, 1960, at A1; S. A. Davis, *Uncle Toms*, Daily Defender, Aug. 1, 1960, at A11; *Say Automation Is Threat*, New York Amsterdam News, Jan. 7, 1961, at 15; *Shun "Toms," NAACP Tells Regional Staff*, Afro-American, Mar. 1, 1969, at 12; *McClelland Quits Race, Shocks Democrat Party*, Pittsburgh Courier, Mar. 17, 1962, at 12.

[13] *Keyes v. School District No. 1*, 413 U.S. 189 (1973) (holding that absent a segregative intent, a school board does not have to integrate its schools).

been purposefully segregated, the court required that Atlanta's school board implement a desegregation plan. Afterward, the school board and Atlanta's NAACP branch heatedly negotiated an agreement. The NAACP Legal Defense Fund (LDF), the organization's national legal arm, had been handling the case from its New York headquarters until the president of Atlanta's NAACP branch, Lonnie King, who opposed busing, secured power of attorney and hired different counsel. With new counsel, the Atlanta branch and the school board reached what detractors derided as the "Atlanta Compromise," recalling Booker T. Washington's infamous racial accommodationist speech. The plan only bused 4,000 children. The livid LDF, preferring a scheme that involved far more children, called the plan the unconstitutional concoction of whites and a cadre of *Uncle Toms*. LDF attorney Howard Moore assailed the compromise as like a "slave auctioning himself off, more or less . . . literally selling out the rights of our children."[14]

The Atlanta NAACP branch, however, deemed the plan good for the city even though a majority of Atlanta's blacks favored busing. To defend themselves, the Atlanta branch's officials sampled the rhetorical flourishes of states' rights advocates who wanted to prevent outsiders from interfering in their local affairs. A local NAACP leader claimed that Atlanta residents detested a "New York Yankee coming down here and telling us how to run our school case." The head of the branch sang a similar tune, declaring that the LDF was more "interested in winning civil rights law suits" than promoting "what's good for Atlanta." That they employed the vernacular of the former Confederacy to denounce Northern "carpetbaggers" undoubtedly alienated many. But one had valid reasons to oppose busing. Indeed, busing is not a litmus test.[15]

Another example of opposition to busing being equated to treachery occurred in January 1973 when a black anti-busing crusader, Texas state legislator Clay Smothers, drew "cheers and laughs" during his speech delivered at an anti-busing rally in Oxon Hill, Maryland. Twenty thousand demonstrated against a plan that bused 32,000 of Prince Georges County's 162,000 schoolchildren, a district about one-fourth black. Smothers, with a "mixture of wit and anger," spoke from the flatbed of his truck, drawing the loudest applause of all. Smothers's popularity that day was possibly an astute recognition by the all-white audience that Smothers, because of his race, was the best possible

[14] Stephen G. N. Tuck, Beyond Atlanta: The Struggle for Racial Equality in Georgia, 1940–1980 212 (2001); Kevin Michael Kruse, White Flight: Atlanta and the Making of Modern Conservatism 239 (2005).

[15] Tomiko Brown-Nagin, Courage to Dissent: Atlanta and the Long History of the Civil Rights Movement 366 (2011); Tuck, Beyond Atlanta 212; Jeff Nesmith, *Atlanta Busing Compromise Leaves NAACP Bitterly Split*, Washington Post, Nov. 24, 1972, at A15.

busing antagonist. Blacks, however, had a far different response: Smothers was an *Uncle Tom*. His foes likely took exception to his antics in front of a white crowd, and concluded that he was performing for white folks who, motivated by racial animus, disapproved of busing. Smothers, who said he was "against blacks ... talking to me about their rights," had a terrible reputation among blacks back home in Texas. He was deemed "a black Archie Bunker" and a "black Theodore Bilbo."[16]

Although segregation by law was waning, black integrationists in the 1960s and 1970s still had to work diligently to complete the desegregation process. In the South, school boards vociferously fought the Supreme Court's increasing demand for school desegregation. Many social places, like Southern lunch counters, still refused to serve black patrons. The North had its own problems with segregation. Although segregation was not legally codified, many Northern cities were just as segregated as their Southern counterparts. To get all on board, integrationists often depicted their black opponents as *Uncle Toms*. If a critical mass of blacks said that integration was not necessary, that America had done enough to fix its racial ills, many blacks feared the nation would listen. Here, blacks managed norms in response to the concern that whites would use any crack in the black populace to halt the already tortoise-like pace toward integration. As in the previous period, when blacks discharged *Uncle Tom* to attack blacks insufficiently antisegregation, in this period, *Uncle Tom* was lofted at conservative blacks who opposed integration.

UNCLE TOMS DO NOT SIT-IN OR PROTEST

The strategy to strangle segregation had to be as mighty as the practice itself. Jim Crow was once the boss in the South, particularly the Deep South. Blacks were segregated not just in public education, but also in social settings such as hotels and restaurants. Because the latter discrimination was usually not state sponsored, the Fourteenth Amendment provided little remedy. Blacks could not enter a courtroom armed with an equal protection argument and exit with the right to stay at a Memphis hotel. Jim Crow could block such conventional maneuvers. Blacks, therefore, had to devise creative attacks. Protests generally, and sit-ins specifically, became the most popular. Sit-in demonstrators, often heralded as heroes, were commonly juxtaposed to purported *Uncle Toms* who

---

[16] *No Busers Make Hero of Black On Their Side,* New Journal and Guide, Jan. 20, 1973, at B3; Charles J. Ogletree, All Deliberate Speed: Reflections on the First Half Century of Brown v. Board of Education 67 (2004); *The Ten Best and Ten Worst Legislators,* Texas Monthly, July 1977, at 100.

were maligned for avoiding conflict. Blacks, that is, enforced racial loyalty norms to incite blacks to be active fighters in social movements.

The sit-in has long been in blacks' repertoire. In 1867, blacks in Charleston, South Carolina, used it to boycott the city's first horse-drawn streetcars. Blacks could ride on the front or rear platforms but were forbidden from sitting inside the cars. After a few sit-ins, the company relented and implemented a non-discriminatory policy. Blacks rode the streetcars shortly thereafter until Jim Crow laws were passed after the turn of the century.[17] Blacks in Richmond similarly devised a plan in April 1867 to attack the local streetcar company's "whites only" policy. In the wake of the sit-ins, the company announced that there would be six streetcars, two of them reserved for white women, and children and blacks were permitted to ride in the others. Blacks in other Southern cities, including New Orleans and Mobile, in 1867, in the first months of congressional Reconstruction, likewise staged sit-in streetcar demonstrations and earned the right to ride. Even in the nineteenth century, blacks could unite to affect public policy.[18]

Blacks carried the sit-in into the twentieth century. Students at Howard University organized one in April 1943 and one in April 1944, protesting segregation in public places in the nation's capital. They successfully desegregated Little Palace Cafeteria, but their campaign ended after the university's president forced them to stop. Howard relied heavily on the federal government's money, and the racist Senator Theodore Bilbo controlled the purse strings.[19]

Although those students involuntarily discontinued their operation, their form of student protest was adopted by other black college students. In May 1943, blacks at the University of Chicago, using the sit-in, integrated Jack Spratt Café, a restaurant in the South Side of Chicago.[20] More famously, Franklin

---

[17] William C. Hine, *The 1867 Charleston Streetcar Sit-Ins: A Case of Successful Black Protest*, 77 South Carolina Historical Magazine 110, 110–14 (1976).

[18] Id. at 112; Peter J. Rachleff, Black Labor in Richmond, 1865–1890, 42 (1989); Eric Foner, Reconstruction: America's Unfinished Revolution 1863–1877 281–82 (1988); *Street-Car Difficult in Richmond*, New York Times, Apr. 24, 1867, at 1; *The Richmond Street Cars*, New York Times, May 2, 1867, at 5; Roger A. Fischer, *A Pioneer Protest: The New Orleans Street-Car Controversy of 1867*, 53 Journal of Negro History, 219, 219–33 (1968); *The Street-Car Question in Mobile*, New York Times, Apr. 21, 1867, at 1.

[19] Flora Bryant Brown, *NAACP Sponsored Sit-ins by Howard University Students in Washington, D.C., 1943–1944*, 85 Journal of Negro History 274, 278–80 (2000); Beverly W. Jones, *Before Montgomery and Greensboro: The Desegregation Movement in the District of Columbia, 1950–1953*, 43 Phylon 144, 144–54 (1982); Charles E. Cobb Jr., On the Road to Freedom: A Guide Tour of the Civil Rights Train 2 (2008); Theodore Gilmore Bilbo, Take Your Choice: Separation or Mongrelization (1947).

[20] *Break Down Race Bars at 47th Street Café*, Chicago Defender, May 15, 1943, at 8; August Meier and Elliott M. Rudwick, CORE: A Study in the Civil Rights Movement, 1942–1968 (1975).

McCain, Ezell Blair Jr., Joseph McNeil, and David Richmond of North
Carolina A&T University conducted sit-ins at a Greensboro Woolworth's
department store in February 1960. By month's end, similar protests were
being conducted in thirty-one cities in seven Southern states.[21]

The young black college students who launched sit-in efforts in the South
were frequently distinguished from the supposed *Uncle Toms* of yesteryear.
One reporter described the frays between the two camps as "showdowns" and
"no place is left for Uncle Toms." Another wrote, "Young Negro America –
version 1960 – has been emancipated from fear, untied from Uncle Tom's
apron strings and weaned from the milk of patience." One man who penned
a letter to the editor in the *Afro-American* was dismayed that "[m]any of our
contemporary uncle toms advise our young progressive minded people to
relinquish their strategy in promoting betterment for our race." Writing to the
Philadelphia Tribune, another man thought that black youth had reformed
the image of the Southern Negro, scribing, "When the sit-ins demonstrations
started in the South a friend of mine said to me, 'there are no more Uncle
Toms in the South, they all moved up north!'"[22] Another agreed, postulating
that "85 per cent of the colored people in the South are rebelling against the
segregated customs, about 10 per cent are 'straddling the fence' and about
five per cent are 'Uncle Toms.'" Such pronouncements helped promote black
solidarity around the righteousness of active protests. Indeed, they not only
compelled blacks to fight, but also established that blacks who advocated
timidity would be deemed traitorous.[23]

A couple of months after the Greensboro sit-ins, blacks managed racial loyalty norms to push blacks into active resistance. In Columbus, Ohio, protestors
staged a rally during which they implored blacks to "drop their 'Uncle Tom
attitude.'" After dropping the "Uncle Tom attitude," the protestors hoped,
blacks would begin participating in sit-ins and similar demonstrations and
specifically promoting the boycotting of places like Woolworth's, notorious
for segregated lunch counters in the South. The protestors understood that a
strain of thought in the black community taught blacks to suffer, rather than
boldly confront racism. Imploring blacks to eschew the "Uncle Tom attitude"

[21] Kenneth T. Andrews and Michael Biggs, *The Dynamics of Protest Diffusion: Movement
Organizations, Social Networks, and News Media in the 1960 Sit-Ins,* 71 *American Sociologic
Review* 752, 754 (2006); Gretchen Cassel Eick, Dissent in Wichita: The Civil Rights
Movement in the Midwest, 1954–72 1–11 (2001).

[22] Daniel Collins, *Uncle Tom's Funeral,* Afro-American, June 11, 1960, at 4; Petre McCloud,
Readers Say, Philadelphia Tribune, July 12, 1960, at 4.

[23] *Divide and Conquer White Man's Device, Says "Ten City" Head,* Afro-American, Feb. 25,
1961, at 7.

constructively built solidarity and helped disabuse blacks of the notion that waiting until it gets better was a proper rejoinder to racism.[24]

In the spring of 1960, Savannah, Georgia, like many Southern cities, witnessed sit-ins. When the youthful leader of the local NAACP and others sought to rip apart the restraints of segregation, the city's mayor countered that their activities were sullying the city's reputation. The demonstrations started with student sit-in protests at a "dime store." Other economic boycotts followed. Demonstrators held placards in front of stores that read: "Is Our Money Separate?," "Don't Buy Where You Can't Eat," and "Off Limit for Negro Patrons." By the first week of May, the four-week-old boycott had cost local merchants more than a million dollars. Some blacks disagreed with the tactics. At first, local "Uncle Toms" ignored the boycotts. But then they were under siege when the boycotters began publically calling them out by name. No blacks, subsequently, defied the boycott. None wanted to be the "Uncle Tom," perfectly illustrating why blacks are wise to manage racial loyalty norms. Constructive norms help promote unity and encourage racial progress.[25]

As the previous tale established, blacks who insisted that the race should eschew protest methods needed to take cover. *Uncle Tom* was inevitably headed their way. Take Dr. J. S. Nathaniel Tross, a black minister and editor of the *Charlotte Post.* Tross claimed that most of Charlotte's blacks frowned on black protestors. In a radio interview, Tross called the demonstrations "uncalled for, unnecessary, ill-advised and inexpedient." In response, students at Johnson C. Smith University, a historically black college in town, hung, from the university's main campus gate, a dummy with "Dr. Ross, Uncle Tom" painted on it. One can never be certain what compelled Tross's derision of student protestors. The students perhaps thought that he was akin to Percy Greene and Rev Humes; perhaps, that is, at the behest of white supremacists, he derogated the aims of civil rights advocates. Or maybe they fathomed that he was simply part of an old guard. He was accustomed to the antiquated mindset that coached blacks into silence rather than loud shouts for racial fairness. Blacks, nonetheless, had a definite interest in rousing blacks into action, and maligning those attempting to subvert those aims was a worthy enterprise.[26]

In 1963, with the help of comedian Dick Gregory, black Mississippians demonstrated against disfranchisement and segregation in the state. After a

---

[24] *Urges, End of "Uncle Tomism,"* Chicago Defender, Apr. 23, 1960, at 9.

[25] Louis Martin, *Sit-In Pickets Startle Southern "Paradise,"* Chicago Defender, May 7, 1960, at 1.

[26] *"Race Relations Sunday" Comes at Opportune Time,* New Journal and Guide, Feb. 20, 1960, at 13; Miles Wolff, Lunch at the Five and Ten: The Greensboro Sit-ins: A Contemporary History 153 (1970).

day of protesting, Gregory announced to the crowd of demonstrators that "we can end this mess this week if enough of you decided to do so.... With the salaries you're making, you ain't got nothing to lose. Half of you would be eating better in jail." That is, Gregory implied that discrimination could not continue absent blacks' compliance. Dallas' Rev. W. R. Fairley, "Mr. Goodwill," disagreed with Gregory's advice to agitate the status quo that day. Fairley tried to steer the crowd away from protest but was derided as an "Uncle Tom." A black attorney spoke after "Mr. Goodwill," saying, "I'm glad to know we have an emissary from the other side who can go back and take this message.... You go tell them this: White folks, it's not like it used to be." Fairley attempted to rebut criticism, but stopped, unable to reply over the raucous *Uncle Tom* calls. Gregory invited Fairley to join the demonstrators and offered to "take the bandana off [his] head."[27]

In 1964, residents of Chester, Pennsylvania, staged an interracial protest of the city's segregated public schools. The protestors wanted to end school segregation and equalize the conditions between black and white schools. A local clergyman, Donald G. Ming, pled for blacks to eschew the "unlawful" demonstrations. Ming said he was for racial progress, but thought the proper setting was "the bargaining table, not the streets." Stanley Branche, a Ming critic, headed a local organization affiliated with the protests. Branche believed that the biggest obstacle was not whites, but *Uncle Toms*. Branche hung an effigy of Ming and called him an *Uncle Tom* and a "part-time Negro." When Ming visited the demonstrations, protestors jeered him, saying, "We don't want no Uncle Toms."[28]

Social protests continued into the 1970s, confirming that blacks still saw a prominent color line. These protests also confirmed that local black communities were fissured, impeding unity. A boycott in Vicksburg, Mississippi, illustrates both points. The boycott's impetus occurred on February 23, 1972, the day black seven-year-old Doreen Wallace was allegedly raped by J. D. Hunt, a fifty-eight-year-old white man. Hunt was only charged with contributing to the delinquency of a minor after the grand jury found the evidence insufficient to support a rape charge. Blacks in the city used this as fuel to ignite and sustain a mass boycott of city stores. Their demands were fairly aggressive: increased black representation in city employment, a police review board, the disciplining of certain police and judges, a majority black school board, and finally,

---

[27] Miss. *Police Take Photos of Vote Marchers to Stop Registration*, Chicago Defender, Apr. 6, 1963, at 1.

[28] Kay Anderson, *Jail Leader after Chester School Boycott*, Philadelphia Tribune, Feb. 15, 1964, at 1; Mark Bricklin, *State Police Invade Chester for Boycott*, Philadelphia Tribune, Feb. 11, 1964, at 1.

better jobs in the stores that were being boycotted. With blacks comprising roughly half of the city's population, the boycott devastated local business. Stores reported about a 40 percent decline in receipts. Some blacks opposed the boycott and a small group of them asserted that the boycotters were intimidating them. Black opponents of the boycott were known in the city as *Uncle Toms* for being unwilling to assist in improving the black plight.[29]

Generally, blacks who opposed protest activities were inexcusably meek. Protest activities did, however, come with the severe threat of violence. James Chaney, Andrew Goodman, and Michael Schwerner are indelibly stamped in American history as the three young civil rights workers who were murdered in Mississippi in 1964. The work was dangerous. If a black person cautioned against demonstrations for fear of death, then the inexcusable meekness norm should not have been enforced.

But the preceding supposed *Uncle Toms* were not cautioning against protest because of its inherent dangerousness. Rather, these folk simply exhibited the sheepishness that was no longer tolerable in the 1960s and 1970s. In the 1920s, with a stifling racial climate and the ever-present threat of lynching, to assail protest activities was forgivable. One could cite various reasons, including the low chance of success, against the propriety of group protest. In the 1960s, when blacks achieved victories from protests, arguments against it were baseless. Branding those who bemoaned protest actions as *Uncle Toms* not only lessened the chance that such detractors would exist, it also likely transformed many into willing participants. In this context, loyalty policing helped blacks further their legal interests.

Although some blacks questioned the protest movement, few held the power to actually quell the passion of young blacks. But black college administrators did. Black administrators of Southern historically black colleges were often criticized for obstructing student protests. In 1961, for instance, Southern University suspended eight and refused to readmit forty others because of their participation in off-campus antisegregation protests. The university even closed for a brief period because university president Dr. Felton Clark asserted that the protests had "disrupted ... campus life." More than 100 faculty members condemned the decision in a statement. The students called the school's administrators *Uncle Tom* Rev. B. Elton Cox, a Congress of Racial Equality field secretary who helped quarterback the student protests, called Clark "a modern day, intellectual Uncle Tom."[30]

[29] Austin Scott, *Black Boycott, Job Demands Quiet Vicksburg Downtown*, Washington Post, May 28, 1972, at A16.

[30] *Bias Fight Closes University in La.*, Philadelphia Tribune, Jan. 23, 1962, at 1; Adam Fairclough, Race & Democracy: The Civil Rights Struggle in Louisiana, 1915–1972 266–71 (2008).

Similarly, M. K. Payne, the president of Savannah State College, confronted treachery allegations. In 1963, Payne continued the school's segregation policy, denying admission to white students. Jim Crow, though frequently overlooked, operated in two directions. Racial separation barred blacks from white schools and the opposite held true too. Cleveland Christophe, a professor at the college, was fired when he permitted white students from a nearby Air Force base to take his economics course. About 80 percent of the students at the college protested the decisions with students parading signs reading "Let's Kill Jim-Crow Education." More inflammatory, students burned Payne in effigy to protest the continuation of segregation in Southern schools. The *Defender* reported on the ordeal and included a picture of the scene with the caption: "Effigy of an Uncle Tom."[31]

The firing of black professors at the all-black Grambling College in 1966 precipitated another showdown between blacks and the perceived *Uncle Toms* leading a historically black college, this one after the 1964 Civil Rights Act made segregation illegal. Three professors at Grambling participating in the Great Society Movement (GSM) were fired. The GSM was a civil rights organization comprised of Grambling students and faculty members. Grambling's president, Dr. R. W. E. Jones, denied that the professors' civil rights activities led to their dismissal. He insisted, instead, that the teachers in question were only temporary instructors who failed to meet the minimum standards of permanent faculty members. The students and fired professors, however, rejected that explanation, asserting that Jones bowed to white pressure to stunt any civil rights activities from taking place on campus. One of the fired professors said that it was twice as hard to fight "Uncle Tom Negroes as it is to face the white man in our struggle for equal rights." He wanted to run people like President Jones "out of the community." The GSM started its goal by marching across to the state capital.[32]

Writing in the *Cleveland Call and Post*, William Walker argued that the happenings at black colleges confirmed that black educators "have done a complete Uncle Tom act on the issue of school integration." Walker explained that wherever nonviolent student protests occurred, powerful whites forced black school officials to punish black students to intimidate them from contesting their subordination. There was, however, a silver lining; Walker believed that

---

[31] *700 Students Blast Jim Crow at Savannah State College*, Chicago Daily Defender, May 1, 1963, at 4.

[32] *Rights Fighting Profs Fired; Students March*, Chicago Defender, July 30, 1966, at 32; *Prexy Denies Firing 3 Professors Over Their Rights Activities*, Chicago Defender, Aug. 13, 1966, at 5.

the students' protest efforts exposed "the Uncle Toms with college degrees."[33] Walker's belief that black educators danced whenever their white bosses played music had real merit. Segregationists were known to deliver speeches claiming that they had local black allies in their fight – schoolteachers, bus drivers, and similar employees whose jobs depended on segregation.[34]

The life of the Southern black college president, though, was arduous. Thomas DeSaille Tucker, for instance, a president of a Florida black college, was fired for hiring too many Northern teachers who supposedly scoffed at "Southern institutions" and taught their students to deride "the agricultural and industrial life of the race." Because of white state officials, black administrators were simply unable to support the sit-in movement. If a black president voiced support, Southern state politicians had no qualms about replacing him with a more compliant steward. More harmful, states were even open to closing disobedient schools entirely. If a black president felt that his duty was to educate young black minds, then surely he cannot be faulted for ensuring that the school remains open to serve its mission. The real problem was that the federal government would not enforce the law in the South.[35]

Because of the supreme pressure under which they operated, black presidents should not be automatically condemned if they proved unwilling to support sit-in protests. They could have been true soldiers in the war for racial progress, but concluded that retreat was wise in this particular battle. Some will malign them for not resigning. But to stay was not treacherous. Their detractors unsuccessfully prosecuted them for violating constructive norms.

UNCLE TOM CARRIES A BADGE

About the criminal justice system regarding blacks, W. E. B. Du Bois remarked:

> The laws are made by men who have little interest in him; they are executed by men who have absolutely no motive for treating the black people with

---

[33] 500 Students Boycott Classes at Two Schools in Louisiana, Georgia, Philadelphia Tribune, Feb. 3, 1962, at 1; William Walker, Southern Educators Stand in Way of School Integration, Cleveland Call and Post, June 30, 1962, at 2C; Bias Fight Closes University in La., Philadelphia Tribune, Jan. 23, 1962, at 1; William Walker, Down the Big Road, Cleveland Call and Post, Jan. 20, 1962, at 2B.

[34] Mississippi Is Still Looking to Uncle Toms, Cleveland Call and Post, June 9, 1962, at 2C.

[35] Fairclough, Tuskegee's Robert R. Moton and the Travails of the Early Black College President, at 65; Adam Fairclough, Tuskegee's Robert R. Moton and the Travails of the Early Black College President, 31 Journal of Blacks in Higher Education 94, 100, (2001); Gerald L. Smith, A Black Educator in the Segregated South: Kentucky's Rufus B. Atwood 150 (1994); Jeffrey A. Turner, Sitting In and Speaking Out: Student Movements in the American South, 1960–1970 71 (2010).

courtesy or consideration; and finally, the accused law-breaker is tried, not by his peers, but too often by men who would rather punish ten innocent Negroes than let one guilty one escape.[36]

In 1969, Louis L. Knowles and Kenneth Prewitt captured the essence of blacks' critique of the criminal justice system. "To [black] citizens," they wrote, "the law symbolizes white oppression. Those who represent the legal system are almost exclusively white and reflect the prejudices and ignorance of white society." "The very structures of the system because they are created by whites," they continued, "invariably operate to disadvantage the culturally different, regardless of who is in control." After his tour of the segregated South, Swedish sociologist Gunnar Myrdal reported that "the Negro's most important public contact is with the policeman. He is the personification of white authority in the Negro community." The police officer's chief function regarding the color line was to "keep the Negro in his place." The white officer – the first line of defense – was integral in preserving white supremacy.[37]

For much of American history, popular culture routinely portrayed blacks as enemies of the state, a stain on an otherwise beautiful American fabric. The silent film *Birth of a Nation*, for example, depicted free blacks as naturally violent brutes. That image has grown fainter with time. But when it was vivid, it animated harsh antiblack law enforcement practices. When blacks were lynched, police departments often behaved as though investigative responsibility lay with some other entity. But when blacks were accused of a crime, they were generally denied the constitutional protections that white criminal defendants took for granted. Blacks, therefore, developed hostility and suspiciousness toward the criminal justice system and its police officers. Despite significant progress, those ill feelings remain. In the 1960s and 1970s, they were ubiquitous.[38]

---

[36] Du Bois, The Souls of Black Folk 176.

[37] Louis L. Knowles and Kenneth Prewitt, *Racism in the Administration of Justice, in* Race Crime and Justice 13 (Editors Charles E. Reasons and Jack L. Kuykendall 1972); Gunnar Myrdal, An American Dilemma: The Negro Problem and Modern Democracy 535–42 (7th printing 2009). Homer Hawkins and Richard Thomas are decidedly more vivid. They write, "In every major city where blacks lived in large enough numbers to be noticed and feared by whites, the white police-force was allowed and often encouraged to keep 'the niggers in their place.'" Homer Hawkins and Richard Thomas, *White Policing Black Populations: A History of Race and Social Control in America, in* Out of Order?: Policing Black People 65 (Editors Ellis Cashmore and Eugene McLaughlin 1991).

[38] Even when the police stepped in to stop a lynching, "All too often a lynching prevented by the police merely presaged a legal lynching by a kangaroo court. Blacks thus faced a double bind: while weak legal institutions failed to protect them against lynching, strict and 'efficient' law enforcement hit them harder than any other racial or ethnic group." Manfred Berg, Popular Justice: A History of Lynching in America 164 (2011). There have

During the 1960s, though, police departments began hiring blacks in response to increasing crime in black neighborhoods and urban riots, and because some presumed that blacks were more capable of policing black neighborhoods. Police departments, furthermore, began diversifying their ranks to quiet civil rights organizations' loud demands. By 1971, however, cities had failed miserably at recruitment. Only Washington, DC had meaningfully integrated its police force. And even there that integration was hollow. Indeed, black cops in the nation's capital rarely interacted with their white peers. As a result, two-thirds of black cops trusted few or no white officers. Employment discrimination around the country was rampant, and those few black cops were confined below the glass ceiling on which their white peers walked.[39]

But one high hurdle to recruitment was the low opinion blacks held of police officers. A black Indianapolis man, for example, declined to join the force because "the image is too bad" and his friends would tease him. Considering their history with police, many blacks looked suspiciously at their brethren who opted to become cops, puzzled that anyone would voluntarily immerse themselves in a bigoted environment. Blacks who cashed checks that police departments wrote paid a stiff price: *Uncle Tom*.[40]

Being a police officer is inherently dangerous. Each night, an officer's family wonders if their loved one will return home. But for the black officer the consternation is amplified. The black officer is "much more than a Negro to his ethnic group because he represents the guardian of white society, yet he is not quite a policeman to his working companions because he is stereotyped as a member of an 'inferior' racial category." Blacks had difficulty defending their decision to become police officers because they accepted a position long identified with white supremacy. Norman Randall, a Maryland police

been numerous books written about lynching. See William Fitzhugh Brundage, Lynching in the New South: Georgia and Virginia, 1880–1930 (1993); James H. Madison, A Lynching in the Heartland: Race and Memory in America (2003); Ken Gonzales-Day, Lynching in the West, 1850–1935 (2006); Amy Louise Wood, Lynching and Spectacle: Witnessing Racial Violence in America (2009). One of the main constitutional protections denied to blacks was a criminal trial where members of their race were not purposefully excluded from the jury. See generally Brando Simeo Starkey, *Criminal Procedure, Jury Discrimination & the Pre-Davis Intent Doctrine: The Seeds of a Weak Equal Protection Clause*, 38 *American Journal of Criminal Law* 1 (2011); Ann Martin, *The Police and the Black Community*, 3 *Journal of Police Law Quarterly* 22 (1974); Manfred Weidhorn, An Anatomy of Skepticism 106 (2006).

[39] John L. Cooper, The Police and the Ghetto 116–17 (1980); Paul Delaney, *Recruiting of Negro Police Is a Failure in Most Cities*, New York Times, Jan. 25, 1971, at 1. Cooper writes, perhaps some disagree, that history does not validate the prediction that black cops would be more sympathetic to blacks. Cooper, The Police and the Ghetto 117; Delaney, *Recruiting of Negro Police*, at 1; Kenneth Bolton Jr. and Joe R. Feagin, Black in Blue: African-American Police Officers and Racism 121 (2004).

[40] Bolton and Feagin, Black in Blue 121; Delaney, *Recruiting of Negro Police*, at 1.

officer, said it well in 1962 when he declared, "If you were black and you joined the white establishment, you were an Uncle Tom." A decade later, the idea that black cops were susceptible to *Uncle Tom* accusations persisted. In 1972, Washington, DC officer John W. Littles disclosed that he was often derided as an *Uncle Tom*, a "White Man's Nigger," and "Oreo." This was the life of the black police officer.[41]

As Randall and Littles's testimonies reveal, black folk were wary of the Negro with the shield. Many feared that blacks would forget their roots if they became police officers. No true "race man," according to this reasoning, could long survive as a policeman. The black cop was supposed to help recreate the character of law enforcement. Many frequently believed, however, that they were the ones who were recreated, becoming nothing more than a white cop inside a black shell. This dynamic is evident upon investigating the inconsistency of blacks imploring police departments to hire more black officers but then maligning them as *Uncle Toms*.

In the 1960s and 1970s, violent crime, especially in black neighborhoods, grew alarmingly high. Many contended that whites policing black areas was difficult because of ingrained distrust. Departments across the country concluded that black cops could better police those communities. Police recruiters, then, toured black colleges, advertised in black newspapers, and visited black churches in search of potential candidates. The Washington, DC police department even sent a "recruitmobile" to black slums.[42]

Departments were stunned, however, that black cops were denounced as *Uncle Toms* when venturing into black neighborhoods. "The negro citizenry," proclaimed one white Los Angeles police officer, "was crying for the department to add more Negro policemen. Then when we send Negro officers out into areas where mostly Negroes live, these Negro officers are openly called all kinds of names and instantly become objects of thrown trash, bricks and bottles." Sacramento Sheriff John Misterly also reported that blacks desired inclusion. "But," said Misterly, "we have very few black applicants per year, probably because they feel they will be labeled 'Uncle Toms' if they enter police work." Misterly's hunch – that *Uncle Tom*, a scarecrow, intimidated potential recruits – was correct. As one black student said in 1970, "Black policemen can't do much because of the way the system is.

---

[41] Nicholas Alex, Black in Blue: A Study of the Negro Policeman 13–14, 32 (1969); Anne Arundel, *City Honors Its First Black Police Officers, Integration Came 40 Years Ago*, Washington Post, Dec. 14, 2000, at M03; Ron Shaffer, *Compassion Wins Honor for Officer*, Washington Post, Aug. 20, 1972, at B1.

[42] Carl Husemoller Nightingale, On the Edge: A History of Poor Black Children and Their American Dreams 4 (1993); Alex, Black in Blue 28.

Blacks call them 'uncle toms.' I wouldn't become one." Blacks in Los Angeles were so distrustful of the local criminal justice system the LAPD had to recruit at Southern universities.[43]

Los Angeles Sentinel columnist Bill Lane faulted the white power structure for blacks' cynicism. "[I]t all points up a display of harvest now being reaped from a crop of racial Jim Crow sown over the past 30 years in police departments," Lane wrote in the black newspaper. His critique concerned Los Angeles, but applied elsewhere with equal vigor. Employment discrimination within police departments denied entrance to only a few blacks. An unmistakable stink of racism, therefore, emanated from law enforcement. Black cops had to accept the stench, many blacks presumed, to remain on a police force. The black officer who endeavored to air out the department, purifying it of its prejudiced elements, would face quick dismissal. The true race man would never survive, but the accommodating one, however, could persevere. Perhaps this explains why, in 1968, when Winston Moore, superintendent of the Cook County Jail in Chicago, became the first black head of a major penal institution, he declared, "I am not an Uncle Tom. I have never been one and will never be one."[44]

This discussion might cause some to believe that blacks enforced a racial loyalty norm holding that black cops were inherently treacherous. But such a reading is mistaken. Black cops, rather, were sometimes deemed *Uncle Toms* because negative traits were assumed. Black officers, that is, were sometimes considered *Uncle Toms* because many anticipated that they would invariably develop the repugnant characteristics identified with duplicity.

The account of Bob Oliver, who shed the *Uncle Tom* label, supports this interpretation. Oliver, first baseman for the Anaheim Angels, was also a part-time officer in the 1970s. "I wasn't accepted too well at first," Oliver recounted. "I was just another black pig. An Uncle Tom ... But the kids saw I was a good guy and started gaining confidence in me." If being a black cop inherently violated a social norm, Oliver could never have redeemed himself. The *Sentinel's* explanation of why young blacks refused to become cops further buttresses this point. "[T]o date," the newspaper claimed, "perhaps the major reason most young men from this community shun the blue uniform is because they have been led to believe that the police department is a racist group and there is no future for a black man in the department unless he takes on the garnements

---

[43] Bill Lane, *The Inside Story*, Los Angeles Sentinel, May 12, 1966, at D2; *Sheriff Says Recruiting Snag on Written Tests*, Sacramento Observer, Jan. 29, 1970, at B31; *Roving Reporter: What People Think*, Sun Reporter, Sept. 26, 1970, at 14.

[44] Lane, *The Inside Story*, at D2; *"I'm No Uncle Tom" Says New Jail Boss in Chicago*, New Journal and Guide, Mar. 23, 1968, at 8.

[*sic*] of an 'Uncle Tom.' This he refuses to do." Black cops were deemed *Uncle Toms* – which evidenced that they broke a social norm – because the community expected treasonous inclinations from them.[45]

Derek Ackeridge, a black officer, explained that not all black cops were *Uncle Toms*. Ackeridge understood blacks' hostility toward the police and black officers specifically. Police departments, he posited, symbolized oppression. But Ackeridge contended that some black cops were worthy of adulation, holding that they came in two varieties: the black cop and the *Uncle Tom* cop. The black cop was devoted to his people, whereas the *Uncle Tom* cop was self-interested, an enemy to the black cop and the entire black community. "The Uncle Tom cops," Ackeridge indicated, "shun [the black cop] out of fear that he might make waves in the police department standing up for justice and ... in so doing create problems for them. These Uncle Toms, to achieve their status, had to disregard their manhood to become boot licking lackies [*sic*] for the bosses. They tap danced while the boss was whistling Dixie just to become head nigger in charge." Ackeridge's maligning black cops for kowtowing to white bigotry for their own self-interests was constructive. Black officers who acquiesced to bigotry not out of fear for their own occupational future, but as a strategy to further their own career, had shown themselves to harbor gross impurities in their devotion to the race and violated the norm that required blacks care about the group.[46]

Ackeridge touched on the salient issue animating loyalty enforcement of black police officers. Many blacks, including Ackeridge, believed the social climate within police departments encouraged conduct and attitudes that would render black cops unwilling or unable to push for positive change in the criminal justice system. Within police departments, many presumed, blacks were pressured to comport subserviently, avert their eyes to injustice, or worse, actively perpetrate abuse on blacks. And blacks' fear was justified because "[i]n the process of adaptation, many black officers conform to the informal norms of" police departments. Indeed, "[t]heir lower occupational status, coupled with a desire to maintain a positive self-image as a good professional officer, can lead ... to ... conforming." Many black cops, in other words, refused to buck the system and instead became police officers who perpetrated injustices on fellow blacks. A segment of the black community countered by pressing black cops to neither debase themselves nor further

---

45 Dave Distel, *This Is Interesting Work*, Los Angeles Times, Feb. 12, 1974, at C1; *Where Are Black Officers?*, Los Angeles Sentinel, June 10, 1971, at A6.
46 Patrolman Derek T. Ackeridge, *The Policeman: A Black Nationalist*, New York Amsterdam News, July 31, 1971, at A7.

their career at blacks' expense. Blacks needed a counterbalance to compete with the pressure black cops faced within police departments. The solution was enforcing racial loyalty norms that instructed black cops to neither exhibit servility nor abuse other blacks. Norm breakers were punished with *Uncle Tom* denunciations.[47]

Concluding that an officer is guilty of betrayal without individualized evidence is quite unfair. But black cops were often put in situations where eschewing black solidarity was very tantalizing. Alerting them that treachery would be penalized was constructive because it put the race at the forefront of black officers' minds. They were members of a group that was treated poorly by the criminal justice system of which they were also members. This racial loyalty enforcement could coax blacks into seeing themselves as engines of reform that could reshape the criminal justice system, rendering it fairer. Such norm management could, furthermore, compel black cops to respect the black citizenry and treat them with dignity, a manner in which many white cops did not.

Perhaps in part because they feared violating norms, some black officers refused to remain quiet amid the racial hostility and inequality of the 1960s police department. Many black cops felt they were treated differently than their white peers. Black officers contended that employment standards were higher for them in terms of hiring, retention, and promotion. Oftentimes blacks were only permitted to police black neighborhoods and could only occupy low-level positions. Studying the data, one scholar concluded that the black officer "is far from achieving the full status that the job implies for his white counterpart."[48]

Melvin Jackson, a black Philadelphia policeman, harbored such grievances. Jackson's insider status, as true with Ackeridge, provides a unique position from which to study how the loyalty of black cops was policed. Jackson, who resigned in 1967 after a fifteen-month stint, disclosed that discrimination pervaded in the force. He claimed that blacks were continuously passed over for promotions in favor of whites with less seniority. Blacks, moreover, were confined to the lowest duties. "This is the way it is throughout the whole police department," he claimed. "You have to be an Uncle Tom to get ahead. If you 'make waves' or 'create problems' they discipline blacks." Jackson, in other words, considered blacks who acquiesced to the racism within police

[47] Bolton and Feagin, Black in Blue 121; John Cooper writes that black officers were "informally ... discouraged from being too helpful or friendly with residents of the ghetto." Cooper, The Police and the Ghetto 117.
[48] Alex, Black in Blue 112.

departments as *Uncle Toms*. Such comments notified black police officers that the black community frowned upon accommodation.[49]

His criticism, however, was only constructive if the blacks in question consciously maneuvered to further their own careers by taking on the persona of "the black man who won't complain." One is not inexcusably meek if one remains silent on bigotry within one's professional setting if speaking out will effectively terminate one's employment. But purposefully being silent to reap personal benefits is a patently obvious disloyal tactic deserving swift censure.

Jackson's testament further underscores the impetus for creating social norms to regulate the behavior of black cops. The system rewarded black cops who avoided challenging the status quo. The self-interested black officers, therefore, realized the personal benefits to be acquired by playing the role of the "compliant Negro." A tactic to dissuade blacks from pursuing that portrayal was announcing that any who accepted the role incurred a heavy penalty. The cost for racial treason had to be high. Raising the price of duplicity was the function of racial loyalty norms and *Uncle Tom*.

The behaviors that Jackson reported appear mild in comparison to other findings. Take the events of a northeastern black family into consideration. A mother of four, Mrs. Anna Hill was beaten by white thugs in her predominantly white neighborhood just a week after the family moved into their new home. On a July afternoon in 1970, Mrs. Hill sent her fourteen-year-old son and her thirteen-year-old daughter to a local store. On their trip, white youths hurled bottles at the siblings and sexually threatened Hill's daughter. "We're going to get some nigger," they shouted. Mrs. Hill approached white women nearby to discuss the incident. The women, unwilling to converse, handed bats to two nearby white boys who proceeded to bludgeon Hill. She then called the police. Two policemen arrived on the scene, one black, one white. The black police officer told her that he refused to intervene. Later, when discussing the unfortunate events, Mrs. Hill said, "That [U]ncle Tom told me that 'this is a white neighborhood and that he couldn't protect a few of us blacks.'" Hill's use of *Uncle Tom* was constructive because the officer clearly had no concern for the race.[50]

On par with the previous supposed *Uncle Tom* cop was an officer Charles Evers recalled in his autobiography. Evers's awareness of "Tom," as he derisively labeled him, began after Evers helped launch an economic boycott in Port Gibson, Mississippi. The boycott was immensely successful, resulting in blacks being hired in stores and two black police officer placements in addition

---

49 Len Lear, *Quits Police Force; Charges Harassment*, Philadelphia Tribune, Nov. 28, 1967, at 1.
50 *Mob Armed with Baseball Bats Beat Mother of 4*, Philadelphia Tribune, July 21, 1970, at 1.

to one deputy sheriff appointment. The city also agreed to take accounts of police brutality seriously and to cease referring to adult blacks as "boys" and "girls." Emboldened by their victory, blacks next agitated for better schools, streets, and sewers. But the more blacks pushed, the more whites defended the status quo. Desiring to maintain the integrity of their prized racial caste, city bigwigs hired a white police chief, an assistant police chief with a reputation of abusing blacks, and Tom, a black policeman. Tom's assignment was to spy on and intimidate blacks. Tom, an obvious derivative of *Uncle Tom*, was a natural target of derision. By willingly serving as a sleuth for whites who wanted to stunt racial progress, Tom revealed himself as amenable to throwing the race overboard as he navigated a self-serving strategy.[51]

Tom violated the norm that requires blacks to care about the race and also the norm that prohibits furthering the enemies' interests. Blacks needed to discipline those using their police shield to serve as a saboteur; doing so helped build black solidarity that could serve as a launching pad for implementing strategies for full racial emancipation. Tom was unlikely to be brought back into the fold after being branded a race traitor. But those who learned about the censure he received would be less likely to follow his path, producing a population that contained less betrayal and more unity.

Many might find the behavior of Captain Chester Gethers, who was deemed an "Uncle Tom" cop in June 1965, less troubling. Gethers, a Philadelphia police officer, ordered the arrest of two black demonstrators at Girard College who were blocking street traffic and disturbing the public while participating in a political protest. Cecil B. Moore, head of the local chapter of the NAACP, claimed that Gethers failed to first ask the two gentlemen to move. During a later protest, Moore denounced Gethers as an "Uncle Tom in charge of that West Philadelphia cotton patch." Moore pushed the protestors to picket Gethers's police station and even his home to "let his children see what kind of Uncle Tom they have for a father."[52]

Gethers, seemingly, would have avoided ostracism had he simply warned the protestors instead of quickly arresting them. Working against him was that he easily could be viewed as the black marionette cop who hindered a civil rights protest at the behest of his white bosses manipulating his strings. Whether Gethers attempted to curry favor with whites by showing that he too could be tough on the "unruly blacks" is unknowable. Thus, appraising the constructiveness of the use of *Uncle Tom* here is impossible. But given

[51] Evers, Evers 176–77.
[52] Art Peters, *Official Vows "Won't Take It Lying Down,"* Philadelphia Tribune, June 8, 1965, at 1.

the circumstances, some blacks were predisposed to negatively interpret his actions. Gethers, therefore, became an archetype of the black cop who sacrificed the race's interests for his own.

What was true for Officer Gethers was common throughout the era – a segment of the black population sought to foster group unity to improve their condition. The black cop, as a component of an unequal criminal justice system, faced perhaps added burden to be an agent of change. Any hint of failure resulted in group ostracism. But the norm management in this context was generally constructive. Blacks used *Uncle Tom* and enforced racial loyalty norms in ways that promoted black solidarity, which provided a starting point to contest inequities and mobilize blacks around important legal goals.

BLACK MILITANTS, MALCOLM X, AND *UNCLE TOMS*

The 1960s saw a new era of black militancy, featuring a worldview contrasting deeply with that of mainstream civil rights organizations. Where moderate organizations like the NAACP and its peers advocated for integration and preferred to work within the system to generate better outcomes, militants concluded that the system was fundamentally flawed, only producing racist outcomes. Despite their deep differences, the two camps did share an important similarity – management of racial loyalty norms. Moderates, on the one hand, sanctioned segregation accommodationists. Militants, on the other hand, directed their ire at integrationists, which was, outside of Garveyism, a completely new viewpoint.

But not only did they throw *Uncle Tom* jabs, militants leaned into their punches much more than anyone else. That militants were particularly aggressive users of *Uncle Tom* was obvious even to those who lived during the era. In 1963, for instance, Associated Negro Press columnist P. F. Prattis reported that militants wielded *Uncle Tom* as a sledgehammer against foes. Prattis believed that unless black leaders embraced their brand of militancy they would be stuck with *Uncle Tom*. And he claimed, "[o]nce known as an 'Uncle Tom' [the leader's] career is over."[53] Similarly, columnist Stanley G. Robertson said that black militants call anyone who disagrees with their positions an "Uncle Tom" and a sellout to the "Power Structure."[54]

This sort of racial loyalty norm management, however, was deeply destructive, a point amplified in the next chapter. The norm managed here was that not being a militant was treacherous. Loyal blacks, that is, agree with

[53] P. L. Prattis, *Issues Good and Bad*, Los Angeles Sentinel, Dec. 26, 1963, at A6.
[54] Stanley G. Robertson, *L.A. Confidential*, Los Angeles Sentinel, Oct. 12, 1967, at A7.

black militants' critique of America and their aggressive solutions to the color line. This idea failed to reach norm status, not deemed legitimate by a broad enough swathe of the black community. Although black militants criticized their foes for betrayal, to build black solidarity, their efforts actually fractured the black community, weakening the bonds of racial kinship.

An example of such destructive norm management occurred during an NAACP commemoration of the seventh anniversary of *Brown* in Harlem. In May 1961, the African Nationalist Action Council, a militant organization, prevented the event from starting. Bearing signs that read "2,000 cops could not stop protest against the 'Uncle Tom' NAACP," the militants demanded that Robert F. Williams be allowed to speak. Williams, of Monroe, North Carolina, was a leading black militant in the '50s and '60s espousing "armed self-reliance." His local NAACP chapter was a unique "well-armed and disciplined fighting unit." In 1959, the NAACP suspended Williams for preaching violence. He continued his work, and militant blacks considered him a cultural hero of sorts. When Williams spoke, he announced his goals of "fighting the enemy, with arms [and] not turning the other cheek" and denounced the "Uncle Toms" who advocated passive resistance. After his speech, the meeting was called off because the militants refused to let anyone else speak. The destructive norm here compelled blacks to be supporters of violent resistance or be deemed a sellout.[55]

Black Muslims, particularly those linked with the Nation of Islam, were also frequent and destructive purveyors of sellout rhetoric. As once said by a black man sympathetic to the teachings of Elijah Muhammad, the faith's religious leader, integrationists "willingly or blindly accept Uncle Tom leadership and allow their puppet leaders to lead them to certain disaster." Integrationists endured frequent *Uncle Tom* criticisms. But believing that integration offered blacks their best hope for racial progress was not tantamount to betrayal. As was true in the age of Garvey and Du Bois, a disagreement between two camps was unwisely equated to racial treachery.[56]

The most historically significant Black Muslim of the era was Malcolm X, a pugnacious wielder of *Uncle Tom*. The documentary *The Hate that Hate Produced* (1959) brought Malcolm X into the public eye. From there, he matured into one of the most visible black leaders until his death in 1965. His race relations views were a product of various hardships. The murder of his father by the KKK, the racism he endured from white teachers and fellow

[55] Alfredo Graham, *NAACP Rally Wreckers Denounced*, Pittsburgh Courier, May 27, 1961, at A3; *Nationalists Break Up NAACP's Harlem Rally*, New York Amsterdam News, May 27, 1961, at 13.

[56] W. F. Scotty, *Likes Muhammad*, New York Amsterdam News, Sept. 23, 1961, at 13.

students as an adolescent, and his imprisonment all shaped the thoughts of a man who profoundly impacted the 1960s. Malcolm openly displayed his hatred of so-called *Uncle Tom* Negroes in many colorful musings. Malcolm X appropriated "animal imagery" in his speech to free blacks from their image of whites as a moral people. His imagery was a device to convince blacks to come together to solve their own problems.[57]

Malcolm repudiated both integration and assimilation. Actually, he conflated the two. Malcolm's adversaries – moderate civil rights leaders – sought integration. Assimilation, however, entailed adopting white cultural norms. But Malcolm argued that racial amalgamation accompanies integration, which he vehemently opposed. Instead, he sold black nationalism – the "control of politics and economics within black communities." By linking integration with assimilation, Malcolm strengthened his argument and leveled a heavy blow against his opponents. "He rejected the idea of becoming part of white society by positing the idea that to become part of this society was to become something that the black person was not: *white*."[58]

As a spokesman for the Nation of Islam, Malcolm championed a separate black existence. He described blacks' parting from America as the breaking up of a marriage. "We can't get along, so let's be intelligent and get a divorce," he once remarked. Martin Luther King rebutted Malcolm's argument, insisting that "[w]e are here in America and we are home to stay.... We aren't going nowhere." But Malcolm considered integration a fool's errand. "I know from personal experience," he wrote in his autobiography. He told one audience, "[y]ou can't please the white man ... You just can't please him. You can't satisfy him. Why, you're out of your mind trying to make love to a white man." And the result of integration was interracial marriage and biracial children, two things Malcolm abhorred.[59]

Those seeking integration were middle-class blacks, Malcolm argued, and he had no "love for the black bourgeoisie." Malcolm, instead, identified with working-class blacks who were most likely to be disenchanted with the illusory American dream. Using his past as a poverty-stricken child and ex-convict who turned his life around, Malcolm was a person with whom these blacks could relate. Malcolm was real. Unlike other black leaders, he, at least initially, steered clear of attempting to change white attitudes. Not until his hajj in

---

[57] Frederick D. Harper, *The Influence of Malcolm X on Black Militancy*, 1 Journal of Black Studies 387, 390 (1971); Hank Flick and Larry Powell, *Animal Imagery in the Rhetoric of Malcolm X*, 18 Journal of Black Studies 435, 435–37 (1988).

[58] Dean E. Robinson, To Forge a Nation, to Forge an Identity: Black Nationalism in the United States, 1957–1974 13, 25–26, 31 (PhD dissertation 1995).

[59] Bruce Perry, Malcolm: The Life of a Man Who Changed Black America 187–88 (1991).

1964 did Malcolm X "bec[o]me less and less doctrinairely antagonistic towards whites." Malcolm was devoted to getting blacks to break the stronghold white Americans had on their psyche, encouraging independent thought.[60]

Among his peers in the Nation of Islam, Malcolm was the most critical of upper-class blacks. He assailed them as "house slaves," "Nincompoops with Ph.D.s," "Quislings," "sell-outs," and, of course, Uncle Toms. Malcolm assailed "bourgeois Negroes" and thought the group featured three distinct types. First were "working-class black folk with upper-class pretensions" who attempted to be the true bourgeoisie, but actually did not have money. They created, nonetheless, a "black elite culture." The second group was wealthy blacks with lives very comparable to their white peers. Malcolm rebuked this class for ignoring the underprivileged black masses. The third class is relevant for the purposes of Uncle Tom. This class contained the "self-proclaimed black leaders," holding top posts within integrationist organizations. Malcolm believed that all three classes of the black bourgeoisie tried their best to imitate white cultural norms while degrading anything identified with blackness.[61]

Their viewpoint, Malcolm felt, affected the racial uplift strategies the black bourgeoisie endorsed. More pointedly, this worldview prompted the black bourgeoisie's desire to seek integration. The "self-proclaimed black leaders" wanted to join coalitions with whites in order to precipitate racial change. This, to Malcolm, was nonsensical. Malcolm argued that "integration was a myth, a false solution, a panacea that had served to deceive blacks and to reinforce white superiority, that reduced blacks to a level of dependency on the white man, and that few blacks supported." This belief sparked Malcolm X to equate integration to racial treachery.[62]

In 1962, Malcolm X delivered one of his earliest, but fairly obscure, ruminations on Uncle Tom. He was speaking as a witness in the trial of black Muslims in Buffalo. While on the stand, he was asked what an Uncle Tom was and responded in detail, conjuring slavery analogies to sketch the character. Malcolm maintained that Uncle Tom lived closely to his master and was the "liaison" between the master and the rest of the slaves. The Uncle Tom lived better than did other slaves, Malcolm said, and identified more with his master's problems than those of his fellow bondsmen. Uncle Tom did not perish with abolition, Malcolm contended. Rather, he was updated.

---

[60] Robin D. G. Kelley, House Negroes on the Loose: Malcolm X and the Black Bourgeoisie, 21 Callalo 419, 420 (1998); Hank Flick, Malcolm X: The Destroyer and Creator of Myths, 12 Journal of Black Studies 166, 166 (1981); Raymond Rodgers and Jimmie N. Rogers, The Evolution of the Attitude of Malcolm X toward Whites, 44 Phylon 108, 108 (1983).

[61] Kelley, House Negroes on the Loose, at 420, 423–33.

[62] Flick, Malcolm X: The Destroyer and Creator of Myths, at 175.

"In the Negro community today you have a modern counterpart who usually operates or plays the same role today as was played by Tom on the plantation." Malcolm argued that like the slave who enlightened his master on what the slaves thought, Uncle Tom gave the white man that same useful information. Malcolm averred that many prominent blacks fit the description because very few blacks could reach national prominence without serving whites' interest. "They (the white men) will put in one of the national Negroes and they will set forth that all is all right. When Negroes express resentment, Uncle Tom is an apologist to the white man for what the Negroes say, rather than a spokesman for Negroes trying to get an unjust situation solved."[63]

Malcolm X, on November 10, 1963 in Detroit, delivered perhaps his most indelible and powerful monologue on *Uncle Tom*. In his "Message to the Grassroots" speech, Malcolm again adopted slave imagery, comparing the relationship between the house Negro and the field Negro to *Uncle Tom* and his followers. The house Negro, like an *Uncle Tom*, asserted Malcolm, was propped up by whites to discipline other blacks. The white man, Malcolm said, "takes a Negro, a so-called Negro, and makes him prominent, builds him up, publicizes him, makes him a celebrity. And then he becomes a spokesman for Negroes – and a Negro leader." He continued, "Just as the slavemaster of that day used Tom, the house Negro, to keep the field Negroes who are nothing but modern Uncle Toms, twentieth-century Uncle Toms, to keep you and me in check, to keep us under control, keep us passive and peaceful and nonviolent." Malcolm lamented the 1960s incidents seared into the country's memory when white police officers pummeled and turned fire hoses and attack dogs on black protestors who refused to reciprocate violence because of "Uncle Tom leaders." "To keep you from fighting back, he gets these old religious Uncle Toms ... to teach you and me, just like Novocain, to suffer peacefully. Don't stop suffering – just suffer peacefully."[64]

On another occasion, in his 1963 speech entitled "Twenty Million Black People in a Political, Economic and Mental Prison," Malcolm added flesh to his thesis that there are two types of Negroes: *Uncle Toms* and blacks. *Uncle Toms* identified with whites' problems and their institutions. That is, *Uncle Toms* truly believed they held ownership stake in America. Thus, when disaster struck, an *Uncle Tom* assumed his interests were also imperiled. Malcolm said:

> And when you say, "your army," he says, "our army." He hasn't got anybody to defend him, but anytime you say "we" he says "we." "Our president," "our

[63] *What's a Muslim? Malcolm X Answers*, New York Amsterdam News, Nov. 17, 1962, at 1.
[64] George Breitman, Malcolm X Speaks: Selected Speeches and Statements 3–17 (1989).

government," "our Senate," "our congressmen," "our this and our that." And he hasn't even got a seat in that "our" even at the end of the line. So this is the twentieth-century Negro. Whenever you say "you," the personal pronoun in the singular or in the plural, he uses it right along with you. When you say you're in trouble, he says, "Yes, we're in trouble."

Uncle Toms' antithesis, however, never harbored such delusions. When he overheard white folk fret over their misfortune, his response was, "Yes, you're in trouble." Instead of having a seat at whites' table, real blacks preferred a table of their own.[65]

One additional musing completes Malcolm's view on *Uncle Toms*. In a 1963 speech at the Michigan State University, Malcolm X asserted that blacks should be granted their own separate nation within the United States. Integration, he felt, was a disastrous policy championed by misguided Negroes. Those who espoused integration, he said, were the "new Uncle Toms. They have been brainwashed into thinking of themselves as whites. They deny their own history, culture and brothers in Africa." Malcolm, however, "scorns his former master and sees him only as an oppressor."[66]

Even though Malcolm wisely targeted racial betrayers with scorn, he equated both support for integration and passive resistance with treachery, leading to deeply destructive uses of *Uncle Tom*. Championing integration as blacks' best hope for racial progress was not racially treacherous; it did not violate any constructive racial loyalty norms. Ethnic Europeans used just that very strategy to become full participants in American democracy. Unlike blacks, these ethnic Europeans shared a common skin color with the existing white ruling class. Blacks, nevertheless, should have been permitted to debate whether integration was the best strategy for racial progress without fear of being sanctioned for racial treachery. Malcolm attacked a straw man, wrongly averring that integrationists, essentially, wanted black people to "pass over" and become whites. That was untrue. Rather, integrationists wanted blacks to have the same access to the tools for success that whites took for granted. People championed integration precisely because they were activated by a love for their group and a dedication to their well-being. Maligning those who committed to the cause damaged the race's ability to work together to improve the lives of black folk.

The tactic of nonviolent resistance, moreover, did not indicate treachery either. It was an imminently defensible tactic to highlight the perniciousness of bigotry that helped blacks procure legal gains. If the goal of black solidarity

---

[65] Perry, Malcolm X 25–57.
[66] *Muslim Leader Asks Negro Nation in U.S.*, Chicago Defender, Jan. 26, 1963, at 3.

is to get all blacks invested in the group to work together, then branding as sellouts those who come, with pure motives, to the bargaining table to offer solutions to the race problem hinders that goal.

ANALYSIS

The black cultural practice of purging supposed elements of racial betrayal from black America continued in the second epoch of *Uncle Tom's* use. The period, interestingly enough, began with blacks thinking that *Uncle Tom* had perished.

Many blacks assumed that *Brown*, decided in 1954, completed the puzzle. Robert L. Carter, an NAACP attorney who helped implement the strategy to overturn *Plessy*, revealed that his comrades were "certain that the civil rights fight had been won" with *Brown*. Blacks, however, needed to solve many other puzzles because Supreme Court holdings were not the only roadblocks to racial equality. Once blacks understood that their business was unfinished, they once again noticed that *Uncle Toms* were as prevalent as ever. From 1960 to 1975, *Uncle Tom* generally marched toward two different targets: segregationist sympathizers and integrationists.[67]

Traditional civil rights advocates used the epithet against blacks who continued to help prop up segregation. These same blacks, during the first epoch of *Uncle Tom*, scoffed at the idea of desegregation. The management of norms here was generally constructive. The same, however, cannot be said about the second manner in which *Uncle Tom* was wielded – by black militants against integrationists. Black militants destructively policed racial loyalty, wrongly branding their ideological opponents as traitors.

Rev. J. W. Jones, the Baptist minister who tried but failed to discourage James Meredith from enrolling at Ole Miss, was an *Uncle Tom* of the first variety. Jones feared Meredith's pursuit simply because it would rile up white folks. The father of a soldier killed in Vietnam who the city of Wetumpka, Alabama refused to bury in the local cemetery because he was black, leveled similar criticism at local blacks. Although he contended that they needed to unite to resist rampant discrimination there, he realized that because local blacks were docile *Uncle Toms* the great clash between black folk and their oppressors would never occur. Criticizing blacks for shirking from a battle for racial equality helped instill a fighting spirit in the race.

---

[67]   Robert L. Carter, A Matter of Law: A Memoir of Struggle in the Cause of Equal Rights 135 (2005).

In the South, school boards fought vociferously against the Supreme Court's increasing demand for progress in school desegregation. Social places, like Southern lunch counters, still refused to serve black patrons. Many Northern cities were as segregated as were their Southern counterparts. Integrationists, therefore, knew that their work could hardly tolerate blacks wilting before segregation. To get all on board, integrationists often depicted their conservative black opponents as *Uncle Toms*. Here, blacks policed loyalty in response to the fear that whites would use any crack in the black populace to trip the already meandering stride toward integration. Like in the previous epoch, when blacks used *Uncle Tom* as a weapon against blacks who were insufficiently antisegregation, in the 1960s, *Uncle Tom* was used against those who were not pro-integration.

Sit-in demonstrations and protests generally were the context in which integrationists used *Uncle Tom*. Sit-ins, freedom walks, and the like forced the powerful "to move faster than they would have otherwise to redress grievances." Demonstrators were frequently lauded for personifying the true race warriors. Some, however, opposed their methods, and being branded as an *Uncle Tom* was the cost of dissent. Some blacks derided the sit-in efforts and dissuaded blacks from participating largely because the activity was too aggressive. With the success the tactic was having, however, such viewpoints were inexcusably meek.[68]

The most prominent black detractors of sit-in efforts may well have been presidents of Southern black colleges. Whether they honestly opposed student protests or they were carrying out the dictates of powerful whites is difficult to know. Black college presidents who simply obeyed the command of their superiors should not have been faulted, though. That is not to say that blacks should always follow the dictates of the ill-meaning. But black college presidents were pressured by bigwigs, and if they were dedicated to both racial justice and educating young black minds, then relenting to pressure did not deserve rebuke. The best-case scenario after a black college president refused to stop black students' protests was that he would be replaced. The worst-case scenario was the closing of the school. Thus, branding as *Uncle Toms* college presidents who operated under such conditions was wrong, absent evidence establishing that they wanted to obstruct student protests.

Militant blacks, however, like one does an attack dog, sicced *Uncle Tom* onto traditional civil rights organizations and the people who commanded them, a point that shines through in the next chapter. Rather than seeking to be a part of white America, militants emphasized self-reliance as the best

---

[68] *Sit-Ins Prove Effective*, Science News Letter, Apr. 3, 1965, at 215.

option and contended that blacks needed their own boat. Militants concluded that America would never chart a new path toward a place where the country was truly racially egalitarian. And those wanting to integrate into a racist society were their targets.

This tension between integrationists and militants created many of the uses of *Uncle Tom* in this epoch. The evidence of integrationists heaving *Uncle Tom* at militants, however, is scant. Although integrationists stressed that militancy and separatism was wrong-headed, a perceptible movement to associate it with racial betrayal never eventuated. Militants, though, continuously depicted integrationists and their organizations as controlled by whites, which establishes that without the specter of whites behind the scenes pulling the strings, *Uncle Tom* accusations were unlikely to fly.

Some targets of *Uncle Tom* accusations went beyond the integrationist-militant dichotomy, most notably, the black police officer. They were not derided as turncoats because of their philosophy on racial transformation. Rather, their problem was that police departments were the first line in sustaining a racial pecking order where blacks were treated as perpetual basement dwellers and an enemy from within. More pointedly, cops maintained racial subordination. They promulgated and enforced racism. When blacks entered the threshold of a police station donning not handcuffs but the cop uniform, blacks assumed they were white officers wearing black masks.

Uncle Tom underwent a significant and unbecoming facelift during the second epoch. After the change, *Uncle Tom* looked far more destructive. It was indeed often used in ugly and regrettable ways. *Uncle Tom* was equated, for instance, with education and success. In 1965, one black child wrote a letter to an advice columnist because his friends called him an *Uncle Tom* "for going to school dressed up and speaking courteously to my white teachers." Two years later, a black girl relayed an analogous account to that same columnist, writing that "the kids at school make fun of me because I study hard, try to make good grades, and don't want to wear my hair natural." The child, who signs her anonymous letter "Left Out," felt isolated from kids who believed that school is for "squares" and that the only way for black youths to progress was "by hustling on the street." In 1967, Bertram Gardner, writing in the *Cleveland Call and Post*, too noticed that successful blacks were called *Uncle Toms* by those who want "unity in blackness."[69]

[69] Arletta Claire, *"Arletta's Advice,"* Chicago Daily Defender, Dec, 15, 1965, at 23; Arletta Claire, *"Arletta's Advice,"* Chicago Daily Defender, Jan. 25, 1967, at 21; Bertram Gardner, "A *Time for Decision,"* Cleveland Call and Post, Mar. 18, 1967, at 1A.

Such usages led Comedian Dick Gregory to claim that *Uncle Tom* was the "most misused word in America today." Gregory wanted to keep the epithet; he used *Uncle Tom* himself. But Gregory felt that the pejorative was hurled indiscriminately. "You smile, some people say you're Tomming; say thank you, you're Tomming." Indeed, actions that hardly signal racial betrayal were considered *Uncle Tom* acts. Gregory claimed that if "a married man walks into church on Sunday and he got a girl on the side and he sits there with an expression on his face like he doesn't do these things – that's a form of Uncle Tom." In situations, moreover, where a person checked their ego to escape punishment, that too was considered *Uncle Tom* behavior, Gregory said. "A cop stops you for speeding and you try to talk him out of it; you let him say things to you in a tone and language you'd never let anyone ordinarily. And *that's* a form of Uncle Tomism.... You're not doing anything more'n try to get out of that ticket."[70]

George Schuyler, who like Gregory wielded the slur, agreed. Especially before 1960, *Uncle Tom* constantly appeared in his *Views Reviews* column in the *Pittsburgh Courier*. He, nonetheless, felt that the pejorative was used to "isolate and destroy everybody with a contrary view" as conveyed in a 1961 column. He went further, writing:

> Anybody who didn't believe that school integration would solve the Negro problem, who didn't believe that vertical ghettos were better than horizontal ones he means by that some Negroes are consciously or [sub]consciously asking the white folk to jim-crow Negroes on the basis of individuals rather than lump them all together ... who didn't believe that racial sweetness and light would result from carting Negro children two or three miles off to attend school with white kids would begin the millennium, or that passing laws would mean the end of all racial restrictions, was promptly labeled a beast and enemy of the people ... and "Uncle Tom."[71]

Others concurred with Gregory and Schuyler. Columnist Bill Weathersby, for instance, wrote that the "phrase has been so commonly used it is now considered cliché." Relatedly the *Cleveland Call and Post*, in criticizing Adam Clayton Powell's reliance on black-led coalitions instead of also considering interracial coalitions, wrote that "An important step ... is to stop calling a Negro an 'Uncle Tom' simply because he attempts to make organization or political alignments which cut across racial lines." And Dr. Peyton Gray Jr., a civil rights activist, contended that too many blacks proffer arguments that

[70] Gilbert Millstein, *A Negro Says It With Jokes*, New York Times, Apr. 30, 1961, at SM34.
[71] Nat D. Williams, *Dark Shadows*, Chicago Daily Defender, Nov. 8, 1961, at 11.

equate to "I'm Blacker than you in my approach to the problem. Therefore you must be an Uncle Tom."[72]

Some events during this era illustrate how *Uncle Tom* was being expanded way beyond its proper limits and that blacks were managing incredibly destructive norms. For instance, in 1961, a black couple from Los Angeles found a bag containing $240,000 that fell out of an armored car. The janitor and his wife returned the money and received a $10,000 reward. They did the morally right thing. But blacks around the country wrote letters demeaning them. One wrote, "Go back South where you belong and pick cotton." Another penned, "You're a disgrace to the colored people, an Uncle Tom, a white folks' nigger. You could have played it 'cool' for a year or two. I hope your black hides starve." That blacks were called *Uncle Toms* for returning lost money further establishes that destructive norm management abounded in the 1960s and 1970s.[73]

At its most deplorable, *Uncle Tom* appeared in connection with overt violence. Take a usage stemming from events during the 1967 Detroit riots. Although participants said the riots were a response to white exploitation, middle-class blacks too found themselves caught in the spider's web. Melvin Johnson, one black victim, was a leading black business owner of a beauty supply company. His business building was burned to the ground. Many other middle-class blacks in the city reported that they were awakened at night by telephone callers who said that "[t]onight is the night 'Uncle Tom.' Either join with the black rebels tonight or your home will be blown up."[74]

What happened to middle-class blacks in Detroit was not an isolated occurrence. Rather, *Uncle Tom* was continually discharged in violent contexts, disfiguring the pejorative. In a 1968 *Playboy* interview, for instance, Eldridge Cleaver, a member of the Black Panther Party, said that he respected blacks who robbed stores when racism precluded their ability to pursue an honest living more than the "Uncle Tom who does nothing but just shrink into himself and accept any shit that's thrown into his face." Yet in a 1972 interview, Huey Newton, also a Panther, outdid Cleaver in maiming *Uncle Tom* while throwing the pejorative back at him. Newton gave Cleaver a choice of bringing

---

[72] Bill Weathersby, *Bill's Beat*, Chicago Defender, Apr. 3, 1965, at 16; *Adam Powell's "Black Position" Paper*, Cleveland Call and Post, June 19, 1965, at 8B; Peyton Gray Jr., *Peyton's Place*, Philadelphia Tribune, Oct. 26, 1968, at 8; Marc Meltzer, *Dr. Peyton Gray Jr., Civil Rights Activist*, Philly.com, Nov. 29, 1996, available at: http://articles.philly.com/1996-11-29/news/25649031_1_substitute-teacher-civil-rights-italian-culture.

[73] *Honest Janitor Who Returned Brinks Cash Damned and Praised*, Philadelphia Tribune, May 16, 1961 at 1.

[74] Mordecai Jones, *Rioters Threaten to Kill Leaders*, Philadelphia Tribune, July 29, 1967, at 1.

about a violent revolution or being an *Uncle Tom*, saying "if you do anything to stop the process then you are reactionary–either pick up the gun now and win the revolution or you are an Uncle Tom."[75]

A murder produced another unfortunate use of *Uncle Tom* that mangled the epithet. Eugene Banks, black, shot and killed a disabled white man. As Banks tried to flee the scene, three black men held him down, preventing his escape. One of the black men reported that he later received threatening telephone calls from folk who said that he was an *Uncle Tom*. Some considered it racial treachery, that is, to stop a murderer, if the assailant was black and his victim was white. Such usages of *Uncle Tom* demonstrated that racial loyalty policing had gone deeply awry. By finding racial treachery where none existed, the racial loyalty police, ostensibly attempting to build black solidarity, actually kneecapped efforts to unite around shared oppression. These destructive uses rendered *Uncle Tom* unseemly, calling attention to some of the ugliest conversations taking place among black folk. When the eyes of the 1960s and 1970s looked at *Uncle Tom* they saw an almost grotesque epithet.[76]

[75] Eldridge Cleaver, Eldridge Cleaver 182 (1969); *Will Seek Changes Within System*, Los Angeles Times, Jan. 31, 1972, at A3.
[76] *Harassed Hero Called a "Tom*," Cleveland Call and Post, Dec. 14, 1968, at 3A.

5

No Man Was Safe

UNCLE TOM CIVIL RIGHTS (INTEGRATIONIST) LEADERS

B Y THE 1960s, BLACK PUBLIC figures understood that racial snipers tracked their every act, scoping for any misstep that signaled betrayal. In fact, missteps were frequently unnecessary for loyalty enforcers to rifle *Uncle Tom* accusations into situations clearly devoid of duplicity. Even the highest of cultural icons drowned in waves of criticisms during the 1960s and 1970s. Indeed, some whose lofty cultural status has posthumously grown too exalted to criticize were once submerged face first into a pool of *Uncle Tom* ridicule. Simply put, amid the second epoch, no status was too well fortified or too elevated to keep anyone safe from *Uncle Tom*.

This was especially true for integrationist civil rights leaders. Integrationists were ambivalently perceived, being among the most adored and reviled among their race. Many blacks considered them cultural heroes. They pushed presidents, Congress, and the Supreme Court to achieve equality under the law. John F. Kennedy orated in 1963, "One hundred years of delay have passed since President Lincoln freed the slaves, yet their heirs, their grandsons, are not fully free." The black advocates for that full freedom were civil rights leaders, influencing Kennedy, his predecessor, Lyndon Baines Johnson, and congressional leaders to pass legislation granting blacks the equality that *Brown* failed to secure. Such leaders firmly believed that blacks' road to full emancipation was racial integration.

Some blacks disagreed vehemently with the voyage toward racial integration. Whether they self-identified as black militants, black nationalists, or black Muslims, many rejected all efforts for blacks to set sail in the white man's boat. To this camp, integrationists were imploring blacks to walk the plank, advocating that they lie with the enemy, relinquish their cultural identity, and pursue a path that would take an already lost people way off course.

Seeking closer proximity to the enemy, they contended, was the worst possible move. And thus they denounced integrationists as *Uncle Toms*, a regrettable occurrence that nearly destroyed the chain that links black folk together and corroded blacks' ability to architect their ultimate racial triumph. The norms managed in this context were especially destructive, more so than any other.

Integrationists violated no constructive racial loyalty norms. Recalcitrant whites opposed integration. Thus, to pursue it certainly was not to advance the interests of the antiblack. The idea that integrationism, furthermore, indicated meekness was similarly fallacious. Integrationists believed that the best opportunities to advance were through access to traditional paths to success. To champion integrationism was not meek. And last, black radicals failed miserably in establishing that integrationists were supporting a racial program that was so obviously antithetical to the race's interests that any proponent necessarily betrayed the race. Black radicals managed exceedingly destructive norms, indicting many venerable blacks with treachery.

That even includes Martin Luther King Jr. Not only was King branded as an *Uncle Tom*, but, surprisingly, associating one of the most revered black Americans with betrayal became commonplace. One of his first public forays with *Uncle Tom* was in September 1958, the day Izola Curry stabbed him with a letter opener, a near fatal injury. King was inside Blumstein's Harlem department store signing copies of his book *Stride Toward Freedom* (1958). Outside of the store, African nationalist protestors carried various anti-King signs, one of which read, "Uncle King are you an Uncle Tom too?"[1]

The overwhelming majority of the instances when King was called an *Uncle Tom*, though, were during the 1960s. His indicters invariably cited his nonviolent resistance as supporting their charges of disloyalty. Stokely Carmichael, H. Rap Brown, and LeRoi Jones all labeled King as an *Uncle Tom*. New York congressman Adam Clayton Powell called him "Martin Loser King." The black nationalist publication the *Razor* dubbed him America's "biggest Uncle Tom" because "[a]nyone who teaches his people not to fight the enemy ... is a traitor." King correctly noted that his militant detractors distorted his message. King argued for nonviolent resistance, not nonresistance as his adversaries often claimed. King wanted blacks to peacefully contest their subordination. He never encouraged blacks to sit idly and accept injustice. He simply disagreed with violent strategies, viewing them as immoral and unwise.[2]

[1] Les Matthews, *Says Martin Luther King Humiliated by Own*, Chicago Daily Defender, Sept. 29, 1958, at A8; Taylor Branch, Parting the Waters: America in the King Years, 1954–63 243–44 (1988).

[2] *Two Americas, Many Americas*, Washington Post Magazine, Oct. 22, 1978, at 21; *The Razor*, Vol. 2 No. 2; Martin Luther King, Jr. King, The Autobiography of Martin Luther King, Jr.

Malcolm X, too, joined the castigation. Malcolm frequently tore into famous blacks. He posthumously called Booker T. Washington a "white man's nigger." Jackie Robinson and Joe Louis, two men he admired, were "stooges" for whites. And Dr. King was no different. Malcolm routinely called Dr. King an "Uncle Tom" and a "chump" for his integrationist nonviolent outlook. Malcolm even incited violence against King. During a June 29, 1963 rally, Malcolm said, "Go up there (to Salem Church) tomorrow and let Uncle Tom (King) know that we are against him and do not believe what he preaches." The next day, at Harlem's Salem Baptist Church, King was pelted with eggs.[3]

King recounted the incident in his autobiography. He felt he was targeted because some believed he was "a sort of polished Uncle Tom." A month after the Salem incident, Malcolm said that King was "not a modern Moses but a modern Uncle Tom." In November 1963, at a Philadelphia rally, Malcolm criticized the audience for participating in sit-in demonstrations and other forms of nonviolent protests that King championed. Calling King a "handkerchief headed Uncle Tom," Malcolm wondered why blacks wanted to integrate lunch counters and the like. "[A]nd what are all you 'Toms' doing all this demonstrating and picketing for? A desegregated cup of coffee? This is no revolution ... this is a 'beg-o-lution' ... you 'Toms' are begging the white man for a cup of coffee at a lunch counter."[4]

---

266 (2001). The *Uncle Tom* insults did not solely originate from American sources, coming from abroad as well. During the early 1960s, Soviet spies tried to influence King to further inflame America's racial tension. Preferring a radical, the KGB was "frustrated" that the moderate had become the most influential voice on race in America. Its goal was to either radicalize King or have someone like Stokely Carmichael supplant him. The plan was to get the "American Communist Party to influence King by putting secret party members within King's entourage." When that failed, the KGB plotted to paint King as an *Uncle Tom*. In 1967, the KGB ran stories in African newspapers depicting him as an *Uncle Tom* "who was secretly being paid off by the Government so that he would make sure the civil rights movement would not threaten President Lyndon B. Johnson." These attempts, however, were fumbling. "News that the K.G.B. was attempting to plant false stories in the African press portraying Dr. King as an 'Uncle Tom,' at the very time when Dr. King was harshly attacking Johnson's conduct of the Vietnam War indicates that American police agencies were not the only Keystone Kops active in the 1960s." Bert Roughton Jr., *Author: KGB Failed to Sway King*, News, Atlanta Journal and Constitution, Sept. 23, 1999, at 1A; James Risen, *K.G.B. Told Tall Tales about Dallas, Book Says*, New York Times, Feb. 12, 1999, at 4.

3   Michael Dorman, *Military Spying on Dr. King Reported*, Seattle Times, Mar. 14, 1998, at A3.

4   Perry, Malcolm X: The Last Speeches 203; King, The Autobiography of Martin Luther King, Jr. 266; Ron Zyla and Mark Bricklin, *Malcolm X Tells Camden Crowd "Christianity White Man's Religion,"* Philadelphia Tribune, July 2, 1963, at 3; Bill Alegander, *"Blood Must Be Shed," Malcolm X Tells Muslims*, Philadelphia Tribune, Nov. 19, 1963, at 4; Edward E. Curtis IV, Black Muslim Religion in the Nation of Islam, 1960–1975 3 (2006).

In a PBS interview with Kenneth Clark in 1963, Malcolm fully unpacked his critique of King.

> A hundred years ago they used to put on a white sheet and use a bloodhound against Negroes. Today they've taken off the white sheet and put on police uniforms, they've traded in the bloodhounds for police dogs, and they're still doing the same thing. And just as Uncle Tom, back during slavery, used to keep the Negroes from resisting the bloodhound, or resisting the Ku Klux Klan, by teaching them to love their enemy, or pray for those who use them spitefully, today Martin Luther King is just a 20th century or modern Uncle Tom, or a religious Uncle Tom, who is doing the same thing today, to keep Negroes defenseless in the face of an attack, that Uncle Tom did on the plantation to keep those Negroes defenseless in the face of the attacks of the Klan in that day.

Through his anachronistic historical recitation – the Klan sprang up post-slavery – Malcolm painted Dr. King as a double agent working on behalf of white oppressors to dupe his comrades into dropping the proverbial pitchfork. Rather than rebelling against blacks' overseers, Malcolm insisted, Dr. King's nonviolent tactics were akin to submission.[5]

Uncle Tom also marred Dr. King's close comrade, civil rights strategist Bayard Rustin. "More than anyone else," Rustin biographer John D'Emilio wrote, "Rustin brought the message and methods of Gandhi to the United States. He insinuated the nonviolence into the heart of the black freedom struggle." After Congress passed the Civil Rights Act of 1964, Rustin championed a shift from "protest to politics," whereas many blacks, especially black youth, were increasingly becoming nationalistic and militant. Rustin, however, supported interracial coalition politics between white liberals and blacks. He was an integrationist who wanted to work within the political system to engender positive change.[6]

---

[5] Malcolm X interview with Kenneth Clark transcript, available at: http://www.pbs.org/wgbh/amex/mlk/sfeature/sf_video_pop_03_tr_qry.html. Ron Christie wrongfully uses this passage to accuse Malcolm X of insinuating that King was "acting white." Far from it, Malcolm is arguing that King was a black agent for whites. Ron Christie, Acting White: The Curious History of a Racial Slur 109–10 (2010). Martin Luther King Sr., like his son, was dismissed as an *Uncle Tom*. "Daddy King," as he was called, was also influential in the civil rights movement. A stalwart in the movement said, "He's the daddy of the movement. Without him, there wouldn't have been a movement." During the 1960s, for instance, he was a mediator between sit-in protestors and their white targets. But not all revered Daddy King. While he was serving on the board of Morehouse College, black students made demands of the faculty. One of the young students called King, likely seen as pro-administration, "a white man's Uncle Tom." Kathryn Johnson, *Dr. King Sr. Still Preaches Social Gospel*, Los Angeles Times, Aug. 29, 1973, at A2.

[6] John D'Emilio, Lost Prophet: The Life and Times of Bayard Rustin 1 (2003); Jerald Podair, Bayard Rustin: American Dreamer 80 (2008).

But more than just being an integrationist, militants like Stokely Carmichael believed that Rustin opposed organizing around blackness. Rustin, for example, repudiated black nationalism and Black Power. He even disagreed with black studies programs, believing such pedagogy separated blacks from the mainstream. Carmichael charged Rustin with separating himself from black people just when blacks were starting to "embrace their blackness and claim their rights to political and economic autonomy." With this being his worldview, why militants branded Rustin as an *Uncle Tom* is clear.[7]

An incident during the Harlem riots in 1965 shows how militants perceived Rustin. Rustin entered the maelstrom wanting to quell the disorder, but he was hammered with bottles and *Uncle Tom* instead. He responded that he would "be a 'Tom' if that would save the lives of women and children." The event pained Rustin, who dedicated his life to his race. "The biggest hurt is to be considered an Uncle Tom by your own people.... [It hurts me when the] people I love most would misunderstand my motives."[8]

Another central figure in the movement, A. Philip Randolph, too felt the misery Rustin knew all too well. When Randolph stood against Black Power, a "Los Angeles Negro editor" knocked him down as an *Uncle Tom*. Malcolm X also dismissed Randolph as an *Uncle Tom* for championing integration. But here, *Uncle Tom* started no rift between the two men as it so often did. In spite of their differences, Malcolm X and Randolph mutually respected one another. "[All] civil rights leaders [were] confused," Malcolm thought, "but Randolph [was] less confused than the rest." Randolph was one of the few mainstream civil rights leaders who invited Malcolm to events. Malcolm hated to attend because "he didn't believe black people were going to get anything from such meetings, that whatever they got they would have to take."[9]

Unlike with Randolph, Malcolm was unable to replicate that mutual respect with Thurgood Marshall. The animosity was deep between the two. Marshall, the lead counsel in *Brown*, staunchly supported integration and rejected black nationalism. Marshall deemed the Nation of Islam (NOI) a useless sect "run by a bunch of thugs organized from prisons and jails, and financed, I am sure, by [Egyptian President Gamal] Nasser or some Arab group." Malcolm X, a member of the NOI at the time, called Marshall a "twentieth century

7 Devon W. Carbado and Donald Wise, *The Civil Rights Identity of Bayard Rustin*, 82 *Texas Law Review* 1133, 1181–83 (2004).
8 *Died*, Newsweek, Sept. 7, 1987, at 75; Jacqueline Trescott, *The March, The Dream; Bayard Rustin; Contradictions of a Legendary Leader*, Washington Post, Aug. 21, 1983, at H1.
9 Audrey Weaver, *Unity Lost in Civil Rights Fight Must Be Regained*, Chicago Defender, Nov. 26, 1966, at 11; Gregory P. Kane, *Does Self Hatred Doom the Race Dialogue?*, Buffalo News, Nov. 9, 1997, at H5; Jervis Anderson, A. Philip Randolph: A Biographical Portrait 13 (1972).

Uncle Tom." Black Panther Bobby Seale called Marshall "an Uncle Tom, a bootlicker, a nigger pig, a Tonto and a punk."[10]

As an attorney, Marshall devoted himself to shattering segregation. But black nationalists detested Marshall and the NAACP's goals, arguing that integrationists imperiled the race with their blind sycophantic love of whites. As Elijah Muhammad, the spiritual leader of the NOI, remarked:

> Seeking closer relationship between the slaves and their masters only will provide total destruction of the Negroes by the wise, old slavemaster's children.... Thurgood Marshall does not care for the recognition of his kind or for the Black Nation. He is in love with the white race. He hates the preaching of the uplifting of the Black Nation unless it is approved by the white race.

Black nationalists wanted to separate themselves from white America and, according to Marshall, ever the strategist, "[there isn't a] better way to sink the ship than that way."[11]

Some of the anger from black nationalist leaders trickled down to the masses. A graduate of Howard Law School, Marshall returned in the late 1960s to accept an award. A supposed festive occasion went awry when a militant student called Marshall an *Uncle Tom*. Showing strength and confidence, he stood silently then retorted, "Boy, I was litigating civil-rights lawsuits before you were born. Don't you ever use that name with me."[12]

One of Marshall's biggest allies in combatting state-sponsored Jim Crow was social psychologist Dr. Kenneth Clark. His psychological studies of black schoolchildren that found segregation destructive to the black psyche were central to the Supreme Court's *Brown* opinion that overturned *Plessy*. In 1969, Clark, also a resolute integrationist, resigned from the board of directors at Antioch College because the college wanted to create a racially exclusive institute for blacks. From around the country, blacks chimed in to call Clarke an *Uncle Tom*. In his resignation letter, Clark wrote that he disagreed with Antioch's allowing "some of the more hostile Negro students to coerce and intimidate other Negroes and whites." In an interview, Clark disclosed that

[10] Kelley, *House Negroes on the Loose*, at 419–36; Russell Baker, *Observer: The Decline of Insult*, New York Times, Dec. 3, 1968, at 46; *Name-Calling Will Get Rights Movement Nowhere*, Cleveland Call and Post, Dec. 14, 1968, at 4B. Marshall held his grudge against Malcolm X. Decades after Malcolm's death, Marshall said, "I still see no reason to say he is a great person a great Negro.... And I ask a simple question: What did he ever do? Name me one concrete thing he ever did." Thurgood Marshall, Supreme Justice: Speeches and Writings 306 (Editor J. Clay Smith Jr. 2003).

[11] Williams, Thurgood Marshall 278.

[12] Jerry Adler et al., *Their Amazing Grace*, Newsweek, Feb. 8, 1993, at 56.

he was generally thought to be an *Uncle Tom* by young blacks who considered him an "agent" of their "oppressors" who attempted to keep their rebellion in reasonable bounds.[13]

Whitney M. Young Jr. was another such casualty of the complete assault on integrationists. Young, whose most visible position was as the executive director of the National Urban League from 1961 to 1971, contributed enormously to the civil rights movement. Young was crucial in procuring corporate America's financial assistance in the movement. Young "spent most of his adult life in the white world, transcending barriers of race, wealth and social standing to advance the welfare of black Americans. His goal was to gain access for blacks to good jobs, education, housing, health care and social services. His tactics were reason, persuasion and negotiation." Young was a "reformer," not a revolutionary, as he "worked to move blacks into the mainstream instead of effecting significant political change." This approach put him in constant company with whites. Unlike other civil rights leaders, Young did not mingle much with the common black man but rather glad-handed well-to-do Caucasians in ritzy establishments. Young's ability and willingness to become immersed in the "white world" made him a whipping boy for black militants. Although they considered him an *Uncle Tom*, Young carried more influence than anyone in government and corporate circles. But a true racial warrior, the argument went, scrapped alongside his people and tried to defeat the enemy rather than work with him. Young was known for not sullying his hands and was labeled a "sell-out," "Whitey," "Oreo," and "Uncle Tom."[14]

The Revolutionary Action Movement (RAM), a 1960s black radical organization, went far beyond rhetoric. The organization plotted to kill Whitney Young and Roy Wilkins. Wilkins was an NAACP leader, serving as assistant secretary, editor of *The Crises*, and then executive secretary. Wilkins, like Young, was an establishment figure. And RAM detested the establishment. RAM was an "'underground' movement" of young, disillusioned, poor black folk that "infiltrated civil rights organizations and encouraged a shift toward Marxism and revolutionary black nationalism." RAM, to incite riots, schemed

[13] Kenneth Clarke, The Reminiscences of Kenneth B. Clark 158 (2003).

[14] This quote is found in Whitney M. Young Jr., and the Struggle for Civil Rights. But I took this particular quote from an online resource, Marc Morial, *To Be Equal: Whitney Young – Mr. Inside*, Los Angeles. Watts Times, Feb. 21, 2013, available at: http://www.lawattstimes. com/index.php?option=com_content&view=article&id=958:to-be-equal-whitney-young-mr-inside&Itemid=121; Nancy J. Weiss, Whitney M. Young Jr., and the Struggle for Civil Rights xi, 75 (1989); *Whitney Young On "Newsmakers"* Sun, Los Angeles Sentinel, Aug. 24, 1967, at B7; Rudi Williams, *Whitney M. Young Jr.: Little Known Civil Rights Pioneer*, American Forces Press Service, available at: www.kingsbayperiscope.com/stories/020702/kin_young001.shtml.

to kill Young and Wilkins but make it appear as though the blood was on white hands. Sixteen members were arrested for this frame-up plot. During their criminal prosecution, RAM members testified that they had no hate for Young and Wilkins, but concluded that the two were whites' puppets and *Uncle Toms* needing to be eliminated. "Apparently," Wilkins wrote in his autobiography, "anyone who didn't believe in machine guns was an Uncle Tom."[15]

Established big shots took aim at Roy Wilkins too. Malcolm X called him an *Uncle Tom*. Celes King III, a Los Angeles civil rights leader, called Wilkins "the No. 1 Uncle Tom in America" who had "become so much of a part of the white establishment he is no longer an effective representative of black people." And black militant Stokely Carmichael publically called Wilkins a "mother fuckin' Uncle Tom." In his biography, Wilkins recounted a letter sent to him that explained why he and similar figures received so much criticism. The letter's author compared Wilkins to Moses, who was "replaced when he couldn't communicate with his followers" by Joshua, "a young militant warrior." The thesis was that young militants should supplant the older more cautionary leaders who were simply out of step with their people. Wilkins responded to this letter by saying:

> Between the beginning of August 1961 and the end of the following year, it sometimes seemed as if the roof had caved in and the floor was about to give way, too. A new generation short on history and long on spleen chased after me and the N.A.A.C.P. day and night. Some said we were just too old, others that we were playing Uncle Tom for white America. If the attacks hadn't been so unfair, so divorced from the actual record, so patently one-sided, they would have hurt more; as it was, they still hurt plenty.[16]

In July 1963, Malcolm X challenged Roy Wilkins in addition to Jackie Robinson, Thurgood Marshall, Martin Luther King, and Congressman Adam

---

[15] Black Studies Research Sources General Editors, John H. Bracey Jr. and Sharon Harley, The Black Power Movement Part 3: Papers of the Revolutionary Action Movement, 1963–1996; Dennis C. Dickerson, Militant Mediator: Whitney M. Young Jr. 302 (1998); *Whitney Young on Stand in Conspiracy Case*, New York Amsterdam News, June 15, 1968, at 17; Roy Wilkins, Standing Fast: The Autobiography of Roy Wilkins 325 (1984); Doug McAdam, Political Process and the Development of Black Insurgency, 1930–1970 189 (1982); Civil Rights: An A-Z Reference of the Movement That Changed America 348 (Editors Kwame Anthony Appiah and Henry Louis Gates Jr.).

[16] Kane, *Does Self Hatred Doom the Race Dialogue?*, at H5; Myrna Oliver, *Obituaries, Celes King III*, 79; *L.A. Civil Rights Leader*, Los Angeles Times, Apr. 14, 2003 at B9; *Wilkins Is Urged to Resign by 3 N.A.A.C.P. Leaders*, New York Times, Nov. 12, 1968, at 35; David A. Canton, Raymond Pace Alexander: A New Negro Lawyer Fights for Civil Rights in Philadelphia 159 (2010); Wilkins, Standing Fast 314–15 (1984).

Clayton Powell to prove that they were neither "20th Century Uncle Toms" nor "parrots for their white bosses." Malcolm asserted that each man refused to join a "united effort" against white supremacy because of their "fear of irking their white bosses, embarrassing their liberal white friends, selfishness and greed, or just plain ignorance." Malcolm's reprimand is worth quoting at length.

> I specifically challenge Jackie Robinson, Thurgood Marshall, Roy Wilkins and Martin Luther King to prove their false charges [that members of the Nation of Islam] are a Black Ku Klux Klan, Black Supremists, or Racial Extremists simply because, unlike them Mr. Muhammad takes an uncompromising stand in his demands for immediate and complete freedom, justice and equality for American Negroes....

> I challenge them to prove before a Harlem audience that in making these charges they speak for Black people, instead of being 20th Century Uncle Toms, parroting charges against us that their white bosses fear to make themselves....

> I challenge Martin Luther King to come to Harlem and prove that "peaceful suffering" is the solution to the atrocities being suffered daily by Negroes throughout America....

> And lastly, I invite Adam Clayton Powell to come out and explain to the people of Harlem why 11 million Negro voters should cast their ballot for the same Southern Senator (Lyndon B. Johnson) that the Solid South also wanted as their President.[17]

Malcolm's diatribe, in part, recalled an oft-promulgated argument that integrationists sacrificed blacks' interests because their organizations were nursed on whites' dollars and minds. For instance, some found the ultimate integrationist organization, the NAACP, unnatural, having a "black body with a white head." That is, some contended whites intellectually led and financed organizations like the NAACP, thereby limiting the policies these organizations would endorse. Because whites abhorred black militancy, traditional civil rights leaders rejected it. Contending that whites wrongly held an ownership stake in supposedly black organizations, Malcolm announced that the black community was poorly served when its leaders depended on folk whose interests were unaligned with theirs.[18]

One had valid reasons to dispute that integration was a wise strategy. Many have argued, for example, that black children would have been better served

---

[17] *Muslim Aide Challenged Wilkins, Marshall, King, Powell, Robinson to Debate,* New Pittsburgh Courier, July 23, 1960, at 2.

[18] *The Hate that Hate Produced* (1959).

through separate but truly equal education. Black integrationists, even after *Brown*, spent their energies on getting black children into white schools, but integration was a mere proxy for a good education. Black radicals should have simply stuck to such arguments, rather than lacing their disagreements with sellout rhetoric. Neither camp had the complete solution to the race problem. The two factions should have publically made their cases. Fencing with each other likely would have sharpened both sides' arguments, which could only accrue to blacks' benefit.

The truth is that both integrationists and black radicals saw the same dilemma – segregation, unequal opportunity, and a discounted citizenship – but the two camps offered different solutions. Integrationists believed that blacks needed to reform existing structures to produce racially egalitarian results. They built nonviolent grassroots protest organizations, such as Dr. King's Southern Christian Leadership Conference, to counteract separate but equal. "Inherent in King's activism was a resilient faith that moral fortitude and nonviolence could and would fundamentally and drastically reconstruct the collective psychology of white people."[19]

Black radical groups, however, believed in racial separation. Rather than working within the American system, they rejected it entirely. The Nation of Islam, in fact, concluded that Dr. King's program of racial integration was the "white man's best ploy to undermine black liberation." The Black Panthers had a similar separatist outlook, calling for whites to relinquish power in black communities so that blacks could pursue self-determination. And more radical groups, such as the Revolutionary Action Movement, believed they were in a war with whites, requiring blacks to band together to "destroy the universal slavemaster."[20]

With their incessant accusations that moderate black civil rights leaders were *Uncle Toms*, black radicals harmed the people for which they claimed to be agents. They pounced on blacks who toiled on behalf of their people as they would staunch segregationists. And heaving *Uncle Tom* at black moderates vicariously injured their many followers. Turning friends into foes, radicals' destructive norm management exacerbated blacks' second-class citizenship. Blacks either too timid to even debate solutions, co-opted by whites seeking to protect the color line, or apathetic about the race's well-being were traitors inside the camp needing to be dragged out. Branding such persons

---

[19] Jeffrey O. G. Ogbar, Black Power: Radical Politics and African American Identity 42 (2004).

[20] Louis E. Lomax, The Negro Revolt 187–92 (1962); Ogbar, Black Power 41–43; The Black Panther Speaks 2–4 (Editor Philip S. Foner 1970); Modern Black Nationalism: From Marcus Garvey to Louis Farrakhan 252 (Editor William L. Van Deburg 1997).

as *Uncle Toms* promotes black solidarity by marginalizing folk who halt racial progress, which dissuades many from exhibiting such characteristics and encourages others into more diligently working on behalf of the race. But ostracizing black moderates was calamitous for solidarity and, therefore, racial uplift.

THE *UNCLE TOM* INSIDER

The narrative was very similar for black insiders as it was for civil rights leaders. From 1960 to 1975, few blacks worked within the system. In the first epoch of *Uncle Tom's* use, that was even truer. And during both periods, black insiders were often thought to carry the *Uncle Tom* scent. But the reason their fellow blacks found them odorous changed from the first epoch to the second. Whereas pre-1960, blacks were usually only faulted for asserted timidity in the battle against segregation, post-1960s criticism lacked such specificity. After *Brown*, blacks were disappointed with the lack of progress, wanting whole-scale changes that never appeared imminent. Black insiders were reprimanded for not doing enough – however enough was defined – in facilitating racial progress.

Ralph Bunch might have been the ultimate black insider. Bunche's legacy is tied to his United Nations work, but his imprint left marks on the civil rights movement as well. After Bunche's death in 1971, Roy Wilkins amorously wrote that "[Bunche] did not forget his domestic racial difficulties or his unhappy experiences with them (how could he?), but he sensed early and knew later that war and hunger and hatred were the enemies of man. His life was devoted to efforts to bring about peace." Born in Detroit in 1903, Bunche became a long-standing member of the UN. From 1947 to 1949 he mediated conflicts between Arabs and Jews in Palestine and won the Nobel Peace Prize in 1950 because of the temporary peace he contributed to the tempestuous region.[21]

But his achievements were used against his black brethren. To some whites, Bunche's personal triumphs proved racial fairness was achieved. No remedies were necessary. Bunche singlehandedly proved the system was egalitarian. As Dr. King posited, Bunche's accomplishments were used to hide the horrors of racial inequality. Dr. King wrote that "[if the] Negro wanted to feel pride in his race? With tokenism the solution was simple. If all twenty million Negroes would keep looking at Ralph Bunche, the one man in so exalted a post would

---

[21] Sondra Kathryn Wilson, In Search of Democracy: The NAACP Writings of James Weldon Johnson, Walter White, and Roy Wilkins (1920–1977) 438 (1999).

generate such a volume of pride that it could be cut into portions and served to everyone."[22]

As some blacks detected chinks in Bunche's armor, whites only perceived a well-crafted Negro. Journalist Sam Pope Brewer, in that vein, heralded Bunche as "the most accomplished Negro in the World." Bunche was a successful black man whose accomplishments allowed whites to excuse the status quo. Bunche allowed whites to sit atop the social ladder in relative comfort. *"Things are fine; look at Ralph Bunche."* As Dr. King stated, Bunche was a token. "Tokenism granted the recipient 'a short-term trip toward democracy,' while permitting an infinite deferral on the part of the white majority for the structural changes necessary to pay for the rest of the journey."[23]

To many, Bunche was an *Uncle Tom*, sometimes derided as an "international Uncle Tom." When an Atlanta hotel denied him a room, the *Cleveland Call and Post* reported the event in an article with the sarcastic headline "Bunche Finds out He's Still a Negro" and added that "[i]n certain circles ... Bunche is known as a Negro who has integrated himself out of the race." Andrew Young, also a member of the UN, chastised Bunche because much of his "energy went into not being black and trying to assimilate." And militants called Bunche an *Uncle Tom* for being an integrationist.[24]

But for Bunche the appraisal was more complicated than the hackneyed "all integrationists are *Uncle Toms*" assessments. One criticism held that he permitted himself to be a status quo-legitimating symbol. And another conceded his personal brilliance but held that he toadied up to white folk rather than help his own people. Harlem congressman Adam Clayton Powell agreed, once remarking that "Black Americans had not heard from Ralph Bunche since we helped fight to get his son into the Forest Hills Tennis Club," suggesting that Bunche was an unreliable advocate focused on his own battles and not that of the race.[25]

Malcolm X served Bunche his most attention-grabbing *Uncle Tom* denunciation. On June 3, 1962, an airliner carrying 121 of Atlanta's white high society crashed during takeoff in Paris. Because the crash victims were from

[22] Ben Keppel, The Work of Democracy: Ralph Bunche, Kenneth B. Clark, Lorraine Hansberry, and the Cultural Politics of Race 61 (1995).
[23] Id., at 88.
[24] Ralph J. Bunche, A Brief and Tentative Analysis of Negro Leadership 23 (2005); *Bunche Finds out He's Still a Negro*, Cleveland Call and Post, July 14, 1962, at 2c; Charles P. Henry, Ralph Bunche: Model Negro or American Other? 177 (1999).
[25] Henry, Ralph Bunche 178; Keppel, The Work of Democracy 90; Peter J. Kellog, Northern Liberals and Black America: A History of White Attitudes 384–85 (PhD dissertation, Northwestern University, 1971); Brian Urquhart, Ralph Bunche: An American Life 436 (1993).

segregationist Georgia, Malcolm X said the tragedy was "Allah's doing." Malcolm delighted in the events. When reporting the news of the crash at a meeting, Malcolm started by saying, "I would like to announce a very beautiful thing that has happened." Malcolm's general point was that whites had persecuted blacks and the plane crash was an act of God on their behalf. Bunche sharply disagreed, however, and said that Malcolm's remark "could come only from a depraved mind." Malcolm retorted viciously.

> I'm challenging this international Uncle Tom, who has become world-famous in the United Nations as a puppet and parrot for the white so-called liberals, to come to this mass rally in Harlem Sunday as our guest speaker and prove that his feelings of love, sympathy and forgiveness for the plane load of Georgia whites who were destroyed by the "Hand of God" in France recently, reflects the feeling of the American Black masses.[26]

Bunche claimed he ignored the many *Uncle Tom* taunts hurled his way, including that delivered by Malcolm X. "Labels always have to do with ignorance. This is why Malcolm X came to apologize personally to [me] after he went to Mecca and found out that the world was round." Malcolm was right to apologize. That Bunche scolded him for rejoicing in the deaths of segregationists did not indicate racial treachery but rather a strong disagreement with Malcolm's words.[27]

Bunche's critics charged him with not being committed to purging anti-black elements from American democracy. Powell's comment that blacks "had not heard from Ralph Bunche since we helped fight to get his son into the Forest Hills Tennis Club" underscores the point that Bunche was supposedly interested only in racism that impaired him. After his son was denied, Bunche remarked that the incident revealed to him that "until the lowliest Negro sharecropper in the South is free, I am not free."[28] A cynic could certainly interpret the comment as proving that Bunche only contemplated black solidarity when personally harmed. Bunche, moreover, was criticized for being a token, a false symbol of racial progress often used to paper over racist realities.

---

[26] Robert Alden, *121 in Atlanta Art Group Killed as Jet Airliner Crashes at Paris*, New York Times, June 4, 1962; Louis A. DeCaro Jr., On the Side of My People: A Religious Life of Malcolm X 187 (1996); Peter Louis Goldman, The Death and Life of Malcolm X 99 (1979); Jack V. Fox, *Negro Leaders Lambaste Malcolm X's Delight in Death of Atlanta Whites*, Chicago Defender, July 14, 1962, at 5; Staycee Hibbert, *Muslims Call Ralph Bunche "International Uncle Tom*," Philadelphia Tribune, July 21, 1962, at 1.

[27] Don Shannon, *Sculptor Fasts For Cause*, Los Angeles Times, June 23, 1972, at G13.

[28] Maya Angelou, The Heart of a Woman 245 (2009).

Bunche was a clear advocate for black folk, however, and none of the criticisms leveled against him supported treachery accusations. He certainly had no Garvey moments on his résumé; he neither lauded the KKK nor repeated its racist drivel. After Powell impugned his black solidarity, Bunche retorted that perhaps Powell had not heard from him because Powell "does not speak in the deep south as I do and seems to avoid NAACP meetings." And Bunche argued that he did not fight the tennis club for his own benefit, but because he believed that if his son could not be a member, then no other black person could be. "There should be no room for bigotry," Bunche proclaimed, "in the house of democracy."

Bunche's positions were well within the mainstream of black thought in the era. He criticized the 1957 Civil Rights Act as "disappointingly weak." He supported student sit-ins in the 1960s and participated in the March on Washington and the march to Selma. His views during the 1960s were reasonable and in no way should have led folk to doubt him. True, Bunche was a token. But even if he poorly responded to whites' attempts to use his success against the group, such a failure was a far cry from racial betrayal.[29]

Fellow black insider William Dawson, a Chicago congressman, was familiar with *Uncle Tom* accusations from the 1940s and 1950s. In the 1960s, Dawson remained unable to elude the epithet. In 1963, "Protest at the Polls," a political group comprised of young militants, announced that their candidate A. A. Sammy Rayner would challenge Dawson in the Democratic primary. The group claimed that as long as "Uncle Tom Dawson" remained in office "[we] will never achieve our goals." Dawson was a cog in the machine rather than the destructor the group desired. Just having a black face was insufficient; Protest at the Polls sought a strong supporter of civil rights. Congressman Adam Clayton Powell previously lambasted Dawson for supposedly blocking civil rights progress. Protest at the Polls likewise questioned Dawson's commitment to civil rights. "Despite the ... influence of the Dawson machine," one member of the group stated, "there has been grand larceny of the quantity and quality of Negro representation. The present thrust of the civil rights movement can be used to break the monopoly."[30]

In 1964, about fifty black and white high school students picketed a Dawson rally and chanted, "Dawson must go! And no more Uncle Toms!" A spokesman for the students revealed that they were simply "sick and tired of the old

---

[29] This and the previous two paragraphs are based on the following sources: Henry, *Ralph Bunche* 218–21; Urquhart, *Ralph Bunche* 431, 439.
[30] *New Group Seeks to Unseat Rep. W. L. Dawson*, Atlanta Daily World, Oct. 13, 1963, at A2.

guard, Uncle Tom, handkerchief-head politicians in our community." The protestors even included *Uncle Tom* in some of their songs. "Ain't Gonna Let No Uncle Tom Turn me 'Round," they sang, while carrying placards that read, "YOU SOLD MY PARENTS, BUT NOT ME – I KNOW YOU."[31]

Dawson's youthful opponents championed the protest method and had no use for the congressman's institutional party-building strategies. During this period, Dawson was also less connected to the issues his black constituents dealt with. Dawson was pushing for national civil rights victories in Congress while back in Chicago blacks grappled with a host of problems, including school segregation and the construction of large segregated public housing projects. And although Dawson was championing civil rights legislation, he, like other black congressmen, garnered scant support for his bills. These factors led his opponents to decry him as an *Uncle Tom*. Dawson's effectiveness as a politician was fairly in question. The idea that he was treacherous, however, was unsupported. Indeed, his critics derogated him for being a lackluster congressman but wrongly concluded that this meant hitting him with *Uncle Tom* accusations was proper. It was not.[32]

Dawson was one of a few blacks in the House of Representatives, but Edward Brooke was the Senate's only black member. The Republican, in fact, was America's first popularly elected black senator, beating Endicott Peabody in 1966. Before becoming a senator, Brooke was Massachusetts's attorney general and in 1963, in that capacity, he opposed the local civil rights community when he found a student boycott of segregated Boston public schools unlawful. "Freedom Stayout" called for black schoolchildren to stay home to protest the segregation in Boston schools. But Brooke argued that because state law required children to attend school absent mental or physical ailments, "[t]he School Committee can direct truant officers to retrieve absent pupils and where necessary seek their attendance through the district or juvenile courts." Many reacted harshly; some called him an *Uncle Tom*. Author James Baldwin said he was one of the people "who are bringing about the ruination of the country."[33]

Brooke's detractors, however, never contended that he wrongly interpreted the law. As Massachusetts's top attorney, Brooke could not ignore state laws. The narrative does highlight, though, how black insiders could not always

---

[31] *Students Picket as Dawson Holds Rally,* Chicago Daily Defender, Apr. 1, 1964, at 22.
[32] Manning, William L. Dawson 140–59.
[33] *The Unfinished Chapter Former US Senator Edward Brooke has Built New Life Since the 1978 Scandal,* Boston Globe Magazine, Mar. 5, 2000, at 14; Brace A. Ragsdale and Joel D. Treese, Black Americans in Congress, 1870–1989 5–6 (1990); John Henry Cutler, Ed Brooke: Biography of a Senator 118–20 (1972).

act as agents for the race, particularly when competing interests were at play. Indeed, the insider's ability to represent the race from the inside was limited. As Brooke once said, "I'm the lawyer for the five million citizens of Massachusetts, not for its ... Negroes."[34]

Brooke acknowledged he was not the "picketing type." His civil rights efforts in the trenches were negligible beyond the "occasional pep talk." Because he was so hesitant in interjecting himself in racial matters, some blacks thought that he was an *Uncle Tom*. Cecil Moore, head of the Philadelphia NAACP, quipped that "Brooke quit being a Negro 20 years ago. He's a sunburned white man now." Stokely Carmichael called Brooke an "Uncle Tom" and a "traitor." Brooke made political use of that last attack in his Senate campaign, stating that a vote for him was a vote against Carmichael. That he used Carmichael's opposition to appeal to white voters only fueled the belief that he was a sell-out. Brooke, an integrationist, believed that the Carmichaels of the world were given too much attention.[35]

In 1970, four years into his first Senate term, Brooke visited a black neighborhood in New Bedford, Massachusetts. The neighborhood was reeling from five consecutive nights of violence. Black leaders implored him to determine why funds earmarked for antipoverty initiatives had not reached the depressed community. As Brooke toured the neighborhood, he walked down a street where one black youth had been shot and killed and several others wounded. As he perused the blighted community, a crowd amassed. They shouted at him, urging him to try to remedy the situation. Others concluded, apparently, that he had already betrayed the community and yelled *Uncle Tom*.[36]

Brooke was not a rabble rouser, or even a fiery orator like Martin Luther King. He was a quieter man. But his opponents' criticism that he was not truly invested in the plight of blacks was unfounded. Although frequently unsuccessful, Bunche coaxed his Republican Party to reach out to black voters by championing policies that would meet their needs. Bunche actually criticized President Lyndon Johnson, author of the Great Society, for not doing enough to counter poverty. He also toured riot-torn areas in the mid-1960s, and used his platform to insist that America needed policy solutions to blacks' problems regarding jobs, education, housing, and health care. And when Nixon's

---

[34] African American Lives 100 (Editors Henry Louis Gates and Evelyn Brooks Higginbotham 2004).

[35] Id. at 101; Thomas J. Foley, *White Backlash Slices Brooke's Senate Lead*, Los Angeles Times, Oct. 19, 1966, at 6; Sterling G. Slappey, *More Negroes Run for Office*, Los Angeles Times, Nov. 29, 1965, at 2; Tom Foley, *Republican Brooke Wins Senate Seat in Massachusetts*, Los Angeles Times, Nov. 9, 1966, at 1.

[36] *Brooke Visits Area Rocked by Violence*, Los Angeles Times, July 14, 1970, at B8.

administration failed to promote black capitalism and nominated anti–civil rights Supreme Court justices, Bunche showered him with criticism. In his book *The Challenge of Change* (1966), Brooke argued that "[t]he nation's most urgent and dramatic domestic problem" was racial equality and that "[n]o achievement, however spectacular, in other areas of our national life can obscure the magnitude of this problem." Blacks remained, he argued, "second-class citizens." And he implored the country to work diligently to solve this pressing dilemma. Bunche had proven his commitment to his people, and it was devoid of gross impurities. Assertions to the contrary were deeply unfair. His critics prosecuted destructive norms.[37]

Tom Bradley, as Brooke before him, was a trail-blazing politician who was wrongly indicted for treachery. He was the mayor of Los Angeles from 1973 to 1993, becoming the first black mayor of a majority white city. In 1969, Bradley unsuccessfully challenged incumbent mayor Sam Yorty. Militant blacks called Bradley the "white man's candidate" and referred to him as an *Uncle Tom*. Militants said that he was not a champion of black rights and never took strong positions on race. Oddly, Yorty contended that Bradley was interjecting race in the contest and trying to appeal to "left-wing militants."[38]

Some black insiders violated constructive racial loyalty norms. See Johnny Ford, the first black mayor of Tuskegee, Alabama. His 1972 election was celebrated as a seminal moment for blacks in Alabama. A state with an infamously troubling history on race relations put a black man into the pilot's seat of one of its major cities. But when Ford endorsed Governor George Wallace's reelection in 1974, that pride evaporated. George Wallace's pronouncement of "Segregation today, segregation tomorrow, segregation forever" firmly etched his face into the national consciousness symbolizing obstinate segregation. He was Jim Crow. After the federal judiciary mandated compliance with *Brown* in terms of school desegregation, Governor Wallace publicly flouted the federal judiciary. Yet Ford endorsed a man who sought to reinforce a social hierarchy that kept blacks perpetually in the basement. Ford said he knew his decision would invite *Uncle Tom* accusations, but affirmed his loyalty to his race. "I'm talking about utilizing the political system that traditionally has kept us down, penetrating that system and becoming a part of that decision-making system and causing it to become more responsive and effective in meeting the needs of the black and all poor people." Ford likely saw Wallace's appointment of Jesse J. Lewis, the first black man to serve in any governor's cabinet since

[37] African American Lives 100–01; Edward W. Brooke, The Challenge of Change: Crisis in Our Two-Party System 148, 158–59 (1966).
[38] *Councilman Bradley Under Sharp Attack from Militants*, Afro-American, May 24, 1969, at 16.

Reconstruction, as proving the validity of his argument that blacks needed to work with Wallace to advance their interests.[39]

But as Ford sold Wallace as providing a possible antidote to their problems, blacks thought that he remained the poisonous serpent he had always been. Because during the 1970 gubernatorial contest, Wallace's political tactics were incredibly racist, blacks were right to view him as the dangerous snake he had long been. Once Wallace's political team discovered that his opponent, Albert Brewer, was popular but that voters feared he would be "soft on integration," Wallace used this weakness to win the Democratic Party's nomination. As Wallace's brother said, to win, "We'll just throw the niggers around [Brewer's] neck." One aide said their plan to win the voters was to "Promise them the moon and holler 'Nigger.'" Wallace's campaign promised the voters that if Brewer won, the state would be run by a "spotted alliance" between black militants and "sissy britches from Harvard." And on election morning, Wallace told voters, "Now don't let them niggers beat us, you hear?" and "If I don't win, the niggers are going to control this state." Through his campaign tactics, Wallace had proven himself an avowed antiblack bigot. Particularly because Brewer was a racial moderate, that Ford supported Wallace was indeed treacherous.[40]

In 1975, Ford reiterated his support for Wallace, commenting, "My governor has been fair and judicious to all Alabamians, rich or poor, black or white." This was just a few years after Wallace was quoted in the *New York Times* referring to Senator Brooke as that "nigger senator from Massachusetts." By lauding a racist politician, Ford violated all three constructive norms. Blacks would benefit from dissuading prominent and powerful members of the group from supporting segregationist politicians instead of their more racially egalitarian adversaries. Calling Ford out for his racial treachery reduced the likelihood that other black leaders would repeat his mistake.[41]

A man who hurled *Uncle Tom* destructively and with relative ease had the slur reversed on him. The story seems petty, but the episode demonstrates how *Uncle Tom* was introduced into unsuitable conflicts. Congressman Adam Clayton Powell was called an *Uncle Tom* for opposing the construction of a state office building in Harlem. Republican New York Governor Nelson Rockefeller supported the construction project, as did many black leaders.

---

[39] Vernon Jarrett, *A Black Mayor Supports Wallace*, Chicago Tribune, Apr. 28, 1974, at A6; James T. Wooten, *Wallace Bars 2 More Integration Plans*, New York Times, Aug. 19, 1971, at 28; Virgie W. Murray, *Gov. George Wallace Picks Black Staffer*, Los Angeles Sentinel, Jan. 16, 1975, at A1.

[40] Dan T. Carter, The Politics of Rage: George Wallace, the Origins of the New Conservatism and the Transformation of American Politics 391–94 (1995).

[41] Id. at 7; Jeff Frederick, Stand Up For Alabama: Governor George Wallace 348–49 (2007).

But Powell said that Governor Rockefeller was "going to learn that his Uncle Toms don't speak for Harlem." Indications suggested, however, that most Harlem residents disagreed with their congressman, and the president of the local NAACP branch attacked Powell for his resistance: "I charge that Adam Clayton Powell, Uncle Tom Adam, is making a deliberate effort to stir up conflict in the community because that's what he thrives on. Is Uncle Tom Adam really upset because the will of the people has proven itself and the work is progressing without conflict?" That an office building could devolve into an *Uncle Tom* controversy showed that the epithet was in a state of decline.[42]

In 1970, Eldridge Cleaver of the Black Panthers learned about an official investigation into whether the Black Panthers were victims of systemic police harassment. After the murder of Fred Hampton, the head of the Illinois Panther Party, a federal panel probed police action against the Panthers. Cleaver distrusted the American government and concluded that the commission was going to cover up "an attempt to eliminate the leadership of the Black Panther party and disrupt its ability to function."

Cleaver had a foundation for believing that a concerted effort to thwart the Panthers' activities existed. Vice President Spiro Agnew called the Panthers a "completely irresponsible anarchistic group of criminals." FBI Director J. Edgar Hoover described them as the "number one threat to the security of the United States." Similarly, Jerris Leonard, assistant attorney general in the Nixon administration, described the Panthers as "nothing but hoodlums" and concluded that "we've got to get them." And the president of the Cleveland Fraternal Order of Police said that "the country doesn't need the Black Panther Party, to my way of thinking they should be wiped out." Such comments supported beliefs that, at all levels of government, there was a concerted effort against the Panthers.[43]

Cleaver condemned the panel. Supreme Court Justice Arthur Goldberg, who Cleaver called a "well-known Zionist," was a member. The black members, too, were attacked on racial grounds. Black Michigan congressmen Charles Diggs and John Conyers as well as Roy Wilkins, Whitney Young, and Bayard Rustin were all called "Uncle Toms" for being on the panel. Cleaver intimated that partaking in an effort he believed would whitewash the illegalities perpetrated on the Black Panthers was a form of racial treason. But he failed to use actual evidence to support his claims of betrayal. Merely being

[42] Thomas A. Johnson, *N.A.A.C.P. Leader Assails Powell*, New York Times, Oct. 2, 1969, at 42.
[43] The sources for this and the preceding paragraph are as follows: Current Biography Yearbook 88 (1970); Charles E. Jones, *The Political Repression of the Black Panther Party 1966–1971: The Case of the Oakland Bay Area*, 18 Journal of Black Studies 415, 416 (1988).

on the panel was not treacherous. As was frequently true during the period, Cleaver destructively managed racial loyalty norms.[44]

Other black congressional Democrats were unjustifiably assailed as *Uncle Toms*. Barbara Jordan, for instance, was called Aunt Jemima and then when that did not work, an *Uncle Tom*, for her close relationship to President Johnson and the Texas establishment by her opponent Curtis Graves. But criticizing Jordan for being close to a president who had done more than all post-Lincoln presidents on civil rights was very misguided.[45]

Black Republicans, like Ed Brooke, were besieged by the epithet as well. The current phenomenon that black Republicans are almost reflexively called *Uncle Toms* began in the late 1960s. As civil rights worker James L. Flournoy wrote in his 1970 open letter to black Americans, "There are those who are quick to equate any black who dares to belong to the Republican Party with being an 'Uncle Tom.'" James Farmer, after he was appointed assistant secretary of the Department of Health, Education and Welfare in the Nixon administration, also disclosed that being a black Republican made him imminently vulnerable to *Uncle Tom* accusations. "I know some people may call me an Uncle Tom," Farmer said, "but I'd rather be on the inside working to change things than stand on the outside and complain." As blacks became solidly Democrat, those venturing to the other side of the aisle were constantly punished with *Uncle Tom* indictments. For instance, T. M. Alexander, assistant Federal Housing Administration commissioner, Arthur Fletcher, assistant labor secretary, and Robert Lee Grant and Melvin H. Humphrey, both of the Housing and Urban Development Department, all dealt with being labeled as *Uncle Toms*. They all, however, denied the charge, insisting they were doing their part to bring about equality between the races.[46]

Robert Brown, a black special assistant to President Nixon, was another Republican denounced for asserted racial betrayal. But whereas others did not fit the mold for an *Uncle Tom*, Brown's measurements were far closer. Brown fiercely championed his boss, who blacks openly reviled. In an interview, Brown derided blacks for being too emotionally charged to work successfully

---

[44] Jesse W. Lewis Jr., *Cleaver Wants to Leave Algiers, Rejoin Panther "Struggle" in U.S.*, Washington Post, Jan. 5, 1970, at 1; Bayard Rustin, *Black Panthers and Their Policy*, New York Amsterdam News, Jan. 17, 1970, at 16.

[45] Mary Beth Rogers, Barbara Jordan: American Hero 135 (2000); Myra MacPherson, *Looking Over Jordan*, Washington Post, Oct. 30, 1977, at C1.

[46] James L. Flournoy, *Open Letter to the Black Community*, Los Angeles Sentinel, Oct. 22, 1970, at A9; Jack Nelson, *Blacks Cite Advances in Administration*, Los Angeles Times, Nov. 8, 1970, at G1; Ethel L. Payne, *Sen. Brooke Praises Nixon Peace Efforts*, Chicago Daily Defender, Aug. 23, 1972, at 8; *Farmer Takes Post as Talent Recruiter for Nixon's Team*, Philadelphia Tribune, Feb. 15, 1969, at 1.

with the Nixon administration. Brown said, "One day, at some point, black people are going to have a look at the record and make judgments based on facts rather than emotion, fiery speeches and demonstrations. The masses of our people respond with emotion, but we've made some inroads with those who want to deal with substance."[47]

In addition to blaming blacks, Brown, many felt, embellished Nixon's record on race. Curtis T. Perkins, head of the National Council of Afro-American Republicans, asserted that Brown damaged the relationship between blacks and the executive branch when Brown "glorified" Nixon. Perkins argued that Brown should have honestly assessed Nixon's record and offered the administration solid advice. Perkins insisted that Brown, instead, embodied "yessirism." Without Nixon seriously addressing black poverty, Perkins warned of significant social unrest and violence. But this could be prevented if "those around Mr. Nixon listened to Blacks and did not pick 'Uncle Toms' in Brook's Brothers suits." Another commenter, reacting to Brown, said that "[i]t seems that the news of Uncle Tom's death was grossly exaggerated."[48]

Brown's criticizing blacks for being too overly emotional to work with Nixon was a baseless charge. The lack of cooperation between blacks and the Nixon administration had far more to do with the president's "retrogressive rhetoric" than blacks' over-emotionalism. True, Nixon's civil rights record is laudable in some respects. His administration instituted affirmative action and set aside programs for minority-owned businesses. But Nixon poked the bear with his Southern Strategy; he aggravated racial tensions when he appealed to racially resentful Southern whites in order to win elections. One cannot fault Brown for supporting his boss. But taking cheap shots at black folk, while glossing over real racism emanating from the White House, could rightfully give off the impression that Brown was being inexcusably meek. He might have been seeking to fit in with an intolerant administration by proving to his bosses that he too could toe the company line and share their antipathy of blacks. But if Brown actually were trying to get closer to the president, it proved unsuccessful. Brown "was not included in most of the President's meetings; Nixon found it hard to talk freely with Brown around" because of Brown's race. Although Brown arguably violated constructive racial loyalty norms – each side had enough evidence to support its case – most black insiders had demonstrated their commitments to their people.[49]

---

[47] *Blacks vs. Labor: A Contrast in Political Action*, Los Angeles Sentinel, Feb. 22, 1973, at C12.

[48] *Nixon Asked to Name Black Lawyer as Aide*, New York Amsterdam News, Apr. 7, 1973, at A1; *A Sad Ending*, Chicago Daily Defender, Feb. 13, 1973, at 13.

[49] Dean J. Kotlowski, Nixon's Civil Rights: Politics, Principle, and Policy 1 (2001); Kenneth O'Reilly, Nixon's Piano: Presidents and Racial Politics from Washington to Clinton 317 (1995).

UNCLE TOM SHOOTS AND SCORES

In 1963 in Birmingham, Alabama, Martin Luther King and the Southern Christian Leadership Conference executed a mass confrontation plan, "Plan C." Black agitators conducted sit-ins, marches, and protests to put Southern "brutality openly – in the light of day – with the rest of the world looking on" to force President Kennedy's hand. They wanted, in other words, a national remedy to racial discrimination. Former heavyweight champion boxer Floyd Patterson and Jackie Robinson announced their intention to travel to the city to assist the effort. Jesse Owens, however, thought the two should stay away. "I can't see where they're going to be of any great help," Owens said. Many blacks felt the quote evidenced that Owens was an *Uncle Tom*.

Owens was of a different time. Born in 1913, the track and field star's athletic pinnacle was his winning four gold medals in Berlin in 1936. Athletes his age were just athletes, not participants in social change efforts. But in the 1960s, many blacks demanded more of their sports heroes. Responding to Owens, one reader wrote to the *Defender*, stating, "[t]he Negro is sick and tired of waiting for the big shot Uncle Toms who won't speak up." Another wrote that Owens's remarks were in keeping with "his usual Uncle Tom self," proclaiming that "Owens has done nothing to make the modern, thinking Negro proud. He might point to the fact that he is liked by white people. He most certainly is[;] they love his antebellum image of the Negro." Owens's comments could be interpreted in many different ways. His adversaries believed he felt that black athletes had no place in fighting for civil rights, a sentiment strongly suggesting inexcusable meekness. Indeed, managing racial loyalty norms that punished blacks for criticizing those willing to fight racism could only help blacks in their efforts to ameliorate racial discrimination.[50]

Muhammad Ali faced a similar issue. Before he changed his name from Cassius Clay, and before he began lambasting his opponents as *Uncle Toms*, Ali had his own *Uncle Tom* experience. In 1963, at an "Afro-American conference" in Oakland, Ali was asked if he would fight in a segregated arena. The young boxer was quoted as saying, "Yes!" Columnist Brad Pye Jr. wrote that Clay had an "Uncle Tom moment."[51]

---

[50] Randall Bennett Woods, Quest for Identity: America Since 1945 175 (2005); Taylor Branch, Parting the Waters: America in the King Years, 1954–63 631 (1988); *Jesse Owens Hits Alabama Trip by Patterson, Jackie Robinson*, Chicago Daily Defender, May 16, 1963, at 3; Stonewall Edwards, *The People Speak*, Chicago Daily Defender, May 29, 1963, at 12; Nelson Turner, *Our Other Enemy*, Chicago Daily Defender, May 23, 1963, at 12.

[51] Brad Pye Jr, *Prying Pye*, Los Angeles Sentinel, Oct. 17, 1963, at A14.

Although Ali beset his opponents with *Uncle Tom* accusations, none of his victims ever endorsed a position as identified with racial treachery as expressing a willingness to entertain a segregated audience. During the less radical 1950s, Louis Armstrong and Nat King Cole were denounced for performing in front of segregated audiences. In that racial climate, it was destructive to brand those two performers as *Uncles Toms*. In 1963, however, in the heart of the civil rights movement, after black students had been successfully waging social protests against segregation, to express support for fighting in front of a segregated audience was inexcusably meek. Nearly a decade after *Brown*, blacks should have never bowed so low to white supremacy as to put on a show before it. And blacks were right to enforce norms to discipline such behavior.

Ali, though, easily weathered his *Uncle Tom* storm and later caused various tempests for his foes. Ali changed his named in 1964 when he officially joined the Nation of Islam. When some of his opponents continued to insultingly call him Clay, Ali countered with a derisive appellation of his own, *Uncle Tom*. Floyd Patterson was his first such victim. In January 1965, before their fight, Ali crashed Patterson's training camp to heckle him. Ali said, "I want to hear my name – my real name!" Patterson, without looking at Ali, said, "the name he was born with was Clay." Ali repeated his demand and yelled again at Patterson, "You white man's Uncle Tom. I'll jump right in there on you now." Patterson also insulted black Muslims and the Nation of Islam. In response, Ali attacked Patterson for being beloved by white America and ridiculed him for living in a white neighborhood. Ali claimed before their contest that he was "going to put him on his back, so that he can start acting black." During their fight, while the two were clenched, Ali again called Patterson an "Uncle Tom." While punishing him, he asked Patterson, "What's my name?" and called him a "White American" and the "White man's nigger."[52]

Some black sports columnists defended Patterson. A. S. Doc Young balked at the idea that Ali could question someone's racial loyalty because Ali was "the biggest Uncle Tom in the history of sports." Young, like many older blacks, strongly opposed the Nation of Islam. Young said with his "yakkity-yakkings about self-segregation, he blasphemes 364 years of Negro fight for equality." Bill Nunn Jr., another sportswriter, scribed that by "calling Patterson an 'Uncle Tom Negro,' the champion showed ignorance and intolerance. Patterson certainly [is no Uncle Tom]." Brad Pye Jr. wrote that Patterson was

---

[52]   Jack Cuddy, *Is Clay Building Floyd Up for Himself*, Los Angeles Sentinel, Jan. 28, 1965, at B3; *Patterson Calls Clay Modest Man*, Chicago Daily Defender, July 21, 1966, at 37; Srikumar Sen, *Undefeated and Still Champion*, The Times, Jan. 11, 1992; Tom Humphries, *Bad Guys Make the Ring Go Round*, The Irish Times, Nov. 9, 1998, at 57.

a life-long member of the NAACP and participated in many important civil rights initiatives. Pye then asked, "What has Cassius Clay done for anyone beside himself?"[53]

Two years later, history repeated itself when Ali gave a televised beating to an opponent who insisted on calling him Cassius Clay. Ernie Terrell, this time, was the victim. In the ring, Ali bashed Terrell and at one point after each punch asked, "What's my name? Uncle Tom! What's my name?" The strife in the ring was a spillover from their hatred outside it. Before the fight, Ali said that he would continue to call Terrell an "Uncle Tom" until "he learns to respect me and call me Muhammad Ali." During a press conference in 1966 that was staged to gin up interest for the bout, *Uncle Tom* nearly drove the two to fists because Ali continuously demeaned Terrell with the pejorative.[54]

Terrell was incensed that Ali questioned his racial loyalty and rebuffed Ali's verbal taunts. "I know that he brings many fans into the fights by running off at the mouth," Terrell said later, "but I will not allow him to call me an Uncle Tom." Terrell further claimed, "calling another man an Uncle Tom that's just plain vicious." A few days before the fight at another press conference, Ali apologized for calling Terrell an *Uncle Tom*. "Ernie Terrell ain't no Uncle Tom and I shouldn't have called him that, but I'm still going to give him a good whopping for calling me Cassius Clay," Ali said. A. S. Doc Young reiterated his criticism of Ali after the champ called Terrell an *Uncle Tom*. "Show me a bigger Uncle Tom than Cassius Clay," he wrote, "and I'll show you Cleopatra, in the living flesh." After the fight, one commenter wrote, "In their pre-fight build-up, Clay called Terrell an 'Uncle Tom' for calling him Cassius Clay and vowed to make him call him Muhammad Ali. There is no evidence that Clay succeeded in this command."[55]

Of all of Ali's fights, his duels with Joe Frazier are the most memorable. Their three matches are indelible. Their fights intrigued the world not solely because of punches and knockouts, but also because of the contempt between the two men. They hated each other. But originally they were friends. In 1969, Philadelphia native Frazier was listening to Muhammad Ali on a local radio station. At first, Ali was discussing political issues. He then, however, abruptly

[53] A. S. Doc Young, *Good Morning, Sports!*, Chicago Daily Defender, June 2, 1965, at 30; Bill Nunn Jr., *Change of Pace*, Pittsburgh Courier, Feb. 6, 1965, at 23; Brad Pye Jr., *Prying Pye*, Los Angeles Sentinel, Jan. 28, 1965, at B1.

[54] *Freedom Fighter; Nicholas Lezard at last Becomes a Fan of Ali*, The Guardian, May 6, 2000, at 11; Frank Keating, *Way Back When…*, The Guardian, Feb. 7, 1997, at 10; *Clay Draft Decision Near*, Chicago Daily Defender, Jan. 9, 1967, at 28; *Ali, Terrell Square Off Over Insult*, Chicago Daily Defender, Dec. 29, 1966, at 34.

[55] Dick Edwards, *Ern Burns at "Tom" Tag Says Clay Will Pay*, New York Amsterdam News, Jan. 21, 1967, at 33; *Terrell Is No "Uncle Tom,"* Los Angeles Sentinel, Feb. 2, 1967, at B3; A. S. Doc

began calling Frazier "clumsy, a fighter without class, an Uncle Tom ... [and] a coward." And as the years went on, so did the insults. To Ali, Frazier was a stupid *Uncle Tom* who was "too ugly to be the champ." Ali strongly interjected race in his taunts, portraying Frazier as "the white man's champion," the inference being that he was that for black folk. "Ninety-eight percent of my people are for me.... If I win, they win. I lose, they lose. Anybody black who thinks Frazier can whup me is an Uncle Tom. Everybody who's black wants me to keep winning."[56]

Frazier, the son of a Southern sharecropper, was born in abject poverty. In many respects, Frazier lived a stereotypically black life marked by struggle and oppression. Considering his hardships, and eventual massive success, one might presume that blacks would have exalted him to heroic status. But such was not the case. With *Uncle Tom*, Ali turned Frazier into a traitor. In the months before their first of three fights, Ali marketed himself as black America's champion and Frazier as the white man's puppet. Of all the blows Ali landed, *Uncle Tom* most pained Frazier. Blacks for decades viewed him skeptically. *Uncle Tom* was the most effective brush in portraying Frazier as a racial scourge. For many years, the humiliated Frazier rebuffed Ali's apologies. He was dumbfounded that a former friend had challenged his racial authenticity.

Shortly before their first brawl, Frazier was apparently fed up with the taunts. Although by then most assumed that Ali threw out *Uncle Tom* barbs merely to agitate his opponents and draw more attention to his fights, Frazier saw something insidious to the black community in Ali's constant barking. Ali, Frazier concluded, was selling the black community a bill of goods and espousing a worldview that would be counterproductive in American society. He lamented, "Clay called me an Uncle Tom! You going to tell me Clay don't have white friends? What color's his trainer, for example? These black people who fall for him and believe him and follow what he says to do will be right where they are 10 years from now."[57]

But Ali was successful in pegging Frazier as white America's chosen Negro. Frazier, in fact, was asked whether it bothered him to be considered the "Great White Hope." Frazier rejected the label, instead pointing again to Ali's white trainers. He retorted, "look at Clay, every time I see him, he's got white folks

---

Young, *Good Morning Sports!*, Chicago Daily Defender, Jan. 26, 1967, at 40; Brad Pye Jr., *Cassius Clay Launders Ernie Terrell's Bag of Dirty Tricks in 15 Rounds*, Los Angeles Sentinel, Feb. 9, 1967, at B1.

[56] William Nack, My Turf: Horses, Boxers, Blood Money, and the Sporting Life 166 (2004).

[57] *Morning Briefing*, Los Angeles Times, Mar. 1, 1971, at C2; Shirley Povich, *For Ali, the Talk Show Is Just About Over*, Washington Post, Mar. 7, 1971, at 39.

in his corner. I call that the real Uncle Tom." Ali's taunts were so successful that people started showing up at Frazier's gym just to jeer him. "The Uncle Tom epithet tripped so incessantly from Ali's lips, and now from the crowd around the gym, that Joe might as well have been wearing a sign." The taunts bothered not only Frazier, but his son Marvin, who had to defend his father in school.[58]

But in 2001, Ali apologized. Ali admitted that he erred in calling Frazier an *Uncle Tom*. "I said a lot of things in the heat of the moment that I shouldn't have said. Called him names I shouldn't have called him. I apologize for that. I'm sorry. It was all meant to promote the fight." Frazier responded graciously. "I'll accept [the apology], shake his hand and hug him when I see him. We're grown guys. This has been going on too long. It's like we've been fighting the Vietnam War.... We have to embrace each other. It's time to talk and get together. Life's too short."[59]

Ali even derided fighters he never faced in the ring. Ali recounted an incident in his autobiography when he called Bobby Foster an *Uncle Tom*. Ali traveled to Albuquerque to attend a banquet honoring Foster, the retiring light heavyweight boxing champion. At the banquet, Ali was conversing with a group of Native Americans who described their plight as worse than that of blacks living in urban ghettoes. Foster overheard the conversation and demanded that Ali stop disparaging his home state. Ali responded, "What kind of Uncle Tom are you[?] ... I came down here to honor you, but if you act like a fool, I'll whip you good."[60]

Ali also called Joe Louis an *Uncle Tom*. Louis openly disparaged Ali. In the ring, Ali danced to avoid blows. Louis hated that. In the early 1960s, Louis knocked Ali's "float like a butterfly, sting like a bee" tactics, insisting, "he can't punch ... He can't hurt you and I don't think he takes a good punch. He's lucky there are no good fighters around.... I would have whipped him." Louis also criticized black Muslims. "I'm against Black Muslims," he said, "and I'm against Cassius Clay being a Black Muslim. I'll never go along with the idea that all white people are devils." Feeling unfairly attacked, Ali retaliated. "Slow-moving, shuffling Joe Louis beat me? He may hit hard, but that don't mean nothing if you can find nothing to hit." He then assured that he would "never ... end up like Joe Louis." Ali ended

[58] George Vecsey, *Frazier Sharp in "Tough" Prison Talk Show*, New York Times, Nov. 9, 1971, at 63; Mark Kram, Ghosts of Manila: The Fateful Blood Feud between Muhammad Ali and Joe Frazier 129–30 (2001).

[59] Richard Sandomir, *Boxing; No Floating, No Stinging: Ali Extends Hand to Frazier*, New York Times, Mar. 15, 2001, at 1.

[60] Muhammad Ali, The Greatest 323 (1979).

his barb with a great insult, declaring that the Brown Bomber should change his name to *Uncle Tom*.[61]

Ali picked fights with non-boxers as well. Wilt Chamberlain was among his targets. Chamberlain was the most offensively dominant NBA player in history, once averaging more than fifty points in a season. His prowess extended off the court; he claimed to have had sex with more than 20,000 women. From his wealth of experience, Chamberlain concluded that black women were inferior in the bedroom. In his book, Chamberlain said he preferred white women because they were more intellectually compatible. Such a comment would naturally perturb Muhammad Ali, a man who, when he had no income because his boxing license was suspended, declined an offer of $400,000 to play boxing great Jack Johnson in a movie because Johnson notoriously romanced white women. Ali thought that white women permitted themselves to become a symbol of white supremacy and preferred to stay with women of color, particularly black women. Ali asked Chamberlain why he found black women "incompatible," but Ali never received a response which, he wrote, "didn't surprise me, as I had never heard of Wilt associating much with black men or women or doing anything worthwhile for blacks. In fact, the association he was most proud of was with Richard Nixon, who used him once as sort of a spear-carrier in his election campaign." For this, Ali called the seven-footer "the world's largest Uncle Tom."[62]

Other sports stars besides Muhammad Ali were at the center of *Uncle Tom* disputes during this epoch. Jackie Robinson was assailed as an *Uncle Tom* while actively playing sports. After retirement, he met the same fate. The older Robinson saw black political culture shift leftward, and the self-described "Rockefeller Republican" was clearly out of step. His relationship with Norman Rockefeller, New York's Republican governor, was compromising, leading to him being called an *Uncle Tom* twice publicly in 1967. When Jackie Robinson joined the governor's staff, he knew that many blacks would consider him an *Uncle Tom* attempting to further his own interests at the race's expense. But he stood up to those who sought to dismiss him. "I feel perfectly secure," he wrote, "in saying that I have not been an Uncle Tom to

[61] Donald McRae, *Heroes without a Country: America's Betrayal of Joe Louis and Jesse Owens* 331–32 (2002); Chris Mead, *Champion: Joe Louis Black Hero in White America* 291–93 (1985).
[62] Ralph Novak, *Wilt Chamberlain: As an Actor, or Anything Else, His Ambition Is Fit for a Giant*, People, July 30, 1984, available at: http://www.people.com/people/archive/article/0,20088351,00.html; Clovis, News-Journal, Feb. 1, 1976, at 5; A. S. Doc Young, *Good Morning, Sports!*, Chicago Defender, Dec. 17, 1975, at 25; Ali, The Greatest 322–23.

him and happy to say that the Governor neither wants me as an Uncle Tom nor believes I could become one."[63]

That Robinson was deemed guilty of violating racial loyalty norms for his relationship with Governor Rockefeller was unfair. Their political bond started after Robinson sent a letter to the governor that criticized the dearth of blacks in upper-level and policy-making positions in his administration. After reading it, Rockefeller telephoned Robinson and invited him to meet and discuss his complaints in person. After their discussion, the governor introduced major reforms. Robinson wrote, "Out of that one meeting came some sweeping and drastic changes, some unprecedented appointments of blacks to high positions, ensuring influence by blacks in the governor's day-to-day policy decisions. Some of the governor's top-level people were very unhappy about these changes." Surely Robinson was not an *Uncle Tom* for serving as an advisor to an important politician who eventually became vice president. That Robinson supported a politician who had shown his willingness to listen to criticisms and make positive changes to improve the lives of black folk disproves the allegation that the relationship portended poorly of his racial loyalty.[64]

Other black baseball players too were caught flatfooted in the changing racial climate where sports icons were expected to sound off on white supremacy and the slow pace of change. Those standing silent were easy targets for *Uncle Tom* denunciations. Willie Mays, who many think was the best all-around baseball player who ever lived, never really showed a social consciousness and was considered an *Uncle Tom*. Mays acquired the reputation of never responding to racism when he experienced it personally or when his hometown of Birmingham was engulfed in racial strife. One bartender in San Francisco once remarked that "Mays was hated by [his black customers]. They called him Uncle Tom." Jackie Robinson agreed. Robinson thought that Mays and Roy Campanella were similar – meek uneducated blacks who relented to oppression – and privately thought of him as an *Uncle Tom*. Robinson once said during a televised interview that Mays "has a personality that is loved by white Americans, and I think he will be one of the first Negroes to move into a front office position [in baseball]." That was not a compliment. Henry Aaron, too, heard the *Uncle Tom* chants, but remarked, "You don't have to be a loudmouth to be heard." Elston Howard, the New York Yankees' first black player, was attacked as well. Many probably felt, as one black New Yorker

[63] Jackie Robinson, *I Must Live With Myself*, Chicago Daily Defender, Jan. 20, 1968, at 10.
[64] Robinson, I Never Had It Made 165–66.

wrote in the *Amsterdam News*, that "It's a pity Uncle Toms get breaks like the one he got."[65]

One does not have to be an outspoken racial advocate to be loyal. But those eschewing the role may have done so for reasons that would have violated the three constructive racial loyalty norms. Mays's, Aaron's, and Howard's detractors, however, did not prove that they were guilty of racial treachery. These occurrences are a perfect reminder that evidence must always accompany accusations of racial treachery.

Arthur Ashe was another famous sports figure wrongly taunted as an *Uncle Tom*. The tennis player and periodic activist took controversial stances on issues like college admissions and its relation to the black athlete and apartheid in South Africa. The former stance resulted ironically in the labeling of Ashe as an *Uncle Tom*. In 1973, Ashe played in the South African Open and, while there, Ashe learned about the plight of the disenfranchised black South Africans. But some blacks, both American and South African, thought his presence in the tennis tournament was "an act of complicity with the white racist government." Even though false – after all the oppressive South African government thought of him as a rabble-rouser – the belief that Ashe legitimated apartheid acquired an aura of veracity and the belief that he was an *Uncle Tom* saturated the air. Before his trip to South Africa, Ashe spoke at Howard University, a historically black university in Washington, DC. During his address, two African students shouted, "Uncle Tom! Uncle Tom! Arthur Ashe is an Uncle Tom and a traitor." Athlete Harry Edwards said that his "first reaction was, Arthur Ashe is an Uncle Tom." He continued, "But then as things went along and he began to speak out, I really came to respect what he called his way. I not only came to respect it, I came to depend on it."[66]

A discussion about *Uncle Tom*, the black athlete, and the 1960s would be incomplete without exploring the much-discussed boycott of the 1968 Mexico City Olympic Games. An Olympic boycott had been discussed for some time. Comedian and activist Dick Gregory had tossed the idea around in 1960. But nothing developed until track and field star Tommie Smith commented on the possibility of a boycott when speaking to a Japanese reporter in 1967. In the fall of that year, black athletes formed the Olympic Project for Human

---

[65] Jeff Prugh, *Where Are the Fans?*, Los Angeles Times, May 21, 1975, at E1; Joe Gergen, *Countdown Starts*, Los Angeles Times, May 19, 1972, at F7; Sam Lacy, *The Achilles Heel of Willie Mays*, Afro-American, May 22, 1971, at 7; Hap Harper, *On Elston Howard*, New York Amsterdam News, Apr. 11, 1959, at 8; *Ashe Lays It on the Line*, Sun Reporter, Feb. 17, 1977, at 39; James S. Hirsch, Willie Mays: The Life, the Legend 6, 234, 469 (2010).

[66] Arthur Ashe and Arnold Rampersad, Days of Grace 103–06 (1993); Joanne Ostrow, *"Icy Elegance" of Arthur Ashe Recalled in HBO Special*, Denver Post, Sept. 27, 1994, at E01.

Rights (OPHR). With Harry Edwards as its organizer and primary athlete spokesmen, OPHR wanted to become part of the activist black movement. Its objective was to broadcast how America used black athletes to falsely depict a benign image of race relations at home and abroad. Its founding statement started with the line: "We must no longer allow this country to use a few so-called Negroes to point out to the world how much progress she has made in solving her racial problems when the oppression of Afro-Americans is greater than it ever was." OPHR initially had three main demands: the restoration of Muhammad Ali's title; the removal of Avery Brundage, an asserted white supremacist, from the U.S. Olympic Committee; and disinviting South Africa and Rhodesia from the Olympic Games. Later, black athletes expanded their list to include the addition of at least two black coaches to the men's track and field staff. The staff already had one black coach, Stanley V. Wright. Wright, though, was consistently called an *Uncle Tom* who the "Black Athletes dislike … intensely."[67]

The idea of the boycott was based on sound logic – blacks would benefit if the country was shamed before the world. Many scholars have revealed how the Supreme Court's declaring separate but equal in *Brown* was in many ways compelled by Cold War realities. Communist regimes sold their ideology to third-world countries inhabited by people of color by noting that blacks in America, a capitalist country, were subordinated. If blacks revealed the enormous imperfections of American race relations, then the country may work toward a remedy.

Immense controversy emanated from the proposed boycott, and older black athletes were questioned about their feelings. In such high-profile situations, blacks are often pitted against each other. If one popular black figure becomes a critic, his words are then shoved down the throat of the other side. Guarding against that, Edwards claimed that "[Jesse] Owens grasps the whole Olympic picture [and] agrees deeply with us." Edwards was wrong. Owens vehemently opposed the boycott. He felt that through sports, blacks could better smash racial barriers than through other ways. Edwards, likely feeling betrayed, responded, "Owens is a bootlicking Uncle Tom." Another said that Owens would be an unacceptable appointee to the U.S. Olympic Committee because of his "'Uncle Tom' stand."[68]

---

[67] Dave Zirin, What's My Name, Fool? Sports and Resistance in the United States 73–74 (2005); John McLendon Jr., *Olympic Boycott?...Yes or No*, Cleveland Call and Post, Aug. 3, 1968, at 7B; William Jackson, *Stars Disagree on Olympic Boycott*, Cleveland Call and Post, Mar. 9, 1968, at 9B.

[68] The information complied for this and the preceding paragraph is as follows: William J. Baker, Jesse Owens: An American Life 207 (1986); McRae, Heroes without a Country, at 339;

Owens's worldview, as expressed in his book *Blackthink: My Life as a Black Man and White Man* (1970), was that of a man who believed that racial equality had been secured. Owens was an individualist. But the black athletes involved in the Olympic racial protest were collectivists, endeavoring to improve the plight of the group. Owens, one the one hand, argued that "[i]f the Negro doesn't succeed in today's America, it is because he has chosen to fail." Harry Edwards, on the other hand, pointed to the structural inequalities that were largely invisible to whites but were vivid to blacks as they stifled their social mobility. Intimately familiar with the ugly side of collectivism, Owens compared the Olympic protestors' viewpoints to that of Adolf Hitler in *Mein Kampf*. Owens believed "that race-thinking of any kind or collective action of any sort was akin to Nazism and fascism, a form of 'tyranny.'" Owens's incredible denial of the salience of race in his 1970 book was quite unfathomable, which is why he wrote a book a few years later, *I Have Changed* (1972), distancing himself from much of what he wrote in *Blackthink*. He realized, for instance, that his claim that blacks' failure was chosen was wrongheaded. Owens, nevertheless, had clearly rejected the idea of black solidarity and, therefore, should have not been denounced as an *Uncle Tom*. He had opted out. And those who do should be allowed that option and not criticized for racial treachery.[69]

Joe Louis, like Owens, opposed the boycott. He believed that black excellence at the games would push the black cause forward more than a protest. In 1938, Louis, the Brown Bomber, became an American hero – an unlikely feat for a black man – after defeating German boxer Max Schmeling. The victory was portrayed as an American triumph over Nazi Germany. As the heavyweight champ, Louis maintained a palatable image that whites embraced. After his retirement, he still maintained a palatable image that whites embraced, engendering antipathy among young blacks who tended to be more militant than their parents and not alive to fondly recall his boxing heroics. Following his retirement, blacks began expecting their public figures, whether they were politicians, writers, or athletes, to speak about the ills of white supremacy. But Louis never did. His problem was that his image was tailored to the 1930s and 1940s. But after his retirement, the racial climate was progressing, yet Louis stood flat-footed. His outlook likely influenced his decision to oppose the 1968 Olympic boycott. Louis was called an *Uncle Tom* as a result.[70]

Jesse Owens, I Have Changed 9–10 (1972); John McLendon Jr., *Olympic Boycott?...Yes or No*, Cleveland Call and Post, Aug. 10, 1968, at 9B.

[69] Jesse Owens, Blackthink: My Life as a Black Man and White Man 43–44 (1970); Douglas Hartmann, Race, Culture and the Revolt of the Black Athlete: The 1968 Olympic Protests and Their Aftermath 231–36 (2003).

[70] Mead, Joe Louis Black Hero in White America 291–93.

But Louis was not the stereotypical sellout who glossed over racism to appease white folk. Lacking education and oratory skills, he was simply unsuited to stand before the world and advocate for blacks, once telling a reporter, "Sometimes I wish I had the fire of a Jackie Robinson to speak out and tell the black man's story." After hearing about a black man who voiced apathy about Southern protests, Louis replied, "He's dumb." Louis was committed to black folk and thus was no *Uncle Tom*. He simply was not a leader on the front lines.[71]

The athletes who mulled over the boycott ultimately dropped the idea. An actual boycott was always unlikely. Athletes train assiduously for an event that takes place once every four years, and to relinquish a dream to win a gold medal is incredibly difficult to do, no matter how noble the cause. Although they did not boycott, the athletes left an atmosphere of black consciousness in Mexico. When boxer George Foreman pranced around the boxing ring with a miniature American flag in his hand after winning gold, he appeared aloof. And *Uncle Tom* accusations followed.

Foreman said he was trying to be patriotic, unaware that his sunny disposition would cast a shadow of betrayal. Other black Olympic athletes invaded the American consciousness with their conveyed message of black suffering – the raised fists, the black gloves of Tommie Smith and John Carlos – a form of silent protest against injustice. Images are often juxtaposed. When that of Carlos and Smith's raised clenched fists are contrasted with Foreman and his dainty America flag, Foreman appears placatory to the establishment, ingratiating himself to white America. "I didn't mean it to be a counter-protest or anything like that," Foreman said. "I wasn't even conscious that the television cameras were on me.... I waved the flag because I was so happy and so proud to be an American." Although deeply unfair, for all of Foreman's talent, he was not seen as a true fighter – at least not one who fought for his people. To black militants, Smith and Carlos were authentic; Foreman was an *Uncle Tom*.[72]

The management of racial loyalty norms in this context was destructive. Muhammad Ali delivered the most historically significant utterances of *Uncle Tom*. The epithet from Ali's lips always hit undeserving targets, typically people with whom he had personal disputes. Because of his popularity, Ali's misuse of *Uncle Tom* likely influenced countless others to replicate his errors. Indeed, more than anyone else, Ali helped mainstream the unjustified *Uncle Tom* accusation. Racial loyalty norms have been managed worse during each

---

[71] Id. at 293.
[72] Arthur Daley, *Sports of the Times*, New York Times, Jan. 25, 1970, at 166; Glenn Dickey, *Boxing's a Mess, But George Is a Delight*, San Francisco Chronicle, Apr. 17, 1991, at D3.

subsequent period. Some of the responsibility for that falls at the feet of one of the most beloved sports heroes grown from American soil.

SINGING, DANCING, ACTING, AND *UNCLE TOMMING*

Engulfed in racial tension during the mid-twentieth century, few blacks transcended race. Even fewer would feel welcomed in white homes. And probably only one would receive a cordial invitation: Sidney Poitier. This peculiar sentiment among whites even led the *New York Times* to publish an article entitled *Why Does White America Love Sidney Poitier So?*[73]

Poitier was Hollywood's first iconic leading black actor. In his movies, he was the "integrationist hero." Poitier's characters were cultured and wise, had impeccable diction, and dressed conservatively. "Sidney was a black man that met [white] standards." The men he portrayed were subdued, had no inclination to attack the status quo, and were devoid of sexual desires. Poitier, essentially, played "mild-mannered toms" that took derision from white characters because their acumen dictated humanity.[74]

Poitier endeared himself to whites, and some blacks – but not all, namely the militants. Stokely Carmichael, H. Rap Brown, and the Black Panthers branded him an *Uncle Tom*. After Poitier won an Academy Award for *Lilies in the Field* (1963), militants called him an *Uncle Tom*, a "lackey," and a "'million-dollar shoeshine boy." In that movie, he is Homer Smith, an ambulatory construction worker who meets East German nuns in Arizona who believe he was God-sent to build them a church. But some thought that Smith was less than a man. He appeared to be solely devoted to working for whites. Those branding him an *Uncle Tom*, however, helped fuel his success. In the South, whites liked him precisely because he was nothing like the black militants. In fact, his interracial kissing scene in *Guess Who's Coming to Dinner* (1967) was only censured in one Southern theater, a remarkably low number given the times.[75]

Poitier wrote candidly about his image in his autobiography. "According to a certain taste that was coming into ascendancy at the time, I was an 'Uncle Tom,' even a 'house Negro,' for playing roles that were nonthreatening to white audiences, for playing the 'noble Negro' who fulfills white liberal fantasies." Poitier got it right. He fostered an image that many concluded was a

---

[73] Clifford, *Why Does White America Love Sidney Poitier So?*, New York Times, Sept. 10, 1967, at 123.

[74] Bogle, Toms, Coons, Mulattoes, Mammies, & Bucks 175–76 (2001 ed.).

[75] Michael E. Ross, *Sidney Poitier on 40 Years of Change*, New York Times, Feb. 18, 1989, at C18; Aram Goudsouzian, Sidney Poitier: Man, Actor, Icon 214, 287 (2004).

net negative for the race. With social conditions needing much improvement, Poitier helped buttress a belief that improvements were unnecessary, things were fine, and the problems blacks had were of their own making. "After all, Poitier wasn't like *that*."[76]

Although blacks should have felt free to debate the quality of Poitier's characters, his cinematic roles were nothing akin to what blacks saw when they sat in theaters and looked up at the silver screen in the 1940s. And even when accounting for improved historical conditions, the *Uncle Tom* roles during the World War II era were far less excusable than Poitier's roles in the 1960s. In fact, one can proffer a very convincing argument that Poitier committed no offense at all. After all, his characters never demeaned the race. He never received a Hollywood paycheck in exchange for performances that defiled black Americans before the entire world. In fact, quite the opposite. Poitier's roles improved the world's perception of black folk. As such, unlike the actors in the previous period, Poitier infringed no constructive racial loyalty norms.

James Brown was another entertainer during this period wrongly accused of racial disloyalty. Looking back on the breadth of Brown's music, rationalizing that he was an *Uncle Tom* is difficult. But amid the racial turbulence of the 1960s, even the Godfather of Soul can have his blackness questioned. In 1968, Brown appeared on television with Democratic presidential candidate Hubert Humphrey to help him win the presidential election, held a televised concert in Boston after Dr. King's death that successfully mitigated riots, and with his band, flew to Vietnam after he released a patriotic song, *America Is My Home*. Brown biographer Cynthia Rose wrote:

> This trio of events poured gasoline on the flaming rhetoric of black militants, who pictured the contradictory icon as an assimilationist, an Uncle Tom. After all, Brown's work had – to use a Hollywood term – made crazy bank during the '60s. And the conspicuous awards he had accrued – the jet, the radio stations he owned, his mansion in St Albans, New York – hardly helped discredit complaints that James had bought into a system ruled by the Man.

Brown countered with his song *Say It Loud – I'm Black and I'm Proud* a few months later. With this soulful classic overflowing with racial pride, Brown affirmed his authenticity.[77]

Other musicians too faced *Uncle Tom* accusations. Jimi Hendrix was one. Hendrix was a great black musician who did not play traditional "black music." Blacks may have created rock 'n' roll, but they had long moved on to

---

[76] Sidney Poitier, The Measure of a Man: A Spiritual Biography 118 (2000).

[77] Cynthia Rose, Living in America: The Soul Saga of James Brown 65–67 (1990).

other genres. Hendrix, however, stayed. He was labeled as an *Uncle Tom* and
rock critic Robert Christgau called Jimi Hendrix a "psychedelic Uncle Tom"
for being a shill for white audiences. Moreover, his propensity for drugs, the
numerous photographs of him surrounded by blondes, and his flamboyant
and eccentric nature struck a negative chord in portions of black America
who viewed him as "a stoned clown acting like a nigger for the amusement of
white folks." But his adversaries condemned him more for his personal flair
rather than any lack of commitment to racial justice. Even if one conceded
that Hendrix failed some standardized black culture test, that means nothing regarding the strength of his bonds concerning black solidarity. Thus,
impugning his racial loyalty was deeply destructive.[78]

As black politicians learned, being connected to Republicans invited *Uncle
Tom* accusations, so too did Sammy Davis Jr. He should have never embraced
Nixon. Davis erred in sleeping with the enemy, or more accurately, hugging
the enemy. In 1972 at a Republican youth rally, actor and singer Davis gave
President Nixon a friendly if awkward-looking hug. "It was all so beautifully
vaudeville, Davis suddenly upon the president, a touchy-touchy hug." As they
embraced, camera bulbs flashed, creating an imperishable image that would
cause Davis great distress. A picture of Davis warm and fuzzy with Nixon –
persona non grata in black America largely for his race-baiting electoral
strategies – was a photographical grenade that exploded in his face. After the
picture surfaced on black America's collective doorstep, Davis received hordes
of mail calling him "nigger" and "Uncle Tom." Many blacks likely saw the
image in *Jet*, and the picture had prompted the largest response ever on a subject in the periodical's history. But like other entertainers before him, Davis
was wrongly pegged as an *Uncle Tom* by those over-policing racial loyalty.[79]

ANALYSIS

Until the 1960s, *Uncle Tom* had usually been thrust at the masses and elites
with equal vigor. Militants, however, changed that, setting their sights predominantly on elite blacks. Once militants let *Uncle Tom* off its chain, the
epithet has mainly hounded blacks with a visual presence, are close to power,

---

[78] Eric Snider, *Capturing the Soul of Jimi Hendrix: Author Charles Shaar Murray Lets the Music
Tell the Story about the Elusive Musician*, St. Petersburg Times, Aug. 26, 1990, at 7D; Charles
Shaar Murray, Crosstown Traffic: Jimi Hendrix and the Post-War Rock 'n' Roll Revolution 4,
22 (1989).

[79] Wil Haygood, *The Hug*, Washington Post Magazine, Sept. 14, 2003, at W12; Nixon "Fans" Are
Booed, Boycotted by Blacks, Philadelphia Tribune, Oct. 21, 1972, at 26.

or are otherwise set apart from ordinary black folk. The influential must brace themselves more than the average folk when it is unleashed.

Although one can see glimpses of how militants policed racial loyalty when they slung *Uncle Tom* at average blacks, to appreciate the full picture, one must step back and also examine the epithet in action against public figures. The most striking aspect of loyalty policing during this era was that militants uniformly vilified integrationist leaders as *Uncle Toms*. Dr. King, Bayard Rustin, A. Philip Randolph, and Thurgood Marshall were all bashed. Black radicals seized control of racial loyalty norm management and vowed that blacks foolishly wanting to hold hands with their oppressors were selling the race down the river. So sure of the veracity of their beliefs, they painted their adversaries as *Uncle Toms*. But under no reasonable analysis were these integrationists treasonous. Spirited disagreement was mistaken for betrayal.

Many radicals maintained that the most loyal blacks championed racial separation as the best solution to the color line, and others endorsed more revolutionary and violent strategies. But in a country where blacks comprised just more than a tenth of the population, the revolution would not be televised because it would not occur. And although black separatism might have relieved blacks from racism, it would have put no dollars into the many empty pockets of black folk. Lacking a true viable panacea to the various contributors to black misery, black radicals were in no position to charge their intellectual adversaries with treachery.

Black insiders faced the daunting task of having to work within the system while also representing a discontent and marginalized people. Determining whether black insiders have violated racial loyalty norms is always difficult; their official capacity often forbids their acting as racial agents. Ed Brooke, for instance, as Massachusetts's attorney general, disagreed with the civil rights community when he found a student boycott illegal. But being the state's head attorney required him to enforce the law even if the black community wished he reached a different result. During this period, moreover, the black Republicans' ever-present fear of *Uncle Tom* started.[80]

Also during this epoch, folk were increasingly denounced as traitors for actions having nothing to do with racial justice. Here, Muhammad Ali was especially culpable. Ali taunted his opponents with *Uncle Tom* when his grievances had nothing to do with racial fidelity. Ali maligned his opponents because they continued to call him Cassius Clay or because he disliked

---

[80] Ken Mack has a wonderful book about blacks representing the race, Representing the Race: The Creation of the Civil Rights Lawyer (2012).

them; none betrayed the race. Yet when Ali said he would fight in front of a segregated audience, he warranted *Uncle Tom* being hurled at him.

Although many athletes were unfairly reprimanded, black solidarity, which racial loyalty norms contribute to, pushed black athletes to be more devoted to bettering the race than they otherwise would have been. The 1968 boycott idea, for instance, was a symptom of a racial mood that encouraged blacks to view themselves as not just individuals who happened to be black, but rather a member of an oppressed racial group. Other black athletes during this period, such as Jim Brown, were also black solidarity participants. In the 1960s, Brown helped form the Black Economic Union, which helped blacks start businesses. The social climate of the 1960s and 1970s almost certainly affected this generation's sports stars, persuading them to use their standing to work on behalf of their people. Thus, even if some managed racial loyalty norms destructively, the enterprise helped produce immeasurable benefits.[81]

But the most salient aspect of loyalty policing during this era is that radicals maimed black solidarity. Many blacks who organized around the need for a separate black existence roamed urban areas, shooting indiscriminately into large crowds, hunting for disloyal members despite picturing the wrong image of disloyalty. Blacks who fan the flames of intra-racial disharmony by dousing innocents with *Uncle Tom* accusations deserve to be scorched with wide-ranging verbal censure. Thus, black militants of this era should have faced severe condemnation for their frequently unfair use of *Uncle Tom*. Their rampage that weakened the bonds of blackness must be a pall upon their legacy.

If those who infringe constructive norms must be disciplined, so too must destructive norm managers, especially habitual transgressors, lest loyalty policing collapse amid loud and constant shrieks of unfair prosecutions. Because it scars black solidarity, each destructive use of *Uncle Tom* adds a brick to the wall that blocks the race's path toward racial progress. Blacks, therefore, must censure those who fire *Uncle Tom* indiscriminately to stop the trigger happy from hitting the undeserving. Just as enforcing racial loyalty norms helps stop treachery, punishing those who overuse *Uncle Tom* impedes destructive norm management. Although black radicals helped to instill race consciousness and pride into blacks, those who maligned black moderates for holding the race back did far more to hinder racial progress. Calling black moderates *Uncle Toms* was indefensible and should be remembered, historically, as fracturing the black community. They hurt the ability for blacks to unite and debate solutions to improve the race's plight.

---

[81] Mike Freeman, Jim Brown: A Hero's Life 15 (2009).

As the book closed on the second epoch, the story of 1960s-style black militancy faded – almost as if in mid-sentence – as did debates over integrationism versus nationalism. But during the period, both camps stared at the same maladies, but devised divergent cures. Integrationists held that the only viable pathway to equality was working from within the system to influence it enough to produce favorable outcomes for the race. Nationalists, though, saw the lack of equality a century after slavery as signaling that black leadership was woefully inadequate and the system would never work for the race. *Uncle Tom* mirrored the intra-racial strife in the black community.

6

Uncle Tom Today: 1976–Present

WHERE IS *UNCLE TOM*?

W RITING WITH CERTAINTY IS HARD here. Nevertheless, I feel confident in claiming that *Uncle Tom* surfaces now far less than previously. Before the mid-1970s, *Uncle Tom* was ubiquitous. A welcome guest sometimes, and sometimes anything but. On good days, *Uncle Tom* helped boost black solidarity, on bad days, the opposite. Constructive or destructive, one never knew which *Uncle Tom* would appear.

But *Uncle Tom* is not missing. We can still document its footprint on American culture, especially when searching twenty-first-century media – Twitter, comments sections to online articles, blogs, and the like. *Uncle Tom* has found society's new venues. Increasingly larger shares of black folk, however, have stopped giving breath to *Uncle Tom*. Well-to-do blacks more so than the man on the street, I think, have developed an unmistakable hesitancy in resuscitating the slur.

Also noteworthy is that average blacks are now much less likely to be accused of racial treachery than are more famous blacks. That is not to say that the common man is never terrified that the specter of *Uncle Tom* will be directed toward him. He is. But influential blacks are much more concerned. The link between treachery and power has strengthened.

Average black folk accused of disloyalty have usually committed some cultural faux pas. Blacks with white partners, for instance, understand that some will deem traitorous their romantic choices. Blacks who "talk white" or "act white" – whatever that means – are similarly criticized. A person's dress, hairstyle, friendship choices, and musical preferences are all possible catalysts that generate negative reactions of treachery. Simply put, some blacks have required adherence to certain cultural norms, and those who stray are duplicitous.[1]

---

[1] Eric J. McCauley, *Is Love Becoming Color Blind*, Ebony, May 2007, at 31.

For example, when a fellow named Gary Jefferson received an upper-level promotion with United Airlines, he believed that his success might trigger some to impeach his racial loyalty. As Jefferson said, "Sometimes I walk a tight rope. The trek is lonely when you know some Black persons think you're an Uncle Tom." Fredrick H. L. McClure, a well-respected attorney in Tennessee, was called an *Uncle Tom* and an opportunist. McClure, the first black partner at a top Chattanooga law firm, was well accomplished in the local legal community. But McClure faced *Uncle Tom* accusations mainly because he grew up poor, yet achieved such success that many blacks thought he had forgotten his roots and "consort[ed] with the enemy – rich, white people." Even a black professional skater encountered detractors who labeled him an "Oreo" and an "Uncle Tom" for his vocation.[2]

The norms that punished the aforementioned behavior, however, are incredibly destructive. How a person talks, or who they choose to date or marry, does not indicate abandonment of black solidarity. Constructive norms generally punish choices and behaviors with political and legal ramifications on blacks' lives. When norms wander from those spheres, they are nearly always pernicious.

UNCLE TOM DOES NOT VOTE FOR THE BLACK CANDIDATE

Norms conforming to those spheres can still be quite destructive, however. Voter preference is quintessentially political. In an effort to elect one of their own, some blacks enforced the norm that not supporting a black candidate was racial betrayal. We saw this behavior during Jesse Jackson's 1984 presidential bid, for instance, when some of his backers called blacks who supported his white opponents "Uncle Toms, Judases, and racial traitors."[3]

For much of American history, voting for a black candidate, especially for national offices, was a fantasy. Not until Reconstruction did blacks have seats in Congress. After Reconstruction, Southern states successfully disfranchised blacks, destroying the growing seedlings from which black representation sprouted. During the early twentieth century, most Southern blacks could never even touch a ballot, much less vote for black candidates. And

---

[2] *Gary Jefferson Named Manager in Detroit*, New York Amsterdam News, Sept. 16, 1978, at B6; Mark Curriden, *Fred McClure Rising Star Works Hard at Law, Has Top Reputation*, Chattanooga Times, Sept. 4, 1995, at B1; John Blake, *Running Afoul of the Soul Patrol*, Chicago Tribune, Apr. 6, 1992, at C17; David Ferrell, *Skateboard Pros: Life on the Edge*, Los Angeles Times, Mar. 6, 1994, at 1A.

[3] Leanita McCalin, *Black Votes and Jesse Jackson*, Chicago Tribune, Nov. 6, 1983, at D3; A. S. Doc Young, Los Angeles Sentinel, Nov. 17, 1983, at A7.

although Northern blacks felt the ballot, they saw nothing appealing on the menu. Blacks' citizenship was discounted. The fantasy of potential black representation becoming reality heightened the pressure to back black. This narrative – the long struggle for suffrage – partly compelled many to maintain that supporting black candidates was required. To choose the white opponent is now to dare to be called an *Uncle Tom*. As columnist Leone Williams wrote in 1989, "Any election where a black is running against a white … any black who votes for or supports the white will be labeled an Uncle Tom and a bootlicker."[4]

One could have observed Williams's thesis when blacks sought to elect a black mayor in Chicago. The city's black vote had long been "captive," meaning influential blacks "delivered" the black vote to white politicians in exchange for political favors. As early as 1975, though, blacks wanted to contest the city's imposing Democratic political machine and elect a black mayor.

In 1977, State Senator Harold Washington launched a failed mayoral bid. Local politician Cecil Partee opposed Washington's long-shot attempt, and Washington called him "the worst kind of Uncle Tom" and "the biggest Uncle Tom on God's green earth." Partee's withholding his endorsement being considered treacherous was foreseeable, particularly in light of recent events. When Mayor Richard J. Daley died in 1976, most expected that the black president pro-tem of the city council, Alderman Wilson Frost, would become the interim mayor. Yet when Frost attempted to assume control of the mayor's office, the white machine ward bosses locked him out. During the next election, blacks punished the Democratic machine and vaulted a white woman, Jane Byrne, into the mayor's seat. That was a hearty yet not fully satisfying victory, an appetizer to the black mayor entrée. Partee not backing Washington meant that he stood against the group effort to elect a race member. Partee was the racial saboteur. The sentiment that he was a sellout pervaded.[5]

---

[4]   Benno C. Schmidt Jr., *Principle and Prejudice: The Supreme Court and Race in the Progressive Era. Part 3: Black Disfranchisement from the KKK to the Grandfather Clause*, 82 *Columbia Law Review* 835 (1982); Leone Williams, *The High Cost of Due Process*, Philadelphia Tribune, Aug. 29, 1989, at 2A.

[5]   This paragraph and the preceding paragraph are based on the following sources: Vernon Jarrett, *Political Fistfight on the South Side*, Chicago Tribune, Mar. 19, 1978, at A6; Twiley W. Barker, *Political Mobilization of Black Chicago: Drafting a Candidate*, 16 PS 482, 482–85 (1983); Axe Man, *The Hot Skillet*, Chicago Metro News, May 7, 1977, at 4; F. Richard Ciccone, *Succession War May Be His Legacy*, Chicago Tribune, Dec. 21, 1976, at 1; Neil Mehler and Robert Davis, *Ald. Frost Asserts He's Acting Mayor*, Chicago Tribune, Dec. 24, 1976, at 1.

Like Partee, other politicians were similarly pressured to better the group by assisting fellow blacks' political triumphs. In 1979, for instance, Democrats in the heavily black populated Kings County, New York (Brooklyn) fielded six judicial candidates. All were white. The county's black officials could have included a black candidate. None did. The *New York Amsterdam News* wanted to know what was lacking with black leadership that caused the failure to nominate black judges. The black officials needed a compelling reason. Or else, the *Amsterdam News* editorial board would conclude that "Uncle Tom is alive and well and living in Brooklyn."[6]

If black candidates would ever encounter success, black solidarity would be valuable in nudging blacks into their camps. Countless blacks were content sitting back while whites' hegemony continued. Take the 1979 Democratic primary for mayor of Philadelphia. Charles W. Bowser, black, sought the party's nomination. One black resident thought that electing him was possible "if the Uncle Tom, self-hating 'Negroes' of this city would vote as a bloc." Another resident overheard fellow blacks revealing their refusal to vote for a black candidate. "It is time," the resident said, "for these people to stop being Uncle Toms and a white man's nigger."[7]

A couple of years later, in Chicago, when many blacks were endeavoring to elect a black candidate to head the city's school board, some black organizations threw their support behind a white candidate. In 1981, the city's black community cast its lot with Dr. Manford Byrd, vying to become the first black general superintendent of Chicago's schools. Some blacks involved with community organizations, however, favored Thomas G. Ayers, a white businessman influential in the city's education policy circles. The president of the Chicago Urban League, Jim Compton, and its former president, Edwin C. Perry, were labeled "establishment Negroes" for not backing Byrd. Leon Finney, a local black leader, also supported Ayers, and was called an "Uncle Tom" and a "sell-out Negro."[8]

The percentage blacks are of the electorate is crucial in determining electoral success. Blacks have long debated which was better: creating one majority black district or spreading black voters across various districts. That discussion happened in Oregon in 1981 during the redistricting process. The *Skanner*, a black newspaper in nearby Seattle, supported spreading the black vote over three districts, resulting in each district being 18 percent to 20 percent black. "This," argued the newspaper, "would create a solid Black vote block; a good

---

[6] *Blacks Betrayed?*, New York Amsterdam News, June 30, 1979, at 18.

[7] Joseph Evans, *Bowser Has Chance to Win*, Philadelphia Tribune, May 15, 1979, at 8; J. Washington, *How Stupid Can You Get?*, Philadelphia Tribune, Mar. 18, 1979, at 4.

[8] Vernon Jarrett, *A Losing Strategy in School Battle*, Chicago Tribune, Jan. 11, 1981, at A6.

beginning for any Black politician who is willing to develop support over a broad base. In addition, this plan utilizes all Black voters, rather than concentrating a high percentage in one district and making the rest inconsequential." The second plan would have made blacks 45 percent of one district. The *Skanner* feared that under that plan, one white candidate and a few black ones would enter a race. The black vote would fracture, allowing the white candidate to saunter to an easy victory. One black representative, Wally Priestley, however, preferred this plan and maligned its critics as *Uncle Toms*. Priestley, the *Skanner* surmised, favored whatever would benefit him, writing, "[I]t is time Black leaders reject his self-serving, disrespectful approach which, under the banner of Black progress, is actually designed only to serve himself."[9]

In 1987, Pittsburgh was the site of a similar debate. That year, the local NAACP branch supported at-large city council elections even though the NAACP's national headquarters strongly preferred district elections. In district elections, because of segregation, blacks usually can finagle at least one black representative onto city councils. But in at-large contests, black candidates must attract white voters to win. As national NAACP chief spokesman James Williams asserted, "at-large elections tend to work against black candidates." A small group of black protestors, detesting its decision, gathered outside the Pittsburgh branch office, burned their NAACP membership cards, and held signs that read: "Uncle Tom Leadership Sold Here" and "NAACP Must Serve The People, Not City Hall."[10]

In 1989, blacks in Buffalo wanted desperately to boot their mayor, James D. Griffin, who many considered racist. "[Blacks] didn't vote for me," Griffin supposedly said, "so I don't owe them anything." Two candidates challenged Griffin in the Democratic primary, William B. Hoyt, white, and Wilbur P. Trammell, who vied to become the city's first black mayor. When Mary Davis, a host of a local black radio show, sympathized with Hoyt's candidacy, black listeners berated her. "I've been raked over the coals," she said, "accused of practicing plantation politics and being an Uncle Tom." The belief that *Uncle Toms* would prevent a black person from being elected to mayor surfaced in Cleveland the same year. The *Call and Post* was delighted that two blacks entered the mayoral race, but feared "Black 'Uncle Toms'" would act as "spies running from one campaign to another spreading hate and fear."[11]

9   *Reapportionment Gaining Steam*, The Skanner, Apr. 22, 1981, at 4.
10 Marty Willis, *NAACP Agrees to Review Board Vote on District Elections*, New Pittsburgh Courier, Jan. 31, 1987, at 1.
11 Howard Kurtz, *Mayor Comes out Fighting in Buffalo Race; Challengers Assail Griffin as Divisive, But Splintered Vote May Result in His Fourth Term*, Washington Post, Aug. 12, 1989, at A3; *The '89 Primary*, Cleveland Call and Post, Aug. 31, 1989, at 4A. Mary Davis, obviously, is a woman and is an unusual target for *Uncle Tom* accusations.

Much harder was a black candidate winning a gubernatorial race in 1990, especially in South Carolina, no beacon of racial progress to be sure. As he campaigned around the state, Theo Mitchell, South Carolina's Democratic nominee for governor, surely understood he was an unwise bet. In order to defeat the incumbent, Republican Carroll Campbell, he had to persuade white Republicans, while securing the black vote. In his ham-handed attempt to accomplish the latter, Mitchell called Campbell's black supporters "house niggers" and "Uncle Toms."[12]

In 1999, after John White Jr., a life-long black Democrat, left the Philadelphia mayoral race, he endorsed a white Republican, Sam Katz, and not John Street, a fellow black Democrat. Blacks were upset. They felt White made them believe that another black candidate would receive his backing if he dropped out. One black Philadelphian said, "It's clear to me that [White is] an Uncle Tom." Another believed that "If people aren't calling him an Uncle Tom by now, they certainly should. Someone should make an Uncle Tom poster and put John White's face on it." Some, however, thought that White's independent thinking showed that he was no *Uncle Tom*. One resident believed White was "a smart man who thinks for himself. A so-called Uncle Tom doesn't."[13]

Nearly ten years later, Barack Obama completed his historic White House run. But initially, black voters were not running with him. Indeed, before the first Democratic primary contest, most blacks supported New York Senator Hillary Clinton. But once Obama's victory in the Iowa caucuses demonstrated that he could appeal to whites, blacks deserted Clinton's camp and fled to Obama's. Blacks who stayed behind, like Delmarie Cobb, a Clinton delegate at the 2008 Democratic National Convention, encountered censure. On the convention's eve, Cobb alleged that Illinois State Senate President Emil Jones, Obama's "political godfather," called her an "Uncle Tom," ostensibly for not backing the eventual first black president. And although blacks now have reached the pinnacle of politics, blacks remain vulnerable to *Uncle Tom* accusations if they do not support black candidates.[14]

When investigating whether racial loyalty norms have been violated in this context, one must appreciate that purging society of its antiblack elements through black solidarity is the goal. Black representation, although a useful

[12] Desda Moss, *S.C. Candidate's Slurs Costing Him Support*, USA Today, Oct. 2, 1990, at 2A; *Wilder Not too Wild About Theo Mitchell*, Philadelphia Tribune, Oct. 9, 1990, at 5A.

[13] Michael J. Rochon, *Voters Boo, Cheer Katz Endorsement*, Philadelphia Tribune, Sept. 17, 1999, at 1A; Michael Dabney, Kendall Wilson, and Nate House, *Has White Sabotaged His Political Future?*, Philadelphia Tribune, Sept. 17, 1999, at 1A.

[14] Abdon M. Pallasch and Dave McKinney, *Did Jones Call Woman "Uncle Tom"?*, Chicago Sun-Times, Aug. 25, 2008, at 6. For his part, Jones denied the story.

tool to accomplish that end, is not the actual end. Blacks are not well served by simply having black politicians, but rather by having politicians who seek to clean the smog of bigotry wherever it permeates. A black politician may be more likely to endorse this worldview, but the worldview is crucial, not the racial makeup of its adherent. After all, if, say, neutralizing employment discrimination is one goal, a sympathetic white politician bests a black one who denies its existence.

With that settled, the blurry picture of what constitutes racial treachery comes into better focus. Blacks should not be considered *Uncle Toms* simply by pulling the lever for the white candidate instead of the black one. That decision lacks the information necessary to determine the existence of treachery. Thus, blacks backing Hillary Clinton over Barack Obama are not necessarily *Uncle Toms*. The same holds true for other elections.

But parts of the picture retain some blurriness. Although the Fifteenth Amendment enshrined black male suffrage in the U.S. Constitution in 1870, black men struggled to actually vote, let alone run for office. Blacks have grown accustomed, therefore, to white representatives. A black face in that role was simply impossible for much of American history. Some blacks, consequently, began to view white politicians as the natural and proper state of affairs. This feeling likely triggered some to prefer white candidates. Such attitudes, though, could only reside in an inexcusably meek mind. These folk truly were guilty of racial betrayal.

During the first epoch of *Uncle Tom's* use, Carter G. Woodson wrote about blacks who believed that whites were their superiors. Whites, not blacks, holding power was right. For example, some black workers complained when blacks were made their supervisors. Some beliefs fade. Others remain. Blacks must malign those still exhibiting this outlook. It establishes repugnant docility.

UNCLE TOM AND THE UNEQUAL JUSTICE SYSTEM

In the previous epoch, the only blacks within the criminal justice system vulnerable to racial loyalty policing were black police officers, largely because they were the only ones inside. Black police officers were rare, of course. But compared to, say, the judiciary, police forces were fairly inclusive. After the civil rights movement, employment opportunities expanded in many sectors, including the justice system. When it came to police officers, for instance, "concerns for the prevention of civil disorders and for equal employment opportunity after 1970 led to a marked increase in the number of blacks ... in some departments," especially in cities with black mayors or black police chiefs or where local governments practiced affirmative action. And although blacks are underrepresented in prosecutorial positions and judgeships, the numbers improved drastically after the 1970s.[15]

The gates that opened to allow blacks to enter the justice system permitted *Uncle Tom* to slip through as well. But *Uncle Tom* did not just badger blacks for merely being darker versions of bigoted whites. That was generally true in the previous epoch. In the third epoch, blacks frequently prosecuted more onerous and destructive norms instead.

Some racial loyalty policing, though, remained constructive. And we see such a rarity in 1992 when Jody Atkins, white, murdered Terrell Royce Rutledge, black, in Cross City, Florida. Atkins set the events in motion when he went to the black side of town to buy crack cocaine. After leaving, Atkins discovered that he had been given soap instead of drugs. Atkins then returned to confront his swindlers and demanded his money back. A scuffle ensued. One man struck Atkins's truck with an axe and Atkins responded by shooting and killing Rutledge, an innocent bystander, with a semiautomatic rifle. "All I was doing," Atkins boldly confessed later, "was trying to kill me some niggers." Atkins was charged with homicide. And five black men in the altercation were charged with third-degree murder because they committed felonies – riot and battery – that led to the killing, the state alleged.

In response, Deborah Mitchell, a local black activist, crusaded for the "Cross City Five." Mitchell received no assistance from other blacks. They were too timid to confront whites, she claimed. The city's black chief, Marcellus Dawson, was in her crosshairs as she distributed literature accusing him of being an "Uncle Tom" and a "traitor" who "terrorize[ed] the black community with threats of imprisonment" if they made too much noise about this incident. Blacks thought a racist conspiracy was afoot and that Chief Dawson was its *Uncle Tom* muscle. If Dawson cowed blacks into silence, he was unquestionably treacherous.[16]

Acts of omission too could compel *Uncle Tom* denunciations, as illustrated by the story of black New York correctional officers who overlooked the mistreatment of black inmates. David Jemmott, a black correctional officer, witnessed other officers abusing many black inmates at a medium-security prison

[15] Gerald David Jaynes and Robin M. Williams Jr., A Common Destiny: Blacks and Society 490, 491 (1989).

[16] The sources for this and the preceding paragraph are as follows: Mike Clary, *Deep South, Deep Trouble*, Los Angeles Times, June 17, 1992, at E1, E7. The Cross City Five were subsequently acquitted of murder but found guilty of battery. Mike Clary, *Fast Forward: Jury Acquits "Cross City Five,"* Los Angeles Times, Oct. 12, 1992, at 1E. An all-white jury found Atkins guilty of manslaughter, and he received the maximum sentence, seventeen years in prison. The Cross City Five were acquitted of third-degree murder, though some were convicted of lesser offenses.

in Sarasota, New York. Jemmott continuously reported incidents to his superiors. Inmates considered the other black officers who kept quiet *Uncle Toms.* A black Washington, DC resident witnessed similar misdeeds from white cops. But he "urge[d] Blacks also to look at black officers who do not speak out about this kind of abuse. They are the Uncle Toms in blue who, like their white counterparts, are not friend[s] of yours."[17]

Indicting black insiders for their silence concerning antiblack brutality is complicated. Some, on the one hand, were reluctant whistleblowers because they consciously groomed themselves to be "one of the good ones" to further their own aspirations. This cultivated image dictated their silence should a black person fall victim to a beating. Such folk resided with the inexcusably meek and arguably with those who defied the other two constructive norms. Blacks who muffled their voices fearing employment loss, on the other hand, are different. Norms must not be so taxing that they compel blacks to eschew black solidarity. Requiring blacks to sacrifice their jobs meets that standard. Although invested in the absence of brutality within the criminal justice system, blacks cannot require that one stand on the soap box if doing so might lead to one standing in a bread line.

Although blacks being criticized for their silence in the face of brutality was seemingly more common, sometimes black police officers were criticized because the brutality of white officers was projected onto them. Such was true in the Rodney King incident. On March 3, 1991, Los Angeles officers severely beat King, a heinous attack famously caught on camera. Once the pounding was broadcast in a perpetual nationally televised loop, the city's black cops were routinely derided. Black officers were reminded of their membership in a reputedly racist organization and were painted as traitors. Officer Garland Hardeman went to a black neighborhood and heard a woman shout, "What are you going to do, beat me like Rodney King? ... You black cops are just Uncle Toms. You're no better than the white boys!" Hardeman felt "ashamed" and empathized because, as a black man, he was "exposed to the same kind of discriminatory treatment they are."[18]

A jury acquitted the four LAPD officers tried for the beating. "King was interpreted as perpetually threatening to beat the police who beat him," writes

[17] Leonard Colvin, *Former N.Y. Guard Seeks Compensation for On-the-Job Abuses,* New Journal and Guide, Feb. 7, 1996, at 1; John Washington, *Views from Our Readers,* New Journal and Guide, Dec. 13, 1989, at 6.

[18] Tracy Wood and Faye Fiore, *Beating Victim Says He Obeyed Police; Law Enforcement: He Is Freed from Jail. D. A. Files No Charges Against Him,* Los Angeles Times, Mar. 7, 1991, at 1; Robert Deitz, Willful Injustice: A Post-O.J. Look at Rodney King, American Justice, and Trial by Race 189 (1996); Charisse Jones, *Black Cops Caught in the Middle,* Los Angeles Times, Apr. 15, 1991, at 1A.

Linda Williams. And "this threat," she continues, "embodied in the sight of the powerful black male body, made his beating defensible in the eyes of both white police and white jurors." For six days after the verdict, the city was engulfed in the flames, destruction, and mayhem that were the 1992 Los Angeles riots.[19]

Los Angeles's black police officers likely recall it as the period when their race deemed them dastardly sellouts. During the riots, one black police officer said that he was called an "Uncle Tom" and a "traitor" while wearing his uniform in his own predominantly black neighborhood. Another officer was spat on and yelled at when trying to quell a group of rioters. "You sell-out! You sell-out! Why are you working for a white man?" one shouted at the officer. The officer's nearby partner was asked, "Whose side are you on?" and called an *Uncle Tom* and an Oreo.[20]

Black members of the National Guard brought in to assist were likewise condemned. Guardsman Wade Morris, for example, was beset by the treachery trifecta; he was called a sellout, an *Uncle Tom*, and a house Negro. The epithets brought Morris, trained to fight in war, to tears. But he understood the venom behind the bite. "In this city," Morris relayed, "if a brother just wears baggy pants, he gets searched." "And if five brothers are in a car," he continued, "they will be pulled over.... It's accepted as fact of life here for black men. But we still have a job to do and that is to protect innocent people. I can't worry about the other stuff." Even when Willie L. Williams took over as police chief of the LAPD in May 1992, two black organizations in the city called him an "Uncle Tom" for taking the job.[21]

Some might contend that these officers were deemed traitorous solely for being officers. A better reading, however, is that the brutality of the Rodney King incident was attributed to them. They were *Uncle Toms* by association. Large swaths of L.A.'s black community refused to treat black cops as being any different than those who showered King with blows. If they remained in the LAPD, the city's black officers would be treated as if they too were caught on camera cracking King's bones with their nightsticks.

---

[19] Richard A. Serrano, *All 4 Acquitted in King Beating*, Los Angeles Times, Apr. 30, 1992, at 1; Linda Williams, Playing the Race Card: Melodramas of Black and White from Uncle Tom to O.J. Simpson 266 (2001); Mark Baldassare, The Los Angeles Riots: Lessons of the Urban Future 136 (1994).

[20] Karen M. Thomas, *Riots Tore at Black L.A. Cop's Soul*, Chicago Tribune, May 9, 1992, at C11; Stephen Braun and Leslie Berger, *Chaos and Frustration at Florence and Normandie*, Los Angeles Times, May 15, 1992, at A1.

[21] Paul Shepard, *Black Guardsmen Put Duty First in L.A.*, Plain Dealer, Apr. 16, 1993, at 10A; John Brazington, *King Case May Go to Federal Court*, Philadelphia Tribune, May 1, 1992, at 1A.

But putting these officers on trial for racial betrayal based on membership within the LAPD was destructive. Racism very well might have bustled through Los Angeles police precincts. Only solid evidence, however, builds a successful case for racial treachery. That was wanting here. Some might contend that these officers violated the norm proscribing blacks from cooperating with the race's enemies; they worked on behalf of an antiblack organization, the LAPD, detractors might insist. But that norm requires one to promote the enemies' antiblack interests. Thus unless these officers personally participated in the degradation of black folk, they must be exonerated. Maligning these officers as *Uncle Toms* impaired the cause of black solidarity. Indeed, if blacks believe they may be branded as traitors for such flimsy reasons, many will reject the cause of joint action. Such incidents underscore the point that although policing loyalty can reinforce black solidarity, the cause can be severely hamstrung by inept efforts to manage social norms.

In the previous examples, the supposed *Uncle Toms* were accused of mistreating fellow blacks. But blacks being considered *Uncle Toms* for failing to provide preferential treatment, or more precisely, for helping produce an outcome that negatively affected a black person, pervaded during this epoch. As blacks began occupying positions with power, some blacks required that power holders exercise their clout to benefit blacks, no matter what. Some, that is, defended the notion – a notion that the norm entrepreneur wanted to be a racial loyalty norm – that blacks must use their status to generate positive outcomes for other blacks, a very destructive norm.

In 1982, we see an example of a black judge being called an *Uncle Tom* almost certainly for this reason. Wayne Williams was convicted of murdering two men in Atlanta, and the police uncovered that he was the infamous Atlanta Child Murderer, killing more than twenty black children, slayings that haunted the city from 1979 to 1981. The prosecution's circumstantial case was reputedly of "unprecedented strength." This did not foreclose some blacks, however, from believing that a racist conspiracy was afoot, even though Atlanta's black police chief apprehended Williams along with a black FBI agent and despite Williams being convicted by a majority black jury before a black judge. Rev. Joseph Lowery, an Atlanta civil rights icon, remarked that skepticism was understandable because, "Let's face it, blacks have been victimized by the courts.... Blacks are naturally suspicious." Williams's parents contended that their son was innocent. After the conviction, Williams's father called the white prosecutor a "[s]on of a bitch." His mother said her son was convicted because of a conspiracy between the "conniving prosecutors" and "Uncle Tom" Judge Clarence Cooper. A mother losing her son to a lifetime in prison is undoubtedly painful. The grief, not any substantive transgression

Judge Cooper may have committed, likely ignited the fuse that launched that *Uncle Tom* accusation. Indeed, one cannot help but presume that if her son was found not guilty, Cooper would not have even bothered heaving the slur.[22]

A black state judge presiding over an obscenity case was likewise called an *Uncle Tom* for, essentially, irking another black person. In 1989, raunchy rap group 2 Live Crew released their album *As Nasty as They Wanna Be*. After performing their sexually explicit songs during a Florida concert, the group was arrested by police and hauled off to jail for obscenity. The arraignment judge told them that they and their music were detestable. Luther Campbell, 2 Live Crew's front man, called the judge an *Uncle Tom* in response. But many agreed with the judge. San Antonio stores pulled the album from their shelves. The solicitor general of South Carolina gave storeowners ten days to stop selling it. Forty-nine weeks after the album was released, Florida storeowners who sold the album were arrested. Michele Moody-Adams, a black philosophy professor, argued that Campbell wrongly sought to rally blacks around his cause by playing on their understandable fears of white racism "to protect a right that has nothing to do with race … This means that no black person can ever criticize any other black person's conduct without being called … an 'Uncle Tom.'" Moody-Adams's critique was convincing. Campbell, like many others, attempted to turn a nonracial situation into a racial loyalty event. Because the black judge violated no constructive norm, Campbell's use of sellout rhetoric was indefensible.[23]

The factual background in *Ohio v. Ward*, a 1986 shoplifting case, mimics the previous examples where a destructive norm enforcer launched *Uncle Tom* at a black person who failed to extend sufficient support or favoritism. Brenda Ward, the defendant, was inside a Dayton supermarket, attempting to steal food with her friend. When they left the store, the cashier noticed "bulges" in their coats. The security guard followed them, demanding their return. The two fled. The guard pursued them, but only apprehended Ward. After the guard escorted Ward back into the store, the police arrested her. Before she was taken away, she called the guard a "mother fucker, Uncle Tom nigger." Ward apparently thought that because the security guard was black

[22] BACM Research, Atlanta Child Murders: Wayne Williams FBI Files 449 (1983); James Baldwin, The Evidence of Things Not Seen 12 (1995). See generally Bernard Headley, The Atlanta Youth Murders and the Politics of Race (1998); Art Harris, *Atlanta's Doubts*, Washington Post, Mar. 1, 1982, at A1; Editorial, *The Atlanta Verdict*, Washington Post, Mar. 2, 1982, at A16; Charles Madigan, *Many in Atlanta Not at All Comforted by Guilty Verdict*, Chicago Tribune, Mar. 7, 1982, at B6.

[23] Larry McShane, *Raunchy Rappers Meet Geraldo and Phil*, Associated Press, June 14, 1990; Hugh Garvey, *Getting It Up in Smoke*, Vibe, Aug. 1998, at 48; M. Moody-Adams, *Don't Confuse 2 Live Crew With Black Culture*, New York Times, June 25, 1990, at A16.

he owed allegiance to her, even though she was a thief and his job required him to stop her.[24]

In this next tale, an interesting dilemma presented itself for a black criminal defense attorney in a high-profile case. The 1986 story began when Steven Roth hired two black men, Darren Norman and Steven Bowman, to assault his tenant Marla Hanson. Hanson, an ex-model, drew Roth's ire when she pressed for the return of her $850 security deposit and rejected his flirtatious advances. After Roth's conviction of first-degree assault, Bowman and Norman were tried jointly. Each had their own black attorney. Alton Maddox represented Bowman. Plummer Lott represented Norman. Throughout the three-month trial, both Maddox and Lott argued that Roth disfigured Hanson's face and their defendants were framed. But during his closing argument, Lott pinned the crime entirely on Bowman, stunning the courtroom. Maddox was livid. Bowman's family and blacks in the courthouse called Lott an *Uncle Tom* and a "snitch."[25]

Shrugging off the criticism, Lott noted that his "obligations run to my client."[26] But, because Lott blamed his client's codefendant, who happened to be black, he was branded an *Uncle Tom*. If Lott and Maddox agreed to not pin the crime on the other's client, Lott's gambit was indeed treacherous. But it was not racially so. If his client's codefendant was white, no one would have assailed him for racial betrayal. The voracity of Lott's legal defense should not have been limited by the melanin of his client's cohorts. Lott owed Maddox's client no special deference because of racial kinship.

Philadelphian Judge Abram Frank Reynolds, well respected locally, received *Uncle Tom* accusations after leniently sentencing two white teenagers convicted of raping an eleven-year-old black girl. The two had to undergo sex-offender treatment, residential treatment, house arrest, and lengthy court supervision, but no jail time. Here was a black preteen sexually assaulted by white teenagers, and the black judge felt that jail time was unsuitable. If the races were reversed, most blacks would assume that jail time would have been a given, certainly reducing any leniency that critics might have afforded to

---

[24] *Ohio v. Ward*, 1986 Ohio App. LEXIS 9836, at 1–5 (Ohio Ct. App., 1986).

[25] Todd S. Purdum, *Model Slashed, an Ex-Landlord Is among 3 Held*, New York Times, June 6, 1986, at 3B; Robert D. McFadden, *Wounded Model Retains Her Faith in Career and City*, New York Times, June 7, 1986, at 29; Kirk Johnson, *Prosecutor Says Rejection Caused Razor Assault on Fashion Model*, New York Times, Nov. 25, 1986, at 2B; Kirk Johnson, *Slashed Model Accused of Race Bias by Defense*, New York Times, Mar. 22, 1987, at 34; Associated Press, *Defense Lawyer Says He Is "the Victim,"* New York Times, Mar. 28, 1987, at 31; Peter Noel, *Was Maddox Betrayed in Model Slashing Case?*, New York Amsterdam News, May 16, 1987, at 1.

[26] Noel, *Was Maddox Betrayed in Model Slashing Case?*, at 1.

Reynolds. A man true to his race, his detractors would argue, would have severely punished the rapists. His detractors, though, provided no evidence that he violated constructive norms. Reynolds might have erred; perhaps a better judge would have been harsher. Yet even if true, that blunder was not racial betrayal. His detractors prosecuted a very weak case.[27]

Sometimes circumstances wedged black police officers into awkward positions, forced to protect the enemy, rendering them highly exposed to *Uncle Tom*. One such scenario occurred when black officers had to defend the Klan from black protestors. The events began when U.S. District Judge Louis Oberdorfer permitted the KKK to march between the Washington Monument and the Capitol in Washington, DC. DC officials wanted to limit the march to four blocks, fearing that the city would fail to keep the peace. DC officials' prediction was correct; more than a thousand protested the KKK march and the police struggled to quell the violence. Some demonstrators threw rocks at the Klan, but the cops were frequently pelted instead. In fact, one police officer was trapped for fifteen minutes in his police car as projectiles bombarded it. Having to defend the Klan made black cops the objects of ridicule. "All these people were throwing bottles and calling us 'Uncle Tom,'" one officer said. "We couldn't put our personal beliefs into the situation. I'm hoping they [the Klan] don't come back any time soon. It was rough." These officers committed no crime against the race; they were employees whose jobs put them in an uncomfortable position. These officers, that is, were unfairly scolded for doing their jobs, which, unfortunately for them, was protecting the Klan.[28]

The treatment of Christopher Darden, the tormented O. J. Simpson prosecutor, best demonstrates the pain the black insider endured. Blacks would dissect the evidence. They would evaluate it earnestly. And they would conclude that O. J. Simpson was guilty of double homicide. Darden sincerely believed the truth was obvious. "I had believed that African Americans ... would convict a black icon when they saw the butchery, the pattern of abuse, and the overwhelming evidence."[29]

Darden miscalculated. "I was branded an Uncle Tom," he wrote, "a traitor used by The Man." He received faxes saying, "You're an Uncle Tom." People telephoned him, calling him an *Uncle Tom*, warning, "don't ever refer to yourself as black, 'cause you ain't," and asking, "how could you allow yourself

---

[27] Jacqueline Soteropoulos, *Judge Dedicated to Children Calls It a Career. Abram Frank Reynolds Saw no Higher Professional Calling than Family Court*, Philadelphia Inquirer, July 19, 2003, at B01.

[28] Mary Jordan and Linda Wheeler, *14 Hurt as Anti-Klan Protestors Clash with Police*, Washington Post, Oct. 29, 1990, at A1.

[29] Christopher Darden, In Contempt: Christopher A. Darden 11 (1996).

to be used like that?" Public opinion about Simpson's guilt divided along racial lines. The invective that Darden received was undoubtedly amplified because many felt he was chosen because of race. As Elise Cose scribed, "the endless media coverage and Darden's subsequent best-selling book created a compelling and indelible portrait of the black prosecutor as a tortured soul – as a conflicted laborer in a perfidious place where celebrity, crime, and conflicting racial perceptions collide." For being on the side that sought to punish Simpson, who many blacks felt was framed by the racist LAPD, Darden was *persona non grata* in his own community.[30]

Some scholars, including law professor Kenneth Nunn, have argued that blacks should never be prosecutors. Nunn insisted that because of systemic racism within the criminal justice system, which blacks are powerless to remedy, blacks "should not contribute to the oppression of other" blacks. Although he did not use the term *solidarity*, the belief that blacks should eschew endeavors that subordinate their brethren undergirded Nunn's argument. One who agrees might sanction Darden as a traitor.[31]

Nunn is correct in holding the criminal justice system liable for perpetuating racial inequality. And as law professor Paul Butler has forcefully argued, "power-drunk prosecutors" are integral in reproducing subordination. In the context of racial betrayal, however, I reject a standard that considers prosecutorial work inherently treacherous. Black prosecutors, rather, should be judged on how they discharge their duties. Prosecuting the drug offenses of black youth more than white youth, for instance, would obviously warrant sanction. But Darden was simply a prosecutor in a high-profile case, not some cruel lawyer looking to punish the most famous Negro he could find. Darden was no *Uncle Tom*.[32]

Occasionally, individual blacks held themselves out as the arbiters of blackness, determining the normative code of conduct in a specific situation. In these scenarios, the supposed *Uncle Toms* did not necessarily even retain positions within the criminal justice system. Rather, they could be participants in a criminal justice debate with important voices. This racial loyalty norm required one to embrace the position that a self-proclaimed racial agent announced.

[30] Id.; Christopher Darden, *The Trials of a Black Former Prosecutor*, Essence, Nov. 1997, at 62; Williams, Playing the Race Card 5, 265.

[31] Kenneth B. Nunn, *The "Darden Dilemma": Should African Americans Prosecute Crimes?*, 68 Fordham Law Review 1473, 1478 (2000); Margaret Russell, *Beyond "Sellouts" and "Race Cards": Black Attorneys and the Straitjacket of Legal Practice*, 95 Michigan Law Review 766 (1997).

[32] Paul Butler, *Gideon's Muted Trumpet*, New York Times, Mar. 27, 2013, available at: http://www.nytimes.com/2013/03/18/opinion/gideons-muted-trumpet.html?ref=opinion&_r=0.

Perhaps the best example of this norm stems from a now infamous hoax. In the late 1980s, Tawana Brawley, a black teenager, gained national attention after claiming that six white men, including a police officer, sexually assaulted her. A grand jury subsequently concluded that she had concocted the entire tale. Until the deception was revealed, however, the controversial allegation consumed New York State. Al Sharpton, the bombastic Harlem activist, incited anger by playing on black resentment. Sharpton sought to define the parameters of the debate and provoke outrage. Assemblyman Roger Green upbraided Sharpton for his "tactics that encourage race war." Sharpton retorted that Green was a "state-sponsored Uncle Tom." New York Governor Mario Cuomo revealed that some black ministers found Sharpton's public pronouncements deplorable. These clergymen, however, relayed their concerns privately because, "They were ... concerned that they'll be called 'Uncle Toms.'" Members of the local chapter of the NAACP also criticized Sharpton's tactics, and they were likewise called "Uncle Toms" and "Aunt Thomasinas."[33]

A few years later, Sharpton again attempted to marginalize his foes with *Uncle Tom* when he and his associate, attorney Alton Maddox, traveled to New Jersey. On April 10, 1990, Phillip C. Pannell, a black teenager, was shot in the back while running away from Gary Spath, a Teaneck, New Jersey police officer. Whereas Sharpton and Maddox inflamed the wound, others, like Jesse Jackson and the nearest NAACP chapter, opted to soothe it. "They," Sharpton proclaimed, "are calling on people who can bring calm to the area rather than ask them to demand justice." "Rev. Jackson and others only want us to be quiet," he continued. Sharpton alleged that the local power structure and "Uncle Toms" in the area colluded to keep the peace. But Sharpton "intend[ed] to turn the streets inside out until justice is done." Sharpton here defined what the black community's temperament should be – fiery indignation – and the noncompliant were disloyal.[34]

[33] Esther Iverem, *Bias Cases Fuel Anger of Blacks*, New York Times, Dec. 14, 1987, at B1; Mike Taibbi and Anna Sims-Phillips, Unholy Alliances: Working the Tawana Brawley Story (1989); Robert D. McFadden, Outrage: The Story Behind the Tawana Brawley Hoax (1990); Edwin Diamond, *The Brawley Fiasco*, New York Magazine, July 18, 1988, at 20; Robert D. McFadden, *Brawley Made up Story of Assault, Grand Jury Finds*, New York Times, Oct. 7, 1988, at A1; Howard Kurtz, *Political Fracas Overshadows New York Probe of Racial Assault*, Washington Post, Mar. 2, 1988; Jeffrey Schmalz, *Racial Puzzle for Cuomo*, New York Times, May 9, 1988, at B1; Jesse Walker, *NAACP Counsel Cracks Down on Tawana's Reps*, New York Amsterdam News, Mar. 19, 1988, at 3.

[34] *150 Teaneck Marchers Protest April Shooting*, New York Times, July 23, 1990, at B4. Spath was acquitted of criminal charges. *Jury Acquits White Cop in Death of N.J. Teen That He Shot in the Back*, Jet, Mar. 2, 1992, at 26; Simon Anekwe, *Al Sharpton Vows March Protest in Teaneck Killing*, New York Amsterdam News, Apr. 21, 1990, at 1.

The case of the racially motivated 1986 murder of Michael Griffith in New York City likewise reveals how some sought to define the race's official position and punish dissenters. Griffith died after a car hit him as he fled white youths who were beating him and his three friends. Local black leaders successfully pressed Governor Andrew Cuomo to appoint a special prosecutor in Griffith's death. Queens District Attorney John Santucci was the initial prosecutor, but under his stewardship, the case against the alleged perpetrators floundered. Black leaders wanted a special prosecutor because they felt that Santucci "either botched or covered up" what really happened. Those leaders felt vindicated after the special prosecutor indicted twelve "white thugs" for Hawkins's murder. Many who demanded a special prosecutor called blacks who disagreed "Black 'Uncle Toms and Tomasinas.'"[35]

Various norms were at play here in the context of the criminal justice system, most of them destructive, none more than that of the self-appointed black spokesman. Policing racial loyalty helps blacks pursue racial progress, in part, by helping reduce the number of treacherous blacks who can sabotage the debates blacks must have. The self-appointed spokesman, however, took it upon himself to settle the debate on his own, and tossed *Uncle Tom* at any who dared disagree.

UNCLE TOM DOESN'T BELONG ON THE SCHOOL BOARD

The Supreme Court decided *Brown* in 1954, yet a quality education still remains out of reach for many black children. The racial achievement gap is wider than ever. The black high school graduation rate is dismal. In 2005, the college graduation rate for blacks was 42 percent, twenty percentage points lower than that of whites. And from the ivory tower of academia to popular culture, discussion abounds concerning whether black children eschew education because academic success is associated with whiteness.[36]

---

[35] Peter Noel, *12 Youths Indicted for Howard Beach Murder*, New York Amsterdam News, Feb. 14, 1987, at 1. New York saw three such slayings in the '80s. The first victim was Willie Turks in 1982. Turks was beaten to death by a group of whites. Griffith was the second. The third was Yusuf Hawkins in 1989. A white mob beat Hawkins and three friends, and Hawkins was shot twice in the chest. Joseph P. Fried, *Court Is Told Defendant Struck Victim*, New York Times, Mar. 3, 1983, at B3; Felicia R. Lee, *At Youth's Wake, Fried, Anger and Talk of Racism*, New York Times, Aug. 30, 1989, at B4.

[36] Brando Simeo Starkey and Susan Eaton, *The Fear of "Acting White" and the Achievement Gap: Is There Really a Relationship?*, Charles Hamilton Houston Institute for Race & Justice, Oct. 30, 2008; *Black Student Graduation Rates Remain Low, but Modest Progress Begins to Show*, 50 Journal of Blacks in Higher Education 88, 88 (Winter, 2005/2006); *Public High School Graduation and College Readiness Rates in the United States*, Sept. 2003, available at: http://www.manhattan-institute.org/html/ewp_03_appendix_table_1.htm.

After *Brown*, mainstream civil rights organizations sold integration as the best way to ensure that black children were no longer relegated to inferior underfunded schools. But the Supreme Court, with a long line of decisions, rendered integration nearly impossible. In light of this, many blacks pressured local school boards to serve their children well, despite various obstacles that frustrated the mission. Because of residential segregation and white flight, blacks are often the majority in their cities and wield power on local school boards. But this power invites charges that individual school board members are failing students and are consequently treacherous. *Uncle Tom* is often used in this context to attack black educators who supposedly violated racial loyalty norms. Most of these stories do not recount enough details to establish the existence of duplicity. But blacks should monitor racial loyalty in this context because betrayal could hamper the education of black children.

In 1980, we see an example of a black school board member, Lloyd Webb of Inglewood, California, being dismissed as an *Uncle Tom*. That year, Inglewood public schools were the site of racially charged incidents. One white female teacher inappropriately commented on a black student's hair. A different teacher reportedly kicked a student while calling him black. Another teacher told students that they should go to schools in the San Fernando Valley "so you can get a quality education with White kids." And white teachers formed cliques that excluded black colleagues, further aggravating racial strife. Some parents protested, keeping 450 kids home one day and 476 the next. Many claimed that Webb, despite knowing about the racial friction, refused to intervene because of political considerations. Black teachers and a fellow school board member, therefore, called Webb an *Uncle Tom*. Webb, denying he was a traitor, said that "[i]f fighting for justice and quality education for all of the students in the district, regardless of race or color, makes me an Uncle Tom, then I don't apologize for being an Uncle Tom." His detractors, though, would say that he sacrificed the needs of black pupils for personal interest.[37]

Some thought that if blacks were going to serve on school boards, whites wanted them to be *Uncle Toms*. Vincent Reed, head of Washington, DC's board of education, resigned from his position in 1980 because he refused to be an *Uncle Tom*. Reed said that "the board wants an Uncle Tom superintendent ... They want you to bow and scrape before them. I don't intend to bow and scrape.... I'm here to do a job; I'm concerned about 100,000 kids."[38]

---

[37] James H. Cleaver, *Inglewood Schools Near Explosion Point*, Los Angeles Sentinel, Dec. 25, 1980, at A1.
[38] Vincent Reed (interview), *Talk with Vincent Reed*, Washington Post, Dec. 24, 1980, at A11.

Similar thoughts swirled around Wrightsville, Georgia, in the early 1980s. Blacks in the city wanted to help shape the educational policy of local schools. After decades of rampant racism, blacks began protesting the city's gross inequality, achieving noticeable but small gains. The lack of black representation on the school board proved an obstinate challenge, however. Some blacks thought that the city had not progressed enough to allow blacks on the school board. But if a black person made it, "it will be someone ... that whites can control. Another Uncle Tom." No particular person was branded an *Uncle Tom* here. But the speaker nonetheless played an important role in managing constructive racial loyalty norms; they notified all that being controlled by whites who were antagonistic to blacks' interests was intolerable.[39]

Franklin Smith, in that vein, endured allegations that he was an *Uncle Tom*, a marionette who whites allowed to steward education in the nation's capital. Smith, head of Washington, DC schools in the mid-90s, struggled mightily to improve student performance. But when Smith explored having a private company assume control of some of the District's worst-performing schools, onlookers derogated him. He took the idea from Baltimore, which had employed a Minnesota firm to rescue some of its schools. During the hearings to discuss the idea, he was called an *Uncle Tom* and a "slave seller" who wanted to hire "a white-owned company that would make a profit on the backs of African American children." Other school board members supported the idea; they too were called *Uncle Toms*. One member's home was vandalized. Some were even stopped and accosted on the street at night. A director of a local research center said the attacks on Smith were the most vitriolic criticisms he heard in the community. With the inability to garner support, Smith dropped his plan.[40]

Smith seemingly wanted to have an honest debate about what would work best for black students. Destructive norm managers, however, upon unleashing *Uncle Tom*, disallowed it. Constructive racial loyalty norm management benefits such important discussions; it helps prevent disloyal members from corrupting them. But, when folk ascribe nefarious motives to people without evidence, they impede black solidarity and, consequently, racial progress.

Other black educators were tagged with the *Uncle Tom* label without evidence. Jerome Harris was one such educator. In 1994, the Compton Unified School District, serving mostly black and Latino students with poor test scores, hired Harris as its head administrator. Harris was known for aggravating

---

39 *Year after Violence between Blacks, Whites,* Los Angeles Times, Apr. 26, 1981, at 23.
40 Sari Horwitz, *The Final Exam,* Washington Post, May 16, 1995, at C01; DeNeen L. Brown, *Privatization Issue Takes Nasty Turn,* Washington Post, July 28, 1995, at A01.

teachers, principals, and board members so much that he had been dubbed a dictator. But he raised test scores wherever he went. Harris was devoted to kids and claimed that where minorities controlled city governments, they had no excuse; students of color must perform well. Despite his track record, according to Amen Rahh, a local citizen, Harris was an *Uncle Tom* unless he established otherwise. Rahh said, "I don't see Dr. Harris working for the interests of African American and Latino students.... The state of California hates African Americans and Latinos. I see him in the same light as the Uncle Toms throughout history, until he proves that he's not one." Rahh, though, committed a cardinal sin in loyalty policing; one must always base *Uncle Tom* charges on evidence.[41]

Some black college students likewise contended that whites preferred *Uncle Toms* in positions dealing with education. At the University of Virginia in the mid-1980s, for example, the Black Student Alliance held a series of campus protests and meetings, demanding the resignation of the dean of Afro-American affairs, Paul L. Puryear. They charged him with ignoring the concerns of black students, presumably his chief responsibility. Puryear, subsequently placed in a different position, averred that those students sought segregated facilities and services on campus. A former Black Student Alliance president, Louis Anderson, said that, "The problem is 'Uncle Tom' administrators. The university doesn't hire that many blacks to begin with, but then it goes and puts in people who aren't responsive to the concerns of black students." A derelict Puryear was not a traitor but rather a poor employee. A Puryear who was unconcerned with the needs of black students, however, deserved the rebuke that Puryear actually received. Which one was the actual Puryear, though, is impossible to now establish.[42]

At times when a black person receives a position after having been championed by the broader black community, supporters often expect that the recipient will always be in lockstep with their desires. The dissonance between those expectations and what actually occurs can produce unsettling spectacles. Bernard Harleston knows this all too well. Blacks in New York City "rallied diligently" for Harleston to be the president of City College of New York. But by 1992, they began questioning the wisdom of their endeavors when some accused Harleston of trying to eliminate the college's Africana Studies Department reportedly after a professor claimed that Jews and Italians

[41] Howard Blume, *Cover Story: Raising Compton's Bottom Line*, Los Angeles Times, Mar. 10, 1994, at 8.

[42] David Treadwell, *Problem for South; Blacks Still Feel Sting of Campus Bias*, Los Angeles Times, May 25, 1986, at A1.

colluded to disparage blacks in motion pictures. Rev. Calvin Butts, a previous
Harleston backer, was angry, saying, "[N]ow just because a few people didn't
like what Professor Jeffries said, Harleston decided to dismantle the Black studies department." The supposed dismantling was the firing of Professor Jeffries,
who was replaced with Edmund Gordon, former chair of Yale University's
African-American Studies Department. Butts said that Harleston was guilty
of an "Uncle Tom action."[43]

Whether treachery occurred in most of the previous instances is impossible
to determine without more information. Blacks, in any event, were right to
intently monitor the actions of educators. Their work – providing students an
education that will unlock a promising future – was quite the important task.
With so much at risk, blacks had an enormous interest in ensuring that educators effectively discharged their duties.

ANALYSIS

Destructive norm management has increasingly predominated during this
period. Although *Uncle Tom* has been sullied through highly questionable
usages, political and legal concerns still frequently activate the damaged epithet, establishing that some blacks continue to seek to enforce intra-racial discipline through racial loyalty norm management.

This is directly observable when blacks chastise each other for not supporting black political candidates. The trek from emancipation to full suffrage
rights was arduous. And after the passage of the Voting Rights Act of 1965,
the number of black elected officials has steadily increased. That blacks have
the opportunity to elect other blacks undoubtedly drove some to believe that
black representation was a solution to the problem of politicians consistently
ignoring their needs. This put the onus on blacks to support their own. Those
opting instead for the white opponent were accused of racial treachery. And
Uncle Tom was employed to enforce intra-racial discipline.

But linking support for black candidates to racial loyalty is wrongheaded.
Symbolic representation is just that – symbolic – whereas the stubborn
dilemmas facing blacks are anything but. This requires blacks to focus on
electing politicians devoted to racial progress, regardless of skin color. Blacks
who support white politicians because of their submissive belief that leadership positions are reserved for whites, however, were proper targets. They are
inexcusably meek.

[43] Kenneth Meeks, *Rev. Butts: Harleston Sold Us Out*, New York Amsterdam News, July 13, 1992, at 3.

Tracing *Uncle Tom* in the context of the criminal justice system leads to some remarkable stories. The norm management in the context of the criminal justice system, though, was far more destructive than during the previous epoch. The earlier promulgators and enforcers were more cautious. Charles Evers, for instance, exercised care when dubbing a black cop who spied on civil rights activists in Mississippi "Tom." The 1960s and 1970s featured relatively sober-minded enforcers. In this period, however, we see folk like 2 Live Crew's Luther Campbell calling a judge an *Uncle Tom* because the judge deplored his raunchy musical content and was not inclined, ostensibly, to be a sympathetic jurist. Al Sharpton's actions were even more condemnable. The norms in this epoch were destructive because the cast of characters who policed loyalty were careless.

Educators were perhaps surprising recipients of *Uncle Tom*. But, not upon reflection. They were entrusted with overseeing black youth's education. Their duties were instrumental in ensuring that the next generation of blacks had better life outcomes than those of their parents. Blacks on school boards who fail to shoulder their responsibilities are considered disappointments who sold the race out. Ascertaining whether the accusations of racial disloyalty are accurate, however, is incredibly difficult with the incomplete information at hand.

But in this epoch, *Uncle Tom* mainly targets prominent blacks. Even in this chapter dedicated to the black masses, most of those nursing *Uncle Tom* injuries were prominent in their community. They just lacked national recognition. Now, the most vulnerable are black conservatives. *Uncle Tom* is practically a rite of passage for members of the black right. But calling black conservatives *Uncle Tom* is in total harmony with the legacy of the epithet. *Uncle Tom* was a device used to regulate black behavior to contest blacks' subordinate status. Blacks who attempt to compel blacks to resist joining the conservative ranks are making a critique – that conservatism is antithetical to blacks' interests. That is not to say that it is fair to sideline black conservatives as social pariahs. It certainly is not. But the usage is at least consistent with the epithet's history.

7

So What About Clarence?

THE HISTORY OF A JUSTICE

HERE HAS TO BE ONE. That one who best understands the pain of *Uncle Tom's* piercing stiletto plunge. That one who has been gored so repeatedly that his name is now synonymous with racial treachery. That one who has caused blacks to actually debate whether they should cease naming their children the same name as his. That one without whom the biography of *Uncle Tom* could not be written unless he was given a central role. That one is Supreme Court Justice Clarence Thomas.[1]

Clarence was born on June 23, 1948 in Pin Point, Georgia, into an impoverished community that lacked sewage and paved roads. When Clarence was two years old, his father abandoned the family while his mother was pregnant with his brother Myers. Pin Point was segregated, and the same year the Supreme Court decided *Brown*, 1954, Clarence started first grade at a Jim Crow elementary school.[2]

In 1955, Clarence's mother, unable to financially support them, sent him and his brother to live with her parents in Savannah. Moving in with his grandparents greatly improved the trajectory of Clarence's life. There, his grandfather taught him to work hard and rely on no one. His grandfather once told him,

1 Tonya B. Lewis, *Derogatory Language Damages African-Americans*, Oklahoma Daily, Feb. 25, 2003, available at: http://oudaily.com/news/2003/feb/25/column--derogatory-language-damages-african/; Michael Thelwell wrote, "Perhaps black people ought to give serious thought to retiring Clarence from general use as a name in our communities." Kevin Merida and Michael Fletcher, Supreme Discomfort: The Divided Soul of Clarence Thomas 21 (2007).

2 Clarence Thomas, My Grandfather's Son: A Memoir 2–4 (2007). Justice Thomas was a member of the Geeches or Gullash, blacks who lived in the barrier islands and low country areas of Georgia, South Carolina, and Florida who spoke with a distinctive dialect; Jane Mayer and Jill Abramson, Strange Justice: The Selling of Clarence Thomas 33 (1994); Andrew Peyton Thomas, Clarence Thomas: A Biography 60 (2001).

"I never took a penny from the government because it takes your manhood away." After Clarence and Myers left Pin Point, Clarence writes, the "vacation [was] over." They lived in a strict household but in relative luxury.[3]

After two years of high school in Savannah, Clarence attended St. John Vianney Minor Seminary, an all-white boarding school outside of Savannah that trained future priests. His classmates ostracized and racially harassed him. "Smile, Clarence, so we can see you," a student said to him once. Clarence was in a self-described "self-hate" period where "you hate yourself for being a part of a group that's gotten the hell kicked out of them." To fit in, Clarence avoided being stereotypically black. He spoke perfect English. He resolved to get good grades. He tried to fit in. But nothing seemed to work at St. John Vianney.[4]

In 1967, after graduating from high school, Clarence attended the Immaculate Conception Seminary in Missouri to further his goal of becoming a priest. He was unhappy there, though. The low point was the day Martin Luther King Jr. was assassinated. One classmate rejoiced, hoping that "the s.o.b. dies." Clarence then reconsidered his desire to become a priest. Greatly disappointing his grandfather, Clarence left the seminary in May 1968, after only eight months.[5]

Clarence enrolled at the College of the Holy Cross that same fall. At Holy Cross, he was something of a black nationalist, helping create the Black Student Union, eventually becoming its treasurer. Clarence also headed a free-breakfast program for local black schoolchildren and championed a student protest of apartheid in South Africa. He admired the Black Panthers and a poster of Malcolm X hung from his college dorm room wall.[6]

Clarence subsequently entered Yale Law School as one of twelve black students. There, he attempted to not be seen as "a black student." He avoided his professors, sitting in the back of the classroom. He did not take civil rights courses, instead studying tax, accounting, antitrust, and property law. He felt he had a "monkey on his back" because his white classmates assumed that blacks were only there because of racial preferences.[7]

3   Peyton Thomas, Clarence Thomas 8, 12; Clarence Thomas, My Grandfather's Son 73.

4   Peyton Thomas, Clarence Thomas 81; Juan Williams, A *Question of Fairness*, The Atlantic Online, February 1987, available at: http://www.theatlantic.com/politics/race/thomas.htm.

5   Peyton Thomas, Clarence Thomas 105; Michael Eric Dyson, April 4, 1968: Martin Luther King Jr.'s Death and How It Changed America (2008); Williams, A *Question of Fairness*.

6   Merida and Fletcher, Supreme Discomfort 103–12; Williams, A *Question of Fairness*.

7   The JBHE Foundation, *Justice Clarence Thomas: A Classic Example of an Affirmative Action Baby*, 18 *Journal of Blacks in Higher Education* 35 (1997–98); Williams, A *Question of Fairness*.

Clarence struggled to find post–law school employment. Although he received interviews, prospective employers treated him differently than they did his white peers. Interviewers told him that he could do pro bono work—an experience his white classmates never reported. The disparate treatment angered Thomas. "I went to law school to be a lawyer, not a social worker. If I want to be a social worker, I'll do it on my own time." Attending an elite law school, many assume, ensures immediate career success. But that was not the case for Clarence. "You know, I was in debt," he said. "I needed a job, and I couldn't get a job." He remarked that his Yale Law "degree meant one thing for whites and another thing for blacks," adding that it was "discounted."[8]

Thomas finally found employment with Missouri's Republican attorney general, John Danforth, serving as counsel to the state department of revenue and the tax commission. He refused to work on racial matters, fearing that others would consider him a "second-rate" thinker hired solely because of his race. After three years of working in Missouri, Justice Thomas took a job at Monsanto, a chemical company. Two years later, he resumed working with Danforth, who had become a U.S. senator, as a legislative aide. Thomas worked on energy and environment matters, again avoiding race. By then, Thomas had also become a Republican.[9]

In 1981, Thomas became assistant secretary for civil rights at the Department of Education for the Reagan administration. Thomas initially declined the position, not wanting to be "pigeonholed" as a token, but accepted after some coaxing. Thomas turned down a lower-level policy position with Sen. Danforth to do the work he always spurned: "black work." He quickly antagonized integrationists when he overturned a departmental policy of insisting that Southern states unify their separate white and black college systems. Thomas feared that the policy endangered historically black universities, which educated most of the nation's black professionals.[10]

Eight months later, Reagan nominated Thomas to head the Equal Employment Opportunity Commission (EEOC), a position he assumed in February 1982. While at the EEOC, Justice Thomas infuriated the civil rights community. He ended the EEOC's use of timetables and numeric goals that relaxed rules for employers already found guilty of violating civil rights laws.

[8] Steve Kroft, 60 Minutes: The Justice Nobody Knows; Justice Clarence Thomas Discusses His Childhood, His Career, Anita Hill and His Book (CBS News television broadcast Sept. 30, 2007).

[9] Id.; Williams, A *Question of Fairness.*

[10] Merida and Fletcher, Supreme Discomfort 76. Kevin Merida and Michael A. Fletcher, *Supreme Discomfort: More Than a Decade after His Bitter Confirmation Battle, African Americans Are Still Judging Clarence Thomas Guilty. Is That Justice?*, Washington Post Magazine, Aug. 4, 2002, at W08; Williams, A *Question of Fairness.*

He also stopped the EEOC from bringing class action lawsuits that relied on proving discrimination through statistics. By putting the kibosh on statistics, his detractors contended, Thomas helped discriminators. Direct evidence of discrimination is typically unavailable, and often statistical evidence provides the only way to prove racial harms.[11]

Thomas helped Vice President George Bush's presidential election efforts in 1988. Once elected, in 1990, Bush repaid Thomas with an appointment to the prestigious U.S. Court of Appeals for the DC Circuit. On June 27, 1991, Justice Thurgood Marshall announced his retirement from the Supreme Court. On July 1, President Bush nominated Thomas to fill the seat.[12]

His nomination seemed assured until an FBI interview with Anita Hill, during which she claimed that Justice Thomas sexually harassed her, leaked. Democrats used the allegations to derail the nomination of a conservative black man some feared could potentially dislodge blacks from their party. With his Supreme Court seat on the line, Thomas fought back during his Senate confirmation hearings:

> This is not an opportunity to talk about difficult matters privately or in a closed environment. This is a circus. It's a national disgrace. And from my standpoint, as a Black American, it is a high-tech lynching for uppity Blacks who in any way deign to think for themselves, to do for themselves, to have different ideas, and it is a message that unless you kowtow to an old order, this is what will happen to you. You will be lynched, destroyed, caricatured by a committee of the U.S. Senate rather than hung from a tree.

Justice Thomas was eventually confirmed by a 52–48 vote, the narrowest margin ever by a successful nominee.[13]

JUSTICE THOMAS MEET *UNCLE TOM; UNCLE TOM* MEET JUSTICE THOMAS

One of the first times Thomas publicly dealt with *Uncle Tom* was when he headed the EEOC. The civil rights community criticized his stewardship

[11] Williams, *A Question of Fairness*; Juan Williams, *Black Conservatives*, Washington Post, Dec. 16, 1980, at A21.

[12] Meyer and Abramson, Strange Justice 15–16, 18–19; Merida and Fletcher, Supreme Discomfort 167; Linda Greenhouse, *The Supreme Court; Bush Picks a Wild Card*, New York Times, July 2, 1991, at A1.

[13] Merida and Fletcher, Supreme Discomfort 182, 189, 193–94; Meyer and Abramson, Strange Justice 136–39; Hearing of the Senate Judiciary Committee on the Nomination of Clarence Thomas to the Supreme Court, Oct. 11, 1991, available at: http://etext.lib.virginia.edu/etcbin/toccer-new-yitna?id=UsaThom&images=images/modeng&data=/lv6/workspace/yitna&tag=public&part=24; *The Thomas Nomination; On the Hearing Schedule: Eight*

because he never consistently backed traditional antidiscrimination policies. As Thomas recounted, "They have called me an 'Uncle Tom,' 'a foot shufflin' (man) with a water-melon eatin' grin" for simply taking "a different stand."[14]

Before Thomas heard his first Supreme Court case, many blacks already considered him an *Uncle Tom*. According to a July 1991 poll, 49 percent thought that he was not an *Uncle Tom*, 30 percent thought he was. Since his confirmation, those numbers have undoubtedly worsened. Clarence Thomas's popularity with blacks is in a state of perpetual decline, and many make their displeasure known. Spike Lee, for instance, said, "I think Malcolm X, if he were alive today, would call Supreme Court Justice Clarence Thomas a hand-kerchief head, a chicken-and-biscuit-eating Uncle Tom." Daphne Barbee-Wooten, an attorney for Hawaii's ACLU branch, said that extending Thomas an invitation to visit "sends a message that the Hawaii ACLU promotes and honors Black Uncle Toms who turn their back on civil rights." Jocelyn Elders, former U.S. surgeon general, called Justice Thomas an *Uncle Tom*, feeling "that he has used all the advantages he had to get himself [to the Supreme Court], and now he wants to make sure that he is perceived as a conservative white man." Columnist Alicia Banks wrote an "Open Letter to a Supreme Uncle Tom" where she vented, "We do not hate you because of your opinions. We hate you because you have the power to wield your twisted opinions as weapons of oppression upon millions of us. We hate you for your brutal legal actions. We see you as [a] star player on a deadly neocon team."[15]

Law professor Derrick A. Bell Jr. wrote a scathing indictment and without using *Uncle Tom*, Bell legitimates its application against Justice Thomas:

> The addition of Judge Clarence Thomas to [the Supreme Court], as the replacement for Justice Thurgood Marshall, is likely to add deep insult to the continuing injury inflicted on civil rights advocates. The cut is particu-larly unkind because the choice of a Black like Clarence Thomas replicates

Further Witnesses, New York Times, Oct. 13, 1991, at 34; Ruth Marcus, *One Angry Man: Clarence Thomas Is No Victim*, Washington Post, Oct. 3, 2007, at A23.

[14] Chester A. Higgins Sr., *EEOC Chief Beset by Cries of "Uncle Tom," Budget Woes and Growing Backlog of Cases*, Michigan Citizen, June 18, 1988, at 13; Merida and Fletcher, Supreme Discomfort 152–60; Howard Kurtz, *EEOC Drops Hiring Goals, Timetables*, Washington Post, Feb. 11, 1986, at A1; Howard Kurtz, *EEOC to Resume Hiring-Goal Efforts*, Washington Post, July 24, 1986, at A1; Lena Williams, *Washington Talk: Equal Employment Opportunity Commission*, New York Times, Feb. 8, 1987, at 54.

[15] Greenhouse, *The Supreme Court*; Public Opinion Online, July 30, 1991, Sponsored by Time, Cable News Network; Matthew Cooper, *Washington Whispers*, U.S. News & World Report, July 22, 1991, at 16; Kelley O. Beaucar, *Hawaii ACLU Members Compare Thomas to "Hitler," "Anti-Christ,"* Fox News (June 26, 2001), available at: www.foxnews.com/story/0,2933,28108,00.html; *Trash Talk*, St. Petersburg Times, Mar. 21, 1997, at 8T; Alicia Banks, *Open Letter to a Supreme Uncle Tom*, http://stewartsynopsis.com/clarence_thomas.htm.

the slave masters' practice of elevating to overseer and other positions of quasi-power those slaves willing to mimic the masters' views, carry out orders, and by their presence provide a perverse legitimacy to the oppression they aided and approved.[16]

In 1995, the Supreme Court held in *Miller v. Johnson* that the Equal Protection Clause prevented Georgia from purposefully creating majority black electoral districts to increase black representation in Congress. Without such districts, proponents argued, Congress would have few minority representatives. Georgia Congressman Billy McKinney, black, said of the Supreme Court decision, "I think it's a day of infamy for … black people in the South.… I'm saying that four racist white people and one Uncle Tom made this decision."[17]

Leonard Small, who has known Thomas since they were both teenagers, says Thomas "wishes almost sociopathically to be white," adding that "he not only hates himself, he hates his history." Small said, "in the novel *Uncle Tom's Cabin*, Eliza ran from slavery and Uncle Tom stayed. While we are trying to run for freedom, Justice Thomas is not only staying, he's telling."[18]

Justice Thomas's opinion in *Hudson v. McMillan*, to Small, was treacherous. In *Hudson*, three Louisiana prison guards shackled Keith Hudson, a black inmate, then pummeled him in seclusion, leaving him with facial bruises, loosened teeth, and a cracked dental plate that was "unusable for several months." A majority of Supreme Court justices held that the beating violated the Eighth Amendment, constituting cruel and unusual punishment. Justice Thomas dissented, writing, "In my view, a use of force that causes only insignificant harm to a prisoner may be immoral, it may be tortuous, it may be criminal … but it is not 'cruel and unusual punishment.'" Small retorted, "What does that mean? That guards have free course to beat on Negroes in prison?" Justice Thomas's opinion angered Hudson's fellow inmates too. "They were calling him Uncle Tom, house nigger, things like that. Some of them were saying, 'I wish he were in here with us.'"[19]

Blacks still living near where Justice Thomas grew up are likewise sour on their native son. In May 2001, Thomas returned to Savannah and met up with old acquaintances. They toured the library where Thomas spent much of his youth. While they regaled in old stories, a local black activist and retired

---

[16] Derrick A. Bell, Jr., *Racial Realism*, 24 *Connecticut Law Review* 363, 370 (1992).

[17] 515 U.S. 900, 907 (1995); Cal Thomas, *Base Political Campaign on a Candidate's Ideas*, The Times Union, July 17, 1996, at A9.

[18] Merida and Fletcher, *Supreme Discomfort.*

[19] 503 U.S. 1, 4 17, 18 (1992) (Thomas, J., dissenting); Merida and Fletcher, Supreme Discomfort 245.

schoolteacher, Abigail Jordan, walked up to the group and said, "I just wanted to see what a group of Uncle Toms look like."[20]

Clarence Thomas is principally censured for his conservatism. To his indicters, his worldview is fundamentally inconsistent with racial loyalty. As Manning Marable wrote, "One might condemn Clarence Thomas as an 'Uncle Tom,' but that would be an insult to 'Uncle Toms.' Thomas, the 'race traitor,' ... actively oppose[s] the black community's interests." But Thomas swats the many *Uncle Tom* charges that fly his way with the same basic response: Blacks punish dissenters. "I am not an Uncle Tom. I do not pay attention to that nonsense. That is one of the problems we have as black people. We don't allow differing views." Another time he remarked, "does a black man instantaneously become insensitive, a 'dupe' or an 'Uncle Tom' because he happens to disagree with the policy of affirmative action? ... Does it make sense to criticize someone who says all Blacks look alike, then praise those who insist that all Blacks think alike?" Henry Louis Gates was right when he contended that Justice Thomas is held up for special scorn because he attacks affirmative action. Gates defends Justice Thomas's right to disagree, stating that there is not "one way to be black."[21]

Indeed, one can still be loyal and a contrarian. Black solidarity permits differing viewpoints. Thomas has said that he's "trying to help Black America." His detractors seek to dismiss him as an *Uncle Tom*, but their arguments essentially equate conservatism with treachery. Thomas, however, can sincerely believe that affirmative action is a bad policy that hurts blacks. His positions are not so out of bounds that he must be guilty of treason.[22]

By concentrating solely on his policy positions, Thomas's critics have consistently failed to prove his guilt. What should Thomas do if he finds that racial preferences and the welfare state stunt black progress by making blacks dependent on government? If he legitimately believes this, would not the true harm be for him to silence himself? His many detractors contend that his brand of conservatism is so obviously antagonistic to blacks' interest that it constitutes betrayal. But they have not proven that his worldview violates constructive norms. In order to dismiss ideas as tantamount to betrayal one must explain their incompatibility with black solidarity. Thomas's castigators have fallen short of their burden. But Thomas may nonetheless be *Uncle Tom*.

---

[20] Merida and Fletcher, Supreme Discomfort 2–3.
[21] Dr. Manning Marable, *"Bush's Blacks: Race Traitors?"* – *Part One of Two*, The Free Press, Aug. 8, 2002, available at: http://www.freepress.org/columns/display/4/2002/486; *Clarence Thomas Says: "I'm no Uncle Tom,"* Jet, Nov. 14, 1994 at 4; Merida and Fletcher, Supreme Discomfort 375.
[22] Merida and Fletcher, Supreme Discomfort 29.

THE CASE AGAINST A JUSTICE

Justice Thomas's antagonism toward affirmative action activates most of the betrayal allegations. The criticism is easy to recite: Thomas benefited personally from affirmative action, but to further his career, he began criticizing the very same programs instrumental to his success. Georgia Congressman John Lewis stated that Thomas "wants to destroy the bridge that brought him over troubled waters.... He wants to pull down the ladder that he climbed up." Although opposing affirmative action is perfectly acceptable, fashioning an anti–affirmative action persona to benefit oneself, without concern for its impact on the race, is disloyal, violating the norm that blacks care about the group.[23]

Thomas has often recounted his poverty-stricken upbringing in Pin Point, using his experience as a once poor youngster yet immensely successful man to bolster his opposition to affirmative action. In 1988, building his conservative bona fides, Thomas argued against the welfare state, declaring that "[w]e [blacks in the South] learned to fend for ourselves in a hostile environment ... not only without the active assistance of government, but with its opposition." Jeffrey Toobin, in reviewing Thomas's memoir, described it as conforming to "a familiar American archetype, that of the determined outsider who, by dint of intelligence and hard work, transcends the meager circumstances of his birth."[24]

Thomas's Booker T. Washington "up from his own bootstraps" image – what Vernon Jordan called the "bootstrap myth" – bolsters his anti–affirmative

[23] Linda P. Campbell, *Black Debate on Thomas Carries Over to Hearings*, Chicago Tribune, Sept. 20, 1991, at 1. Justice Thomas's statements against racial preferences are numerous. In a 1986 letter to *Playboy*, for example, responding to an article critical of the Reagan administration's civil rights record, Justice Thomas wrote that people should be evaluated "on the basis of what they can do and not on the basis of irrelevant personal characteristics." In 1987, while a participant in a panel discussion in Santa Barbara, CA, Justice Thomas said that "ultimately any race-conscious remedy is no good." Id. And, when Joseph H. Duff, another participant, said that when he was admitted to law school under an affirmative action program, it was "good for society," Justice Thomas shot back, "No that was good for you." Neil A. Lewis, *On Thomas's Climb, Ambivalence about Issue of Affirmative Action*, New York Times, July 14, 1991, at 1. The desire to analyze Justice Thomas in the black community is indeed a remarkable phenomenon. I myself have participated in conversations with friends and family on what exactly motivates Justice Thomas to think the way he does. Merida and Fletcher report similarly, writing, "As we saw it, no other public figure in American life had the ability to spark such intense passions among Blacks – if not seething anger, then the restless need to analyze him, to come up with some piece of sideline sociology to explain the vast gulf between arguably the most powerful African American in the land and so many members of his own race." Merida and Fletcher, Supreme Discomfort 8.

[24] Karen Grigsby Bates, *Are You Doubting Thomas?*, Los Angeles Times, Nov. 9, 1994 at B7; Meyer and Abramson, Strange Justice, at 32; Jeffrey Toobin, *Unforgiven: Why Is Clarence Thomas So Angry?*, The New Yorker, Nov. 12, 2007, at 86.

action credentials. If a black man reared in abject poverty can climb to the Supreme Court, then perhaps the playing field requires no leveling. Justice Thomas's life, as he portrays it, certainly supports the arguments he dispenses against affirmative action. White House advisors, when selling his Supreme Court nomination to the American public, used this compelling narrative, labeling it the "Pin Point Strategy." Thomas's poor Pin Point upbringing truly enamored them. The family's wooden shack insulated with newspapers, the lack of electricity, and the outhouse they shared with neighbors was the perfect narrative to ride on the road to confirmation.[25]

I see at least two problems, however. First, reports of Thomas's poor upbringing have been greatly exaggerated. And second, Thomas did not simply benefit from affirmative action, it was instrumental to his success.

After they moved in with their grandparents in Savannah, Thomas and his brother were not poor. Financial advantages, not poverty, shaped Thomas's life. After all, he received nine years of parochial school education when the majority of black pupils languished in underfunded Jim Crow schools. His high school peers report that he was not impoverished. Charlie Mae Garrett, Thomas's classmate at St. Pius X High School, recalls that Thomas's life was not a "struggle," adding that "[h]e had a good life. I think all of us who went to Catholic school were somewhat privileged." Garrett was baffled while watching Thomas accentuate his poor upbringing in Pin Point during his televised confirmation hearings. Garrett said, "I was like, 'When did he live in Pin Point?'" Another classmate disclosed, "Personally, I thought he was rich," at least compared to fellow blacks in the neighborhood. Childhood friend Floyd Adams stated although "[e]veryone is emphasizing that [Thomas] grew up in Pin Point in poverty, ... when his grandfather took over, Clarence moved into what would be considered a fairly successful black middle-class family." Thomas's life trajectory, therefore, when told honestly, is far less powerful in the context of affirmative action.[26]

More important, though, is that Thomas's career was built on affirmative action. He formerly admitted this. In 1983, to his EEOC colleagues, Thomas stated, "[b]ut for [affirmative action laws], God only knows where I would be today. These laws and their proper application are all that stand between the first 17 years of my life and the second 17 years." At Yale Law,

25 Booker T. Washington, Up From Slavery (1900); Robert J. Norrell, Up From History. The Life of Booker T. Washington (2009); Toobin, *Unforgiven*; Merida and Fletcher, Supreme Discomfort 36.
26 Merida and Fletcher, Supreme Discomfort 36, 55, 56; John Lancaster and Sharon LaFraniere, *Thomas: Growing Up Black in a White World*, Washington Post, Sept. 8, 1991 at A1.

his classmates recalled him claiming that had he not been black he would not have been admitted. Even in a conversation with friend Frank G. Washington shortly after his Supreme Court nomination, Thomas appears to have shown private support for affirmative action. Washington relayed that "Thomas said that he thought such programs were acceptable when they were based not simply on race but 'on some notion that we were actually underprivileged.'"[27]

But since his Supreme Court confirmation, Thomas has routinely denied that affirmative action helped his career. In 1996, Thomas delivered a speech wherein he disclaimed benefiting from affirmative action. On a separate occasion, Thomas told journalist Juan Williams that "this thing about how they let me into Yale – that kind of stuff offends me. All they [Yale] did was stop stopping us." Another time, Thomas stated that when he "went to Yale Law School, they had reduced black admissions from 40 to 12. We were all there on our own merit." Even his conservative backers have shielded him from assertions that he was admitted to Holy Cross because of race. Thomas Sowell, a fellow black conservative, argued that racial preferences at Holy Cross began after Clarence enrolled. Ensuring that Thomas is untarnished by the affirmative action brush is seemingly very imperative to the political right.[28]

But facts are stubborn things. Racial preferences benefited Thomas at Holy Cross, Yale Law School, the Department of Education, the EEOC, and even in his appointment to the Supreme Court. But for affirmative action I would not know who Clarence Thomas is. The Clarence Thomas of 1983 was correct. God only knows where he would be.

In 1968, Thomas was a beneficiary of the Martin Luther King scholarship program that Holy Cross established to increase black representation at the school. When Holy Cross President John E. Brooks was asked if Thomas benefited from affirmative action, he retorted, "Certainly." At Yale Law, affirmative action was likewise decisive in his admission. Yale used affirmative action the year he was admitted less than in previous years. Thomas was accurate on that point. But the school still considered race in hopes of ensuring that a tenth of an entering class would be black. And, even though Thomas had excellent grades, Yale Law School's dean during Thomas's years said that he had "no doubt … that in some measure Clarence was preferred because of his background." James Thomas, Yale Law admissions offer when Clarence

[27] Neil A. Lewis, *On Thomas's Climb, Ambivalence About Issue of Affirmative Action*, New York Times, July 14, 1991, at A1.
[28] Id.; Williams, *A Question of Fairness*; JBHE Foundation, *Justice Clarence Thomas*, at 35; Thomas Sowell, *How "Affirmative Action" Hurts Blacks*, Forbes, Oct. 6, 1997, at 64.

Thomas applied in 1971, said "it's pretty clear" that affirmative action helped Thomas get accepted into Yale.[29]

The positions the Reagan administration offered to Thomas similarly would have been denied to him had he not been black. Thomas's first appointment was as assistant secretary for civil rights at the Department of Education and from there he headed the EEOC. The Reagan administration chose Thomas largely for racial considerations. Why else would Thomas, who concentrated mainly on commercial law, receive two civil rights job offers other than that Reagan's administration was looking for a black face? That Thomas particularly disdained civil rights work only makes the selection odder. Assistant Attorney General Brad Reynolds confirmed that Thomas was chosen because of his race. During a toast to Clarence Thomas's second confirmation as EEOC chairman, Reynolds cheered him as "the epitome of the right kind of affirmative action working the right way."[30]

His appointment to the Supreme Court too was an exercise of affirmative action for one by the Republican Party professing to oppose racial preferences. When he nominated Thomas to the Supreme Court, President George H. W. Bush said that Thomas was "the best qualified person for the job on the merits." Bush proclaimed, "the fact that [Thomas] is a black and a minority had nothing to do with" his nomination. Thomas insisted that his race was irrelevant to his nomination. Few actually believed this. Thomas had scant judicial experience and had an unremarkable stint as the head of the EEOC. And Bush faced heavy pressure to replace Justice Marshall, the first black Supreme Court justice, with another black lawyer. As Senator Joseph Biden said, "Had Thomas been white, he never would have been nominated. The only reason he is on the Court is because he is black."[31]

---

[29] JBHE Foundation, *Justice Clarence Thomas*, at 35, 36.

[30] Id. at 34–35; Christopher Edley Jr., *Doubting Thomas: Law, Politics and Hypocrisy*, Washington Post, July 7, 1991, at B1. Oddly enough, Justice Thomas, prior to this, actively decided not to choose jobs that would result in the pigeonholing of him as a black man. Thomas Edley writes:In the 1970s, Thomas proudly focused on corporate matters, considering it important that he not be "typed" as a civil rights specialist. The best way to avoid being treated like a nigger is to avoid nigger jobs, as striving Blacks have long counseled one another – I've heard it since seventh grade. Then, the Reagan administration put him in two successive such jobs – first as assistant secretary for civil rights in the Department of Education and then as head of the EEOC.See also the words of Neil Bernstein, who was quoted as saying that Justice Thomas:[w]as very strong on the notion that he wanted to make his mark as a business lawyer and not have anything to do with civil rights. . . . But he wound up going down the path he swore he would never go down. He was always conflicted. He was opposed to getting jobs based on race when that turned out to get him everything he got. . . . Merida and Fletcher, Supreme Discomfort 140. Merida and Fletcher, *Supreme Discomfort.*

[31] Bush, though, was supposed to say that Justice Thomas was the "best man" instead of "best qualified." John Greenya, Silent Justice: The Clarence Thomas Story 171 (2001); *The Supreme*

One might argue that because he benefited from affirmative action Thomas must always support it. As columnist Maureen Dowd wrote, "It's impossible not to be disgusted at someone who could benefit so much from affirmative action and then pull up the ladder after himself." But Dowd's views are too simplistic. One can benefit from a policy that one later rejects.[32]

But criticizing race-conscious hiring while positioning oneself for jobs that one knows will only be extended because of race is indefensible. And this is how Thomas comported for a possible Supreme Court seat. Thomas laughed at the idea that he positioned himself for the Court, joking that his path there – from Danforth's legal office in Missouri, to the Department of Education, to the EEOC – was unlikely. "The problem I have with that," Thomas quipped, "is there is a lack of precedence." Those who knew him, however, understood that Thomas gunned for the top spot. Michael Middleton, who worked with Thomas at the Department of Education and at the EEOC, said, "[Thomas's] feeling was, 'I am the highest ranking African-American lawyer in government and Thurgood Marshall is getting up in age. When they start looking around for a replacement, I want to be in position for that." Middleton said that, during their first meeting, Thomas actually told him he would be on the Supreme Court. Thomas understood that, with a Republican in the White House, he was the most prominent conservative black lawyer when Justice Marshall neared retirement. Thomas, the audacious alchemist, endeavored to turn black skin, gumption, and an average résumé into gold, a Supreme Court seat. And his formula worked.[33]

As a justice, Thomas believes that to answer constitutional questions, one should determine the Constitution's "original meaning," that is, what it meant when it was written. He is, in other words, an Originalist. Many conservatives champion Originalism, including Justice Antonin Scalia. Thomas, as common for conservative Originalists, concludes that the Fourteenth Amendment's Equal Protection Clause renders the Constitution colorblind. Thus, Thomas contends that all race-conscious government decision making, namely affirmative action, is presumptively unconstitutional. In his *Grutter v. Bollinger* (2003) dissent, for instance, Thomas quoted Justice Harlan's *Plessy v. Ferguson* dissent: "Our Constitution is color-blind and neither knows

---

Court; *Excerpts From New Conference Announcing Court Nominee*, New York Times, July 2, 1991, at 14. Justice Thomas said, responding to the assertion that people think he was nominated only because he is black, "I think a lot worse things have been said. I disagree with that, but I'll have to live within it." Angela Onwuachi-Willig, *Using the Master's "Tool" To Dismantle His House: Why Justice Clarence Thomas Makes the Case for Affirmative Action*, 47 *Arizona Law Review* 113, 118 (2005). Mayer and Abramson, Strange Justice 21.

[32] Maureen Dowd, *Could Thomas Be Right?*, New York Times, June 25, 2004 A25.

[33] Merida and Fletcher, Supreme Discomfort 18, 139–40.

nor tolerates classes among citizens." *Grutter* concerned the affirmative action admissions policy of University of Michigan Law School. A 5–4 majority found the school's plan constitutional. Thomas dissented.[34]

Conservative Originalists like Thomas, however, have a huge problem. Their claim that the Constitution is colorblind, which drives their aversion to affirmative action, cannot be supported by any historical account of the Fourteenth Amendment. As the states ratified the Fourteenth Amendment, Congress passed numerous race-conscious statutes solely to benefit blacks. Indeed, "A great deal of historical work suggests that affirmative action was accepted by those who ratified the equal protection clause. In the aftermath of the Civil War, Congress engaged in numerous race-conscious efforts, singling out African Americans for special help." In 1866, for instance, Congress passed an act that appropriated money for "the relief of destitute colored women and children." In 1867, Congress passed another act assisting poor blacks in the District of Columbia. Other congressional legislation passed before, during, and after the ratification of the Fourteenth Amendment appropriated money for "colored" soldiers and sailors in the Union Army. These acts prove "that those who profess fealty to the 'original understanding,' who abhor judicial 'activism,' or who hold that the legal practices at the time of enactment 'say what they say' and dictate future interpretation, cannot categorically condemn color-based distribution of governmental benefits as they do."[35]

Also significant, the congressmen who drafted and passed the Fourteenth Amendment originally understood it to permit segregation. A Constitution that is colorblind, yet permits segregation, is irreconcilable. Alexander Bickel, a law clerk for Justice Frankfurter when the Supreme Court heard *Brown*, researched the amendment's legislative history, learning that its purpose was to extend civil rights to the freedmen. Bickel observed that the "civil rights" formula ...

> covered the right to contract, sue, give evidence in court, and inherit, hold, and dispose of real and personal property; also a right to equal protection in the literal sense of benefiting equally from laws for the security of person and

34 Clarence Thomas, *The Higher Law Background of the Privileges or Immunities Clause of the Fourteenth Amendment*, 12 Harvard Journal of Law and Public Policy 63, 63 (1989); Clarence Thomas, *Toward a "Plain Reading" of the Constitution – The Declaration of Independence in Constitutional Interpretation*, 30 Howard Law Journal 983, 993 (1987); Samuel Marcosson, *Colorizing the Constitution of Originalism: Clarence Thomas at the Rubicon*, 16 Law & Inequality Journal 429, 458–59 (1998); *Grutter*, 539 U.S. at 312–16, 336, 364 (Thomas, J., dissenting) (quoting *Plessy*, 163 U.S. at 559) (Harlan, J., dissenting).

35 Cass R. Sunstein, *Affirmative Action in the Higher Education: Why Grutter Was Correctly Decided*, 41 Journal of Blacks in Higher Education 80, 80–81 (2003); Jed Rubenfeld, *Affirmative Action*, 107 Yale Law Journal 427, 430–32 (1997).

property, including presumably laws permitting ownership of firearms, and to equality in the penalties and burdens by law.... But there is no evidence whatever showing that for its sponsors the civil rights formula had anything to do with unsegregated public schools; Wilson, its sponsor in the House, specifically disclaimed any such notion.[36]

The 39th Congress that drafted the Fourteenth Amendment stopped short of including language in the Civil Rights Act of 1866 that would have invalidated segregation, further suggesting that Congress had no intent to attack it. The Fourteenth Amendment, after all, was Congress's attempt to enshrine into the Constitution the 1866 act. The same Congress that drafted the Fourteenth Amendment, furthermore, supervised segregated education in Washington, DC. That Congress which has power over the capital's schools would allow segregation to continue there, yet "to invade State sovereignty, which the framers were zealous to preserve, in order to impose a requirement of desegregation upon the States" is implausible. Thus, because the Fourteenth Amendment was understood to permit segregation, one cannot claim that the "colorblind Constitution" forbids affirmative action.[37]

Originalism, though, is an "inconstant term." Adherents have various Originalism recipes and Justice Thomas's version has its own distinct flavor. Thomas's judicial philosophy uses Originalism as a base and adds a dash of natural law for a twist. Because the historical record alone does not maintain a construction of the Fourteenth Amendment that mandates colorblind governmental decision making, Justice Thomas is compelled to use other legal ingredients to support this interpretation. The result is an exotic, if hard to swallow, mélange.[38]

Specifically, Thomas asserts that a "promise of equality of rights" guaranteed by the Declaration of Independence ("all men are created equal") should have led the Supreme Court to a different decision in *Dred Scott v. Sandford* (1857). In *Dred Scott*, the Court famously held that the Constitution denied blacks citizenship. Justice Taney wrote that blacks were "so far inferior that

---

[36] Klarman, From Jim Crow to Civil Rights 304; Alexander M. Bickel, *The Original Understanding and the Segregation Decision*, 69 *Harvard Law Review* 1, 56 (1955).

[37] The Fourteenth Amendment was designed to "constitutionalize" the Civil Rights Act of 1866. Raoul Berger, Government by Judiciary: The Transformation of the Fourteenth Amendment 32, 138, 201 (2nd edition 1997). Looking to the debates surrounding that act, therefore, aids in understanding the original public meaning of the Fourteenth Amendment.

[38] Greene, Selling Originalism, 97 *Georgetown Law Journal* 657, 661 (2009); andrè douglas pond cummings, *Grutter v. Bollinger, Clarence Thomas, Affirmative Action and the Treachery of Originalism: "The Sun Don't Shine Here in This Part of Town,"* 21 *Harvard Blackletter Law Journal* 1, 13 (2006); Bret Boyce, *Originalism and the Fourteenth Amendment*, 33 *Wake Forest Law Review* 909, 1027 (1998).

they had no rights which the white man was bound to respect." That decision, Thomas contends, was wrong. The promise of equality of rights renders the Constitution a colorblind document, Thomas argues, and should have compelled the Court to declare that slavery "was inconsistent with the Declaration, and hence, with the Constitution."[39]

Thomas's reliance on natural law and the Declaration of Independence to undergird his contention that the Constitution is colorblind is unconvincing at best and downright odd at worst. The notion of equality that Thomas construes from the Declaration of Independence is the instrument that Thomas uses to transform the Constitution into a colorblind document. But the Fourteenth Amendment's Equal Protection Clause also guarantees equality. The question is not whether the Constitution guarantees equality, but rather what equality means. Thomas's use of the Declaration of Independence merely moves the issue of defining "equality" nearly a century earlier, from the post–Civil War era to the founding of the Republic.[40]

As discussed, the post–Civil War conception of equality was inconsistent with a colorblind Constitution. The issue then becomes whether the American Revolution generation defined equality as requiring race-neutral decision making. The short answer is no. First, the Founding Fathers who drafted the Declaration of Independence, in an early version, criticized the king of England for trying to end the slave trade and for inciting slave rebellions. People this devoted to African slavery are curious and ultimately unpersuasive champions of race neutrality. The Constitution they drafted and ratified a decade later allowed for race-conscious government decision making. The "We the People" in the Constitution's preamble excluded black slaves who were disallowed from participating in American democracy.[41]

A historical analysis of federal laws from 1789 to 1791 further establishes that the accepted meaning of equality rejected colorblindness. The first Congress drafted the Bill of Rights. Laws enacted during this period are particularly helpful in appreciating this generation's conception of equality. In 1789, for instance, the first Congress passed the Federal Judiciary Act that incorporated into federal law various state laws that discriminated on the basis of race. In 1790, Congress enacted the first color-conscious law, the "Act to Establish an Uniform Rule of Naturalization," which permitted "any ... free white person" residing in the United States for two years to apply for American citizenship.

---

[39] Thomas, *Toward a "Plain Reading" of the Constitution*, at 984; Marcosson, *Colorizing the Constitution of Originalism*, at 458; *Scott v. Sandford*, 60 U.S. 393, 407 (1857).

[40] U.S. Const. amend. XIV, § 1; Marcosson, *Colorizing the Constitution of Originalism*, at 459.

[41] Thurgood Marshall, *The Constitution: A Living Document*, 30 *Howard Law Journal* 915, 916–17 (1987).

In 1792, Congress passed another color-conscious law, the first federal Militia Act. When the bill was first introduced, the language was colorblind, allowing free blacks to serve. But Congress eventually changed it specifically to prevent black participation in militias. Thomas, therefore, cannot define equality during the formation stages of the Union to equate to colorblindness. In affirmative action cases, Thomas suddenly becomes a living constitutionalist. He deemphasizes the original meaning of the Equal Protection Clause and reinterprets the breadth and scope of words, phrases, and constitutional language to promote his sense of justice and fairness.[42]

Thomas's departures from Originalism extend beyond his mystifying use of natural law. Originalists define a judge's role as boiling down to interpreting text and arriving at decisions. Judges must never allow their race, for instance, to color their opinions. As Thomas once remarked, a judge "must become almost pure, in the way that fire purified metal, before he can decide a case. Otherwise, he is not a judge, but a legislator, for whom it is entirely appropriate to consider personal and group interests." Thomas, however, often infuses his personal views into cases where race is salient.[43]

Thomas's concurrence in *Jenkins v. Missouri*, for instance, is not "impartial." *Jenkins* concerned a district court order that required the state of Missouri to remedy past legal segregation by implementing a host of educational reforms designed to repopulate Kansas City public schools with white suburban students. A 5–4 majority overturned the district court order. Thomas's personal experiences as a black man drove his disdain for these integrationist policies as his concurrence reflects.[44]

In addition to his inconsistent Originalism, Justice Thomas committed a flagrantly dishonest foul. In his *Gutter* dissent, Justice Thomas quotes Frederick Douglass in his speech "What the Black Man Wants":

> In regard to the colored people, there is always more that is benevolent, I perceive, than just, manifested towards us. What I ask for the negro is not benevolence, not pity, not sympathy, but simply justice. The American people have always been anxious to know what they shall do with us.... I have had but one answer from the beginning. Do nothing with us! Your doing with us has already played the mischief with us. Do nothing with us!

[42] Stephen A. Siegel, *The Federal Government's Power to Enact Color-Conscious Laws: An Originalist Inquiry*, 92 *Northwestern University Law Review* 477, 514–16, 520–21 (1998); Edwin Chemerinksy, Constitutional Law 11 (2005); cummings, Grutter v. Bollinger, *Clarence Thomas, Affirmative Action and the Treachery of Originalism*, at 5.

[43] Marcosson, Colorizing the Constitution of Originalism, at 459; Justice Clarence Thomas, Judging, 45 *University of Kansas Law Review* 1, 4 (1996).

[44] *Jenkins v. Missouri*, 515 U.S. 70, 98–101 (1995); Id. at 115 (Thomas, J., concurring).

If the apples will not remain on the tree of their own strength, if they are worm-eaten at the core, if they are early ripe and disposed to fall, let them fall! ... And if the negro cannot stand on his own legs, let him fall also. All I ask is, give him a chance to stand on his own legs! Let him alone! ... Your interference is doing him positive injury.

Justice Thomas uses Douglass's words as a launching pad to conclude that "blacks can achieve in every avenue of American life without the meddling of university administrators." That is, Thomas contends that Douglass would have rejected affirmative action because, as the speech shows, Douglass abhorred government interference.[45]

Aside from the futility of trying to predict what policies a person would endorse based on a weak data point, here a speech delivered before the Thirteenth Amendment was even ratified, there are two problems. First, Douglass championed the Freedmen's Bureau. In 1865, Congress enacted the Freedmen's Bureau Act, creating the Bureau of Refugees, Freedmen and Abandoned Lands. The bureau's main responsibility was aiding blacks in the enforcement of lease and work contracts and to assist blacks in renting land that the Union Army confiscated during the Civil War. Although the Freedmen's Bureau also aided poor whites displaced as a result of the war, assisting blacks was priority.[46]

The Freedmen's Bureau was the federal government's first attempt at remedying slavery's innumerable vestiges. If Justice Thomas culled the correct message from Douglass's speech – that the government need not meddle in black folks' lives – Douglass's endorsing of the Freedmen's Bureau is hard to explain. In fact, he almost became its director in 1867 although ultimately he turned it down. Douglass was particularly interested in the government providing education to freedmen, lauding efforts in creating colleges and schools throughout the South. Thomas rails against affirmative action, a policy designed to increase minority representation in college, by using the words of a man who applauded the government for promoting black education at a time when many whites were not getting the same educational assistance. Thomas hasn't the skills to slip on the shoes of men long passed and speak for them.[47]

---

[45] *Grutter*, 539 U.S. at 349–50 (Thomas, J., dissenting).

[46] Eric Schnapper, *Affirmative Action and the Legislative History of the Fourteenth Amendment*, 71 *Virginia Law Review* 753, 760. 761 (1985); Toni Lester, *Contention, Context and the Constitution: Riding the Waves of Affirmative Action Debate*, 39 *Suffolk University Law Review* 67, 90–91 (2005).

[47] David Blight, Frederick Douglass' Civil War: Keeping Faith in Jubilee 198 (1989); The Life and Writings of Frederick Douglass 205 (Editor Phillip S. Foner 1955).

Second, and more important, Justice Thomas, by eliding a crucial line from the quote, completely changed its character. Douglass said, referencing blacks:

> Let him alone. If you see him on his way to school, let him alone, don't disturb him! If you see him going to the dinner table at a hotel, let him go! If you see him going to the ballot box, let him along, don't disturb him! If you see him going into a work-shop, just let him alone, – your interference is doing him positive injury.

That is, Douglass was not telling whites not to assist blacks, but instead not to harm them. Douglass, a preeminent intellectual of his day, understood the racial realities. The white masses were not begging to help blacks reach equality. Douglass was much too busy a man to squander his time by telling whites, who would not dare touch the black skin they reviled, to withhold their helping hand. Thomas is right to conclude that Douglass's speech is all about convincing whites to leave black people alone. But the intervention Douglass was warning against was whites disallowing blacks from being full participants in American democracy. Indeed, Douglass appreciated that whites, particularly in the South, were willing to do anything to maintain white supremacy, including segregation, disenfranchisement, physical intimidation, and murder. Douglass cautioned against those ills, not something akin to affirmative action.[48]

Justice Thomas not only abused Douglass's legacy but has mocked the depravity of black suffering. In *Fisher v. University of Texas*, Thomas compared affirmative action to slavery and segregation. "The University's professed good intentions," Thomas wrote, "cannot excuse its outright racial discrimination any more than such intentions justified the now denounced arguments of slaveholders and segregationists." Justice Thomas, in *Parents Involved v. Seattle School District No. 1* (2007), further insulted victims of segregation. In *Parents Involved*, the Court prohibited the use of race in assigning children to public schools to integrate schools. Justice Thomas concurred, writing that those endorsing the integrationist practices of Seattle and Louisville "give school boards a free hand to make decisions on the basis of race – an approach reminiscent of that advocated by the segregationists in *Brown*.... This approach is just as wrong today as it was a half-century ago." The comparison is insulting. Creating an inclusive learning environment is wholly dissimilar from machinating to entrench racial apartheid in education. The plaintiff group, Parents Involved in Community Schools, champions neighborhood schools, racial

---

[48] DeWayne Wickham, *Thomas Distorts Douglass' Speech*, USA Today, July 1, 2003, at 13A.

code words used by whites who fought desegregation and school busing. But to Justice Thomas, these folk and not the integrationist educators of Seattle and Louisville are the rightful heirs of the *Brown* legacy. As Justice Stevens noted, it is a "cruel irony."[49]

Justice Thomas also has fostered warm relationships with overt racists. He is close friends with Rush Limbaugh, a man who once said about blacks, "They're 12 percent of the population. Who the hell cares?" In fact, Thomas officiated Limbaugh's wedding. Thomas also befriended North Carolina Senator Jesse Helms. Helms was close enough to Justice Thomas that the dean of University of North Carolina's law school enlisted Helms's help in convincing the justice to visit the school. Helms's bigotry surpassed that of Limbaugh. Helms once said, "[i]t is time to face honestly and sincerely the purely scientific statistical evidence of natural racial distinction in group intellect." Perhaps this is why he defended segregation as not wrong "for its time." Helms even followed Carol Moseley-Braun, the first black female senator, into an elevator, telling fellow senator Orrin Hatch, "Watch me make her cry. I'm going to make her cry. I'm going to sing 'Dixie' until she cries." Then, accentuating the lyrics concerning how great life was before slavery's demise, Helms sang "Dixie." Helm's "white Hands" attack ad against his black opponent Harvey Gantt in their 1990 Senate contest is perhaps his highest racist accomplishment. The ad featured a white man's hands crumbling up a rejection letter with an ominous-sounding voiceover saying, "You needed that job and you were the best qualified. But they had to give it to a minority because of a racial quota." Helms race-baited for political gain, but Thomas saw no wrong. "I can say that I've only seen Senator Helms treat people with dignity and I think that when we judge him," Thomas once said, "we should judge him as he treats the least among us."[50]

[49] 551 U.S. 701, 748, 751 (2007); Berger, Government by Judiciary 137; *Fisher v. University of Texas*, 133 S. Ct. 2430 (2013) (J., Thomas concurring); *Parents Involved*, 551 U.S. 701 at 748 (Thomas, J., concurring). *Parents Involved*, 551 U.S. 701 at 799 (Stevens, J., dissenting). Parents Involved in Community Schools Home Page, available at: http://www.piics.org/; Frank Brown, *Nixon's "Southern Strategy" and Forces Against Brown*, 73 Journal of Negro Education 191, 192 (2004); Lawrence John McAndrews, The Era of Education: The Presidents and the Schools, 1965–2001 71 (2006).

[50] Merida and Fletcher, Supreme Discomfort 223; Cash Michaels, *Jesse Helms' Revisionist History*, BlackPressUSA.com, available at: http://www.Blackpressusa.com/news/Article.asp ?SID=3&Title=National+News&NewsID=4342; Virginian Pilot, July 8, 2008, at B11; John Nichols, *Jesse Helms, John McCain and the Mark of the White Hands*, July 4, 2009, The Nation, available at: http://www.thenation.com/blogs/thebeat/334586; Peter Applebome, *Racial Politics in South's Contests: Hot Wind of Hate or Last Gasp?*, New York Times, Nov. 5, 1990 at A5; The commercial is available at http://www.youtube.com/watch?v=KIyewCdXMzk; *The 1990 Elections: State by State*, New York Times, Nov. 8, 1990, at B8; John Dodd, And the

Whereas he can overlook Helms's racism, showing similar magnanimity to blacks who have committed no offense is difficult for Thomas. See his criticism of Thurgood Marshall, for example. Justice Marshall delivered a speech in 1987, the bicentennial of the Constitution's adoption. His thesis was that he revered neither the original Constitution for it sanctioned slavery, nor the Founding Fathers for they produced a document that was immoral and defective from its inception. Justice Thomas, in response, wrote that Justice Marshall's "sensitive understanding" was an "exasperating and incomprehensible ... assault on the Bicentennial, the Founding, and the Constitution itself." Recounting historical truths is no assault, though. As Judge A. Leon Higginbotham argued, Marshall's speech recognized that "some may more quietly commemorate the suffering, the struggle and sacrifice that has triumphed over much of what was wrong with the original document, and observe the anniversary with hopes not realized and promises not fulfilled."[51]

Yet that Thomas would defend the original Constitution and the Founding Fathers from such critiques is strange. The document declared that blacks were three-fifths of a person, and the Founding Fathers entered into a union that was premised on denying the humanity of his race. What motivated his peculiar defense is unclear. Perhaps Thomas maligned Marshall upon appreciating the possible benefit in defending the Founders from the reproaches of a jurist detested by the same conservatives whose support would be instrumental in him becoming a justice. That might explain why he differentiated himself from Justice Marshall once to a conservative audience, reassuring listeners that he was "wild about the Constitution."[52]

Thomas also reproached his own sister, portraying her as a welfare queen. "She ... gets mad when the mailman is late with her welfare check.... That is how dependent she is." Unlike Clarence and his brother Myers, his sister Emma Mae did not live a privileged middle-class life in Savannah. She was left behind in poverty in Pin Point and raised by her Aunt Annie. When

World Came His Way – Jesse Helms' Contributions to Freedom 8 (2002), available at: http://www.jessehelmscenter.org/jessehelms/documents/ClarenceThomasexcerpt.pdf; John O. Calmore, *Airing Dirty Laundry: Disputes among Privileged Blacks – From Clarence Thomas to "The Law School Five"*, 56 *Howard Law Journal* 175, 184 (2003). If an outright racist was nice to them personally, few blacks, I believe, would be quoted praising the individual. I have seen no record of Justice Thomas rebuking Helms's stances on racial issues. Merida and Fletcher, Supreme Discomfort 65.

[51] Merida and Fletcher, Supreme Discomfort 65–66; Marshall, The Constitution, at 915, 917; Clarence Thomas, *Black Americans Based Claim for Freedom on Constitution*, San Diego Union & Tribune, Oct. 6, 1987, at B7; A. Leon Higginbotham, Jr., *An Open Letter to Justice Clarence Thomas from a Federal Judicial Colleague*, at 1010.

[52] Meyer and Abramson, Strange Justice 14.

Justice Thomas denounced his sister, moreover, she no longer was on welfare. She was working two jobs. She had been on welfare previously, but only because she quit work to care for their aunt, who was bedridden after a stroke. Publically, however, Thomas portrayed his sister as the stereotypical black woman whose most strenuous activity was going to and from the mailbox to collect her check. His description affected both his sister and black women regardless of whether they are on government assistance. He gave life to a stereotype that is better off dead. Justice Thomas's critique of the welfare state should be debated. The reliance on stereotypes that demean black women, however, is unnecessary.[53]

In his defense, sometimes when a black judicial nominee's candidacy is stalled in Congress, Thomas will advocate on their behalf. Justice Thomas has done this for various federal judges, including Eric Clay, Henry H. Kennedy Jr., and Victoria A. Roberts. Regarding Roberts, Thomas's friend, Judge Damon Keith of the Sixth Circuit, also black, called Thomas to put in a good word for her. Justice Thomas then met up with Roberts. It went well. Afterward, Thomas called Republican senators Orrin Hatch and Trent Lott, who then dropped their objections to her nomination and the Senate confirmed her. Roberts was deeply appreciative stating, "He has, in his own way, helped me and others like me.... And we're on the bench, and we're making decisions that may be very contrary to those he may make."[54]

THE *UNCLE TOM* AMONG US

Justice Thomas has said, "I am not an Uncle Tom ... I have not forgotten where I came from.... I feel a special responsibility to help our people." The quote demonstrates that Thomas has not opted out. Thomas's supporters, therefore, cannot inoculate him from criticism by contending that he has no racial obligations. He believes he does. Thus, if after weighing the evidence, a race member concludes that Thomas is more likely than not apathetic toward the group, then sanction is permissible.

---

[53] For more on the use of the black welfare recipient as a racial stereotype see, e.g., Note, *Dethroning the Welfare Queen: The Rhetoric of Reform*, 107 *Harvard Law Review* 2013 (1994); Williams, *Black Conservatives*; Meyer and Abramson, Strange Justice 40, 75.

[54] Merida and Fletcher, Supreme Discomfort 354–56. Additionally, Justice Thomas has a close relationship with Leah Sears, a black judge from Georgia's Supreme Court who has been described as "relatively liberal." Ward was supposedly on the short list of judges who President Obama might have nominated to the Supreme Court when Justice Sotomayor was appointed. Krissah Thompson, *Supreme Court Prospect Has Unlikely Ally*, Washington Post, May 10, 2009, available at: http://www.washingtonpost.com/wp-dyn/content/article/2009/05/09/AR2009050902519_pf.html.

After investigating his life, judicial opinions, and statements, the answer is clear. I would treat the man who claims that Clarence Thomas is not an *Uncle Tom* no differently than the man who claimed he was in two places at once, no differently than the man who claimed to have bested father time, no differently than the man who claimed to have caught fish in a desert. I have weighed the evidence. And the scales are lopsided. Justice Thomas is an *Uncle Tom*. He is uncommitted to the black plight.[55]

The case against Justice Thomas starts with his concocted rags-to-riches fairytale, his stage from which he attacks affirmative action. But if affirmative action is such a bad policy, why does he promulgate the myth that he lived an impoverished life and by sheer grit made it to the Supreme Court? Thomas has deceived the public about the impact these preferences have had on him. If he wants observers to view him as honest, why not simply admit that affirmative action impacted his life but tell the public how it harmed him? Does he not choose this route because affirmative action actually helped him? Worse yet, he positioned himself to benefit from affirmative action despite assailing it as a bad policy for other blacks. What is so special about him that he should benefit from affirmative action but no one else?

A good lawyer never asks questions to which he does not already have the answers. And I know Thomas has no decent replies to my queries. He, first, created a fictitious backstory; second, he railed against affirmative action while, third, positioning himself for opportunities that he knew would otherwise be denied to him if he were white. Affirmative action was good for him but no one else because his career in the conservative movement would flounder unless he opposed it. Panacea or poison, what Thomas truly believes about affirmative action is irrelevant. He told the rest that it was toxic while clandestinely ingesting it – that's what matters. These fouls are reprehensible enough on their own for one to conclude that Justice Thomas is more likely than not out for himself. The case is already that strong.

But Thomas has committed many more fouls. His friendships with Rush Limbaugh and Jesse Helms further corroborate Thomas's racial apathy. Justice Thomas's willingness to defend and befriend racists is repugnant. Helms endorsed blacks' genetic inferiority, racially harassed a black colleague, and race baited in elections. Lauding Helms would have been an impossible task for most blacks. His racist stench would disallow them from even coming close. It becomes far easier, however, if one is indifferent to the victims of Helms's attacks. Thomas appears impervious to the stench. The case strengthens.

[55] Ken Foskett, Judging Thomas: The Life and Times of Clarence Thomas 276 (2004).

Thomas's criticism of Justice Marshall should be joined with that of his sister, rendering it one powerful piece of evidence. Justice Thomas apparently found some benefit in publically attacking the two because the substance of both criticisms is weak. Marshall maligning the Revolutionary War era figures for their inhumane treatment of blacks should be innocuous; all should sympathize with that critique. Marshall, guided by historical truths, nonetheless perturbed some who prefer to whitewash historical injustice. Thomas ingratiated himself to those folk by censuring Marshall. Rather than recall racial injustice, he gave approval to those who wish to glorify a racist chapter in American history.

Thomas once remarked that to appease conservatives, "a black was required to become a caricature of sorts, providing sideshows of anti-black quips and attacks." Although conservatives distrusted him after this comment, he was right. Ronald Reagan was ushered into the White House, in part, on whites' backlash against the welfare state. Publicly lampooning his sister as a welfare queen matched a common appraisal of blacks: They would rather rely on the government than do hard work. But Thomas criticizing his own sister was dastardly, especially because the remark was based on a lie. His sister was not on welfare. Thomas's criticism sounds more like the antiblack quip that he once bemoaned. Thomas was the caricature. Thomas was the sideshow. And given his affirmative action deceptions and his willingness to befriend bigots, that he attacked Marshall and his sister to realize his personal ambitions is easy to believe. Blacks should debate Thomas's critique of the welfare state. But embarrassing one's own sister and giving credence to malicious characterizations of black women is a poor conversation starter. And the case strengthens more.[56]

Justice Thomas's deeply misguided attempt to place his worldview within the tradition of Frederick Douglass is just another damning piece of evidence. The contention that affirmative action hurts blacks is an acceptable argument that blacks should examine. But to completely alter a quote to make the point is beyond reprehensible. Butchering a speech of a treasured black icon to serve one's own personal interests is hard to overlook. Thomas knew the quote could not reasonably be interpreted as anti–affirmative action. Thus he doctored it. His *Fisher* and *Parents Involved* concurrences are likewise offensive. Again, perhaps affirmative action and state-enforced integrationism are pernicious. But equating University of Texas's affirmative action program to slavery and

---

[56] Meyer and Abramson, Strange Justice 16, 18; Kimberlé W. Crenshaw, *Race, Reform, and Retrenchment: Transformation and Legitimation in Antidiscrimination Law*, 101 Harvard Law Review 1331, 1336–37 (1988).

Jim Crow is insulting as is likening integrationists to segregationists. The case gets even stronger.

Justice Thomas's inconsistent Originalism and bizarre equal protection jurisprudence can be interpreted in many ways. Perhaps he is simply proffering a shoddy and unconvincing argument. Supreme Court justices' superior intellect is wrongly often assumed because they often purvey tortured logic behind substandard prose. Maybe that's the correct explanation. Or perhaps it's politics. Justice Scalia similarly departs from Originalism in affirmative action cases. Observers typically decry him for transparent political calculations. Justice Scalia opposes affirmative action and uses whatever math will get him to his preferred sum. That's the typical refrain of his detractors. Justice Thomas could likewise be charged with being disingenuous for the sake of reaching his preferred outcome.

But another interpretation is that Justice Thomas's arguments are pretextual. His sudden departure from Originalism and his strange reading of history can be deemed a cover for hidden motives. The argument is that his status relies on being against affirmative action. And, even if he knew it to be constitutional under Originalism, he would have to ignore that. Inconsistent Originalism, by itself, is insufficient to establish racial treachery. Yet it reveals the depth of his intellectual dishonesty. It is indeed another piece of evidence that further substantiates a well-supported narrative. And the case is complete.

Thomas, of course, will deny the charge. Perhaps his best exculpatory evidence is the work he does on behalf of black federal judge nominees. But a thousand highly respected black judges could defend him and they would make no difference. The sins remain. Thomas, a black conservative well positioned to test many assumptions in the black community, has so much evidence suggesting that he is racially indifferent. That should dishearten all. Thomas hinders the ability of blacks to assess the propriety of black conservatism. Indeed, anyone who agrees with his arguments can be sullied by concurring with one who purposefully distorts quotes of revered black leaders to suit one's own ends. Among blacks, Thomas can ruin an idea simply by endorsing it.

Justice Thomas, nonetheless, cannot allege that I prohibit dissent. Thomas likes to wage wars against his critics on accustomed terrain – the idea that blacks punish nonconformists. His overly worn rhetorical weapons still work well there. His substantive political opinions, however, are not the theater of this battle. My argument has nothing to do with his contrarianism. In fact, I argue that blacks should debate his positions. Rather, he is being charged with being unconcerned about the black plight. His musket will no longer do; he must pick up new arms. Blacks deserve his response.

One can predict one of Thomas's likely retorts. In fact, law professor Angela Onwuachi-Willig has already written a comprehensive defense of Thomas that matches my prediction. Onwuachi-Willig was compelled to defend him because, like Thurgood Marshall, Thomas is constantly slighted as lacking intellectual heft and derided as a puppet for a more respected jurist, in Thomas's case Justice Scalia, in Marshall's case Justice Brennan. Onwuachi-Willig contends that Thomas's ideas are all his own. She defends Thomas as being racially loyal, arguing that race is an important part of one's identity and manifests itself differently in each person. Thomas, Onwuachi-Willig holds, "is conservative precisely because he is black." She continues, "Much like black liberals whose life experiences have shaped their reactions to issues such as affirmative action in a way that makes them liberal, Justice Thomas's experiences with race have led him to adopt ideologies that are strictly based on self-reliance without government interference in a way that makes him conservative." She even concedes that his opinions take on a personal tone in racial cases, but argues that this is owed because of his "life experiences." I would imagine most would find this defense unavailing. I certainly do. That is not to say that Onwuachi-Willig's defense might not be convincing to some. But to my mind, Thomas is clearly an *Uncle Tom*, an especially reprehensible one at that.[57]

[57] Angela Onwuachi-Willig, *Just another Brother on the SCT?: What Justice Clarence Thomas Teaches Us about the Influence of Racial Identity*, 90 *Iowa Law Review* 931, 933–38 (2005). I am sympathetic because the idea that Justice Scalia is considered a cerebral heavyweight but Justice Thomas is not is a risible idea owed to racist assumptions of black intellect.

8

The Curious Case of *Uncle Tom*

BLACK CONSERVATIVES – THE NEW *UNCLE TOMS*

THE BURN OF JUST ONE *Uncle Tom* accusation is agonizing. To endure prolonged exposure to the epithet as has Clarence Thomas is a harrowing experience known to but a few. One might imagine the agony being so acute that he commiserates with his similarly afflicted kin: black conservatives. Like Thomas, they insist that they have been wronged. And many are right. Conservative ideology, like conservative jurisprudence, should not place adherents directly in the fire. As always, the key inquiry is whether the person defied constructive norms. The burn black conservatives endure is sometimes defensible, although not for the typical reasons.

The black right comprises a deep pool of intellectual thought, including a viewpoint holding that antiblack attitudes, discrimination, institutional racism, and structural inequalities have no appreciable effect on blacks' lives and thus are unworthy of much attention. Discrimination against whites, however, namely affirmative action, is a scourge on society, requiring an immediate cure and constant discussion. That is, some black conservatives insist that whites, not blacks, are the true casualties of racial injustice.

But this viewpoint is erroneous. Blacks should debate the seriousness of racism – overt, covert, and unconscious – and structural inequality. And some might contend that blacks would fare best by focusing solely on self-help measures and ignoring protest activities. Such views do not signal betrayal. Those denying the salience of racism in all of its many forms, however, are likely, although not certainly, cooperating with antiblack interests.[1]

[1] Ian F. Haney Lopez, *Institutional Racism: Judicial Conduct and a New Theory of Racial Discrimination*, 109 *Yale Law Journal* 1717 (2000); Michael C. Dawson, Black Visions: The Roots of Contemporary African-American Political Ideologies 289 (2001).

This is true for at least two reasons. First, a wealth of evidence so convincingly establishes how discrimination injures blacks that deniers warrant suspicion. Job applicants with black-sounding names, for instance, are 50 percent less likely to receive interview callbacks than are identical candidates. Employers even prefer whites with criminal records over blacks without one.[2]

When blacks try to use their income to improve their lives, discrimination persists. A study using data from 2004 to 2008 revealed that mortgage lenders were more likely to push black borrowers into high-risk subprime mortgages than whites even when keeping credit scores constant. "[A]mong borrowers with a FICO score of over 660 (indicating good credit), African Americans … received a high interest rate loan more than three times as often as white borrowers." In 2011, the Justice Department reached a $355 million settlement with Bank of America for discrimination against minority borrowers.[3]

When blacks sue their discriminator, race shortens the long arm of justice. Law professor Regina Austin found that racial stereotypes diminish damages awarded to blacks in civil cases. An all-white jury, for instance, lowered damages awarded to a deserving plaintiff because she was a "fat, black woman on welfare who would simply blow the money on liquor, cigarettes, jai alai, bingo or the dog track." Courts, moreover, still allow juries to use race-based actuarial tables when determining monetary damages. As torts scholar Martha Chamallas notes, "When lost earnings are calculated using race-based tables … the awards [for blacks] are considerably lower than they would be for comparably injured white victims." The factors that produced these economic harms scar blacks in every facet of their lives. The idea that discrimination poses no threat to blacks is, therefore, fictitious.[4]

The second reason supporting suspicion of blacks discounting the power of discrimination is that antiblack interests want black defectors to voice such arguments. In the previous epochs of *Uncle Tom*'s use, the most condemnable blacks excused or condoned discrimination, appreciating white supremacy rewards its black caregivers. An encyclopedia of sorts, this book catalogues

---

[2] Marianne Bertrand and Sendhil Mullainathan, *Are Emily and Greg More Employable than Lakisha and Jamal? A Field Experiment on Labor Market Discrimination*, available at: http://www.nber.org/papers/w9873.pdf?new_window=1.

[3] Devah Pager, *The Mark of a Criminal Record*, 108 *American Journal of Sociology* 937, 960 (2003); Debbie Cruenstein Bocian and Roberto G. Quercia, Lost Ground, 2011: Center for Responsible Lending, Disparities in Mortgage Lending and Foreclosures 5 (2011); Charlie Savage, *Countrywide Will Settle a Bias Suit*, New York Times, Dec. 22, 2011, at B1.

[4] Martha Chamallas and Jennifer B. Wriggins, The Measure of Injury: Race, Gender, and Tort Law 33 (2010); Martha Chamallas, *Civil Rights in Ordinary Tort Cases: Race, Gender, and the Calculation of Economic Loss*, 38 *Loyola Los Angeles Law Review* 1435, 1438–39 (2005).

treachery, teaching a valuable lesson: Some blacks promote the degradation of the race. *Uncle Toms* are among us and to deny this is to give them aid and comfort at the expense of blacks' well-being.

In the 1940s, for instance, Rev. E. M. Wilson, working with local segregationist leaders, participated in a plot that forced local black businessmen to sign onto a statement that supported the governor of Alabama's desire to discriminate in the assigning of war contracts. That same decade, a black man named Ned Davis told a South Carolinian businessmen's club that whites would always be blacks' "masters." The likelihood that he benefited after that speech is high. In the 1950s, Percy Greene and Rev. H. H. Humes, black newspapermen from Mississippi, were paid by the White Sovereignty Commission to disparage the civil rights movement in their newspapers. In the 1960s, Charles Evers, a local leader, noted that black Mississippians still collaborated with white supremacist organizations in exchange for rewards. Also in the 1960s, Rev. Clinton Boone of Hempstead, New York, dissuaded blacks from joining the NAACP and implored them to stop racial protests. Local blacks surmised that he sought to curry favor with the mayor. This is just a sampling of the blacks charged with participating in racial subordination. Each endorsed positions or completed tasks that would serve antiblack interests. In this epoch, blatant offenders are worthless. Calling whites the "masters" would be fruitless in contemporary discourse. The zeitgeist calls for subtlety.

Those antagonistic to blacks' plight always seek to distance blacks from power that could intervene to improve their condition. The arguments furthering this goal have changed throughout time. Slavery defenders denounced the efforts of abolitionists by maintaining that blacks' inferiority and innate brutality necessitated the peculiar institution. During Jim Crow, scientific racism supported the racial caste system. Blacks' flaws, that is, always render government intervention improper, according to blacks' foes. Understanding this history enables one to predict that the racially hostile would proffer the following three-pronged argument.

First, racism has no or only a negligible effect on the lives of black people. Second, blacks are subordinate because of their own failures. And third, public policy must therefore not intervene. The third prong never truly changes. The antiblack argument always has the same conclusion: The state should not seek to improve the status of the race. Black problems require black solutions.

To admit that discrimination diminishes the quality of black life is to offend this worldview. Just as ardent slavery and segregation defenders appreciated that conceding the equality of the Negro would undercut their positions, those demanding that blacks are culpable for their sorrowful present understand that they must never acknowledge that discrimination still injures blacks. It so happens that a contingent of blacks espouse the "black fault ideology."

This ideology is related to two works, Charles Murray and Richard J. Hernnstein's *The Bell Curve* (1994) and Dinesh D'Souza's *The End of Racism* (1996). Whereas *The Bell Curve* asserted that blacks' genetic intellectual inferiority explained their subordinate status, *The End of Racism* blamed blacks' cultural inferiority. The two books agreed, however, that the government must not intervene on blacks' behalf because public policy offered no remedy. Blacks' own failures, whether genetic or cultural, fully account for the race's subordinate status. Racism – which has been vastly overstated – has had no impact. The goal of the right-wing movement out of which these books sprang seeks first, to marginalize blacks; second, to rebuff all attempts to treat black ills as worthy of national solutions; and third, to frame blacks as the sole author of their melancholy saga. This is the thinking among the antiblack to which the black fault ideology is inextricably linked.

The tribulations of black economist Glenn Loury anchor this discussion. Loury had membership within this movement before fleeing in the mid-1990s. Loury decried *The Bell Curve*, *The End of Racism*, and Stephen and Abigail Thernstrom's *America in Black and White* (1997). The Thernstroms's book too held blacks' own supposed pathological behaviors responsible for the lack of racial progress. Loury penned a critical review, charging the Thernstroms with being so wedded to the idea that public policy offered no solutions to the race problem that they misread their own data.[5]

While a part of this movement, Loury realized that his black skin limited his group privileges. White neoconservatives were permitted kinship with their ethnic groups. Jewish neoconservatives, for instance, could show affinity for their people. Yet, when he expressed black solidarity, his white colleagues would, in his words, "begrudge me." Drinking from the fountain of ethnic pride, that is, was for whites only. After denouncing *The Bell Curve*, Loury claimed he was implored to "get off the fence. You're either with us or you're with them," confirming that he was expected to contribute to a team that wanted its black players to champion works that endorsed their own genetic inferiority. "It felt as if they expected me to be a self-hating black," he said, "in order to be a neoconservative."[6]

[5] Glenn C. Loury, *The Conservative Line on Race*, The Atlantic, Nov. 1997, at 144–54, available at: http://www.theatlantic.com/past/docs/issues/97nov/race.htm.
[6] Id.; Christopher Alan Bracey, Saviors or Sellouts: The Promise and Peril of Black Conservatism from Booker T. Washington on Condoleezza Rice 135–42 (2008).

Loury recounted going to a 1990s Harvard event attended by popular left-leaning black Harvard professors, the Cornel Wests and Charles Ogletrees of the world. Jesse Jackson too attended. Loury approached Jackson and apologized for a 1980s article he wrote assailing Jackson for supposedly abusing the civil rights legacy for his own personal gain. Loury regretted writing it. He wrote the piece, he disclosed, to appease his white bosses for whom he wanted to work in the future. "I was doing someone else's bidding," Loury revealed. Black linguist John McWhorter, who too formerly moved in the same circles, revealed that this camp obsessively desired that he criticize Jesse Jackson. The movement fixates on disproving liberals, particularly on racial matters. Loury, in reviewing *America in Black and White*, wrote that when "[r]eading it, one cannot escape the impression that the enemy is being engaged."[7]

Lowry's firsthand observations while inside the gates provide valuable intelligence. Discarding the white sheets and forsaking the segregation-defending rhetoric, the antiblack have once again emerged and formed a movement that would throw a million sticks and stones if it would hurt racial progress. This cannot be denied. Every black member violates the norm against furthering the enemy's interests. Expressing the black fault ideology strongly indicates affiliation within this movement. The problem, however, is that this movement is nebulous. It's unlike the KKK or a White Citizens Council with clearly defined memberships. There must be a rebuttable presumption, therefore, that anyone who conveys the black fault ideology works on behalf of antiblack interests. Blacks who fit this definition will certainly argue that they are not what they appear. And they may be able to establish that even though they may look like *Uncle Toms* they actually are not. But observers should feel comfortable concluding that they are at least wearing an *Uncle Tom* uniform.

Some will discourage ascertaining whether championing this ideology is sanction-worthy. Just deal with the argument, they will aver. That position, however, must be rejected. The black fault ideology, when proffered by non-blacks, appears unduly harsh, causing listeners to question its propriety. But blacks can use their race to dispel those questions. Black skin, in this context, conveys to listener that the speaker necessarily has the group's best interest at heart. The listener's skepticism consequently dissipates. In response to the power of racial identity in this context, blacks must interrogate the righteousness of the speaker. Blacks who are in position to inspect the Trojan horse but fail to do so have opened the gates to bad faith actors who will corrupt national race conversations that produce the policy decisions affecting blacks'

7   The Glenn Show, bloggingheads.tv, Feb. 18, 2013, available at: http://bloggingheads.tv/video
    s/10084?in=22:09&out=24:54; Loury, *The Conservative Line on Race.*

lives. The stakes are high. Permitting blacks belonging to a hostile intellectual movement to sabotage the group's welfare would be a strategic blunder.[8]

Thomas Sowell, perhaps stronger than any other, espouses the black fault ideology. Sowell, "the patron saint of modern-day black conservatism," constantly defends himself from accusations of racial betrayal. "If you're black and don't think of yourself as a victim," he wrote, "you must be a self-loathing Uncle Tom." Sowell, however, does not just play defense; he attacks his critics with equally harsh language. Sowell claims that "black leadership is not about leading black people, but extracting what they can from white people and – above all – maintaining themselves in office or in positions of visibility." Sowell delights in condemning black leaders. He puts the word *leaders* inside quotation marks (i.e., black "leaders"), obviously poking his adversaries. Sowell denies that liberal black leaders are faithful race representatives. Rather, he finds them to be solely self-interested. Sowell, therefore, cannot fault others for examining him to determine whether he too is compromised. Hypocrisy is a terrible quality.[9]

As early as the 1970s, Sowell declared that the civil rights struggle was complete. He disfavors antidiscrimination laws, arguing that because racism is inefficient and economically irrational, the free market discourages it. A white employer, in other words, will not opt for an inferior white candidate over a better black one because the decision hurts the employer's bottom line. Sowell also refuses to attribute racism to blacks' subordinate status, instead arguing, through innumerable books and articles, that cultural failings explain lagging socioeconomic indicators. And Sowell harvests deep ire for affirmative action, insisting that it hurts blacks by making their accomplishments appear undeserved while also fostering white resentment.[10]

In 1981, Columnist Carl T. Rowan wrote, "These are times when I want to ask the Lord to deliver us back to the days of Stepin Fetchit, Aunt Jemima and Uncle Tom" because although those types were embarrassing, Sowell and his "educated" ilk were far more dangerous. Rowan was responding to a television interview where Sowell refused to admit that employment discrimination affected black employment rates. The black fault ideology brooks no assertion that discrimination diminishes black opportunity.[11]

---

[8] Cheryl Harris, *Whiteness as Property*, 106 *Harvard Law Review* 1707, 1714 (1993).

[9] Rona Marech, *S.F. State Prof Writes the Book on Black Politics*, San Francisco Chronicle, Aug., 29, 2003, at E8; Peter Worthington, *Black Vs. Black: A Bitter War of Words Erupts over Affirmative Action in America*, Toronto Sun, June 1, 2002, at 15; Thomas Sowell, *Black "Leaders" Ignore Real Needs*, Chicago Sun-Times, July 19, 1998, at 26.

[10] Andrea Yvette Simpson, Race, Class and African American Political Ideology 56 (PhD dissertation 1994); Bracey, Saviors or Sellouts 128–32.

[11] Carl T. Rowan, ... *Or Quisling?*, Washington Post, Sept. 29, 1981, at A19.

Sowell contends, moreover, that affirmative action programs, minimum wage, and government intervention hurt blacks. In that vein, in 1981, he wrote a column entitled "Affirmative Action Harms the Disadvantaged," asserting that affirmative action had actually impeded black progress. He argued that since the implementation of quotas and affirmative action, minorities' income gap widened. But an economist with Sowell's experience knows that correlation does not mean causation, especially because the economic climate of the late 1960s was decidedly better than that of the early 1980s. The average unemployment rate in 1981 was 7.6 percent. When President Nixon implemented the Philadelphia Plan in 1969, often considered a lodestar for affirmative action programs, the unemployment rate for the year was 3.5 percent. The United States was in the beginning of a recession when Sowell wrote his column, and most economists understand that blacks fare far worse in economic turmoil relative to whites. For an economist to ignore these basic facts when determining the efficacy of affirmative action was a grave error. Disagreeing with affirmative action is fine. But to employ patently specious arguments to knock the program is unscrupulous and rightly raises suspicions. Columnist Charles E. Belle concurred, responding to Sowell in an editorial with the subtitle "Uncle Tom Is Not Dead." "Some people reading Sowell's article will believe that white America has at last found what it has always wanted," Belle asserted, "a black American soul sold for a little money, a minute amount of media limelight, and the promise of eternal whiteness from the White House."[12]

Sowell further lowered himself in the eyes of many when he called *The Bell Curve* "one of the most sober, responsible, thorough and thoughtful books to be published in years." *The Bell Curve* was pilloried in the national press. In an editorial, Sowell praised the authors, Herrnstein and Murray, and condemned their critics. He actually recommended the book as a Christmas gift. Simply put, Sowell showed much more warmth toward polemicists who disparaged blacks with flawed and discredited methodology than he did the media who defended blacks. To be clear, Sowell did not endorse the genetic intellectual inferiority premise of the book. But that he would support the authors of such a racist book further evidences that Sowell cooperates with antiblack interests and, moreover, is apathetic toward blacks. The case of Glenn Loury informs that this right-wing movement views itself as engaged in a battle with the

[12] Thomas Sowell, *Affirmative Action Harms the Disadvantaged*, Wall Street Journal, July 28, 1981, at 28; Charles E. Belle, *Business in the Black*, New Journal and Guide, Sept. 3, 1981, at 8; *Databases, Tables & Calculators by Subjection*, available at: http://data.bls. gov/timeseries/LNU04000000?years_option=all_years&periods_option=specific_ periods&periods=Annual+Data; Kevin L. Yuill, Richard Nixon and the Rise of Affirmative Action: The Pursuit of Racial Equality in an Era of Limits 136 (2006).

enemy: liberals. Thus, Sowell operates in a space that dictates that when the authors of a book endorsing black inferiority are warring with the supposed liberal media, Sowell had better defend those denigrating blacks. Sowell, however, should have done what Loury did – left.[13]

Sowell's kindred spirit, conservative economist Walter Williams, has suffered a similar fortune. Like Sowell, Williams decries governmental intervention in the economy, believing that social programs meant to alleviate poverty actually exacerbate it. But his controversial racial musings explain his frequent run-ins with *Uncle Tom*. Williams wrote, for instance, that blacks prospered from slavery because "[m]ost black Americans are in the solid middle class ... [and] if we totaled the income black Americans earned each year, and thought of ourselves as a separate nation, we'd be the 14th or 15th richest nation." On another occasion, Williams questioned whether apartheid served South African blacks better. In light of high crime and rampant AIDS infections, Williams wrote that "Africa's past experience should give Western anti-apartheid activists some pause for thought. Wouldn't it be the supreme tragedy if South African blacks might ponder at some future date ... whether they were better off under apartheid?"[14]

Walter Williams praised the *End of Racism*. Glenn Loury and Robert L. Woodson, another black conservative, both left the American Enterprise Institute in 1995 because its author, Dinesh D'Souza, was also a research fellow at the think tank. D'Souza argued in the book that African slavery was not the evil that it is portrayed to be. He insisted, furthermore, that segregation protected blacks. Defending Jim Crow, D'Souza wrote that only "an infinitesimal fraction of the black population" was lynched. And he scribed that "a natural hierarchy of racial abilities would predict and fully account for" blacks' lower socioeconomic status. Columnist William Raspberry believed that D'Souza took "delight" in demeaning blacks. As proof, Raspberry quoted the book's discussion of varying slave identities. "Slaves developed widely different personalities on the plantation: the playful Sambo, the sullen 'field nigger,' the dependable Mammy, the sly and inscrutable trickster. Some of these personality types are still recognizable." Publically rebuking the *End of Racism* was important to both Woodson and Loury because, Loury said,

[13] Michael L. Ondanntje, Black Conservative Intellectuals in Modern America 19 (2010); Thomas Sowell, *Why Can't We Talk About Intelligence Intelligently*, Seattle Times, Oct. 26, 1994, available at: http://community.seattletimes.nwsource.com/archive/?date=19941026&slug=1937979.

[14] Walter Williams, *Reparations for Slavery*, Capitalism Magazine, Jan. 12, 2001, available at: capmag.com/article.asp?ID=89; Walter Williams, *Were Blacks Better Off under Apartheid?*, available at: www.jewishworldreview.com/cols/williams010902.asp.

silence "in the face of this book, written by a conservative colleague, would make us Uncle Toms."[5]

Sowell and Williams were not only silent, they supported the book. Williams praised it, as did Sowell, calling it "[p]erhaps the most important new book" in 1995. And as with *The Bell Curve*, Sowell recommended *The End of Racism* as a Christmas gift. Loury was correct; their support for the book was treacherous. Both are guilty of disobeying the norm that proscribes collaborating with those hostile to blacks.[16]

Dealing with Sowell first, he not only endorses the black fault ideology, he wrote the song. And he has been singing that one hit forever. Indeed, he has repeated the same lyrics in his unending stream of books and editorials that has flowed for five decades. He writes in other areas. But that music has few listeners. His high standing in the right-wing movement has been wholly earned with his undying adherence to the black fault ideology. That creates a presumption that he has violated constructive norms that his warm support for *The Bell Curve* and *The End of Racism* confirms. Championing those books and even advocating that people buy them as a Christmas gifts is unforgiveable.[17]

Sowell's kindred spirit, Walter Williams, commits the same misdeeds. Arguing that blacks are better off because of slavery and that black South Africans were better off under apartheid rightly strikes observers as comments a black conservative proffers to prove himself, the price of initiation. Loury revealed that his unfair criticism of Jesse Jackson was an act of appeasement. Walter Williams's arguments appear analogous.

When Loury was implored to "pick a side," he deserted a movement that lauded books arguing that blacks are intellectually and culturally inferior. Woodson, who moved in the same circles, went AWOL for the same reasons. Sowell and Williams stayed, however, and have continued cavorting with blacks' enemies. Blacks not actually invested in the group should be criticized when they poison the debate. And these men are pure arsenic. Sowell and Williams may try to avoid punishment by opting out. They have necessarily opted in, however, because both use their blackness to further their racial politics. And these men are not alone. Indeed, the mold remained after Sowell and Williams were made. Other blacks have the same look and feel, including Larry Elder, Armstrong Williams, and Shelby Steele.

---

[5] Ondanntje, Black Conservative Intellectuals in Modern America 19; William Raspberry, *"End of Racism" Can Only Serve to Perpetuate It*, Chicago Tribune, Sept. 18, 1995, at A19.

[16] Thomas Sowell, *Some Last-Minute Gift Ideas*, San Antonio Express-News, Dec. 20, 1995, at 1.

[17] Id.

Like Williams and Sowell, Ward Connerly, the anti–affirmative action crusader, has been perpetually targeted. Connerly rose to prominence in 1996 when he successfully campaigned for the passage of Proposition 209, which banned affirmative action in California state universities. In 1999, Connerly went to Florida to end affirmative action in public universities there. During a speech at Florida State University College of Law, one student called Connerly an "Uncle Tom." In 2003, Connerly campaigned against affirmative action in Michigan and was censured as a "segregationist" and "Uncle Tom of the new millennium" at University of Michigan. In his *Boondocks* comic strip, Aaron McGruder dubbed Connerly a "self-loathing traitor to [his] people" and a "boot-licking Uncle Tom." The *Oakland Tribune*, too, airs its grievances against Connerly in editorial art, calling him an "Uncle Tom," an "Oreo," and "lawn jockey for the ruling class."[18]

In his book *Creating Equal: My Fight against Race Preferences* (2000), Connerly recounted a conversation he had with Reverend Amos Brown, a San Francisco preacher. "Brown began by apologizing for having characterized me in one of his sermons as an 'Uncle Tom,'" Connerly wrote, "but he said that the apology was directed to Tom ... not me, because Tom had at least come to the defense of his people against their slave masters, while I was selling them out." "'So you don't actually deserve to be accorded the title of 'Uncle Tom,'" Brown told Connerly. Black public intellectual Tony Brown, who himself opposes affirmative action, asserted that Connerly "flat out hates black people."[19]

Ward Connerly allies with the Pacific Legal Foundation, a California legal organization that brings lawsuits focusing on racial equality under the law. Their lawsuits are generally on behalf of whites complaining of state-sponsored racial discrimination. Connerly has no voice for blacks with similar complaints. Courts, for instance, can use race-based actuarial tables to determine damages in lawsuits. Connerly is silent on this. He, instead, backed the Racial Privacy Initiative, which would have proscribed California agencies from collecting racial data "that makes it possible to identify, track, monitor or prove discrimination." The state ballot measure was defeated by Californians by a 2 to 1 margin. But had it passed, enforcing civil rights laws would have been impossible. One *San Francisco Chronicle* editorial quipped that the initiative

---

[18]　Tyler Bridges, *Ballot Drive Will Seek Affirmative Action Ban Florida Campaign Targets Public Sector*, Miami Herald, Mar. 15, 1999, at 1A; Kim North, *Activist Targets U-M Policy*, Detroit Free Press, July 9, 2003, Page 1A; *The Boondocks*, Nov. 17, 2003; Deborah Kong, *Backer of Proposition 54 Challenges the Way Californians Look at Race*, Associated Press State & Local Wire, Sept. 15, 2003; Noemie Emery, *Connerly's Courage; and His Foes' Cowardice*, The Weekly Standard, Apr. 3, 2000, at 35.

[19]　Ward Connerly, Creating Equal: My Fight against Race Preferences 82 (2000); Allen-Taylor and Jesse Douglas, *Conscious of Color*, 6 ColorLines 8, 8–11 (2003).

should have been renamed the "You Can Discriminate and No One Will Be Able to Tell Initiative."[20]

Connerly is not an *Uncle Tom* for disagreeing with race-conscious admissions policies. Connerly's broader actions, however, are inconsistent with one who cares about the race. The case against Connerly is fairly straightforward. First, a black man making a livelihood against affirmative action is suspicious. Many blacks who undoubtedly care about the welfare of black people oppose affirmative action. But few individuals, regardless of race, make it their cause célèbre. Connerly finds racial preferences to be impermissible under the Equal Protection Clause and bad policy. That's fine. But he is utterly silent on discrimination aimed at blacks. That Connerly collaborates with an organization that fights racial discrimination but nearly all of its clients are white further suggests his priorities. And the clincher was championing the Racial Privacy Initiative, which would have rendered it impossible to enforce antidiscrimination law or combat racial profiling and other forms of racial discrimination. Each of these pieces of evidence, when stacked together, builds a case so strong that it cannot be toppled. About the plight of blacks, Connerly cares not.[21]

Not all black conservatives defy constructive norms. Take John McWhorter, for instance. Although McWhorter denies that he fits into the black conservative box, many of his views do. A linguistics professor and author, McWhorter has opined on issues ranging from black speech to black culture – the latter generating great controversy. In his book *Losing the Race: Self-Sabotage in Black America* (2000) McWhorter beset black culture, offering three explanations for racial inequality: "the cult of victimology, cult of separatism, and the cult of anti-intellectualism." In one chapter he averred that blacks stunt their progress by perpetually thinking of themselves as victims. "Separatism Makes Us Inferiors," he asserted in another. His most striking point relates to the lack of intellectual curiosity among blacks. He opined that "black students do so poorly in school decade after decade because of a virus of Anti-intellectualism that infects the black community." His proof is anecdotal evidence pulled from his experiences as a Berkeley professor. He claimed that although he has had

[20] Andy Barlow and Troy Duster, *Racial Privacy/ An Invitation to Racial Discrimination*, San Francisco Chronicle, May 10, 2002, available at: http://www.sfgate.com/opinion/openforum/article/Racial-Privacy-Initiative-An-invitation-to-2838443.php; John Rossomando, *California Initiative Seeks to End Racial Classifications*, cnsnews.com, available at: http://cnsnews.com/news/article/california-initiative-seeks-end-racial-classifications; Brandi Wilkins Catanese, The Problem of Color[blind]: Racial Transgression and the Politics of Black Performance 4 (2011).

[21] Eva Jefferson Patterson, *And Still We Rise*, 6 *African-American Law & Policy Report* 15, 16 (2004).

"slackers" of all races, "black undergraduates at Berkeley tended to be among the worst students on campus, by any estimation." One who reproached black culture as broadly as McWhorter did, particularly with largely anecdotal evidence, provokes *Uncle Tom* accusations.[22]

Whereas Sowell and Williams reflexively deny racism, McWhorter decries it when he sees it. During the 2012 presidential race, for instance, Republican nominee Mitt Romney produced campaign television advertisements falsely accusing President Obama of gutting welfare work requirements. When voters think of welfare, they imagine lazy blacks sitting on plastic-covered couches choosing government checks over employment. Many onlookers thought the Romney campaign was playing on racial fears, falsely implying that the black president was handing out free gifts to shiftless Negroes. McWhorter agreed, calling it "a clear example of race baiting."[23] Likewise, McWhorter had no qualms with denouncing Republican efforts to pass voter identification laws, measures enacted to reduce minority voter participation. McWhorter wrote that the "laws have a viciously disparate impact on blacks, and they should be condemned." And McWhorter criticized Newt Gingrich's suggestion that because poor youth lack work role models they should serve as janitors in their schools, claiming the comment recalled negative stereotypes about blacks.[24]

[22] The Glenn Show, bloggingheads.tv, Feb. 18, 2013, available at: http://bloggingheads.tv/videos/15533; James Joyner, *What Sarah Palin Can Teach Us About Writing*, Outside the Beltway, June 18, 2011, available at: http://www.outsidethebeltway.com/what-sarah-palin-can-teach-us-about-writing/; Michael A. Fletcher, *The Linguist's Fighting Words*, Washington Post, Jan. 3, 2001, at C01; Bracey, Saviors or Sellouts 146–48; McWhorter, Losing the Race 1–49, 81, 83, 89.

[23] Jamelle Bouie, *In New Ad, Mitt Romney Repeats False Attack on Obama's Welfare Policy*, Washington Post, Aug. 13, 2012, available at: http://www.washingtonpost.com/blogs/plum-line/post/in-new-ad-mitt-romney-repeats-false-attack-on-obamas-welfare-policy/2012/08/13/92cda562-e547-11e1-9739-eef99c5fb285_blog.html; Ed Kilgore, *Romney's Utterly Mendacious (and Effective) New "Welfare Queen" Attack*, New Republic, Aug. 8, 2012, available at: http://www.newrepublic.com/blog/plank/105911/romneys-utterly-mendacious-and-unfortunately-effective-new-attack-obama-and-welfar.

[24] John McWhorter, *Mitt's Despicable Welfare Attack*, New York Daily News, Aug. 9, 2012, available at: http://www.nydailynews.com/opinion/mitt-despicable-welfare-attack-article-1.1131974; Amy Bingham, *Trump, Gingrich to Create Apprentice-Style Program for Poor School Kids*, abcnews.com, Dec. 5, 2011, available at: http://abcnews.go.com/blogs/politics/2011/12/trump-gingrich-to-create-apprentice-style-program-for-poor-school-kids/; John McWhorter, *Is Romney a Race Baiter?*, The Daily Beast, Aug. 29, 2012, available at: http://www.thedailybeast.com/articles/2012/08/29/is-romney-a-race-baiter.html; John McWhorter, *Letter to a Young Conservative: Why They Call Us Uncle Toms*, The Root, Dec. 7, 2010, available at: http://www.theroot.com/views/why-they-call-us-uncle-toms?page=0,1; John McWhorter, *No More Forums about a Black Agenda*, The Root, Mar. 16, 2011, available at: http://www.theroot.com/views/no-more-forums-about-black-agenda?page=0,1,; Elicia Dover, *Gingrich Says Poor Children Have No Work Habits*, abcnews.com, Dec. 1, 2011, available at: http://abcnews.go.com/blogs/politics/2011/12/gingrich-says-poor-children-have-no-work-ethic/.

McWhorter should not be grouped with the likes of Sowell and Williams who would never articulate such comments, possibly because doing so would threaten their standing in various right-wing intellectual circles. As happened to Loury, they would be told to "pick a side." Because of *Losing the Race,* some may seek to brand him with the *Uncle Tom* label. But that would be an error. McWhorter does not subscribe to the black fault ideology. He deems the idea that black uplift cannot occur outside of blacks going it alone "unduly pessimistic." McWhorter argues "that there are societal interventions short of a new civil rights revolution that must be drummed up by blacks and fellow travelers because they have been shown to make a difference in poor black people's lives." *Losing the Race* might have greatly suffered from over-claims, an over-reliance on anecdotes, and an overall lack of academic rigor. Yet McWhorter is not a voice that blacks should discount by lumping him with the likes of Sowell and Williams.[25]

ALTHOUGH FEW IN NUMBER, BLACK Republican politicians have been uniformly assigned to the *Uncle Tom* camp. Unlike black intellectuals, however, the requisite evidence to locate them there is lacking. Black Republican politicians lack the library of musings that Sowell and Williams have. Many might be Sowell and Williams clones. But the evidence says they look different. In short, those who have charged them with racial treachery have failed to prove their case. They are not *Uncle Toms.*

Gary Franks, for example, a Republican congressman from Connecticut, fell victim to destructive norm management. In 1994, Franks testified in federal court in Georgia that intentionally creating black districts amounted to a "form of apartheid" and was bad policy. Some blacks favor the deliberate creation of such districts, insisting they best ensure black congressional representation. Outside the courthouse, protestors toted signs telling "Uncle Tom Gary Franks [to] Go Home." Georgia Democratic representative Bill McKinney called Franks "a White Judas" who should "be ashamed of [himself]." Democratic Missouri representative William Clay dubbed Franks "a Negro Dr. Kevorkian, a pariah, who gleefully assists in suicidal conduct to destroy his own race" with his "foot-shuffling, head-scratching 'Amos and Andy' brand of 'Uncle Tom-ism.'" Clay added that Franks was a "gun for hire willing to assassinate ... blacks" who desires "to maim and kill other blacks for the gratification and entertainment of ... white racists."[26]

25 McWhorter, *Letter to a Young Conservative.*
26 Rhonda Cook, *11th District "Apartheid," Congressman Testifies,* Atlanta Journal and Constitution, July 26, 1994, at C3; Jeff Jacobs, *Name Calling: Liberals Get a Free Ride,* Times-Picayune, Jan. 2, 1997, at B7.

Franks's prosecutors erred. His argument – concentrating black voters into single districts hurts society – was well within acceptable debate, certainly nothing eyebrow raising. In fact, the idea that majority-minority districts benefit blacks is questionable. Some political scientists posit that outside the South, blacks' political power in congressional elections is maximized by distributing blacks equally across electoral districts. In the South, power is maximized with as many districts that are as close to 47 percent black as possible and the remaining black voters are evenly distributed throughout the other districts. Wedging Southern blacks into 80 percent black districts actually reduces blacks' electoral strength, meaning that Franks's detractors were wrong to even criticize him. Franks, in short, was not an *Uncle Tom*.[27]

During Franks's congressional stint, only one other black Republican roamed Capitol Hill, J. C. Watts. And he too endured *Uncle Tom* jeers. The case was not proven against him either. The Oklahoma congressman recounted, "I have been called an Uncle Tom, a sell out [*sic*], [and] a national disgrace" for being a black Republican. Even his father quipped that "[a] black person voting for a Republican is like a chicken voting for Colonel Sanders." His uncle, a civil rights leader who marched with Dr. King, agreed, saying that Republicans "have brainwashed him real good."[28]

Watts denied that Republicans have hoodwinked him, instead arguing that black Democrats are the ones who had been duped. In 1997, he told a reporter that "some so-called leaders out there are 'race-hustling poverty pimps'.... They talk a lot about slavery ... but they're perfectly happy to have just moved us to another plantation. What scares them the most is that black people might break out of the racial groupthink and start thinking for themselves." As true with Franks, Watts is simply a conservative politician. No evidence proves that he has violated any constructive norms. His detractors are merely deeming that being a Republican is per se evidence of duplicity. That thinking must be rejected.[29]

Michael Steele, like Franks and Watts, was likewise wrongly denounced as an *Uncle Tom*. Steele made history when he was elected to head the Republican National Committee in 2009. When running for the vacant Senate seat in Maryland in 2006, he was called an *Uncle Tom* and a liberal

[27] Lani Guinier, *Groups, Representation, and Race-Conscious Districting: A Case of the Emperor's Clothes*, 71 *Texas Law Review* 1589 (1993); Charles Cameron, David Epstein, and Sharyn O'Halloran, *Do Majority-Minority Districts Maximize Substantive Black Representation in Congress*, 90 *The American Political Science Review* 794, 807–08 (1996).

[28] Jim Myers, *Controversy Lingers over Watts' Remarks, Lawmaker's Ties to Other Black Leaders May Suffer*, Tulsa World, Feb. 9, 1997, at A15; Toby Harnden, *America's "Great Black Hope": Congressman and Former Ottawa Rough Rider J.C. Watts Says He's Tired of Being Singled Out because of His Race*, Ottawa Citizen, Jan. 4, 2003, at A10.

[29] J. C. Watts Jr., *What Color Is a Conservative? My Life and My Politics* 199 (2002).

Web site depicted him as a minstrel character. But other than simply being a black Republican, why he has been called an *Uncle Tom* is unclear. When leading the RNC, Steele demonstrated that he was no apologist, criticizing the GOP for its Southern Strategy "that alienated many minority voters by focusing on the white male vote in the South." And he also argued that life is tougher for black politicians. "Barack Obama has a slimmer margin [of error]. A lot of folks do," he said. "It's a different role for me to play and others to play and that's just the reality of it." Blacks seeking to be custodians of the racial status quo cannot and will not make such statements. These comments cause the antiblack to recoil in horror; he dared say race impacts blacks' lives. Steele is no *Uncle Tom*, and indicting him with racial treachery is wrongheaded.[30]

A far closer call is Allen West, a Florida Republican congressman who lost reelection in 2012. West, an intemperate speaker, never wanted for camera time during his two-year congressional stint. White conservatives fancied his flavor of invective rhetoric. Blacks, however, typically had no taste for it and routinely denounced him as an *Uncle Tom*. West stridently criticized Obama to the delight of his right-wing friends, once remarking, "I can't stand the guy. I absolutely can't stand him." West also chastised blacks for voting for Democrats and black Democratic leaders, who, he claimed, "pacify … the black community." Blacks typically denounce West for supposedly placating disgruntled whites by harshly attacking Obama and to a lesser extent the black masses. During a Fox News interview, for instance, West said:

> So you have this 21st century plantation that has been out there. When the Democratic Party has taken the black vote for granted and you have established certain black leaders who are nothing more than the overseers of that plantation. And know the people on the plantation are upset because they have been disregarded, disrespected and their concerns are not cared about. So I'm here as the modern day Harriet Tubman who kind of leads people on the Underground Railroad away from that plantation into a sense of sensibility.[31]

[30] Rod Paige and Elaine Witty, The Black-White Achievement Gap: Why Closing It Is the Greatest Civil Rights Issue of Our Time 141 (2009); Michael Sokolove, *Why is Michael Steele a Republican Candidate*, New York Times Magazine, Mar. 26, 2006, at 32; Michael McAuliff and Corky Siemasko, *GOP Boss Michael Steel Says He and Barack Obama Have One Thing in Common: It's Tough Being Black*, New York Daily News, Apr. 4, 2010, available at: http://www.nydailynews.com/news/politics/gop-boss-michael-steele-barack-obama-common-tough-black-article-1.163992; Jim Newell, *Michael Steele Admits GOP Has Been Strategically Racist For 40+ Years, Hooray!*, Wonkette, Feb. 8, 2014, available at: http://wonkette.com/414991/michael-steele-admits-gop-has-been-strategically-racist-for-40-years-hooray.

[31] Katie Sanders, *Allen West Says Democrats Distributed His Social Security Number in Mailers*, PolitiFact, July 21, 2011, available at: http://www.politifact.com/florida/statements/2011/jul/21/allen-west/west-says-democrats-distributed-his-social-securit/; The O'Reilly Factor, Fox News, Aug. 17, 2011.

Denouncing West is problematic, however, because he is often outlandish. He once said that Hitler's minister of propaganda, Joseph Goebbels, would be "proud" of the Democrats. He remarked that anyone with an Obama-Biden bumper sticker was a "threat to the gene pool." And he claimed that the "Democratic appetite for ever-increasing redistributionary handouts is in fact the most insidious form of slavery remaining in the world today." When Allen West's lips separate crazy comes out. Thus his contention that he was the modern-day Tubman, when put through "a normal man translator" is that "blacks are voting for politicians who do not offer them the best solution to their problems and hopefully I can convince them that conservative policies are better for them." Such a statement is not deserving of rebuke; it is the comment of a man convinced that conservatism offers the best solution to the color line.[32]

A REPUBLICAN WHO OCCUPIES THE WHITE HOUSE typically appoints a few blacks to government positions. These appointments are in part overtures to black voters. Republicans are receptive to blacks' concerns – that's the intended message. Republicans hope that these appointments will disabuse blacks of the perception that voting for the GOP is an act against one's own interests. These hopes, however, are never realized. Rather than improving blacks' perceptions of the Republican Party, the credibility the appointee has with the black community drops. Republican appointees are constantly chased by accusations of racial abandonment. And like their congressional counterparts, they are too slow to outrun *Uncle Tom*.

President Ronald Reagan's black appointments were often vilified in part because the black community abhorred him. In 1984, California politician Maxine Waters, for example, wrote that Reagan ran on a platform "which snidely suggested that he was going to put Blacks in their place once and for all." She labeled his black supporters "Uncle Tom" and "Aunt Tomasina." In 1987, Paul Robeson Jr. called Reagan "the most racist President in modern U.S. history and has acted repeatedly like a political gangster."[33]

Clarence M. Pendleton, chairman of the U.S. Civil Rights Commission, was probably the most derided of Reagan's appointments not named Clarence Thomas. Pendleton strongly embraced the conservative line on civil rights. He called affirmative action "immoral." He argued that quotas "create[] a new class of victims" and hindered equal opportunity. He was

---

[32] *Rep. Allen West's 15 Most Outrageous Statements*, Thinkprogress, Feb. 16, 2012, available at: http://thinkprogress.org/politics/2012/02/16/417174/allen-west-15-worst-quotes/.

[33] Maxine Waters, *Blacks Must "Reassert" Their Identity*, Los Angeles Sentinel, June 13, 1985, at A8; Paul Robeson Jr., *On Whose Side Is Andy Young*, New York Amsterdam News, May 23, 1987, at 15.

an "'Uncle Tom' fool" for contending that white males were being discriminated against. In 1986, Pendleton wanted to suspend minority set-aside
programs while Congress and the president studied the issue. A "Black
leader," in response, called him an *Uncle Tom* who was "bad news for Black
folks." Historian Manning Marable joked that Pendleton made "the original Uncle Tom look like Malcolm X." According to columnist Deborrah
Wilkinson, "[i]f the Amos and Andy serial is ever revived, Penny would be
up for a leading role." Carol and Anatasia Weaver wrote, "We can only say
Reagan knows how to pick 'em. With this Uncle Tom as a leader of our
U.S. Civil Rights Commission we can only expect things to get worse. Lord
have mercy."[34]

Most Washington bureaucrats oppose the termination of the bureaucra-
cies that they head. But oddly, Pendleton flirted with Congress defunding
the Civil Rights Commission because he felt it might be unnecessary in
the future; there may be no racism to study. Not only did Pendleton discount its importance going forward, he also absolved past generations of
their racism. "I don't happen to believe that the government owes me anything just because my ancestors were slaves," Pendleton said. "I think it's
paid that debt. All it owes to me is to keep the doors open." These sorts of
stances led Manning Marable to conclude that Pendleton follows in the
"Uncle Tom tradition." Pendleton denied being treacherous, calling his
critics "racists," "immoral," and "part of a race industry and ... a problem
for black progress."[35]

Overstating the level of antipathy toward Pendleton is difficult. As Tony
Brown noted, it was "a badge of honor in many circles to poke fun at Clarence
Pendleton and his 'uncle tom' views." But more than that, some blacks
framed antagonism toward Pendleton as a measure of self-preservation. In
that vein, Congressman Gus Savage wrote that blacks must strongly oppose

[34] Carol M. Weaver and Anatasia V. Weaver, *The Lash and the Cross*, New York Amsterdam
News, June 5, 1982, at 4; Constance Dougherty, *A Matter of Civil Rights*, Chicago Tribune,
Feb. 3, 1984, at D18; A. S. Doc Young, *His Name: Julius Erving*, Los Angeles Sentinel, May
15, 1986, at A7; Tony Brown, *Tony Brown's Comment: Why Cast Blacks as Competitors*,
The Skanner, Dec. 11, 1985, at 5; Tony Brown, *Tony Brown's Comments: Black Business
Owners Must Help Each Other*, The Skanner, Apr. 30, 1986, at 5; Calvin W. Rolark, *Let's
Talk; Exercise in Futility*, Washington Informer, Apr. 30, 1986, at 16; Manning Marable,
Along the Color Line; Search for a New Booker T, Tri-State Defender, Feb. 6, 1985, at 5;
Deborrah Wilkinson, *Reagan's Anti-Quotas Move Isn't Surprising*, Philadelphia Tribune,
Feb. 24, 1984, at 3; Hanes Walton Jr., When the Marching Stopped: The Politics of Civil
Rights Regulatory Agencies 143 (1988); *The Pendleton Prose*, Washington Post, Mar. 10,
1985, at c6.
[35] Dr. Manning Marable, *Pendleton: In the "Uncle Tom" Tradition*, Los Angeles Sentinel, Aug.
29, 1985, at A7; About Time Vol. 13, 8 (1985).

any "Judas goat" lest "President Reagan and other powerful, reactionary whites will be tempted to appoint more Clarence Pendletons to frustrate and dishearten us."[36]

Pendleton is criticized for being unconcerned about the plight of black people. In many ways, his political choices track closely with those of Ward Connerly. Both premised their career largely on protecting whites from the expansion of antidiscrimination law. But here exists no equivalence to the Racial Privacy Initiative, that unexplainable piece of evidence confirming Pendleton's lack of commitment to eradicating society of antiblack discrimination and thus gross impurities in his devotion to black folk. Holding that Pendleton violated constructive norms based on his antagonism to affirmative action and other liberal policies is to require that blacks eschew conservatism. Racial solidarity must not compel such beliefs.

Samuel Pierce, another Reagan appointee, was secretary of Housing and Urban Development. Columnist Deborrah Wilkinson said that Pierce should win the "Uncle Tom of the Year" award because of "his present role of Reagan's most obedient and honorable Black." Pierce was the only black member of Reagan's cabinet. Yet, during a White House reception for mayors, Reagan walked up to Pierce and said, "How are you, Mr. Mayor? I'm glad to meet you. How are things in your city?" Afterward, the *Amsterdam News* called Pierce an *Uncle Tom*.[37]

During a 1983 union rally of HUD employees, one worker yelled out that Pierce was an *Uncle Tom*. Texas Congressman Henry González retorted that Stepin Fetchit was a more accurate doppelganger. Benjamin Hooks, the NAACP's executive director, offered Pierce, floundering in a morass of betrayal accusations, a helping hand. Hooks lauded Pierce as a "quiet warrior in the ongoing hostility towards Blacks" eager to save him. But Hooks's gracious gesture caused others to shove him into a morass of his own. Indeed, columnist Nathaniel Clay asserted that black leaders who defended Pierce contributed to the "suffering" of the "Black masses" because of "their disgusting cowardice and Uncle Tomism."[38]

After Pierce's stint as HUD secretary, both the U.S. Office of Independent Council and Congress investigated HUD for corruption and political

[36] Honorable Gus Savage, *Philadelphia Bombing Must Be Condemned*, New Pittsburgh Courier, June 22, 1985, at 4.

[37] Fred Weaver, *The Lash and the Cross*, New York Amsterdam News, Jan. 9, 1982, at 4; Bill McAllister, *HUD's "Stealth Secretary,"* Washington Post, Jan. 24, 1987, at A1; Peter Dreier, *Urban Suffering Grew Under Reagan*, Newsday, June 10, 2004, at A45.

[38] McAllister, *HUD's "Stealth Secretary"*; Nathaniel Clay, *"Silent Sam" – President Reagan's Stepin Fetchit*, Chicago Metro News, Mar. 7, 1987, at 3.

favoritism. Although Pierce was never charged, many under him were convicted of felonies. Al Sharpton, in defending himself from prosecution on tax and fraud charges, said that Pierce "show[s] you that even Uncle Toms are subject to indictment." Pierce was disparaged seemingly for being tethered to the detested Reagan rather than anyone catching him committing some treacherous act. That is, his detractors provided no evidence to support their accusations and, therefore, destructively managed norms.[39]

Colin Powell too suffered from *Uncle Tom*'s aching sting. Powell has enjoyed appointments in various Republican administrations. He was national secretary advisor, member of the Joint Chiefs of Staff, and secretary of state. *Uncle Tom* is thrown at him, but not for his domestic worldview. The moderate Republican is pro–affirmative action and rejects the black fault ideology. Powell is typically reprimanded, instead, for foreign policy reasons. In 1991, for instance, Spike Lee claimed that Powell's foreign policy views made him an *Uncle Tom*. Lee said, "So what? So we've got a black general that's going to be head of the Army that kills black people in Panama? Kills black people in Nicaragua? People of color in the Middle East?" Far harsher, in October 2002, Harry Belafonte likened Colin Powell to a house slave.

There's an old saying in the days of slavery. There are those slaves who lived on the plantation, and there were those slaves who lived in the house. You got the privilege of living in the house if you served the master. Colin Powell was permitted to come into the house of the master.

Voicing displeasure with the policies of George W. Bush and Powell's role from within the administration, Belafonte's words give haven to those who call Colin Powell an *Uncle Tom*.[40]

But as true for the other Republican administration members, Powell's detractors were destructive norm managers, failing to prove their charge that he committed racial treachery. In fact, the idea that a foreign policy view could ever result in racial treachery seems farfetched. The black solidarity I am contemplating involves collective action among blacks in America. Unless one claims that blacks should be put on the front lines of all American wars, for instance, loyalty enforcers must focus on domestic matters.

---

[39] Harold L. Jamison, *Judge's Impeachment Trial Called Witch Hunt*, New York Amsterdam News, Aug. 12, 1989, at 3; Deborrah Wilkinson, *New Year Looks Like a Rerun of the Old Year*, Philadelphia Tribune, Jan. 4, 1983, at 2; Mark Grossman, Political Corruption in America: An Encyclopedia of Scandals, Power and Greed 171–73 (2003).

[40] Sonya Live, CNN, Mar. 19, 1992; Charles Trueheart, *Without "News," The Weeklies Delve Further*, Washington Post, June 4, 1991, at B7; Larry King Live, CNN, Oct. 15, 2002; Bracey, Saviors or Sellouts 160–68.

UNCLE TOM IS NOT JUST FOR CONSERVATIVES

Non-conservative black thinkers are typically less concerned with the specter of racial betrayal. The chilling *Uncle Tom*, however, still haunts them. They must take caution. Because championing unpopular causes or disagreeing with a destructive norm enforcer can enliven the epithet that is typically dormant unless conservatives are near. Whereas *Uncle Tom* sometimes disturbed deserving conservatives, nonpartisan blacks and blacks on the left have generally always been unwarranted targets. Norm management in this context, as is the general rule for this era, has been deeply destructive.

Ask Milton Coleman. In 1984, Jesse Jackson made his first of two unsuccessful attempts to win the Democratic Party's presidential nomination. In February 1984, when he derisively referred to Jews as "Hymies" and New York City as "Hymietown," his unlikely bid became impossible. *Washington Post* reporter Milton Coleman, black, was present for the remarks. And he reported the story. Many blacks judged Coleman as having put his personal ambitions above racial loyalties. If Coleman kept quiet, no one would have ever known about Jackson's utterances. Perhaps Coleman then would not be a villain among some blacks who remember this incident. Such speculation, however, is inconsequential. Coleman did his job. He revealed what he heard. And Coleman was pilloried. Louis Farrakhan, head of the Nation of Islam, was strikingly outspoken.

> I say why did not you all rise up and censure this Judas Uncle Tom, member of your class? But since you don't have the courage to do it, I will do it. I know the reason you won't do it is because the same rottenness that is in his house is also in your own. I said, but we're going to make an example of Milton Coleman. I'm going to stay on his case until we make him bear us this example for the rest of them. What do you intend to do to Mr. Coleman? At this point no physical harm. One day soon we will punish you with death.

Farrakhan's followers agreed and sold buttons that read "Milton Coleman is a Judas, weak-kneed coward Uncle Tom."[41]

Despite Farrakhan's discontent, in this tale, Coleman was not a treacherous character. He was more of a sympathetic protagonist: the intrepid reporter who, despite potential condemnation, reported a newsworthy event. Perhaps

---

[41] Rick Atkinson and Milton Coleman, *Peace with American Jews Eludes Jackson*, Washington Post, Feb. 13, 1984, at A1; *Black Unemployment; Covering Jesse, Space Service Call; Nicaraguan Blockade; Unfriendly Neighbor*, The MacNeil/Lehrer NewsHour, Apr. 6, 1984; *Muslim Suggests Succession of Blacks*, New York Times, Apr. 22, 1984, at 16; Mattias Gardell, In the Name of Elijah Muhammad: Louis Farrakhan and the Nation of Islam 251 (2006); Pamela Newkirk, Within the Veil: Black Journalists, White Media 146–47 (2000).

the best argument against Coleman would have been that he was uncon-cerned about the black plight. That argument, however, is unconvincing. At best, Coleman's decision to report the story evidenced indifference toward Jackson's slim political chances. But mistaking Jackson's political interests with those of black people is misguided. A white reporter certainly would have recounted the tale. Coleman's skin color did not necessitate different behavior.

A few months after Coleman reported the "hymietown" remark, Walter Mondale's and Jesse Jackson's delegates fought over the party's platform dur-ing the 1984 Democratic National Convention. Andrew Young, Mondale sup-porter and Atlanta mayor, implored delegates to oppose Jackson's plan to end dual primaries. In response, Jackson's delegates booed Young. One delegate yelled out, "You goddamn turncoat, you!" Another called Young an *Uncle Tom*. Their grievance with Young was probably less about dual primaries than an influential black politician supporting a white man over Jackson.[42]

Three years later and before the 1988 Democratic primaries, Young rekin-dled his heated opposition to Jackson's presidential aspirations. In January 1987, Young supported Bill Bradley for president, despite Bradley not even declaring, because Young believed he was the "best defense [against] Jesse." Paul Robeson Jr. wrote that Young ignored that Jackson voiced the concerns of black Americans better than any other candidate. Robeson argued, moreover, that Young limited the potential influence blacks had in electing the leaders of their choosing. Young's worldview, Robeson concluded, "sounded like an updated version of Uncle Tom's tradition." What Robeson was really saying, though, was that Young was an *Uncle Tom* because Young opposed the black people's candidate. Yet Young backed Bradley. And racial loyalty enforcement must allow Young that decision, unless, that is, Robeson could demonstrate that Bradley was an antiblack politician or that Jackson was so incredible that no racially loyal black person could stand against him.[43]

In 1984, a black reporter reporting Jesse Jackson's anti-Semitic remark was betrayal as was opposing Jesse Jackson's candidacies. In 1991, then, meeting with Jackson should be a perfectly benign act. But such was not the case. Racial betrayal was a mercurial concept, Rev. Al Sharpton learned. Sharpton and Alton Maddox were close allies in New York throughout the 1980s. In 1991, however, their bond ruptured when Maddox called Sharpton an *Uncle Tom*

[42] Richard E. Meyer, *Jackson Delivers Poignant Apology, Will Back Ticket*, Los Angeles Times, July 18, 1984, at B1; Ze'ev Chafets, *The Tragedy of Detroit*, New York Times, July 29, 1990, at 22.
[43] Maralee Scwartz, *Sen. Bradley Matches Andrew Young's Profile Party's '88 Nominee*, Washington Post, Feb. 1, 1987, at A10; Paul Robeson Jr., *On Whose Side Is Andy Young*, at 15.

for meeting with Mayor David Dinkins and Jesse Jackson. Maddox ordered two members of the duo's organization, the United African Movement, to alert the rest that Sharpton "was no longer in charge." Apparently, Sharpton had become too cozy with black insiders, thereby tarnishing the image of the UAM, what *New York Magazine* once described as "a grassroots group bent on agitating against everyone from the white Establishment to black 'sell-outs.'" Yet, for others, criticizing Jackson still engendered antipathy in the early 1990s. Indeed, *Chicago Tribune* columnist Clarence Page wrote in 1992 that he "risk[ed] being labeled an 'Uncle Tom'" when chiding Jackson. Both criticizing and supporting Jesse Jackson was treacherous. What racially loyalty requires is impossible to determine in this period.[44]

Non-conservative blacks were involved in destructive *Uncle Tom* hullabaloos for actions not concerning Jesse Jackson. For instance, Cornel West, at the time a Harvard professor, was lambasted in the African United Front's 1993 *Open Letter to Cornel West & Other Uncle Toms*. West's supposed offense was putting Jews above blacks. The AUF criticized West for lecturing blacks about their anti-Semitism. "But, apart from occasional references to 'Jewish racism' and the 'demonizing' of Minister Farrakhan, you have yet to fully inform Jews of Black grievances against them." The letter also targeted Henry Louis Gates Jr., ostensibly one of the "Other Uncle Toms" to which the title alludes. Gates, a renowned Harvard professor, was likewise beset for supposed pro-Jewish biases.[45]

At the time, Gates had been well acquainted with *Uncle Tom*, with folks "questioning his marriage to a white woman and why the country's leading black-studies program is housed at Harvard and not at a black university." Gates ignored the negativity, however, especially that concerning his alleged pro-Jewish preferences. "Somebody in my position," he said, "has to stand up against [anti-Semitism]. You can be mad at an individual, but to write off a whole ethnic group – if that makes me an Uncle Tom, I say what I believe."[46]

More perplexing was Spike Lee calling journalist Carl Rowan an *Uncle Tom*. Rowan criticized Lee for telling blacks to skip work and take their kids

---

[44] J'Zamgba Browne, *Moses Stewart Stoutly Defends Sharpton Against Media Reports*, New York Amsterdam News, Mar. 16, 1991, at 4; Stephen Rodrick, *Payback Time*, New York Magazine, July 28, 1997, at 30; Clarence Page, *Blacks and Jews, Words and Deeds*, Chicago Tribune, Aug. 2, 1992, at 3; Clarence Page, *Tawana Brawley and the Exploiting of Racial Problems*, Chicago Tribune, Oct. 5, 1988, at 29; Clarence Page, *Why do the Media Begrudge Jackson's Effectiveness*, Chicago Tribune, Sept. 5, 1990, at 15.

[45] An online version of the open letter can be found at: http://www.blacksandjews.com/Open_LetterAUF.html.

[46] Lola Ogunnaike, *From Abyssinia to Zulu- It's In There*, Daily News, Dec. 13, 1999, at 46; Nat Hentoff, *Quicksand on Campus; Jewish Students Hope for an Attack on Black Antisemitism by a Prestigious Black Man or Woman*, Washington Post, Aug. 11, 1992, at A17.

out of school to see Lee's newly released movie *Malcolm X* (1992). "He's irresponsible," Rowan wrote, "in asking kids to stay out of school and black people to risk precious jobs to go see it." Lee responded that Rowan was a "handkerchief-head Uncle Tom negro." Why Lee believed that Rowan's remark rendered him an *Uncle Tom* is impossible to comprehend, exemplifying how common irrational norm management is during this era.[47]

Three years later, Rowan was again called an *Uncle Tom*. In 1995, Rowan reported that Benjamin F. Chavis, NAACP's executive director, used the organization's funds to settle a former employee's sexual discrimination lawsuit. After Chavis's subsequent resignation, Rowan targeted William Gibson, chair of the NAACP, demanding that he too resign. Rowan was an "Uncle Tom," responded Gibson, "who eats from the white man's table." Other blacks were furious too. Rowan, they claimed, "wash[ed] African-American linen in public." Howard University professor Ronald Walters was one of those furious blacks. "Blacks are powerless enough as it is," Walters maintained. "To expose these problems," he added, "makes the organization even more vulnerable than it already was." Rowan's detractors believed that reporting malfeasance within the NAACP warranted repudiation.[48]

In making private facts about the NAACP popular fodder, Rowan did air dirty laundry in public. That is undeniable. His reporting, moreover, dulled the luster of a venerable racial uplift organization. Rowan, nevertheless, infringed no constructive norms. William Gibson's comment suggests that he believed Rowan was benefiting the enemy by revealing the NAACP's tawdry internal issues. Perhaps Gibson believed that because some might use the information against the organization, Rowan furthered the interests of the other side. But even if Rowan's reporting delighted the NAACP's foes that proves nothing. Rowan's critics would need to demonstrate that some antiblack organization directed him to publically sully the NAACP. And that never occurred. Rowan's columns actually benefited black people. Blacks need well-run organizations. If the NAACP mishandled funds, then the organization needed to be cleaned, and public attention is often the best disinfectant.

ALTHOUGH UNCLE TOM IS MORE likely to pelt Republicans, Democrats must keep their shields up. *Uncle Tom* has often been hurled in their direction. But the epithet rarely hits deserving targets. Norm management here has been purely destructive.

---

[47] *CBS This Morning*, November 20, 1992.

[48] Barbara Matusow, *Visible Man*, Washingtonian, Feb. 1995, available at: http://articles.latimes.com/1994-11-17/news/ls-63971_1_columnist-carl-rowan; Abdon M. Pallasch, *Honored Columnist Carl Rowan Dies at 75*, Chicago Sun-Times, Sept. 24, 2000, at 2.

In 1980, amid Jimmy Carter's failed attempt to deny Ronald Reagan the White House, Reverend Charles Kenyatta, a leading Harlem community activist, decided to support Reagan. Kenyatta was disillusioned with the Carter administration for doing "absolutely nothing for America's Black masses." Although Carter's black supporters likely believed Kenyatta exaggerated the administration's faults, they nonetheless deemed Carter the "lesser of two evils." That a group of black supporters, led by Jesse Jackson, continued to back Carter, incensed Kenyatta, who remarked that the group represented the "'hat-in-hand,' Uncle Tom plantation 'nigger attitude.'" Kenyatta, in other words, implied that black leaders who supported Carter, including Jackson, were inexcusably meek for backing a politician who supposedly ignored blacks. But Jackson and his comrades proffered a perfectly acceptable argument, that a flawed Carter was better than the Reagan alternative. Kenyatta disagreed with Jackson and his cohorts about who was better. That disagreement is a healthy facet of intra-racial debate. But Kenyatta hurling *Uncle Tom* here was pernicious, for he maligned as race traitors folk who were doing the same thing as he: participating in democracy.[49]

When Ralph Abernathy endorsed Reagan, he likewise endured unfair *Uncle Tom* insults, meaning that supporting either Carter or Reagan was considered treacherous. Abernathy, once a high-ranking member of the Southern Christian Leadership Conference, was disappointed with the Carter administration and endorsed Reagan in 1980. Coretta Scott King blamed Abernathy's endorsement on "sinister 'forces.'" Other black folk put it more bluntly and called Abernathy "Judas" and "Uncle Tom."[50]

Illinois Comptroller Roland Burris too was accused of duplicity on indefensible grounds. In the wake of the 1984 presidential election landslide, the losers, the Democratic Party, held elections for leadership positions within the Democratic National Committee. Burris vied for the vice chairmanship. The Congressional Black Caucus (CBC) supported Gary, Indiana Mayor Richard G. Hatcher, the former chairman of Jesse Jackson's presidential campaign. The CBC asked Burris to step down but after he refused he handily beat Hatcher.

The Democrats' shellacking in the 1984 general election was an ominous warning. Their unpopularity with whites, especially white men, denied them the presidency and would for the foreseeable future, absent adjustments. Because he was close to Jackson who alienated white voters, Democrats likely

[49]   *Kenyatta Disenchanted*, New York Amsterdam News, Sept. 6, 1980, at 6.
[50]   Dr. Manning Marable, *Black Leaders and Conservative Cults*, New Pittsburgh Courier, Oct. 4, 1986, at 4.

concluded that Hatcher was toxic by association. Burris was a safer alternative. Hatcher called his defeat "the end of effectiveness" of minority caucuses. Congressman Mickey Leland, the CBC's chairman, compared Burris to blacks who aided whites during slavery. "The classic term is Uncle Tom," Leland said. Burris, that is, was denounced as an *Uncle Tom*, not for any personal inadequacies – other than not being Hatcher – but because white Democrats supported him. Such patently destructive norm management has been all too common during the era.[51]

Khalid Muhammad, who was expelled from the Nation of Islam and later formed the New Black Panther Party, destructively managed norms as well. In 1999, Muhammad attempted to organize a Million Youth March Rally in Harlem. Muhammad, an inflammatory speaker, referred to whites as "white devils," said that Jews and Arabs were "sucking the blood in the black community," called Pope John Paul II a "cracker," stomped on a picture of Jesus while screaming, "Jesus wasn't no cracker," and lambasted the "chicken-winged angles" of Christian iconography. For his asserted hate speech, city officials denied him a permit for the march. Federal Judge Denny Chin reversed that decision, however. He understood the city's rationale. But "even hateful, racist and offensive speech," Judge Chin wrote, "is entitled to First Amendment protection."

Most local black Democrats ignored his event but some, including Harlem councilman Bill Perkins, dissuaded blacks from participating. And Muhammad's followers took exception. One night, a few attacked Perkins, pulling on his arm and yelling, "We are going to kill Uncle Toms like you. You are supposed to be supporting us." Assemblyman Keith L. T. Wright likewise condemned the march and State Comptroller H. Carl McCall disclosed that he "cannot abide by Khalid Muhammad's evil message, and I cannot support his march." In response, Muhammad linked himself to Malcolm X, asserting that Malcolm too was ostracized by "bootlicking, Uncle Tom" politicians.[52]

---

[51] The sources for this and the previous paragraph are as follows: Dan Balz, *Kirk Elected Democratic Chairman*, Washington Post, Feb. 2, 1985, at A1; David Paul Kuhn, The Neglected Voter: White Men and the Democratic Dilemma 1 (2007). Burris is now more known for being the infamous recipient of a Senate appointment extended by disgraced Illinois governor Rod Blagojevich.

[52] David Barstow, *Rebuking Giuliani, U.S. Judge Orders Permit for Rally*, New York Times, Sept. 1, 1999, at 1A; Lynne Duke, *The Right to Bear Bars; Court Says "Hateful" Speech, "Million Youth March" Are Protected*, Washington Post, Sept. 3, 1999, at A02; David Barstow, *Black Politicians Turn against Planned Harlem Rally for Youth*, New York Times, Aug. 26, 1999, at 1A; Bob Herbert, *In America; Endless Poison*, New York Times, Aug. 29, 1999, at 15; Solomon Moore, *Obituaries*, Los Angeles Times, Feb. 18, 2001, at B7.

A few years later, Al Sharpton called Jesse Jackson's son, Democratic Illinois congressman Jesse Jackson Jr., an *Uncle Tom* for not endorsing him during the 2004 Democratic Party primaries. Jackson Jr. backed Howard Dean instead. "Any so-called African-American leader that would endorse Dean despite his anti-black record," Sharpton contended, "is mortgaging the future of our struggle for civil rights." Jackson Jr. rebutted, claiming Sharpton was "over the top," "mostly inaccurate," and "ridiculous." Sharpton harshly retorted. "I'm ready to put out ads telling all Uncle Toms at least send me part of the money you get from selling out because if I wasn't in the race they wouldn't be offering you nothing. I put a whole new generation of Toms in business." Although naming no one specifically, observers understood that Sharpton was referring to Jackson Jr. But the idea that one must endorse Sharpton or else be considered an *Uncle Tom* was unjustifiable.[53]

Racial loyalty norms are managed in confusing and contradictory ways. In many respects, *Uncle Tom* is two-faced. Exploring Jesse Jackson best establishes this. Jackson was called an *Uncle Tom*. Reporting his anti-Semitic remarks was racially treacherous as is criticizing his politics. But simply meeting with him was deemed duplicitous as well. Destructive and inconsistent – that best describes norm management during this period.

Among those residing inside the intellectual or political left, someone will always be further to one's left. On an ideological continuum with 10 being the farthest left, 10s will hurl *Uncle Tom* at 9s, 9s will sling the epithet at 8s, and so on. But this behavior destabilizes black solidarity by attacking folk who have committed no foul against the group. Blacks notice when those they consider true race men or women are ostracized as *Uncle Toms*, which consequently causes many to reject, rather than embrace, black solidarity. Few would want to pledge allegiance to a group that wrongly punishes its members.

UNCLE TOM GOES TO CITY HALL

As blacks migrated to Northern cities, whites relocated to the suburbs, leaving a bloc of black voters that put blacks into mayors' seats. These politicians shouldered an unmanageable expectation. Their black constituents expected they would deliver a solution to structural inequality and poverty. When that solution never came, despair spread, particularly in poor communities. This

---

[53] Hanna Rosin, *The Firebrand Cools It in Carolina; Courting the South, Al Sharpton Puts the Politics of Rage on the Back Burner,* Washington Post, Nov. 10, 2003, at C01; Elizabeth Auster, *Sharpton Slings His Darts Carelessly,* Cleveland Plain Dealer, Nov. 2, 2003, at H3.

dissatisfaction generated many of the *Uncle Tom* taunts these mayors endured. Norm management here was deeply destructive.[54]

In November 1987, Chicago's first black mayor, Harold Washington, died in office, forcing the city council to appoint an interim mayor. Washington's white opponents backed Eugene Sawyer, a long-time black South Side alderman. Most black citizens, however, favored a different black candidate, Alderman Timothy C. Evans, Washington's council floor leader and chief political spokesman. From the start, Sawyer had the numbers. But Evans's supporters, led by Jesse Jackson, sought to change that and attempted to pressure Chicago's eighteen black aldermen into aligning with Evans. During one protest, nearly 4,000 picketers blocked City Hall's lobby and flooded the streets. They held signs, bellowed "Uncle Tom, Uncle Tom Sawyer," and waved dollar bills, mocking Sawyer for selling out. Although having the votes for victory, the dispirited Sawyer considered declining the position. Sawyer ultimately accepted, however, becoming the mayor with the backing of mostly white politicians.[55]

Prevailing black thought in Chicago held that Sawyer was a traitor. Alderman Dorothy Tillman called Sawyer "a shufflin' Uncle Tom" and asserted that he returned blacks to "plantation politics." "I don't want to go back to the plantation. I want to be free," Tillman exclaimed. Evans's backers called Sawyer's supporters "obstructionists," "thieves," and "vultures" and claimed that they formed an "unholy alliance" with whites who opposed Washington throughout his five years as mayor. Tillman asked Sawyer, "Don't you understand what you're doing today? Don't get caught on the wrong side of history. Don't be used. Don't be used by them."[56]

Blacks danced in the streets when Harold Washington won the racially divisive 1983 election. He was their politician. Evans, not Sawyer, was deemed Washington's rightful heir. Because Washington's white adversaries propelled Sawyer into office, one might assert that Sawyer defied the norm against furthering the enemy's interests. But that's specious. Even if one could prove

---

54 Deborah F. Atwater, The Rhetoric of Black Mayors: In Their Own Words x (2010); J. Phillip Thompson III, Double Trouble: Black Mayors, Black Communities, and the Call for a Deep Democracy 3–5 (2006); William E. Nelson Jr. and Philip J. Meranto, Electing Black Mayors: Political Action in the Black Community (1977).

55 George H. Brown, *The Myths and Promise of American Democracy*, 11 *National Black Law Journal* 15, 28 (1988–90).

56 Dirk Johnson, *Chicago in Turmoil as Mayor Is Chosen*, New York Times, Dec. 3, 1987, at A1; Bill Peterson, *In Pandemonium, Chicago Gets a Mayor*, Washington Post, Dec. 3, 1987, at A1; Bill Peterson, *Chicago Council Wavers on Picking Acting Mayor*, Washington Post, Dec. 3, 1987, at A9; Dirk Johnson, *Racial Politics: Chicago's Raw Nerve*, New York Times, Feb 19, 1989, available at: http://www.nytimes.com/1989/02/19/magazine/racial-politics-chicago-s-raw-nerve.html?pagewanted=all&src=pm.

that Washington's white opponents were antiblack, one still must evidence that Mayor Sawyer furthered their antiblack agenda. Sawyer, however, did not promulgate an antiblack agenda and blacks came to support him. Indeed, in the 1989 Democratic primary, Sawyer won more than 90 percent of the black vote. The charge that Sawyer was racially treacherous was destructive. He simply had the misfortune of being the lesser preferred black candidate who was also supported by politicians of which blacks were deeply skeptical.[57]

Uncle Tom had met Los Angeles Mayor Tom Bradley in the 1960s. Two decades later, the epithet reintroduced itself. In 1983, while Bradley attended an in-door luncheon, outside two black protestors carried signs maligning Bradley as they roared, "Bradley is an Uncle Tom. He can't be a man if he takes orders from others." Another citizen, when questioned if he would vote to reelect Bradley, said that the mayor was doing a decent job but that he was an "Uncle Tom ... He's been here this long, and still nothing works for the poor people in this town."[58]

Uncle Tom reappeared in Bradley's life when irreverent comedian Paul Mooney publically embarrassed him. In March 1988, Mooney performed at the 15th Annual Whitney M. Young, Jr. Dinner. Most in the majority-white audience likely were unaware of Mooney's racially explosive comedy. During his routine, as he was wont to do, Mooney delivered black jokes and peppered his punch lines with *nigger* (Mooney subsequently stopped uttering *nigger*). He also called Bradley an *Uncle Tom* who mismanaged Los Angeles. Mooney, soon thereafter, was ushered off stage. Bondie Gambrell, a black real estate developer in attendance, told Mooney that his comedy was "despicable" and directed him to not call a black man an *Uncle Tom* in front of whites. When he learned of Mooney's performance, Jessie Jackson said "nobody should be permitted to abuse a Black leader like that."[59]

Events connected to the Rodney King beating resulted in one last *Uncle Tom* altercation for Mayor Bradley. After the police officers who brutalized King were acquitted, Bradley was to address a huge audience at a local black church. He planned to plead for calm but was booed and shouted down as an "Uncle Tom." This painful incident and the inability to quell the L.A. riots preceded Bradley's not seeking reelection. Two decades as mayor was enough.

[57] Johnson, *Racial Politics*; Eric Harrison, *But Blacks Organize to Oppose Him: Daley Attempts to Mend Race Split in Chicago Vote*, Los Angeles Times, Mar. 2, 1989, available at: http://articles.latimes.com/1989-03-02/news/mn-300_1_black-vote.
[58] Jon J. Harris, *Brown Claims Media Distorted Bradley Remarks*, Los Angeles Sentinel, May 12, 1983, at A2; Jill Stewart, *Registrars Sign Up Possible Voters on L.A.'s Skid Row*, Los Angeles Times, Oct. 5, 1986, at A8.
[59] Betty Pleasant, *"Soulvine...,"* Los Angeles Sentinel, Mar. 31, 1988, at A2.

Throughout those twenty years, *Uncle Tom* hovered over Bradley. He could never escape from it. His prosecutors were usually disappointed in his never solving the herculean problem of black poverty in Los Angeles. California voters in 1978 passed Proposition 13, halving municipal tax revenues. And in the 1980s, the federal government deeply cut social programs. With bare coffers, antipoverty measures went underfunded and poor blacks were further disillusioned. Many questioned Bradley's motives, believing that he strategically adopted conservative policies to win over white voters in the gubernatorial races he lost in 1982 and 1996. After his numerous terms, the distrust was cemented. Bradley was an *Uncle Tom*. But even if one were to concede that Bradley was a pitiful mayor – and I am not arguing that to be true – his critics failed to demonstrate that treachery caused his ineffectiveness. Poor performance is different than betrayal. This is an instance where his critics should have criticized his stewardship of the city rather than pound him as a turncoat.[60]

From the West Coast to the East Coast, *Uncle Tom* made its way across country. In 1990, David Dinkins followed Bradley's lead, becoming New York City's first black mayor and having *Uncle Tom* breathing down his neck. Dinkins's venture into a racial protest demonstrated that black politicians fare poorly in dodging challenges to their racial loyalty. Dinkins called for a peaceful resolution to a black boycott of two Korean stores in Brooklyn that began after a Haitian-American woman was assaulted by a Korean employee at a Korean grocery store. One protestor said, "We are here to close Church Fruits and Red Apple until every merchant learns to respect their customers." After Dinkins publically voiced support for a peaceful end, shoppers returned to the stores. The protestors inferred that Dinkins opposed them and vowed to sustain their efforts. "Nothing can stop us ... We ain't gonna' listen to Uncle Tom Dinkins." The protestors seemingly held that racial loyalty demanded complete support of their efforts. But they failed to demonstrate how calling for an end to the boycott was necessarily treacherous. The protestors, failing in prosecuting Dinkins for disobeying constructive racial loyalty norms, would have been better served by abstaining from sellout rhetoric.[61]

Uncle Tom continued to shadow black mayors. In 1995, Michigan voters approved casino gambling in Detroit. Dennis Archer, Detroit's black mayor,

[60] Murray Campbell, *Los Angeles Race Riots Claim a Black Mayor*, The Globe and Mail, Oct. 3, 1992.

[61] David Gonzalez, *8 Arrested in Boycott of Brooklyn Store*, New York Times, Sept. 23, 1990, at 34. This is one of the few times when a black politician is called an *Uncle Tom* in a situation where the "other side" was nonwhite. Blacks who violated the boycott were called "'Aunt Jemima,' 'Uncle Tom,' Negro, and other nonracial epithets." Claire Jean Kim, Bitter Fruit: The Politics of Black-Korean Conflict in New York City 138 (2000).

awarded licenses to three different developers. Don Barden, a local millionaire businessman, had his bid rejected for being financially unsound. Barden, who would have been Detroit's only black casino owner, claimed his bid was unfairly refused. His advocates called Mayor Archer a "sellout" and *Uncle Tom* but offered no proof that Mayor Archer erred. The destructive norm that Braden's camp attempted to enforce was seemingly that black mayors must look out for their own. Black mayors should absolutely endeavor to ensure that governmental affairs are devoid of discrimination. But requiring them to favor black-owned businesses stretches the limits of black solidarity, especially for politicians.[62]

Uncle Tom, as the case of Washington, DC mayor Anthony A. Williams instructs, shadowed black mayors into the twenty-first century. According to a 2003 *Washington Post* article, unnamed "Black leaders" called Williams an *Uncle Tom*. His rap sheet included various supposed offenses. Williams was dogged for supporting school vouchers and for supposedly encouraging a "white renaissance" when he discussed repopulating the city with 100,000 new residents. And his request to determine the cost of moving the University of District of Columbia, a predominantly black college, from upper Northwest (rich area) to east of the Anacostia River (poor area) was deemed "the latest installment of 'The Plan,' which asserts that whites are lusting after black possessions and want to take back the city."[63]

Norm managers decided that a black mayor must champion a particular set of policy beliefs and Williams's dissent was necessarily treacherous. Williams was a moderate and therefore those to his political left maligned him often. Blacks should have assessed his political ideas and tried to block their implementation if they deemed them wrong-headed. But his critics erred in assuming that Williams's racial identity tied him to a set of policy beliefs.

Although they were managed destructively, racial loyalty norms benefited blacks in this context. The case of Mayor Eugene Sawyer perhaps best illustrates this. White politicians who blacks deeply distrusted ushered Sawyer into office amid loud cries that he was an *Uncle Tom*. Two years later, when he ran in the city's Democratic primary, he received more than 90 percent of the vote. Although calling Sawyer an *Uncle Tom* was unfair, the accusations surely reminded him that he was a member of a group that punished betrayal. Collectively, that is, blacks gain when their leaders appreciate that betrayal

[62] Jim Suhr, *Analysts Hedge Wager on Outcome of Detroit's Divisive Casino Election*, The Associated Press State & Local Wire, July 30, 1998; Jim Suhr, *Would-be Casino Owner Ups the Ante with Help from Michael Jackson*, The Associated Press, July 10, 1998.
[63] Jonetta Rose Barras, *So Far, the Mayor's Been a Bust*, Washington Post, June 15, 2003, at B01.

will be punished. Black Chicagoans understandably fretted about what kind of mayor Sawyer would be. Would he do the bidding of unfriendly politicians? That was a reasonable fear. But calling him an *Uncle Tom* was destructive because he committed no wrongdoing. A constructive strategy here would have been for blacks to simply remind Sawyer that they would not abide by him failing to stand up to local politicians who sought to thwart racial progress, for instance. Blacks can guard against racial treachery without shoving *Uncle Tom* in innocent people's faces.

BLACKS DON'T CHEER FOR *UNCLE TOM*

As in the past, sports figures during this period have been cited for duplicity. These accusations are nearly always destructive. But undisciplined racial loyalty enforcers nonetheless employ *Uncle Tom*, ushering the hobbled pejorative onto a stage where it ought not to appear. *Uncle Tom*, as commonplace during this period, regularly surfaces in situations with no substantive political or legal matter at issue. Instead of introducing *Uncle Tom* to forge solidarity around shared oppression, the epithet is frequently invited merely to deride an athlete who happens to be black, causing racial disunity. That *Uncle Tom* is often an unwelcomed guest has depleted the once potent slur. Its vitality is waning.

We see an example of this in 1976 when Al Sharpton called Muhammad Ali an *Uncle Tom*. Sharpton urged for a boycotting of the Ali-Ken Norton heavyweight title bout in Madison Square Garden because Bob Arum, white, promoted the fight. Sharpton claimed that Ali was treasonous for not selecting a black promoter. "For Muhammad Ali to turn his back on his black promoter [Don King] and fight for white promoters who endorsed his being stripped of his heavyweight title is the epitome of an insult to the black community." Sharpton added that "Ali has become an Uncle Tom and is betraying the black people who stood by him during the darker periods of his career." Sharpton said that Ali had returned to being Cassius Clay and quipped that although he knew Ali danced in the ring, "we did not know that he danced in the white man's business offices, too."[64]

To Sharpton, racial loyalty required that Ali continue his relationship with King, black. But choosing Arum over King, especially because King was a shady businessman to put it mildly, was not treacherous. Blacks must not be

---

[64] Leo Zainea, *Turner Demotes Braves' Robinson*, Chicago Tribune, May 16, 1976, at B7; John Rhodes, *Muhammad Ali Called "Uncle Tom" By Minister*, Philadelphia Tribune, May 18, 1976, at 1.

required to choose black over white in such contexts, especially when black is a crook. Is it duplicitous to choose the white applicant over the black one? Is the black athlete more racially loyal after firing his white agent in favor of a black one? Having these choices factor into racial loyalty burdens the cause of black solidarity because they have no effect on blacks' capacity to resist anti-black racism. Ali, that is, could be a brave warrior against bigotry and have a white fight promoter. The destructive norm management here cripples *Uncle Tom* and frustrates the cause of black solidarity.[65]

The case of former Georgetown Hoyas college basketball coach John Thompson further exposes how *Uncle Tom* has been sapped of its power. Thompson was often labeled a racist for having almost invariably all-black basketball teams despite coaching at a university with few black students. Detractors accused him of intentionally excluding whites from his teams. Yet these whispers failed to prevent *Uncle Tom* accusations premised on having, in his words, "a white secretary or a white academic adviser." Sportswriter Michael Wilbon wrote that he "could hear Thompson called a racist on one side of town, then hear him called 'Uncle Tom' on the other spoke to the contradiction but also reconfirmed he's neither."[66]

Warren Moon, a Hall of Fame quarterback, was similarly hounded by illogical accusations of treason. Moon, a standout quarterback at the University of Washington, had no suitors in the 1978 NFL draft. Racial biases against black quarterbacks' intelligence denied him the opportunity to shine before the brightest lights. But after he starred in the Canadian Football League, the NFL's Houston Oilers provided him the chance he long deserved. And he excelled.[67]

Perhaps his best game was on December 16, 1990 against the Kansas City Chiefs. Moon was stellar, passing for 527 yards, twenty-two shy of Norm Van Brocklin's record. With three minutes left in the fourth quarter, Moon knocked his thumb against a helmet and decided to exit the game. Segments of Houston's black population, including a local columnist, called him an *Uncle Tom* for not pursuing the record of a white quarterback. Their use of *Uncle Tom* was tied to racial stereotypes about black quarterbacks. They aren't smart enough. They can only run. They cannot lead men. Moon taking the record would not have shut the mouths of bigots. But it certainly would have provided black football fans enough ammunition to try. But when Moon left

[65] Jack Newfield, Only in America: The Life and Crimes of Don King 98 (1995).

[66] Juan Williams, *John Thompson's Olympic Trial*, Washington Post, Aug. 28, 1988, at SM18; Michael Wilbon, *A Coach with the Courage to Make America Think*, Washington Post, Jan. 9, 1999, at D01.

[67] David L Porter, African-American Sports Greats: A Biographical Dictionary 215 (1995).

the game, he denied some black fans the possible silver bullet they wanted and they hit him with *Uncle Tom* as retribution. But those who did so not only unfairly attacked Moon, they contributed to making *Uncle Tom* a listless epithet.[68]

The case of basketball great Karl Malone further reveals that *Uncle Tom* is debilitated. In 1995, Derrick Coleman, a fellow NBA player, said that Malone was "an Uncle Tom since the beginning of time. That's how I see him ... as an Uncle Tom.... Because he's an Uncle Tom. He's fake. He's not real." What Coleman's grievances were with Malone – his white wife, his white friends, some character flaw, or his genial relationship with overwhelmingly white Utah, where Malone played basketball for the majority of his career – is unclear. *Uncle Tom* is an insult that typically aggravates the target. But for Malone, such was not to the case. Nicknamed "The Mailman," Malone delivered a comical retort. "You know the old saying, 'You'll look back in a few years and laugh at this?' ... I considered the source and looked back and laughed as soon as I heard it."[69]

A similar perplexing use of *Uncle Tom* can be seen in the case of boxer Evander Holyfield. In 1997, Don King ridiculed Holyfield, saying that he was "personification of Uncle Tom-ism" and a "welfare champion." King's motives are unknown. Most likely, he wanted to verbally attack Holyfield and *Uncle Tom* was a convenient epithet to employ. Such uses sap *Uncle Tom* of all its power.[70]

Former NBA star Charles Barkley too has faced baseless *Uncle Tom* accusations. Barkley is outspoken, and few of his public pronouncements are more indelible than his 1990s Nike commercial where he famously said, "I am not a role model!" Columnist James Strong rebuked him for the statement, arguing that he is indeed a role model with social obligations, especially to black children. Strong also mocked Barkley for quipping that he would do anything for money, including playing basketball for the KKK if the money was good. Barkley's response of "I'm rich," when told that Ronald Reagan favored the wealthy further evidenced, to Strong, that Barkley was uninterested in

[68] Warren Moon with Don Yaeger, Never Give Up on Your Dream: My Journey 115–16 (2000); Mike Sando, *Why Warren Moon Feels How He Feels*, Espn.com, Apr. 1, 2011, available at: http://espn.go.com/blog/nfcwest/post/_/id/35446/why-warren-moon-feels-how-he-feels. The Houston Oilers are no longer an NFL team after having moved to Nashville, becoming the Tennessee Titans.

[69] Mike Wise, *Coleman Speaks, and Beard Cringes*, New York Times, Mar. 17, 1995, at B15; *Warriors' Mullin Battles Rough Season*, St. Louis Post-Dispatch, Mar. 26, 1995, at 12F.

[70] Jeff Schultz, *"Geezer" Foreman Still a Big TV Draw*, Atlanta Journal and Constitution, Nov. 22, 1997, at 07H. Jon Saraceno, *The Wait Is Over Challenger's Basic Strategy: Fight Him Back*, USA Today, Nov. 8, 1996, at 1C.

black solidarity. Because he believed that Barkley shunned his responsibility to the black community, Strong asserted that "[a] reformed thief of any color would make a better role model for black kids than the millionaire Charles Barkley" because he "is not only a superstar but a supersambo as well. He is the Uncle Tom of Pro basketball." Strong claimed that Barkley is "a Tom not only because he's desperate to maintain rapport with whites, but also because he's ravaged by the emotions of an infant." The KKK comment should certainly arouse ire, but Barkley is a jokester and that comment was surely uttered in jest. Needless to say, only serious comments count for racial loyalty policing purposes.[71]

Uncle Tom was brought onto center stage in the 2011 documentary *Fab 5* that detailed the career of the five black freshmen basketball players who entered the University of Michigan in 1991. Jalen Rose, one of the Fab 5, grew up poor in Detroit, even though his dad, Jimmy Walker, was the first pick in the 1967 NBA draft. Rose, like his absentee father, was a great basketball player and was heavily recruited in high school. He had many suitors, but Duke University, a storied basketball program, did not recruit him. And the eighteen-year-old Jalen Rose thought Duke did not court him because he was not an *Uncle Tom*. Rose said in the documentary, "For me, Duke was personal. I hated Duke. And I hated everything I felt Duke stood for. Schools like Duke didn't recruit players like me. I felt like they only recruited black players that were Uncle Toms."

Michigan's Fab 5 and Duke had epic battles on the court when Duke's most prominent black player was Grant Hill. Hill was the son of two well-educated parents. His mother was Hillary Clinton's college roommate; his father was a professional athlete like Rose's father. Calvin Hill, however, a running back for the Dallas Cowboys, raised Grant with his mother in a two-parent household. Because Grant Hill was the most celebrated black player at Duke at the time and because Rose disclosed during *Fab 5* that he was jealous of Grant Hill, most associated the *Uncle Tom* taunt with him. Feeling attacked, Grant penned a response in the *New York Times*. "In his garbled but sweeping comment that Duke recruits only 'black players that were 'Uncle Toms,'" Grant wrote, "Jalen seems to change the usual meaning of those very vitriolic words into his own meaning, i.e., blacks from two-parent, middle-class families." Rose failed to inform observers that his use of *Uncle Tom* was merely what he felt as a teenager and that he no longer felt that way. Thus, he opened himself

---

[71] Wayne Browne, *Charles Barkley, White Media Add Up to an Explosive Mix*, Philadelphia Tribune, June 19, 1992, at 1A; James Strong, *The Baby Huey of Pro Basketball*, New Journal and Guide, July 7, 1993, at 2.

up to Grant Hill's correct reply – it is indefensible to equate indicia of success with selling out.[72]

The salient characteristic of norm management in this context of sports was that trivial matters were mistakenly elevated into events where real racial treachery was a possibility. For instance, Muhammad Ali choosing a white promoter should never have been fodder for norm enforcers. Similarly, under no circumstances should Warren Moon not attempting to break a passing record be equated to betrayal. Norm managers overregulated behavior.

UNCLE TOM TAKES THE STAGE

As true with athletes, norms were managed destructively when entertainers were being policed. The case of Garrett Morris provides an example. As an original member of *Saturday Night Live*, Morris played a variety of roles, some aggravating some blacks. He was one of three panelists, for instance, in a skit lampooning a Carter-Ford presidential debate. The panelists were introduced as: "Liz Montgomery ... of The Washington Post, who was selected ... because of her expertise in economic matters. Tom Burke ... Rolling Stone magazine, for his incisive reporting of the Washington bureaucracy. And Earl Roland (Morris), of the Chicago Tribune ... because he is a Negro." For his *SNL* roles, he received letters impugning his racial loyalty. One stated that "Garrett Morris is a sick Uncle Tom." Morris was also called an *Uncle Tom* for playing the monkey in *The Wiz*. "I got so many years of Uncle Tom letters, especially when I did the monkey in *The Wiz*," he claimed. "Now the same people who criticized me for doing the monkey in 'The Wiz' are doing the donkey in 'Shrek.'" Morris was apparently referencing Eddie Murphy, the voice-over actor for the donkey in the *Shrek* movie franchise.[73]

The standard of measurement in this context is the black actors during the World War II period who played demeaning stereotypes that disparaged the entire race. Morris's roles fall far short of that standard. Perhaps much closer was actor Morgan Freeman, who was panned for his asserted *Uncle Tom* performance in *Driving Ms. Daisy* (1989). In the Oscar-winning movie, Freeman played Hoc Colburn, a black chauffeur for Daisy Wership, a Southern Jewish woman. Some complained about Hoc being too deferential and that he had

---

[72] Grant Hill, *Grant's Unedited Response to the Fab Five's Documentary*, GrantHill.com, available at: http://granthill.com/hilltop/hilltop/grants-unedited-response-to-the-fab-fives-documentary.

[73] Tom Shales and James Andrew Miller, Live From New York: An Uncensored History of Saturday Night Live 176 (2002); *Gospel, Mozart and "Saturday Night" Satires*, Washington Post, Feb. 18, 1978, at B1.

no life of his own, making his world seemingly revolve around his sun, Daisy. Spike Lee ridiculed Freeman for resurrecting *Uncle Tom* stereotypes of the submissive and obedient black man, calling Hoc a, "Bowin', shufflin', Uncle Tom Negro."[74]

Spike Lee similarly knocked Will Smith for playing an *Uncle Tom* role in *The Legend of Bagger Vance* (2000). Bagger Vance, Smith's character, was similar to Hoc. Vance, a magical black caddy in the Deep South during the 1930s, uses his powers to help a white golfer correct his swing. "If this magical black caddy has all these powers," Spike Lee quipped, "why isn't he using them to try and stop some of the brothers from being lynched and [mutilated]? ... I don't understand this!" After the movie tanked at the box office, Smith showed his perceptivity, saying "Black people don't like that whole God-like, subservient black character."[75]

Spike Lee had a right to disparage these characters whose "only function is to highlight and solve the problems of the whites who learn from them." The movies recall an attractive era to some, when blacks were more compliant and dedicated to bettering the lives of their white superiors. Yet Bagger Vance and Hoc Colburn were innocuous compared to the likes of Stepin Fetchit. The roles are incomparable. Whereas the *Uncle Tom* roles in the 1940s helped sully the race around the world, the theatrical performances of Will Smith and Morgan Freeman produced no such harms. Black actors during the World War II era were implored to reject *Uncle Tom* roles that functioned as propaganda to reinforce the racial caste system. Those black actors who nonetheless ignored the loud cries of their brethren violated the constructive norm that requires that blacks care about the group. Panning Hoc Colburn, Bagger Vance, and the actors who portrayed them is fair. But sellout rhetoric should be excluded from the discussion. Freeman and Smith did not accept these roles amid pervasive concerns that blacks not debase the race in popular culture and these roles did not contribute to the degradation of black people. That is, their choosing those roles failed to establish that their devotion to the race was severely compromised.[76]

---

[74] The information for this entry was compiled from various sources. Edward Guntham, *"Fourth" May Be First Vietnam Story Should Win Picture, Director, Actor Oscars*, San Francisco Chronicle, Mar. 25, 1990, at 20; Stan Grossfeld, *Professor Spike*, Boston Globe Magazine, Nov. 8, 1992, at 12.

[75] David Sterritt, *Face of an Angel*, Christian Science Monitor, July 11, 2003, at 13; Ian Nathan, *Role with the Punches*, The Times (London), Jan. 28, 2002.

[76] Mary B. O'Shea, Crazy from the Heat: Southern Boys and Coming of Age in Where the Boys Are; Cinemas of Masculinity and Youth 84 (Editors Murray Pomerance and Frances K. Gateward 2005).

Spike Lee has produced much less deserving victims. In July 1989, Lee called Eddie Murphy an *Uncle Tom* for not using his clout to help blacks break into Hollywood. "I do have a social conscience," Murphy responded. "[B]ut I can't walk into a studio's front office and demand, 'Hire some black people here!' Spike gets overanxious playing that militant-brother role and occasionally says some stupid stuff." Lee called Arsenio Hall, Murphy's good friend, an "Uncle Tom Negro" for placating his white network executives and advertisers when Hall still hosted the *Arsenio Hall Show.* Hall then cancelled Lee's appearance on his show. "I gave him my platform the first time to publicize his film," Hall said, "and my initial thought after hearing what he said on MTV was, 'I wish I could grab this little maggot and choke him'.... The biggest tragedy is that it's black people fighting.'"[77]

In addition to Hall and Murphy, other black comedians were wrongly hit with *Uncle Tom* charges. Bill Cosby was one such supposed *Uncle Tom.* *The Cosby Show,* the first sitcom depicting a black upper-middle-class family, debuted in 1984. The father of the show was a physician, the mother a lawyer, and the two parented good kids. The Huxtables, in short, were exemplary. One critic knocked the show, considering the family black in skin color only. "I don't mean just in their lifestyle," the critic wrote, "even their cultural background, and their whole context of reference, is that of American Caucasians." "Some white liberals and the few blacks who care may think of Cosby as a sellout, but the truth is that he ... no longer qualifies as black enough to be an Uncle Tom." Bill Cosby, that is, had committed desertion by rooting his television show in an inauthentic black experience.[78]

This story demonstrates that prosecutions for "insufficient blackness" fractures black folk while producing no substantive rewards. An identifiable black culture exists and some participate more than others. And to my mind, the Huxtables were a "culturally" black family, one with money, but recognizably black nonetheless. But even if the Huxtables were not, blacks lose by maligning Cosby here. Let's say the Huxtables were insufficiently black. Now what? Blacks should unify around shared oppression, because doing so helps facilitate racial progress. But conducting trials of inadequate blackness distracts the group from what it should have a laser-like focus on: racial inequality. Policing racial loyalty, however, is no distraction because true *Uncle Toms* impede blacks' ability to work together to uplift the race.

[77] Shane Danielsen, *Do the Spike Thing,* The Australian, Nov. 16, 1999, at 13; Jeannie Williams, "*Sex, Lies" and Lavish Praise,* USA Today, Aug. 3, 1989, at 2D; Michael Norman, *TV's Arsenio Hall: Late-Night Cool,* New York Times, Oct. 1, 1989, at 29.
[78] William Raspberry, *Cosby Show: Black or White?,* Washington Post, Nov. 5, 1984, at A27.

Comedian Wayne Brady has faced similar undeserving taunts. Brady rarely curses, certainly never uses *nigger* as do many black comedians, speaks perfect English, and includes improvisational humor in his comedic repertoire. In short, his comedy is not rooted in the black American existence; a non-black comedian could easily deliver his jokes. Brady said one comedian has a "personal mission to talk about me. He did this sketch where he said I pay Black audiences to watch me. I'm White, Uncle Tom this, Uncle Tom that." The comedian Brady referenced was Aries Spears, most known for his work on *Mad TV*, who mocked him in a 2002 episode. In the skit, Spears impersonates Brady as completely unfamiliar with black culture, routinely mispronouncing a rapper's name.[79]

Comedian and actor Jamie Foxx also ridiculed Brady during the 2003 Espy sports awards show. After singing a satirical song about basketball star LeBron James, Foxx joked that the song would be for sale. It was "written by Wayne Brady," he quipped. "[I]t's guaranteed to sell out." Brady defends himself against these attacks, saying he is not attempting to be white, but rather "[i]t's just me doing what I do. Whether it's improv, singing, acting, I have no racial agenda." He added, "I love being Black."[80]

As the cases of Bill Cosby and Wayne Brady show, some loyalty enforcers have wrongly concluded that certain personal styles can ever indicate racial treachery. As noted earlier, blacks have been called *Uncle Toms* for entering into interracial relationships and even for having successful careers. Such norm enforcement greatly over-polices behavior and is unrelated to racial fidelity. The comedic styles of Cosby and Brady must be included in the list of activities that should never cause one to reach to sellout rhetoric.

Richard Pryor, situated on the opposite end of the comedic spectrum, was also charged with being an *Uncle Tom*. Stanley Crouch, a black cultural critic, was his indicter. Pryor, known for his expletive-ridden persona, first introduced *nigger* into stand-up comedy with risqué material like, "Hope I'm funny ... because I know niggers ready to kick ass" and "Niggers never get burned up in buildings ... White folks just panic, run to the door, fall over each other.... Niggers get outside *then* argue." Crouch conceded Pryor's comedic genius but disparaged his style, writing that "the dark side of Pryor used the street-corner level of vulgarity that, in show business retrospect, is no more than minstrelsy. Uncle Tom, cursing his way to the bank." Pryor's naughty comedy was not for everyone. It turned off many. But the idea that Pryor was akin to

---

[79] Nicole Walker, *Cover Story: Wayne Brady*, Jet, Feb. 10, 2003, at 56–59; *Mad TV*, Nov. 9, 2002.

[80] Id.

minstrelsy was unsupportable. Minstrelsy derogated blackness. Pryor, through humor, made insightful racial commentary. To liken Pryor to minstrelsy is to be ignorant of what the practice truly was. Crouch engaged in destructive norm management.[81]

Ben Vereen, however, did perform something that looked very much like minstrelsy. In 1981, actor and dancer Ben Vereen unforgivably erred, some estimated, when he turned his face black and danced during President Ronald Reagan's inaugural ball. The display recalled a painful chapter in American history. Blacks fought hard to bury blackface and to see a black man excavate it, on television no less, was jarring. One media critic wrote that "Vereen's routine … seemed unfortunately shuffly and Uncle Tom-ish – especially considering the fact that the Reagan administration has already been criticized for insensitivity to racial realities." Another wrote that Vereen's performance proved that "Uncle Tom still lives." And black newspapers called it an "Uncle Tom appearance" and an "Uncle Tom act."

Vereen defended his performance, saying it was part tribute to Bert Williams, a legendary black blackface performer, and part cry for racial justice. Some of the performance was unseen by television viewers. If they had watched its entirety, Vereen believed that the point of the performance – that blacks "refuse to be hidden behind a caricature any more" – would have shone through. An embarrassed President Reagan asked during the performance, "Why is he doing this to me?" Most blacks, however, did not perceive Vereen's display as a theatrical protest, instead agreeing with Rex Reed's remark that "Blacks of this great nation should be in a rage over Ben Vereen's 'yard nigger' routine with white lips and the mannerisms of an old porter on the B&O Railroad doing an impersonation of Stepin Fetchit."[82]

Ben Vereen argued that his performance was a racial protest intended to show the ultimate power holder that blacks would not lie down and accept injustice. But blacks' visceral reaction of him performing blackface in front of a distrusted politician was that he was embarrassing the group; he recalled an era when blacks were dehumanized for the enjoyment of whites. He performed in blackface on television. To some, that itself demonstrated racial

---

[81] Stanley Crouch, *Always In Pursuit* 266 (1998); Randall Kennedy, *Nigger: Strange Career of a Troublesome Word* 39 (2002).

[82] The sources for the discussion on Ben Vereen are as follows: Tom Shales, *Inaugural Gala*, Washington Post, Jan. 20, 1981, at B1; *Loose Jaws, The Tattler*, New York Amsterdam News, Jan. 24, 1981, at 7; A. S. Doc Young, *A Convalescent's Notebook*, Los Angeles Sentinel, Feb. 5, 1981, at A7; Major Robinson, *Ben Vereen: Why Should I Be Ashamed of My Heritage?*, New York Amsterdam News, Feb. 7, 1981, at 27; *Ben Vereen Still Under Fire for Blackface Act at Gala; He's Shocked*, Jet, Feb. 12, 1981, at 14–18, 60; Major Robinson, *Vereen Defends Uncle Tom Act*, Afro-American, Feb. 7, 1981, at 1.

betrayal. I am unconvinced, however, that his act violated constructive norms. One might try to convict him for being inexcusably meek in the face of racism. But what was the racism here? Some might insist that he was akin to the black actors during the World War II era. But, again, I remained unconvinced that his performance demonstrated that his devotion to black people was severely compromised, especially because he claimed to be protesting. This was a close call. But norm management during this period did not involve many of those. Racial loyalty norms in this context, as true generally during this period, were gravely mismanaged.

ANALYSIS

In the *Uncle Tom's Cabin* plays and minstrels, Uncle Tom was always a feeble gray-haired man. Tom was old. He was decrepit, past his prime. *Uncle Tom* has much in common with Uncle Tom. The once sturdy epithet has become crippled. *Uncle Tom* was powerful and explosive. That is no longer true. Sure, *Uncle Tom* has its moments, recapturing former glory and punishing deserving targets. But those instances get rarer over time. It has been overtaxed, misapplied, and is now rundown. *Uncle Tom* is not what it once was.

During this epoch, black conservatives – because of their views – are most likely to be called *Uncle Toms*. But holding that black skin bars one from espousing conservatism is indefensible. Some black conservatives, however, are traitorous: those advocating the black faulty ideology which blames racial inequality on blacks' failures and insisting that outside intervention cannot promote black uplift. History demonstrates that blacks working with antiblack interests often champion such arguments. Embracing the black fault ideology is presumptive proof establishing a violation of the norm that prohibits blacks from furthering antiblack interests. Thomas Sowell and Walter Williams, proponents of this ideology, confirm presumptions by supporting *The End of Racism* and *The Bell Curve*. And Williams's claim that blacks benefited from slavery and that black South Africans were better off under apartheid is so outlandish as to be unworthy of public debate.

Black Republican politicians are few in number. But *Uncle Tom* has found nearly all of them. They are typically impugned because they are conservatives and members of the party that most blacks deeply distrust. Their critics, however, have failed to corroborate their charges, unable to demonstrate how their behavior has violated constructive norms.

Although non-conservative black intellectuals are less likely to face *Uncle Tom* accusations, some have suffered the humiliation. Perhaps more non-conservatives have endured the slur, simply reflecting the lack of black conservatives. The most salient point in this context is that what invites condemnation is unpredictable. Opposing and supporting Jesse Jackson propelled charges of duplicity. Both cannot be true. And it turns out neither was. During this period both Cornel West and Henry Louis Gates Jr. were denounced as *Uncle Toms* for decrying anti-Semitism although blacks should certainly oppose bigotry voiced by other blacks.

Black Democratic politicians are much less vulnerable than their Republican counterparts although they too must stay on guard, particularly if they are deemed ineffective leaders. This was true for Los Angeles mayor Tom Bradley. His black constituents anticipated that a black man with power would ameliorate poverty. When it endured, many played the duplicity card. His accusers, and those of other black mayors, however, dealt weak hands and offered no evidence to prove their accusations.

Likewise, athletes during this era were wrongly chided for turning their backs on the race. Quarterback Warren Moon, for instance, was called an *Uncle Tom* because he was disinterested in a passing record. Similarly, boxing promoter Don King branded boxer Evander Holyfield as an *Uncle Tom* apparently for no other reason than personal animus. *Uncle Tom* had no business in these disputes. As true for sports stars, black entertainers were irrationally disparaged. Bill Cosby and Wayne Brady were maligned for their comedy that was supposedly not black enough. Yet Richard Pryor, whose comedy was undeniably culturally black, too was denounced for racial disloyalty, demonstrating how inconsistently racial loyalty was policed.

As the narratives in this chapter demonstrate, during this era, *Uncle Tom* is used wantonly. During the first epoch, being called an *Uncle Tom* suggested that a serious offense occurred. One who was branded an *Uncle Tom* often committed an act that fellow blacks might validly consider harmful in the pursuit of equality. During the second epoch, *Uncle Tom* was wielded more recklessly as those clearly having black interests at heart were targeted. Especially problematic, black militants enlarged *Uncle Tom's* contours, expanding the meaning of the slur to delegitimate integrationist leaders. Although we must fault their condemnation of the likes of Martin Luther King and Thurgood Marshall, nevertheless, their use was connected to a cogent argument concerning how the race should confront legal, political, and social challenges. *Uncle Tom*, that is to say, was at least wielded substantively. Now, more often than not, acts irrelevant to racial injustice are manufactured into crimes against the race. These uses are deeply regrettable.

Indeed, the most destructive facet of racial loyalty norm management during this era was bizarre, not simply wrongful, indictments. For instance, Spike Lee called Carl Rowan an *Uncle Tom* for writing that black people should not skip work and school to see Lee's movie *Malcolm X*. Karl Malone was called an *Uncle Tom* because "he's not real." These irrational uses of *Uncle Tom* have tarnished racial loyalty enforcement.

Racial loyalty enforcers during this period, simply put, have torpedoed the cause of black solidarity. Racial loyalty norms and *Uncle Tom*, in tandem, help forge the black solidarity crucial in promoting racial progress. But destructive norm management has stripped both of their tread, rendering them less useful in helping steer black folk to a better reality. Racial loyalty policing is way off course and in crisis.

Blacks today are more likely to exclude sellout rhetoric from their vocabulary. But those who retain it often employ it in unfitting situations, perpetuating a cycle wherein mainly destructive norm managers police racial loyalty. This drives norm management into further disrepute, increasingly compelling more conscientious blacks to eschew sellout rhetoric partly because they have experienced the pain of unjust accusations of betrayal. The number of those willing to enforce racial loyalty, therefore, becomes even more depleted of more sober-minded thinkers. This cycle has produced a climate that leads many blacks to conclude, wrongly, that enforcing racial loyalty ought to abandoned. Accusations of racial loyalty are presumptively deemed unfair with the presumption often being non-rebuttable.

But since racial loyalty enforcement has been greatly stigmatized, the treacherous have more freedom to sabotage. Indeed, the truly disloyal can avoid punishment by pointing to patently unjustifiable witch hunts. "I am not an *Uncle Tom*. Black people are not allowed to think for themselves." The issue, however, is not independent thought, but rather actions and utterances that subvert racial progress. Calling an innocent person an *Uncle Tom* gives cover to a true *Uncle Tom*. To haven the guiltless and shame the guilty, racial loyalty policing needs to be remedied.

9

What Now, *Uncle Tom?*

THE FOURTH EPOCH OF *UNCLE TOM*

T HIS BOOK FEATURES ONE CENTRAL thesis: policing racial loyalty by enforcing constructive norms strengthens black solidarity, a golden tool in building legal triumphs. Constructive norms discourage actions that hinder a unified people toiling toward a higher existence. A united black citizenry can best construct a path to climb out from the doldrums of American society. Norm violators are dragged before the race to account for their crimes. Their punishment is to withstand debasing condemnation. *Uncle Tom* is the most brutal.

I also proffer three subsidiary arguments. First, blacks have reexamined what it means to be an *Uncle Tom* throughout history. Blacks constantly revisit *Uncle Tom*, ensuring that it fits the era and serves the needs of the race, as individual blacks see it. Betrayal's appearance is constantly changing, sometimes looking very different from one decade to the next. *Uncle Tom* is a chameleon.

Second, destructive norms have increasingly predominated over constructive ones. Even though the first period saw destructive norm managers, proper applications of *Uncle Tom* defined the period. The second era, despite many constructive prosecutions of treachery, witnessed an explosion of blatantly unjustified accusations of betrayal. And during the last era, constructive norm management is an exception to the destructive rule.

That blacks must continue policing racial loyalty through social norms is my third subsidiary argument. But blacks must manage norms constructively. The third period of *Uncle Tom's* use, marked by destructive loyalty policing, must end. A fourth period must supplant it, one where supporting evidence always accompanies accusations of betrayal. The days when blacks are deemed sellouts merely for being conservative, for disagreeing with majority thought, or for otherwise being outside the mainstream must cease.

Some will contend that the preceding chapters, littered with persons wrongly pained by *Uncle Tom* wounds, demonstrate that blacks must put down the epithet as one would an uncontrollable beast. It is too wild and dangerous, careful minds will aver. To advocate for jettisoning the imposition of intra-racial discipline, however, is to promote an idea that would never come to fruition but harm the black community if it somehow did. This book establishes a central truth: Policing racial loyalty is permanent. The use of *Uncle Tom* has fallen since a 1960s peak. Yet sellout parlance, in all its injurious flavors, is never far from the tip of black America's collective tongue. Blacks benefit enormously when race members appreciate that to betray the race is to summon rhetorical punishment. But moving forward, blacks need to have confidence that racial loyalty enforcers will apply norms judiciously. That is the great need of loyalty policing. This book provides the much-needed structure that can end destructive norm management. Although untamed now, *Uncle Tom* is no wild lion that blacks will never be able to control. Blacks can domesticate it if they so choose.

Focusing solely on destructive norm management causes opponents to ignore a valuable benefit to loyalty enforcement. Although destructive norm management is very problematic, fewer violate constructive norms. *Uncle Toms*, in other words, still live but are far scarcer, likely because loyalty has been vigilantly policed for more than a century. Ceasing managing norms would eliminate a powerful deterrent and one should expect treacherous figures to repopulate black America should blacks err and relinquish *Uncle Tom*. The best solution is to eliminate unjustified accusations of betrayal, thus allowing the great benefits of constructive norm management to proceed undisrupted.

What follows is a demonstration of how blacks should police racial loyalty in the twenty-first century. Let this commence the fourth epoch of *Uncle Tom's* use.

JESSE LEE PETERSON

Jesse Lee Peterson, a black conservative from Los Angeles, has constantly had the *Uncle Tom* title forced upon him. It fits him well. Given his statements, and him living in an America that has never been less racially hostile, he is among the most lamentable blacks to have had the misfortune to be considered a traitor.

Peterson, the head of Brotherhood Organization of a New Destiny, claimed that he was on welfare and admired Louis Farrakhan and Jesse Jackson until his awakening, when he found God and Ronald Reagan. He then determined that the "Democratic platform was ... anti-God, anti-values, [and] anti-American."

Peterson subsequently built a career as a right-wing evangelical minister. He is perhaps the most prominent figure of Project 21, a group of ultraconservative black polemicists. Project 21 is partly funded by the Lynde and Harry Bradley Foundation, which has bankrolled studies devoted to the supposed genetic intellectual inferiority of blacks. During the L.A. riots, the National Center for Public Policy Research, a think tank funded in part by the Lynde and Harry Bradley Foundation, arranged for a group of black conservatives to lambaste the rioters and praise the LAPD. Out of this campaign, NCPRR built Project 21. Ever since, should conservative media outlets, most notably Fox News, ever need conservative blacks, they reach into that bottomless well.[1]

Scholar Michael Eric Dyson offered insight establishing why Peterson is routinely dismissed as an *Uncle Tom*. In 2002, Dyson publically debated Peterson on reparations. Peterson argued that "blacks are immoral" to refute Dyson's pro-reparation arguments. "If you've ever wondered what a self-hating black man who despises black culture and worships at the altar of whiteness looks like," Dyson wrote, "take a gander at the Reverend Jesse Lee Peterson." "In Peterson's mind," Dyson continued, "black rates of teen pregnancy, the breakdown of the black family, and black peoples' addiction to civil rights advocacy are the unerring symptoms of moral failures."[2]

The case against Peterson includes far stronger evidence than his "blacks are immoral" claims. Take, for instance, his diatribe on why slavery benefited blacks where Peterson shoved a barrage of words into an empty, morally bankrupt idea.

> I've often said thank God for slavery because you know [without slavery] the blacks that are here would be stuck in Africa and you see how bad Africa is. Everybody momma is trying to get out of Africa and come to America. And so God has a way of looking out for folks and made it possible by way of slavery to get black folks into this country.... I thank God that he saw fit for me to get here. Never mind that we were sold. I mean, I guess my ancestors way back yonder were sold by Arabs and blacks to white folks. And got us here, and brought us to the greatest country in the world. The ride over was pretty tough. It was like riding on a crowded airplane, when you're not in first class. But, you're happy when you get to your destination.... The pain for freedom was tough.... In life when you want to gain something you got to lose something.... [It was] all for the sake of freedom. So I thank God that he got me

[1]   Max Blumenthal, *The Minister of Minstrelsy*, The Nation, Mar. 24, 2005, available at: http://www.thenation.com/article/minister-minstrelsy; Joshua Holland, *Blackwashing*, July 25, 2004, available at: http://www.alternet.org/story/19331/blackwashing.

[2]   Michael Eric Dyson, *Self-hate beyond Debate*, Chicago Sun-Times, Aug. 6, 2002, at 27; Jesse L. Peterson, *Voices*, Los Angeles Times, Apr. 11, 1993, at 24.

here. So to show my appreciation to blacks who suffered as a result of coming here; to the Arabs and blacks who sold us to the white man; the white man for going there and bringing us here, I want to say thanks.[3]

Or see Peterson's post–Hurricane Katrina remarks maligning blacks for being lazy. In an editorial after the tragedy, Peterson questioned "what would you do" if a hurricane is "about to destroy the city you live in?" He then asked, "What would you do if you were black?" "Sadly," he penned, "the two questions don't have the same answer." Instead of leaving the city, blacks in New Orleans were "too lazy, immoral and trifling to do anything productive for themselves."[4]

Peterson's rhetorical assault on blacks continued after the 2008 presidential election. Peterson was extremely disappointed with President Barack Obama's victory. But opposition to Obama is not inherently treacherous; Peterson should have the intellectual freedom to oppose Obama's candidacy. But instead of celebrating the election as signaling racial progress, Peterson described Obama's triumph as partly the product of black racism. "I think we all agree," Peterson remarked on Fox News, "that Barack Obama was elected by black racists and white guilty people. Most black Americans, 96 percent of them, are racist [towards] white Americans. And white folks feel guilty, and they're afraid of being called racist." Blacks deserved scorn, Peterson contended; their bigotry compelled their support for Obama, not his political stances. Later in the broadcast, however, Peterson contradicted himself. He averred that blacks chose Obama because he was a liberal. But if he were "a black Republican conservative, they would not have voted for him," Peterson contended. Apparently, Peterson was unaware that his second argument devoured his first, for if melanin controlled blacks' every whim, they would, in fact, back the "black Republican conservative." Peterson puts assailing black folk far above logic and intellectual consistency.[5]

Peterson does not engage in debate but rather performs it. He has a shtick: deliver incredibly offensive pronouncements that whites cannot lest they be branded racist. And his audience is racially embittered whites. Let's revisit his Hurricane Katrina editorial. He asked his readers what they would have done and then asked his readers what they would have done if they were black. But what if his readers are black? Do blacks not get to participate in Peterson's thought experiment? Peterson never even contemplates that he has black

---

[3] This is transcribed from Jesse Lee Peterson's radio show. The original version is available at: http://www.youtube.com/watch?v=EHsDgCSm11g.

[4] Jesse Lee Peterson, *Moral Poverty Cost Blacks in New Orleans*, Sept. 21, 2005, available at: http://www.wnd.com/news/article.asp?ARTICLE_ID=46440.

[5] *Hannity*, Fox News, February 3, 2009.

readers. Blacks are not invited to view his routine. He has an audience. And their palate prefers analysis marinated in bigotry. His comments only whet the appetite of those with a taste for red meat rhetoric with a prejudiced additive.

Peterson's basic argument is that big government renders blacks lazy, immoral, and incompetent. If big government liberalism produces behavioral pathologies, then blacks' only medicine is small government conservatism. He voices bigotry, that is, to further his political objectives. His affiliation with an organization that is bankrolled by funders of research devoted to proving blacks' genetic inferiority only exacerbates his betrayal. And his worldview makes the black fault ideology seem moderate. Ample support exists for the contention that he has violated all three constructive norms. If Peterson is no *Uncle Tom* then an *Uncle Tom* has not yet been born. Indeed, he singlehandedly demonstrates that blacks must neither relinquish *Uncle Tom* nor stop policing racial loyalty. Blacks must retain valuable arms to combat such figures. And equally important, Peterson's presence establishes that white faces wishing to do blacks harm still appreciate the benefits of a black mask.[6]

But the case of Jesse Lee Peterson highlights another benefit to policing racial loyalty. Antiblack entities are harder to detect now. During Jim Crow, white supremacists, without shame, brandished their scarlet letter for all to see. But nowadays they hide that letter. The antiblack clothe themselves with righteous indignation, using treacherous blacks as additional garments, should anyone endeavor to strip them of their camouflage. They are, however, overdressed. And that outs them. Only one working against blacks' interests has a Jesse Lee Peterson in one's wardrobe. In order for blacks to improve their legal plight, they must disrobe their enemies. Policing racial loyalty helps blacks locate their opposition. From there, blacks can expose them as much as their forbearers exposed themselves. Blacks' legal and political interests depend on it.

JULIUS HENSON ET AL.

Political strategists are infamous for suppressing their opponents' voters. But what's a black political strategist to do when those voters are black? Julius Henson was wedged into that predicament. And he decided to carry out a plan to subdue black participation in the 2010 Maryland gubernatorial race between Republican Robert L. Ehrlich and Democratic incumbent Martin O'Malley. Henson consulted Ehrlich's campaign although he had long been involved with Democratic causes. In fact, in the 2002 Maryland gubernatorial

---

[6] Blumenthal, *The Minister of Minstrelsy.*

race, Henson worked for Ehrlich's opponent, Kathleen Kennedy Townsend. During that contest, Henson called Ehrlich a "Nazi" who "should be running in Germany in 1942, not Maryland in 2002."[7]

He was a Nazi no more. Eight years later, all was forgotten as Henson aligned with Ehrlich, who ultimately failed to unseat O'Malley. Ehrlich hired Henson for $97,000 to reach out to black voters. Henson apparently defined reaching out loosely. On election day, Henson robocalled predominantly black counties. The robocall, an automated telephone call, featured a woman's voice stating that O'Malley had been "successful" and that "[o]ur goals have been met … We're okay. Relax. Everything is fine. The only thing left is to watch it on TV tonight." The message, delivered to more than 110,000 Democrats, gave the misimpression that going to the polls was unnecessary; the race was over.[8]

Henson, along with Ehrlich's campaign manager, Paul E. Schurick, white, was indicted for violating multiple election laws. According to the state, its criminal investigation uncovered a Schurick-conceived plan to suppress the black vote in hundreds of precincts. Henson was entrusted with its implementation. The plan, which was discovered after Henson's home was searched, "centered on what was termed 'The Schurick Doctrine,' which was designed to promote confusion, emotionalism, and frustration among African American Democrats.… The plan stated that [t]he first and most desired outcome [of the Schurick Doctrine strategy] is voter suppression."[9]

Schurick's attorney claimed that the campaign ultimately rejected the scheme. Henson never denied his involvement with the robocalls, but insisted the First Amendment protected the speech. He professed, moreover, that he had no interest in stopping people from going to the polls, as the state maintained, but rather the robocall was a reverse psychology maneuver to push black voters toward Ehrlich. Henson was ultimately found guilty of failing to include a campaign authority line in the robocall and sentenced to six months in prison.[10]

Few would believe that Henson's goal was anything other than the reduction of black electoral participation. And reasonable minds repudiate such

7   Michael Lind, *Not In the Same League*, Washington Post, Oct. 13, 2002, at B02; Craig Whitlock and Lori Montgomery, *At Chamber of Commerce Forum, a Fountain of Promises*, Washington Post, Oct. 24, 2002, at T13; Ovetta Wiggins, *Big Names Boosted Victor in Pr. George's*, Washington Post, Sept. 16, 2004, at B05.
8   John Wagner, *Robocalls linked to Ehrlich's campaign*, Washington Post, Nov. 6, 2010, at B01; John Wagner, *Ehrlich Aide Faces Robo-Call Charges*, Washington Post, June 17, 2011, at A1.
9   Wagner, *Ehrlich Aide Faces Robo-Call Charges*, at A1.
10 Aaron C. Davis, *Document Cited in Md. Robo-Calls Case*, June 18, 2011, at B01; Robert McCartney, *Campaign Tricks Are Enough to Make One Scream*, Washington Post, June 23, 2011, at B01; Yvonne Wenger, *Henson Guilty of 1 of 4 Charges in 2010 Robo-call Scandal*,

behavior as repugnant. He was a bad political actor. That much is certain. But does Henson reside among the racially treacherous as well? Henson hunted Democrats. Black voters overwhelmingly support Democrats. That black skin is a strong proxy for voter preference is mere happenstance. No evidence establishes that Henson fixed black O'Malley supporters in his crosshairs because of their blackness. Henson, that is, targeted black voters because they were Democrats, not because of their racial identity.

Henson, nonetheless, was treacherous. A political operation that decides to suppress the black vote has declared itself to be an antagonist to black folk. It is an antiblack organization. Any black person furthering its goals, therefore, collaborates with the "other side." Henson's behavior violates the norm prohibiting blacks from cooperating with the race's foes.

Let's take another approach. Ponder this question: Do blacks benefit if black political strategists are deterred from suppressing the black vote? The answer is obvious. No one's interests are ever advanced by infringing one's democratic rights. If a black man is permitted to suppress black turnout and be free from *Uncle Tom*, then the pejorative has been sapped of all its blood and rendered a lifeless form. One of the Southern legislatures' first moves after the end of Reconstruction was to devise shrewd ways to strip black men of their Fifteenth Amendment rights. Although robocalls are comparatively ineffective, that Henson is an heir to this Confederate legacy that disfranchised black men is the most damning label one can bestow upon him. And it's so damning because it fits.

That label also applies to blacks who champion other measures that disenfranchise blacks. In the run-up to the 2012 presidential election, various state legislatures, to stop nonexistent in-person voter fraud, adopted voter identification laws that disproportionately disenfranchised blacks. But, as David Schultz, an election expert said, "Voter fraud at the polls is an insignificant aspect of American elections." An election fraud study covering every state and Washington, DC since 2000 only uncovered ten cases of in-person voter fraud. "With 146 million registered voters in the United States during that time," the study states, "those 10 cases represent one out of about every 15 million prospective voters."[11]

Washington Post, May 12, 2012, at B03; Clarence Williams, *Maryland*, Washington Post, June 14, 2012, at B03.

[11]   PEW, *Election Fraud*, Pew State and Consumer Initiatives, Aug. 30, 2012, available at: http:// www.pewstates.org/research/analysis/election-fraud-85899414756; Natasha Khan and Corbin Carson, *Comprehensive Database of U.S. Voter Fraud Uncovers No Evidence that Photo ID Is Needed*, News 21, available at: http://votingrights.news21.com/article/election-fraud/.

Most observers appreciate that voter ID laws are championed by Republicans who understand that because those lacking state-issued identification tend to be blacker and browner than the population at large, requiring voters to show voter ID before voting helps their side. Some Republicans have admitted this. Republican consultant Scott Tranter said publically "that a lot of us are campaign professionals and we want to do everything we can to help our sides. Sometimes we think that's voter ID, sometimes we think that's longer lines, whatever it may be." Mike Turzai, the Pennsylvania Republican House leader, said that the state's newly enacted voter ID law would "allow Governor Romney to win the state" in the 2012 presidential election. Suppressing black turnout was a fixture in the 2012 election with one Florida Republican commenting anonymously that preventing voting on the Sunday before the election in the state "was one of their targets only because that's a big day when the black churches organize themselves."[12]

And as expected, a few blacks have written to defend voter ID laws. Horace Cooper, for instance, wrote an article drenched in tortured logic and methodological errors that argued voter ID laws actually protect black voters. Charles Butler faulted blacks who did not have photo IDs, ignoring the cost, travel, and documentary roadblocks. Butler's column is particularly troubling because he used his having lived during Jim Crow to tell readers that he knew the face of real discrimination and those championing voter ID laws bore no resemblance. Butler, that is, uses his uniquely black experiences to defend bigotry and subordinate the race. Unsurprisingly, both Butler and Cooper are members of Project 21.[13]

---

[12] Aviva Shen, *GOP Consultant: Voter ID, Longer Lines Are Partisan Strategy*, Think Progress, Dec. 11, 2012, available at: http://thinkprogress.org/justice/2012/12/11/1317661/gop-consultant-voter-id-longer-lines-are-partisan-strategy/; Aviva Shen, *Florida Republicans Admit Voter Suppression Was the Goal of the New Election Laws*, Think Progress, Nov. 26, 2012, available at: http://thinkprogress.org/justice/2012/11/26/1234171/florida-republicans-admit-voter-suppression-was-the-goal-of-new-election-laws/; Annie-Rose Strasser, *Pennsylvania Republican: Voter ID Laws Are "Gonna Allow Governor Romney To Win,"* Think Progress, June 25, 2012, available at: http://thinkprogress.org/election/2012/06/25/505953/pennsylvania-republican-voter-id-laws-are-gonna-allow-governor-romney-to-win/.

[13] Charles Butler, *Voter ID Is No Jim Crow – I Know*, Project 21, available at: http://www.nationalcenter.org/P21NVButlerJimCrow90611.html; Horace Cooper, *Victims of Voter Fraud: Poor and Disadvantaged Are Most Likely to Have Their Vote Stolen*, National Center for Public Policy Research, available at: http://www.nationalcenter.org/NPA635.html; Ryan J. Reilly, *Voter Fraud "Study" Authored by Republican Who Pleaded Guilty in Abramoff Scandal*, Talking Points Memo, Aug. 3, 2012, available at: http://tpmmuckraker.talkingpointsmemo.com/2012/08/voter_fraud_study_horace_cooper_jack_abramoff.php. Because Charles Butler explicitly uses his race in debates, he cannot opt out of black solidarity. And membership in Project 21 likely prohibits one from opting out anyway. It is an organization that is premised

Good government does what the individual cannot and citizens are ill suited to do what a voter ID law can. If ineligible voters are walking into the polling places and casting illegal ballots, the government, therefore, is on call. But, as the data proves, in-person voter fraud, the most inefficient manner to affect an election, poses no threat. Thus, reasonable folk must oppose laws premised on combatting it, particularly because, as in Pennsylvania alone, more than 750,000 registered voters lacked photo ID.

Managing racial loyalty in this context will likely have no impact on Cooper or Butler. They write like men undaunted by *Uncle Tom's* power. But to many onlookers, their words will carry no weight. That is, even if one is not afraid of being called an *Uncle Tom*, once the label sticks, one is nonetheless greatly marginalized, reducing one's ability to dupe others into believing that voter ID laws are anything other than a sly attempt to disenfranchise voters.

Michael Steele rejected voter ID laws in 2013 as inconsistent with the Republican Party's efforts to court minority voters. This was undoubtedly difficult for him. Steele sailed directly against the political headwinds within his own party. Perhaps he risked his comrades finding him disloyal because he appreciated that blacks police loyalty too. As the former head of the RNC, Steele's words carry influence, and this episode exemplifies how managing racial loyalty norms promotes blacks' legal interests.[14]

HERMAN CAIN

Herman Cain is a minstrel character. This biting criticism dogged the former CEO of Godfather's Pizza turned presidential hopeful, as the Republican Party searched for its nominee to oust President Obama in 2012. Many will find Cain's failed presidential run largely irrelevant. Historians may ignore it in favor of more supposedly meaningful bids. But an important question can be explored through examining his star-crossed candidacy, a question that this and subsequent generations must answer, particularly because America is increasingly embracing nonwhite political leaders. What behaviors are unacceptable for a black politician courting white voters? This basic

on the idea that blacks offer a unique contribution to political discourse simply because they are black. Members, that is, use their racial identity to further their arguments.

[14] Eric Kleefeld, *Pennsylvania Voter-ID Law Could Disenfranchise Up to 750,000*, Talking Points Memo, July 5, 2012, available at: http://tpmmuckraker.talkingpointsmemo.com/2012/07/pennsylvania_voter_id_disenfranchised.php; Tom Kludt, *Steele: RNC Minority Outreach Incompatible With GOP Voter ID Laws*, Mar. 20, 2013, available at: http://livewire.talkingpointsmemo.com/entry/steele-rnc-minority-outreach-incompatible-with-gop-voter?ref=fpa.

question becomes quite complicated behind the complex background of racial politics.[15]

Although he once led in the Republican primary polls, Cain left the race after he was hounded by various accusations of marital infidelity. But before his exit, some observers bashed him for supposedly acting like a minstrel character to court racially resentful white voters. In the 2012 presidential election, nine out of ten Republican voters were white. The Republican primary electorate was even whiter.[16]

And these were not the more racially egalitarian whites who pulled the lever for Obama. The voters who Cain pursued were much more likely to hold antiblack beliefs. After President Lyndon Johnson signed the 1964 Civil Rights Act, the Republican Party lured Southern white voters into their camp through its Southern Strategy. The GOP played on white voters' racial fears. And many white Democrats became Republicans. The prejudiced sentiments that pushed many to change their party allegiances in the 1960s have proved durable. A 2012 study established that 32 percent of Democrats, 48 percent of Independents, and a whopping 79 percent of Republicans harbor antiblack attitudes. The Tea Party movement, which is rife with these attitudes, wields disproportionate influence in the Republican primaries. Cain had to woo these folk to become the nation's second black president.[17]

The case against Cain is built on various pieces of evidence. While stumping for votes, he sometimes broke off into song. In 2011, he belted an off-key rendition of "He looked Beyond My Faults" at the National Press Club, for instance. He often quoted his grandfather's ungrammatical mantra "I does not care." "Aw shucky ducky," frequently fell from his lips. "Cornbread" was his self-chosen Secret Service name if he would have been granted federal protection. He seemingly beamed with pride, moreover, whenever he exhibited ignorance on foreign policy matters.[18]

---

[15] Herman Cain, This is Herman Cain!: My Journey to the White House 61 (2011).

[16] Matthew Yglesias, *Herman Cain Is Now Leading in the Polls*, Oct. 13, 2011, available at: http://thinkprogress.org/yglesias/2011/10/13/342658/herman-cain-is-now-leading-in-the-polls/.

[17] Joseph A. Aistrup, The Southern Strategy Revisited: Republican Top-Down Advancement in the South 32–37 (1996); Andrew Michael Manis, Southern Civil Religion in Conflict: Civil Rights and Culture (2002); Elizabeth Drew, Richard M. Nixon: The American Presidents Series: The 37th president, 1969–1974 20 (2007); James L. Felder, Civil Rights in South Carolina: From Peaceful Protests to Groundbreaking Rulings 151 (2012); Josh Pasek, Jon A. Krosnick, and Trevor Tompson, *The Impact of Anti-Black Racism on Approval of Barack Obama's Job Performance and on Voting in the 2012 Presidential Election*, at 13, available at: http://www.stanford.edu/dept/communication/faculty/krosnick/docs/2012/2012%20Voting%20and%20Racism.pdf.

[18] Z. Byron Wolf, *Herman Cain's Gospel: "He Looked Beyond My Faults,"* ABC News, Oct. 31, 2011, available at: http://abcnews.go.com/blogs/politics/2011/10/herman-cains-gospel-he-looked-beyond-my-faults/; Geneva Sands, *Cain Explains "aww, shucky ducky" comment on*

There's more. He called Charles and David Koch, conservative billionaires, "brothers from another mother." The Koch brothers have financed various causes that have led onlookers to question their racial motives, including a well-funded and ultimately successful campaign against integrated schools in Raleigh. Wealthy Kansas siblings throwing their financial heft to re-segregate schools in North Carolina spurred accusations of racism. And after former Republican vice presidential nominee Sarah Palin referred to his candidacy as the flavor of the month, Cain began referring to himself as "black walnut," his favorite ice cream flavor.[19]

Some might consider Cain's pronouncement that black people were "brainwashed" into being Democrats more damaging. Cain claimed that blacks were not thinking through the issues and selecting the party whose governing philosophy met their interests. Rather, blacks were being hoodwinked by a party that had cast a spell on them. Jesse Jackson said Cain's remark was "demeaning and insulting." Others thought he, as was true with Allen West who made similar comments, was purchasing white support by derogating blacks' political acumen. Although some whites may have rejoiced upon hearing Cain's brainwashed comment, progressives make comparable statements about low-income whites who support Republicans. One has little reason to believe that Cain does not truly believe that Democrats have duped their black constituents and such a statement does not strike me as inherently impermissible.[20]

"Weel about and turn about and do jis so/ Eb'ry time I weel about and jump Jim Crow." Those lines are from the infamous minstrel song "Jump Jim Crow." Cain's public utterances in no way approximate that minstrel. But during the nineteenth century, minstrels were wildly popular because whites enjoyed the spectacle of disparaging blackness through performance. Cain is accused of this – attempting to ingratiate himself to whites by debasing blackness, thereby allowing potential supporters to consume his political ideas.

"Daily Show," The Hill, Apr. 24, 2012, available at: http://thehill.com/video/campaign/223289-cain-explains-meaning-behind-aww-shucky-ducky-; Maggie Haberman, *Cain's Wished-For Secret Service Code Name: "Cornbread,"* Politico, Nov. 18, 2011, available at: http://www.politico.com/news/stories/1111/68686.html.

[19] Stephanie McCrummen, *Republican School Board in N.C. Backed by Tea Party Abolishes Integration Policy,* Washington Post, Jan. 12, 2011, available at: http://www.washingtonpost.com/wp-dyn/content/article/2011/01/11/AR2011011107063.html?sid=ST2011011202619; Noreen Malone, *Herman Cain Compares Himself to Black Walnut Ice Cream,* New York Magazine, Oct. 4, 2011, available at: http://nymag.com/daily/intelligencer/2011/10/herman_cain_compares_himself_t.html.

[20] Juana Summers, *Jesse Jackson "Plantation" Comments Insult Black Voters,* Politico, Sept. 30, 2011, available at: http://www.politico.com/news/stories/0911/64841.html.

Cain's detractors continuously condemned him, believing all that was missing from his stump speech was blackface and soft-shoe dancing. Columnist Darryl E. Owens contended Cain "acts like a minstrel," adding that "[h]e fans the embers of stereotypes that African-Americans have long labored to extinguish." Sociology professor Laurie Essig had a similar take on Cain's campaign commercial where his white campaign manager champions him as capable of uniting America. The manager seemingly uses his whiteness to vouch for Cain as one of "the good ones." Essig opined that the commercial presented Cain as "a Mr. Bojangles, to make us feel good about being white, about ignoring the ugly foundation of white privilege, like slavery, and just tap dance ourselves away to a better plantation." Dr. Ulli K. Ryder, a racial identity scholar, argued that Cain "uses a certain kind of minstrelsy to play to white audiences." Ryder contended that Cain, to garner white support, intentionally fostered an image of the type of black man who whites enjoyed from the minstrelsy era, the affable and clownish darky who speaks in broken English. And founder of the blog _We Are Respectable Negroes_, Chauncey DeVega, had an even harsher reaction.

> Herman Cain's shtick is a version of race minstrelsy where he performs "authentic negritude" as wish fulfillment for White Conservative fantasies.... Cain in his designated role as black Conservative mascot, absolves the White racial reactionaries ... of their sins. This is a refined performance that Black Conservatives have perfected over many decades and centuries of practice.[21]

Cain has defenders, most notably John McWhorter, who too has faced _Uncle Tom_ allegations. McWhorter rejects assertions that Cain's political style is worthy of rebuke. Instead, McWhorter insists that Cain projects a form of Southern blackness. And rather than hiding his true self, McWhorter contends, Cain has the courage to be black in public, unlike many other black

[21] Darryl E. Owes, _Blacks Can't Afford Cain's Painful Antics_, Orlando Sentinel, Dec. 3, 2011, at A3; Lawrence O'Donnell, The Last Word, MSNBC, Oct. 31, 2011; Laurie Essig, _Minstrelsy, Memory, and Herman Cain_, The Chronicle of Higher Education, Nov. 1, 2011, available at: http://chronicle.com/blogs/brainstorm/my-fuzzy-memory-of-herman-cain/40968; Susan Saulny, _Behind Cain's Humor, a Question of Seriousness_, New York Times, Oct. 19, 2011, available at: http://www.nytimes.com/2011/10/19/us/politics/behind-herman-cains-humor-a-question-of-seriousness.html?pagewanted=all&_r=0; Ulli K. Ryder, _Herman Cain's Use of Racial Language Is Rhetoric We Must Refuse_, New York Daily News, Oct. 23, 2011, available at: http://www.nydailynews.com/opinion/herman-cain-racial-language-rhetoric-refuse-article-1.965787; Chauncey DeVega, _Black History Month Is Herman Cain Playing the Race Minstrel for CPAC_, AlterNet, Feb. 12, 2011, available at: http://www.alternet.org/speakeasy/2011/02/12/black-history-month-is-herman-cain-playing-the-race-minstrel-for-cpac.

politicians. McWhorter holds that blacks should not police Cain's conduct but "should take it as a learning opportunity. At the least, our conception of blackness should be generous enough that conservative black Republicans can afford to be black in public."[22]

McWhorter's defense, however, missed the central issue – that Cain is intentionally using what McWhorter deems to be a form of Southern blackness to appeal to racially resentful whites. McWhorter is right in one sense; black politicians should feel free to be themselves in public. But Cain is lambasted for debasing blackness to gain entry into the hearts and minds of racially resentful whites. McWhorter largely misses the issue.

The general point should be made first. Black politicians can violate the norm against inexcusable meekness when courting nonblack voters. A line exists. And, for instance, a politician who flubs questions on foreign policy and jokingly attributes his failures to blacks not caring about such matters would have crossed it. Such a politician would mirror black actors in the first era of *Uncle Tom*'s use. For their own personal advancement, these actors accepted cinematic roles that tarnished the image of the Negro before the world. Black politicians who debase blackness similarly hurt blacks' interests. Subsequent politicians may be forced to replicate this low archetype or else be deemed unviable candidates. Indeed, if such submissiveness becomes the norm, then self-respecting black candidates may be unable to gain any traction with the sorts of white voters to which Cain had to appeal. Prosecutors, moreover, should not have to prove that black politicians consciously debased blackness in order to appeal to white voters. Intent, in other words, is inconsequential here. Whether deliberate or not, the harm is all the same.

The question is whether Cain is such a politician. The call is close. But the evidence is too unconvincing for me to label Cain an *Uncle Tom*. More convincing is the competing argument – he is an older Southern black man with the cultural affectations common among that demographic who is also a poor politician. Based on his campaign speeches, I find the case too weak to indict him for racial betrayal. Sure, a couple of moments cause self-doubt. His singing at the National Press Club is one. And while campaigning in Tennessee, Cain pointed to a woman in the crowd and said, "she got a sign over there y'all – 'we love black walnut' that's my new name. Just call me black walnut."

---

[22] John McWhorter, *Stop Accusing Herman Cain of Minstrelsy*, New Republic, Oct. 25, 2011, available at: http://www.newrepublic.com/article/politics/96608/herman-cain-not-minstrel; Chauncey Devega, *John McWhorter's Defense of Herman Cain's Race Minstrelsy Is the Very Definition of Piss Poor Thinking*, We Are Respectable Negroes, Oct. 25, 2011, available at: http://wearerespectablenegroes.blogspot.com/2011/10/john-mcwhorters-defense-of-herman-cains.html.

Both spectacles were cringe-worthy. The standard, however, should be black actors and their *Uncle Tom* roles during the 1940s. And Cain's behavior falls short in my eyes. Perhaps Cain made himself look bad. In my view, he certainly did. But his off-putting public displays left the race unscathed.[23]

Although I am unsatisfied, reasonable minds can examine the evidence and disagree with me, ultimately convinced that Cain debased blackness through his political behavior. I concede, though I object, a reasonable mind can find enough there, there. As mentioned, his various critics have studied him and have dubbed him a minstrel character. Cain demonstrates that not every case is clear-cut. Sometimes fair-minded people will disagree. But that racial loyalty norm management be exercised with care is imperative. Cain's detractors, although I disagree with their conclusion, were careful.

BLACK TEA

Whether black Tea Party members have violated constructive norms is a complicated matter, requiring a separate discussion to properly address. Thus, when analyzing some black conservatives, namely Allen West and Herman Cain, I avoided that query. I avoid it no longer.

The Taxed Enough Already Party, or the Tea Party, is a diffuse conservative political movement comprised of various smaller Tea Party organizations. The movement organizes around limited economic principles, namely lower taxes, curtailed spending, and debt and deficit reduction. Keli Carender, a conservative blogger, orchestrated the first Tea Party protest on February 16, 2009, the day before President Obama signed into law the $787 billion stimulus package designed to enliven a decaying economy during the Great Recession. The movement became a defining facet of the American political system as early as April 2009, when Tea Partiers protested across the country, bemoaning President Obama's supposed socialist, big government policies. The Tea Party is a dominant faction within the GOP. Indeed, per a Pew Research survey, in 2013, the Tea Party represented 37 percent of the Republican Party and 49 percent of Republicans who always vote in primaries.[24]

Many observers debate how absolutely the pathogen of bigotry has infected the Tea Party. The weaker critique holds the pathogen responsible

---

[23] A clip of the Herman Cain event at Chattanooga is available at: http://www.youtube.com/watch?v=5g-Pv1HaOek.

[24] Ronald P. Formisano, The Tea Party: A Brief History vii, 1, 25–26, 28 (2012); Alec Tyson, *Tea Party Republicans Exert Stronger Influence in GOP Primaries*, Pew Research Center, Aug. 7, 2013, available at: http://www.pewresearch.org/fact-tank/2013/08/07/tea-party-republicans-exert-stronger-influence-in-gop-primaries/.

for afflicting but a few; some are diseased but the broader movement is unaffected. The stronger critique finds that the entire host has been compromised; the Tea Party itself is the carrier. If either are true, one might contend that Tea Party blacks are *Uncle Toms* for belonging to an antiblack movement. They join the Tea Party, which seeks to spread its strain of racial prejudice, some might say. Tea Party blacks are already accustomed to *Uncle Tom* accusations. Timothy F. Johnson, a black Tea Partier, for instance, has "been told I hate myself. I've been called an Uncle Tom. I've been told I'm a spook at the door." Deneen Borelli, a member of Project 21, said that black Tea Partiers are called "a token, a traitor, an Uncle Tom." Lloyd Marcus recounted that black Democrats who "continue to drink the liberal Kool-Aid" denounced him as an *Uncle Tom*. The question is obvious: Is the Tea Party antiblack?[25]

The repeated claims that the 2 percent black Tea Party is racist deeply angers its members. Tea Partiers, and conservatives generally, are tired of being called racists and decry liberals for "play[ing] the race card in every discussion and every debate." Some rebuff all assertions that racial bias is a feature of the Tea Party. And whenever presented with evidence to the contrary, they accuse liberals of distracting Americans from the real issues. The Tea Partiers willing to concede the existence of racial animus within the movement usually hold that a fringe element has dirtied otherwise good-natured folk with principled beliefs about the role of government.

But much evidence calls such defenses into question. Bush entered the White House with a budget surplus. He then began two wars he never paid for, advocated for and got a prescription drug entitlement that he never paid for, and bequeathed $700 billion to Wall Street in the final months of his administration. Bush's second term ended with a financial catastrophe and a soaring budget deficit and national debt. And his legacy includes the biggest expansion of the federal government since President Lyndon Johnson's Great Society. Yet the Tea Party, supposedly premised around the idea that Washington was fiscally irresponsible by spending money it did not have, was nowhere to be found before Obama's inauguration. Sure, corporate billionaire-funded political organizations, FreedomWorks and Americans for Prosperity, floated the idea for tea party-themed protests years before most Americans knew who Obama was. Many conservatives who later joined the Tea Party, moreover, were truly frustrated with the Bush administration and its "compassionate

[25] *Black Tea Party Activists Called "Traitors,"* FoxNews.com, Apr. 6, 2010, available at: http://www.foxnews.com/politics/2010/04/06/black-tea-party-activists-called-traitors/; Kate Zernike, *Where Dr. King Once Stood, Tea Party Claims His Mantle,* New York Times, Aug. 28, 2010, at A9; Kevin Chappell, *What's Up With This Guy?,* Ebony, July 2010, at 24.

conservatism." But not until the nation's first black president was in the White House did the Tea Party movement gain any momentum. The president had been in office for a few weeks. Suddenly, cable news was seemingly overrun with video clips of Americans' frothy mouths screaming about "taking our country back" (from who?) for reasons that were just as salient in the previous administration. To many, the nearly all-white movement seems animated, at least in part, by fear of a black president.[26]

See Tea Party protests, for instance, where offensive spectacles are all too common. The nostalgic waving of Confederate flags, the proud faces of those holding signs presenting Obama as a primate or as a witch doctor with a bone through his nose, the placards that read "Obamanomics – Monkey see, Monkey spend" are familiar sights at these events. Fox News' Sean Hannity, a conservative, said on his television show that he could find no examples of racist signs at protests, a statement that exposes how candor is in short supply among some ardent supporters.[27]

In March 2010, at a raucous protest against the Affordable Care Act held outside the U.S. Capitol building, Tea Partiers called John Lewis and Andre Carson *nigger* as the black Democratic congressmen walked by. "*Nigger, nigger*" rang out fifteen times, Carson said. At the same protest, a man spat, perhaps accidentally, on Congressman Emanuel Cleaver, another black Democrat. Tea Party leaders, however, quickly denied that these incidents occurred and others flatly accused the congressmen of lying. To them, it was suspicious that at a time when everyone has a camera phone no video evidence surfaced.

---

[26] Scott Rasmussen and Douglas Schoen, Mad as Hell: How the Tea Party Movement is Fundamentally Remaking Our Two-Party System 157 (2010); Michael Graham, That's No Angry Mob, That's My Mom: Team Obama's Assault on Tea-Party, Talk-Radio Americans 4–5 (2010); Eugene Robinson, *What's Behind the Tea Party's Ire?*, Washington Post, Nov. 2, 2010, available at: http://www.washingtonpost.com/wp-dyn/content/article/2010/11/01/AR2010110105086.html; Formisano, The Tea Party, at 11, 26–27. Liberals have criticized the Tea Party movement for being an AstroTurf rather than a grassroots movement. Instead of being a movement of the people, liberals claim, it is a movement funded by wealthy interests. Although it corporate billionaires have given the movement much-needed organizational help and financial backing, without the human capital, the movement would have quickly fizzled out. Eric Zuesse, *Final Proof the Tea Party was Founded as a Bogus AstroTurf Movement*, The Huffington Post, Oct. 22, 2013, available at: http://www.huffingtonpost.com/eric-zuesse/final-proof-the-tea-party_b_4136722.html.

[27] Lauren Loricchio, *Tea Party Attitude Toward Obama Influenced by Race, Researchers Say*, Daily Hampshire Gazette, Oct. 31, 2013, available at: http://www.gazettenet.com/home/9128690-95/tea-party-attitude-toward-obama-influenced-by-race-researchers-say; Christopher Parker, *Race and the Tea Party: Who's Right?*, May 3, 2010, available at: http://www.salon.com/2010/05/03/race_and_the_tea_party/; David Edwards, *Hannity: "I Can't Find Any" Racist Tea Party Signs*, The Raw Story, July 16, 2010, available at: http://www.rawstory.com/rs/2010/07/16/hannity-no-racist-tea-party-signs/.

Footage did later surface of Cleaver being spat on, but many still denied that anyone let *nigger* fly that day.[28]

One can find examples of Tea Party racism outside the emotionally charged atmosphere of a political protest. Reporter David Weigel, for instance, recounted a conversation he had with a group of Tea Partiers outside the Capitol building. They thought Obama was inside. One activist, while peering at the building, repeatedly yelled, "Bring out your boy Obama!" Another shouted, "We took care of one Hussein, we're gonna take care of another one!" That same activist complained about how "they" destroyed Detroit and that "we have one of them in the White House right now." Or see for evidence the president and founder of the Springboro Tea Party, Sonny Thomas, who unfurled a Confederate flag at a Springboro, Ohio, school board meeting in July 2013. At the meeting, he told attendees that blacks "should consider themselves lucky since they are treated better in the United States than they would be if they were in 'Black Countries' with 'genocide.'" Phil Russo, a Tea Party activist, says that one of his Facebook friends posted "something extremely racist" and he voiced his displeasure. Quickly, the friends of that friend "jumped down my throat, calling me a liberal and saying I wasn't a real tea partier."[29]

The odd Obama conspiracy theories bustling throughout the Tea Party further evidence racial hang-ups infesting the movement. Obama was born in Kenya. He's not a citizen. He's the first illegal alien president. He's a secret Muslim. He has ties to anti-American Islamic organizations. The absurdities swarm. According to a 2010 poll, only 41 percent of Tea Partiers acknowledged that Obama was American born. At a protest, Larry Klayman, a founder of a Tea Party organization, implored conservatives "to demand that this president leave town, to get up, to put the Quran down, to get up off his knees and to figuratively

[28] *Rep.: Protesters Yelled Racial Slurs*, CBSnews.com, Mar. 20, 2010, available at: http://www. cbsnews.com/news/rep-protesters-yelled-racial-slurs/; Jesse Washington, *Tea Party Health Care Protests: N-Word Feud Still Rages after Video Discredited*, available at: http://www.huffingtonpost.com/2010/04/13/tea-party-health-care-pro_n_535184.html; Kate Zernike, Boiling Mad 138–39 (2010); Pareene, *Why Did the Liberal Media Believe the Tea Party Racist Smears?*, Gawker, available at: http://gawker.com/5516368/why-did-the-liberal-media-believe-the-tea-party-racist-smears. A video clip of the spitting incident is available at: http://www.youtube. com/watch?v=f7wYt9jee2U.

[29] David Weigel, *Conservative Beat the Press on Health Care Debate "Slurs,"* Washington Post, Apr. 13, 2010, available at: http://voices.washingtonpost.com/rightnow/2010/04/conservatives_beat_the_press_o_1.html#more; Rebecca Klein, *Springboro Tea Partyer Sonny Thomas Unveils Confederate Flag at School Board Meeting*, July 12, 2013, available at: http://www. huffingtonpost.com/2013/07/12/springboro-confederate-flag_n_3587417.html; Phil Russo, *"Tea Party" Is Over: Ex-Activist Says Racism, Hypocrisy Killed the Movement*, The Grio, Apr. 9, 2013, available at: http://thegrio.com/2013/04/09/tea-party-is-over-ex-activist-says-racism-hypocrisy-killed-the-movement/.

come out with his hands up." In 2013, about fifty protestors in Orlando greeted Obama's motorcade with a sign reading, "Kenyan Go Home." That same year, at an Arizona rally, "Impeach the Half-White Muslim!" stained another sign. And the "joke" "The Zoo Has an African Lion and the White House Has a Lyin' African!," to many Tea Partiers, seemingly never yields its comedic value.[30]

Various empirical studies have found that racial animus is a driving factor in the Tea Party. Christopher Parker, a political science professor, studied race and politics in seven states. His data revealed that Tea Party whites were more likely to hold discriminatory beliefs about blacks than white liberals and even conservative whites who were not supportive of the Tea Party.[31]

Alan I. Abramowitz, another political science professor, using different election data, corroborated Parker's findings. Tea Partiers, Abramowitz determined, harbor extraordinarily high levels of racial resentment and very negative views on President Obama compared to the American population and even compared to the Republican Party as a whole. Abramowitz's study, like that of Parker, demonstrated that "racial resentment and dislike of Barack Obama, along with conservatism, merged as the most important factors contributing to support for the Tea Party movement."[32]

Parker's and Abramowitz's work explains why white nationalists have sought to woo Tea Partiers into their ranks. The NAACP commissioned a report detailing the various connections between the Tea Party movement and hate groups. The Council of Conservative Citizens (CofCC), America's largest white nationalist organization, has influenced some regional Tea Party organizations, even organizing and promoting protests. Tea Party activist Roan Garcia-Quintana had to step down from South Carolina Governor Nikki Haley's grassroots reelection steering committee because of his membership with the CofCC. But CofCC members are ambivalent about how receptive

---

[30] Stephanie Condon, *Poll: "Birther" Myth Persists among Tea Partiers, All Americans,* CBSnews.com, Apr. 14, 2010, available at: http://www.cbsnews.com/news/poll-birther-myth-persists-among-tea-partiers-all-americans/; Michael D. Shear, *Score One for Thorn in Government's Side Behind N.S.A. Ruling,* New York Times, Dec. 17, 2013, available at: http://www.nytimes.com/2013/12/18/us/politics/larry-klayman-plaintiff-in-nsa-case-savors-victory.html; available at: Laurie Merrill, Dianna Nanez and Linnea Bennett, *Hundreds Protest Obama Outside Phoenix High School,* AZcentral.com, Aug. 8, 2013, available at: http://www.azcentral.com/news/politics/articles/20130806obama-phoenix-protests-outside-school.html?nclick_check=1; Alex Seitz-Wald, *University of Texas College GOP President: Obama Assassination "Tempting,"* Thinkprogress, Nov 16, 2011, available at: http://thinkprogress.org/politics/2011/11/16/370552/ut-college-gop-preisdent-obama-assassination-tempting/.

[31] Christopher Parker, *Race and the Tea Party: Who's Right?,* Salon, May 3, 2010, available at: http://www.salon.com/2010/05/03/race_and_the_tea_party/.

[32] Matt A. Barreto, Betsy L. Cooper, Benjamin Gonzalez, Christopher S. Parker, and Christopher Towler, *The Tea Party in the Age of Obama: Mainstream Conservatism or*

the Tea Party is to the organization's message, believing that although "the fact that hundreds of thousands of white people got up the nerve to oppose the government [was] astonishing," there is a "negative tendency that plagues Tea Party activism ... to deny the racial dynamic empowering the movement."[33]

The NAACP, in July 2010, passed a resolution during its national convention that condemned the racist elements of the Tea Party and called on others, including those within the Tea Party, to do the same. The Tea Party's response was predictable: Fight back! Mark Williams, a spokesman for the Tea Party Express, wrote one of the first and most corrosive responses to the NAACP's resolution. Williams wrote a fictional letter to President Lincoln that in part said:

> We Coloreds have taken a vote and decided that we don't cotton to that whole emancipation thing. Freedom means having to work for real, think for ourselves, and take consequences along with the rewards. That is just far too much to ask of us Colored People and we demand that it stop!

Williams, soon thereafter, resigned his position.[34]

Shortly after the NAACP passed its resolution, conservative activist Andrew Breitbart, a prominent Tea Party figure, released a heavily edited clip of a speech delivered at an NAACP event by Shirley Sherrod, a worker for the U.S. Department of Agriculture. Breitbart posted the clip on his Web site with the title, "Video Proof: The NAACP Awards Racism." Fox News' Web site trumpeted the clip in a story with the headline: "Caught on Tape: Obama Official Discriminates against White Farmer." In the brief excerpt, Sherrod comes across as a black woman discriminating against a white landowner. Tea

---

Out-Group Anxiety?, 1, 2, 15, available at: http://faculty.washington.edu/mbarreto/papers/teaparty_PPST.pdf.

[33] Rasmussen and Schoen, Mad as Hell 297; Ryan Grim and Luke Johnson, *Is the Tea Party Racist? Ask Some Actual, Out-Of-The-Closet Racists*, Huffington Post, Oct. 24, 2013, available at: http://www.huffingtonpost.com/2013/10/24/tea-party-racist_n_4158262.html; Institute for Research & Education on Human Rights, Tea Party Nationalism: A Critical Examination of the Tea Party Movement and the Size, Scope, and Focus of Its National Factions 60–61 (2010); Devin Burghart, *White Nationalist Tea Partier Co-Chairing South Carolina Governor Re-Election Committee*, Institute for Research & Education on Human Rights, May 24, 2013, available at: http://www.irehr.org/issue-areas/tea-party-nationalism/tea-party-news-and-analysis/item/484-haley-appoints-garcia-quintana; *Gov. Nikki Haley Asks Roan Garcia-Quintana to Step Down Amid Hate Group Controversy*, The Post and Courier, May 26, 2013, available at: http://www.postandcourier.com/article/20130526/PC16/130529364.

[34] Institute for Research & Education on Human Rights, Tea Party Nationalism 64; CNN Wire Staff, *Tea Party Infighting Heats Up*, CNN.com, July 20, 2010, available at: http://www.cnn.com/2010/POLITICS/07/19/tea.party.imbroglio/index.html; Michael A. Memoli and Kathleen Hennessey, *"Tea Party" Leader Resigns after Racist Blog Post*, Los Angeles Times, July 24, 2919, at A14.

Partiers used the clip to sully the reputation of the NAACP, its new foe, and to reinforce a theme attractive to many conservatives – the idea that the real story about race in America, contrary to popular opinion, is that whites are the targets of black racism. Breitbart wrote, "Sherrod's racist tale is received by the NAACP audience with nodding approval and murmurs of recognition and agreement. Hardly the behavior of the group now holding itself up as the supreme judge of another group's racial tolerance." But Breitbart, who claimed to have been sent the speech already edited, proffered a description that was the exact opposite of what was actually true. The hoax ended after the full version of the speech was released. Rather than exemplifying black racism, Sherrod's speech actually concerned how she helped a white landowner and her personal journey to realizing that people are economically disadvantaged regardless of skin color.[35]

Although publically rebuffing the NAACP's assertions, the movement seemingly responded to the organization's concerns, holding diversity rallies, a "Uni-Tea" day event in Philadelphia, and a "Diverse Tea" Web site to promote inclusion and combat "false allegations of racism." The NAACP's head, Benjamin Todd Jealous, believed that real change had occurred, writing, "Yet, amid the threats and denials, something remarkable happened. Tea Party leaders began to quietly take steps toward actively policing explicitly racist activity within their ranks."[36]

Still, race remains problematic for the Tea Party. The *Huffington Post*, in 2013, reported that *Stormfront.org*, a white supremacist online community, has constantly debated the Tea Party in ways that reflect poorly on the movement. The debate arranged into two camps: one holding that the Tea Party has proven to be a fruitful target for white nationalist teachings and one holding that white nationalists waste their time in appealing to Tea Party folk. One poster wrote that he has joined three Tea Party organizations and members were receptive to his message. A different poster revealed that the "Taxed Enough Already movement may not be wholly WN (White Nationalists), however there is plenty of racial awareness out there. That's where it begins; with awareness." And a different one opined that "Saying Tea partiers aren't WNists is like saying Ron Paul supports aren't WNists. While it's true not all

---

[35] Valerie Elverton Dixon, Just Peace Theory Book One: Spiritual Morality, Radical Love, and Public Conversation 447–48 (2012); Frank Rich, *There's a Battle Outside and It Is Still Ragin'*, New York Times, July 25, 2010, at WK8; James Rainey, *On the Media; Short Clip, Untold Harm*, Los Angeles Times, Jul 24, 2010, at 1D; Fae Jencks, Brooke Obie, Eric Schroeck and Christine Schwen, *Timeline of Breitbart's Sherrod Smear*, Media Matters, available at: http://mediamatters.org/research/2010/07/22/timeline-of-breitbarts-sherrod-smear/168090.

[36] Formisano, The Tea Party 111; Institute for Research & Education on Human Rights, Tea Party Racism 5–6.

are, it's also true many are." But when white supremacists attempt to use the banner of the Tea Party for their own gain, Tea Party leaders reject them. In a world where bigotry is openly preferred, many see the Tea Party as a welcome if not wholly familiar place.[37]

Does this evidence prove that the Tea Party is antiblack? The Tea Party certainly is not the White Citizens Councils or White Sovereignty Commissions of the mid-twentieth century that openly attempted to promote white supremacy and sought to put Jim Crow's boot on black America's neck. The idea that the Tea Party is akin to the Klan is too absurd to seriously debate. Thus, at the very least, the Tea Party does not resemble traditional antiblack organizations. It looks a bit different.

That white nationalists often vouch for the bigotry of Tea Partiers is, however, deeply problematic. Who knows a bigot more than a bigot? That many seem energized to oppose the president's black skin rightly calls the movement into question. Indeed, the Tea Party suddenly taking up arms in response to political conditions that predate Obama should induce wariness among observers. The signs, chants, and comments at Tea Party protests are likewise startling. And the work of political scientists confirms what only the delusional would deny: racial resentment flows through the veins of the Tea Party. To find otherwise is to dispute the primacy of empirical evidence and facts and laud emotion and conviction as their equals.

But the bigotry within it does not render the entire movement antiblack. Movements are a merger of principles. Tea Partiers critique the age of Obama for expanding the role of the federal government beyond what is proper. Washington DC, they insist, must provide only a limited social safety net, lower taxes, and focus on reducing the nation's debt. That's their narrative. True, the data says most Tea Partiers harbor racial biases that Americans associate with an era long passed. And the incessant claims to the contrary are farcical. What truly matters, though, are the ends that the movement pursues. When white supremacists reenact *Romeo & Juliet*, they do not render it a racist play. The cast of characters in the Tea Party drama are sometimes repugnant but the overall narrative is perfectly acceptable. Few blacks are drawn to it. The story fails to captivate them. But the NAACP's president, Benjamin Jealous, correctly observed that the Tea Party is not racist but rather has racist aspects. Thus, blacks within the Tea Party do not violate constructive norms necessarily because it is not an antiblack movement.

---

[37] Grim and Johnson, *Is The Tea Party Racist?*; R.E.A.L. Organization, *Florida: Racist "Hate Group" Seeks Own "Tea Party" Event – Rejected by Tea Party Leaders*, Feb. 26, 2010, available at: http://www.realcourage.org/2010/02/florida-tea-party-on-stormfront/.

Blacks should, however, be deeply skeptical of black Tea Partiers. Blacks who participate in the movement do so, I believe, because they agree with its central ideological tenets. They wish to work side by side with like-minded folk. Yet, in their efforts to precipitate change, they willingly put themselves in the position of laboring next to people for whom the verbal grenade "take our country back" has racial implications. When it detonates, and it likely will, black Tea Partiers will have two choices: denounce the racism, or overlook it. If they denounce it, Tea Partiers are likely to enforce their own loyalty norms, and punish them as disloyal team players. When Colin Powell, a Republican, criticized the GOP's "dark vein of intolerance" he was called a RINO, a Republican in Name Only. But to overlook racism is to violate the racial loyalty norm that punishes inexcusable meekness.[38]

Tea Party blacks employ two different strategies in excusing racism within the movement. One is to deflect the Tea Party's race problem by recounting favorable personal experiences. Emery McClendon, a black Tea Partier and member of Project 21, wrote, "I have never encountered racism at any of the events I have attended." But what does McClendon think this means? One can be thrilled that McClendon has never seen anything untoward. Great, McClendon has had nothing but positive experiences. But what about all the patently racist things for which we have proof? Are we supposed to ignore that because McClendon has not personally seen it?[39]

The second strategy is to change the subject and deflect, Deneen Bordello's strategy. To be fair, she once conceded that "offensive signs have been seen at Tea Party rallies." Her use of the passive voice is peculiar. She seemingly cannot find a subject for the sentence, as if she knows no one who has seen these displays and as if she does not know how often the unknown subject has seen them. But, she writes, those signs "are brought by the lone individual." She suddenly finds her subject, "the lone individual," and proffers a statement that, despite her effort, inadequately masks the depth of the problem.

Outside of that small concession, however, Borelli is a master deflector. On Fox News, she said, "The NAACP is nothing but a puppet. They're a puppet organization right now, because they're pushing race politics and it's wrong."

[38] *Black Tea Party Activists Called "Traitors"*, FoxNews.com, Apr. 6, 2010, available at: http://www. foxnews.com/politics/2010/04/06/black-tea-party-activists-called-traitors/; Chris Gentilviso, *Colin Powell: GOP Holds "Dark Vein of Intolerance*," Huffington Post, Jan. 13, 2013, available at: http://www.huffingtonpost.com/2013/01/13/colin-powell-gop_n_2467768.html; Dr. Davis Turner, *Listen to Powell, Jindal*, Feb. 2, 2013, The Inter-Mountain, available at: http://www. theintermountain.com/page/content.detail/id/558964.html/.

[39] Emery McClendon, *I Condemn the NAACP: It Needs to Wake Up!*, available at: http://www. fortwayne912.com/Emery_McClendon.html; Emery McClendon, *The Tea Party is Not Racist*, available at: http://www.nationalcenter.org/P21NVMcClendonTeaParty90710.html.

She criticized the NAACP for changing the subject away from substantive politics and onto race but also chastised the NAACP for not condemning the New Black Panther Party, as if an organization with no followers and no societal impact is supposed to spur people to pull out the condemnatory language. But to malign the NAACP for changing the subject is to perpetuate the fallacy that racism in an immensely influential political movement is a topic unworthy of debate.[40]

The liberal political movement purports to be firmly committed to racial egalitarianism, yet fails often. White liberals frequently extol the virtues of equal opportunity and inclusive hiring and the like, but usually only when any alteration in hiring practices has no effect on their positions. And those familiar with hiring discussions know all too well about the need to find "qualified" minority candidates. The tenor of the conversation is always that the whites in that room are well qualified and great at what they do. The key is to find minorities who belong in that room, those approximating their brilliance. But that's a falsehood. Sorry to say, most people, including whites, are average at their trade. Some exemplary, some terrible, but most are average. When it comes to hiring minorities, however, they require the exceptionalism that they lack, yet strangely think they embody.

Black liberals regularly offer such critiques of political liberalism. If Tea Party blacks are unwilling to put a similar spotlight on bias, then they violate the norm against inexcusable meekness. Black solidarity is premised on lessening the burdens of antiblack racism. Thus, blacks must reject those hemming and hawing in the face of bigotry especially when such folk have proven adept at speaking forcibly in other contexts.

TAVIS SMILEY AND CORNEL WEST

Nurse Eunice Rivers tended to patients during the Tuskegee syphilis experiments. Nurse Rivers, black, worked closely with the black men who were misled into believing that they were receiving free health care from the U.S. government. She was a conduit between the local black community and the scientists who withheld penicillin from patients in order to research the effects of the disease when untreated. The patients were never informed that they had syphilis. They were told that they had "bad blood," a general phrase describing an array of medical maladies. Her black skin, for the doctors, was a commodity that purchased compliant patients. The story is a historical reminder

---

[40] Glenn Beck, Fox News, July 14, 2010; Deneen Borellli, *NAACP Puts Politics Above Civil Rights*, available at: http://www.nationalcenter.org/P21NVBorelliNAACP90710.html.

of how blacks may facilitate the degradation of other blacks. Eunice Rivers has long died. But according to professor and progressive cable news host Melissa Harris-Perry, Nurse Rivers's treacherous spirit lives on in public intellectual Tavis Smiley.[41]

From 2005 to 2009, Tavis Smiley closely aligned with banking giant Wells Fargo. As Wells Fargo held "wealth building" seminars, Smiley was the bank's biggest asset. Smiley's main duties were to deliver opening remarks before the seminars and attract blacks to events. For his services, the bank paid Smiley more than $4 million plus funding for his media ventures. On the surface, nothing appeared improper about the Wells Fargo-Smiley alliance. Smiley provided a valuable service. A business compensated him. Everything looks fine.

But appearances often deceive. And they do here. These seminars were not actually meant to build minorities' wealth. They were a point of contact to potential black and Hispanic borrowers. Smiley, popular and trusted, brought in black crowds. Once Smiley secured their presence, Wells Fargo duped minorities into signing subprime mortgages with exploding interest rates they could never pay back, leading to inevitable loan default and economic calamity. And not only did Wells Fargo target minorities for these loans, the bank gave black and brown customers subprime mortgages at higher rates than worse-situated white borrowers. Discrimination was served with two helpings.

This crushed individual minority borrowers and devastated their communities. Vacant homes littered across minority neighborhoods have ushered in the various perils associated with urban decay. As Lisa Madigan, Illinois attorney general, remarked, "By targeting African-Americans for the sale of its highest-cost and riskiest loans, Wells Fargo drained wealth from families and neighborhoods and added to the stockpile of boarded-up homes that are open invitation to criminals." After numerous states sued Wells Fargo, the bank settled for $175 million.[42]

Kelvin Boston, who joined Smiley in some of the seminars, claimed that they both were ignorant of the predatory lending efforts. "[W]e were just speakers for hire," he said. "We didn't have any role or any control over what else happened. The main point is that we were not involved in any of their discussions or in anything they sold." As of yet, Smiley has not publically apologized for his role. As Harris-Perry strongly intimated on her eponymous television show,

[41] Susan L. Smith, *Neither Victim Nor Villain: Nurse Eunice Rivers, the Tuskegee Syphilis Experiment, and Public Health Work*, 95 Journal of Women's History 96, 105–105 (1996).

[42] Mark Huffman, *Claims Lender Discriminated Against African-American and Hispanic Borrowers*, Consumer Affairs, Aug. 1, 2009, available at: http://www.consumeraffairs.com/news/wells-fargo-news.rss.

whether Smiley's relationship with Wells Fargo was treacherous has caused rumblings among black folk. The question is if Smiley betrayed the race when he opened his palms to the bank and used his personal popularity with black folk to shepherd them to their economic slaughter.

The answer depends on if Smiley knew, or had reason to know, about the nefarious activities. If he had knowledge, then he obviously violated constructive norms. By targeting black folk to dupe them out of their money, Wells Fargo is an antiblack organization. Thus, if Smiley collaborated with the bank, then he would have violated the norm that proscribes collaborating with the enemy. One could convincingly argue, moreover, that by accepting funds in exchange for helping defraud blacks he demonstrated his lack of concern for the race.

The power behind Professor Harris-Perry's Nurse Rivers-Smiley comparison was Rivers's knowledge that the dying men were being deceived. With Smiley, however, the evidence proving awareness is lacking. True, some will be skeptical that such a shrewd operator was completely unaware that Wells Fargo was providing not a path to the American dream of homeownership, but rather a passage to financial wreckage. But skepticism only builds unconvincing cases. Boston did say that Smiley specifically questioned Wells Fargo's bigwigs regarding subprime mortgage loans. But no evidence establishes what he uncovered.[43]

Smiley has been silent about his troubling relationship with Wells Fargo. No apologies, no heartfelt regrets expressed. His silence is in notable contrast to roaring cries about Smiley's racial betrayal. Such accusations are unfair, however; one needs evidence, not hunches, to support such condemnation. If one can provide proof that Smiley knew of the underhanded schemes, or had reason to know, then he should be widely condemned. But such is not the case here. Smiley should be castigated for ignoring his role in this affair and for lacking remorse to those affected. The required proof to prosecute him for racial betrayal, however, is wanting.

Although Smiley's involvement with Wells Fargo has gone largely undetected by mainstream outlets, his repeated harsh criticism of President Obama has received much attention from the mainstream press and the black press alike. Smiley and his close comrade Cornel West, who has been even more disdainful of Obama, have both endured accusations of racial treachery because of their often tough criticisms.

Smiley and West had separate personal disagreements with the president. Smiley's rift began when Senator Obama won the Democratic Iowa primary in January 2008. After the victory, Smiley, on the *Tom Joyner Morning Show*, a popular black radio program, said, "Don't fall so madly in love [with Obama] that you surrender your power to hold people accountable.... I'm not saying overlook Senator Obama, but you now better be ready to look him over." Many listeners thought Smiley was downplaying a historic victory. As radio talk show host Tom Joyner remarked, "He's always busting Barack Obama's chops." A month later, Smiley further chided Obama for missing Smiley's annual State of the Black Union Address. Obama offered to send his wife instead. But Smiley deemed her an unsuitable replacement. On another occasion, Smiley said he hoped that Obama would survive the campaign "with his soul intact." Many blacks concluded that he embodied a "crabs in a barrel" mentality, believing jealousy fueled Smiley's complaints.[44]

Smiley's good friend Cornel West has been even more ornery toward Obama. West used to be Obama's friend. Before their rift, he campaigned for Obama in various cities. But despite his efforts, West complained that Obama never returned his telephone calls. Obama apologized. West subsequently learned, however, that Obama replied to others' calls, just not his.[45]

West was particularly disheartened that he received no invitation to the 2009 presidential inauguration. West went to Washington, DC during the inaugural activities without a ticket. "We drive into the hotel," West said, "and the guy who picks up my bags from the hotel has a ticket to the inauguration." Melissa Harris-Perry was critical of this remark, challenging West for intimating that the lower-class hotel worker should not be at the inauguration if the public intellectual who demands five-figure speaking fees watches from a hotel television. West's attacks on Obama led one writer to scribe that West "uses the language of a jilted lover."[46]

Ever since Obama has become president, both Smiley and West have been strident opponents. They are a duo. Them praising Obama is the only occurrence rarer than seeing one without the other. Their criticism started early.

---

[44] *Tavis Smiley Reportedly Quits Radio Show Over Obama Hate*, Huffington Post, May, 25, 2011, available at: http://www.huffingtonpost.com/2008/04/11/tavis-smiley-quits-radio_n_96246. html; Krissah Thompson, *Blacks at Odds Over Scrutiny of President*, Washington Post, Apr, 6, 2009, at A1; Paul Farhi, *Tavis Smile Will Cut Ties With Joyner Radio Show*, Washington Post, Apr. 12, 2008, at C1.

[45] Chris Hedges, *The Obama Deception: Why Cornel West Went Ballistic*, Truth Dig, May 16, 2011, available at: http://www.truthdig.com/report/item/the_obama_deception_why_cornel_west_went_ballistic_20110516/.

[46] Melissa Harris-Perry, *Cornel West v. Barack Obama*, The Nation, May 17, 2011, available at: http://www.thenation.com/blog/160725/cornel-west-v-barack-obama; Lisa Miller, *I Want to Be Like Jesus*, New York Magazine, May 6, 2012, available at: http://nymag.com/news/features/cornel-west-2012-5/index5.html#print.

Shortly after his 2008 victory, Obama chose an economic team that included Larry Summers, West's former adversary from Harvard. In response, West claimed that Obama had lied about being a man of change. He was a corporate Democrat all along. West said, "He's making it very clear. The working people are not a major priority, they are an afterthought." West has continued to upbraid Obama for supposedly being too close to Wall Street, calling the president a "Rockefeller Republican in blackface" and "a black mascot of Wall Street oligarchs and a black puppet of corporate plutocrats." The inclusion of the word *black* in his anti-Obama taunts is peculiar, as is West's theorizing that Obama is afraid of "free black men." West claimed that because Obama was raised as a white man, he, like other white men, is frightened in dealing with "an independent black brother." West's message is clear: Obama is not a true black man.[47]

Another Smiley and West grievance is their claim that not only has the president failed to address poverty, but that he actually ignores poor people. In August 2011, Smiley remarked, "Say the word poor. Say it Mr. President. We want to hear you say it!" The two do not believe that this is Obama's unique failure. All national politicians, they contend, ignore the poor. This feeling that poverty is being unaddressed by Congress and the president led the two to conduct a country-wide Poverty Tour. Their motivation, they claimed, was to bring attention to the poor and press leaders to devise an agenda to alleviate the burdens of poverty. Poverty is indeed a pressing twenty-first-century issue. But when Smiley demanded that Obama say the word *poor*, he should have realized that just days prior the president had actually discussed poverty.[48]

Obama achieved history with the passage of the Affordable Care Act (ACA), the health care victory that Democratic presidents had been trying to achieve for decades. Smiley and West, however, typically withheld accolades from Obama. Smiley referred to the ACA as "watered down" and "nowhere near what it was supposed to be." And West argued that President Nixon supported more progressive health care legislation than did Obama. On *Meet the Press*, Smiley remarked that although he believed the president "deserves great respect" for passing health care legislation, it was "small change" that was

---

[47] Hedges, *The Obama Deception*; Miller, *I Want to Be Like Jesus*; Touré, *Viewpoint: What's Behind Cornel West's Attacks*, Time, Nov. 15, 2012, available at: http://ideas.time.com/2012/11/15/what-behind-the-bad-blood-between-cornel-west-and-obama/.

[48] Zerlina Maxwell, *West and Smiley's "Poverty Tour" Veers Way Off Track*, The Grio, Aug. 9, 2011, available at: http://thegrio.com/2011/08/09/west-and-smileys-poverty-tour-veers-way-off-the-rails/; Tavis Smiley and Cornel West, The Rich and the Rest of Us: A Poverty Manifesto 5 (2012).

a win for the insurance companies. Smiley contended this even though the health insurance lobby spent more than $200 million to defeat it.[49]

To address poverty, Smiley and West "call for higher taxes on the wealthy, more robust and effective public institutions, and expanded social insurance," moderate policies firmly in line with President Obama's political priorities. Smiley and West also implore Obama to push for reforms just for blacks in explicitly racial terms. "Smiley insists on explicit and repeated acknowledgement of race," Melissa Harris-Perry noted, whereas "Obama typically seeks to address inequality within a racially neutral frame." Obama has rebuffed calls to devise an agenda that caters to blacks. Smiley and West envision themselves as following in the tradition of Dr. King, representatives for black folk who lobby the president to further policies to benefit their people. Obama, however, speaks in race-neutral terms. When asked whether he will work to solve issues that may afflict black people disproportionately, he argues that "a rising tide will lift all boats," meaning he will champion policies that he believes will help all people, including blacks.[50]

Their often loud quarrels with Obama have precipitated many accusations that Smiley and West are simply "haters" upset that their status is being usurped by a black president. Others have held that their grievances exaggerate the faults of the Obama administration. Comedian Steve Harvey has leveled the harshest criticism. He called them both *Uncle Toms*. He later apologized for using the epithet, but not for his underlying grievances. He found their substantive criticism unconvincing and animated by petty personal disputes. Smiley and West, however, argue that they are holding the president accountable. "We're not trying to demonize the president or cast aspersion on him," Smiley remarked. "There is honor in accountability. Our people need to understand this. They can hear everything else the president says, but somehow they miss it every time he says, 'I need you all to hold me accountable.'"[51]

---

[49] *Tavis Smiley, Cornel West on the 2012 Election & Why Calling Obama "Progressive" Ignores His Record*, Democracy Now, Nov. 9, 2012, available at: http://www.democracynow. org/2012/11/9/tavis_smiley_cornel_west_on_the; Meet the Press, Mar. 21, 2010; Meet the Press, Dec. 20, 2009.

[50] Melissa Harris-Lacewell, *Commentary: Don't Hold Obama to Race Agenda*, CNN.com, June 5, 2009, available at: http://articles.cnn.com/2009-06-05/politics/lacewell.race.agenda_1_ tavis-smiley-obama-s-lincoln-barack-obama?_s=PM:POLITICS; Adam Serwer, *All the President's Frenemies*, The American Prospect, Sept. 21, 2001, available at: http://prospect. org/article/all-presidents-frenemies.

[51] Margena A. Christian, *Tavis Smiley and Cornel West Love Obama, Want More*, Ebony, available at: http://www.ebony.com/news-views/interview-tavis-smiley-and-cornel-west-867/2# axzz2KRzzuZqE.

Despite their assertions to the contrary, Smiley and West's criticisms are excessive particularly because their political ideas are far closer to the president's than they let on. One true disagreement, though, concerns Obama's lack of an explicitly black agenda. One would assume that their end goal is the passage of legislation that will alleviate the various dilemmas disproportionately afflicting blacks. If true, then the constant pleas for an explicitly black agenda are perplexing. Such an agenda would have stalled in Congress and secured Obama's fate as a one-term president, resulting in blacks being in the same place – no explicitly black agenda passing Congress – but with a Republican president who would have received less than 10 percent of the black vote.

But that is not to say that Obama should not implement policies that deal with the unique challenges facing blacks. If one community suffers under alarmingly high unemployment, good government responds. In 2010, Al Sharpton told the *New York Times* that Obama was wise to not champion a black agenda. In response, Smiley criticized Sharpton and others who he claimed argued that Obama should ignore black needs. But this is not what Sharpton and others advocated. Rather, they contended that Obama should deal with black issues, but not publically champion an explicitly black agenda. They realized that a black president publically championing a black agenda was political suicide. If Smiley and West seek legislation that ameliorates problems of particular importance to blacks, a more logical approach is for Obama to rebuff an explicit racial agenda in favor of race-neutral policies that combat the challenges facing black folk, not because they are black, but because they are a community suffering under enormous challenges. Obama is not the president of black America. He is a president who happens to be black. But their criticism pulls back the curtains on their archaic mindset that instructs black politicians to wear two hats. The black hat is to be worn when representing black folk and the other hat when handling everyone else's affairs. Smiley and West's viewpoint is outdated and unhelpful to blacks.[52]

More fair is their assessment on Obama and poverty. Through much of his first term, Obama spoke mainly about the middle class and much less so about the poor. But Obama has supported legislation that will benefit low-income people. Obama's tax plan, for instance, lowered taxes on the bottom 20 percent by 80 percent. As tax professor Dorothy A. Brown has documented, Obama's tax plan greatly benefited people of color who are disproportionately poor. The passing of the ACA, furthermore, has proven even more beneficial

---

[52] Sheryl Gay Stolberg, *For Obama, Nuance on Race Invites Questions*, New York Times, Feb. 8, 2010, available at: http://www.nytimes.com/2010/02/09/us/politics/09race.html.

by providing the poor with health insurance. Smiley, nevertheless, criticized it. Again as with the black agenda issue, their criticism reveals a lack of political sophistication.

The Constitution is an invitation to compromise. Presidents cannot turn their ideas into law through sheer will. Legislation must pass Congress. And the ACA was the most progressive piece of legislation that could have passed in 2009. During his 2013 State of the Union address, Obama paid much attention to poverty, announcing, among other things, his goal of increasing the minimum wage. But West's public response after the State of the Union speech was that Obama is a war criminal for his use of drones.[53]

West calling Obama a "Rockefeller Republican in blackface" and "a black mascot of Wall Street oligarchs and a black puppet of corporate plutocrats" is unfair because he cannot support the charge that Obama sold out. The inclusion of the word *black* in the taunts suggests that Obama's blackness somehow requires that he be a different kind of president. President Obama is a defender of capitalism much like anyone who could ever be elected president. And those who criticize him for favoring the rich over the poor have proffered a criticism worthy of debate in the public square. Obama's administration bailed out Wall Street and failed to prosecute Wall Street bankers for their crimes. But Obama is not the Wall Street stooge that West portrays. After all, during the 2012 election, Wall Street strongly opposed Obama and overwhelmingly supported Mitt Romney.

Furthermore, if West considers Obama "a black mascot of Wall Street oligarchs," what is Tavis Smiley, who personally accepted millions of dollars from a bank that essentially stole wealth from black people? West's willingness to defend blacks from any and all harms seemingly dissipates when his friends are the offenders. West was correct in arguing that outsiders must push presidents into supporting sometimes unpopular political ideas that will improve the lives of the American people. But as Touré, a black public intellectual, remarked, "Does the inflammatory nature of his attacks make him eligible for that position?" Melissa Harris-Perry was correct in observing that "West's ego, not the health of American democracy, is the wounded creature in this story."[54]

Smiley and West refuse to accept that Obama is a politician who must deal with electoral realities. They censure him for not endorsing an explicitly

---

[53] Touré, *Viewpoint: What's Behind Cornel West's Attacks on Obama*; Dorothy A. Brown, *Race, Class, and the Obama Tax Plan*, 86 *Denver University Law Review* 575, 575, 582 (2009).

[54] Touré, *Viewpoint: What's Behind Cornel West's Attacks on Obama*; Hibah Yousuf, *Wall Street Overwhelmingly Backs Romney*, CNN Money, Nov. 6, 2012, available at: http://money.cnn.com/2012/11/06/investing/stocks-election-obama-romney/index.html; Melissa Harris-Perry, *Cornel West v. Barack Obama*.

black agenda. But the idea is politically infeasible and ultimately unhelpful to blacks. They disparage Obama for discussing middle-class people and not the poor, without acknowledging that he does discuss poverty and that the middle class determines presidential elections. And the two also seem ignorant on the Republican Party being antagonistic to his every move. He cannot simply pass legislation that would improve the black condition. He's not even a legislator. He's the chief executive. Their criticism reveals them as unserious.

Smiley and West can champion whatever policy they desire. Their names appear on no ballots. They are not even akin to Martin Luther King. Unlike Dr. King and his Southern Christian Leadership Conference, they do not lead a civil rights organization with a broad membership. They head no movement and they have no followers. Smiley and West are accountable to no one. They are public figures who are well compensated for oratory. Obama is a politician, no different than the previous occupants of 1600 Pennsylvania Avenue. He is beholden to the will of the people and 86 percent are nonblack. Because they ignore these basic facts, their criticism must be severely discounted. They are great purveyors of bad thinking.

But do their assessments render them *Uncle Toms*? Those nodding their heads condemn the two for their supposed baseless commentary that jeopardized Obama's political chances during the 2012 presidential election, all in an effort to both bring attention to themselves and avenge old petty grievances. But even if that argument were true – and it has merit – their behavior falls short of betrayal. No meekness whatsoever is afoot here. Although those hostile to blacks' interests likely cheered their criticism, they did not infringe the norm proscribing helping blacks' adversaries. And if self-importance violates the norm that requires blacks care about the race, then they would be in front of a very long line of *Uncle Toms*. Smiley and West, in short, have committed no offense against the race.

Their missteps warrant blacks holding them in lower regard. Before the age of Obama, Smiley and West were popular among blacks. Their popularity has undoubtedly waned and deservedly so. That is unfortunate. They are not, however, *Uncle Toms*. Rather, they are just two fellows who blacks should rightfully pay less attention to going forward. For two men charged with liking attention a bit too much, for loving the camera, that is a tough punishment indeed.

CONCLUSION

Blacks cannot, in the pursuit of racial progress, sacrifice the race's well-being for personal gain. But because saboteurs exist, the race must concern itself with the damage they can generate. *Uncle Tom* is a baleful epithet with the capacity to convince blacks not to cross the threshold to which ostracism is the sanction. For self-defense, *Uncle Tom* must be retained although not handled carelessly. All blacks will never agree on who is an *Uncle Tom*. Absolute harmony is impossible. But if the process mirrors that seen in this chapter, then the results will be defensible.

Final Address

NEARLY FOUR CENTURIES AGO, twenty Africans' feet first hit the shores of a foreign continent that would be the setting of a great human atrocity. They stood in the settlement of Jamestown in the colony of Virginia, land that would eventually be part of the United States of America after its inhabitants and those of the other colonies declared independence from the British government that denied them what they insisted nature gifted every human being. Those who claimed that men have "certain unalienable rights" hypocritically withheld that principle from the ancestral kin of those twenty Africans. That frightful decision has haunted this country, working many horrors upon it; civil war, murder, disenfranchisement, segregation, and the like can all indeed be traced back to the regrettable compromise between slavery's opponents and its defenders.

Men and women of all races have exhausted their brains, bodies, and spirits to atone for that calamity. Their admirable industry has improved the nation. Those with black skin, the target of the wicked, invigorated by a muscular fidelity for their people, have long been leaders. To think of those who have opposed their work, not as individuals, but as a faceless mass of evil – a cloud of bigotry – has been common. But individuals they are; individuals of different colors, genders, ethnicities, and religions. And on the road to unbridled racial equality, blacks must bring overwhelming force to defeat each and every one of them.

Each foe can wage unique offensives. Black foes, inflicting a devastation like no other, obstruct ultimate triumph in various ways. Some cooperate with antiblack entities and become saboteurs or spies. Others' meekness is so unflinching that they retreat from conflict. And many are undedicated to the group and its struggle and thus have proven untrustworthy. To rout the enemy from within, blacks must police racial loyalty, which reduces their ranks and weakens their capacity to achieve objectives.

Many never want to utter *Uncle Tom*. To some, it is a bitter epithet that leaves an aftertaste. It is too acerbic a criticism. For others, policing loyalty is messy. It sullies debate while distracting blacks from evaluating the merits of the supposed betrayer's ideas. But to not deploy this munition is to fight with one arm in the name of being more polite and less messy.

Blacks grapple with other impolite and messy things. That during the sub-prime mortgage crisis big banks waved their wand and made blacks' wealth disappear is impolite and messy. The seemingly unbreakable foundation of structural racism is impolite and messy. The hidden manacle of unconscious bias is impolite and messy. The policies and practices that stack black bodies on top of each other in prisons as though they were cargo on a ship are impolite and messy. Blacks – all blacks – must be completely devoted to reducing the burdens of being black. To those unwilling to use this effective strategy: Pick a seat and have it.

Index